226.4
Kea
   Kealy, John P.
   Luke's Gospel today.

226.4
Kea
   Kealy, John P.
   Luke's Gospel today.

DATE	ISSUED TO
3/9/49	3/30/80

DOMINICAN PRIORY LIBRARY
7200 Division St.
River Forest, Ill. 60305

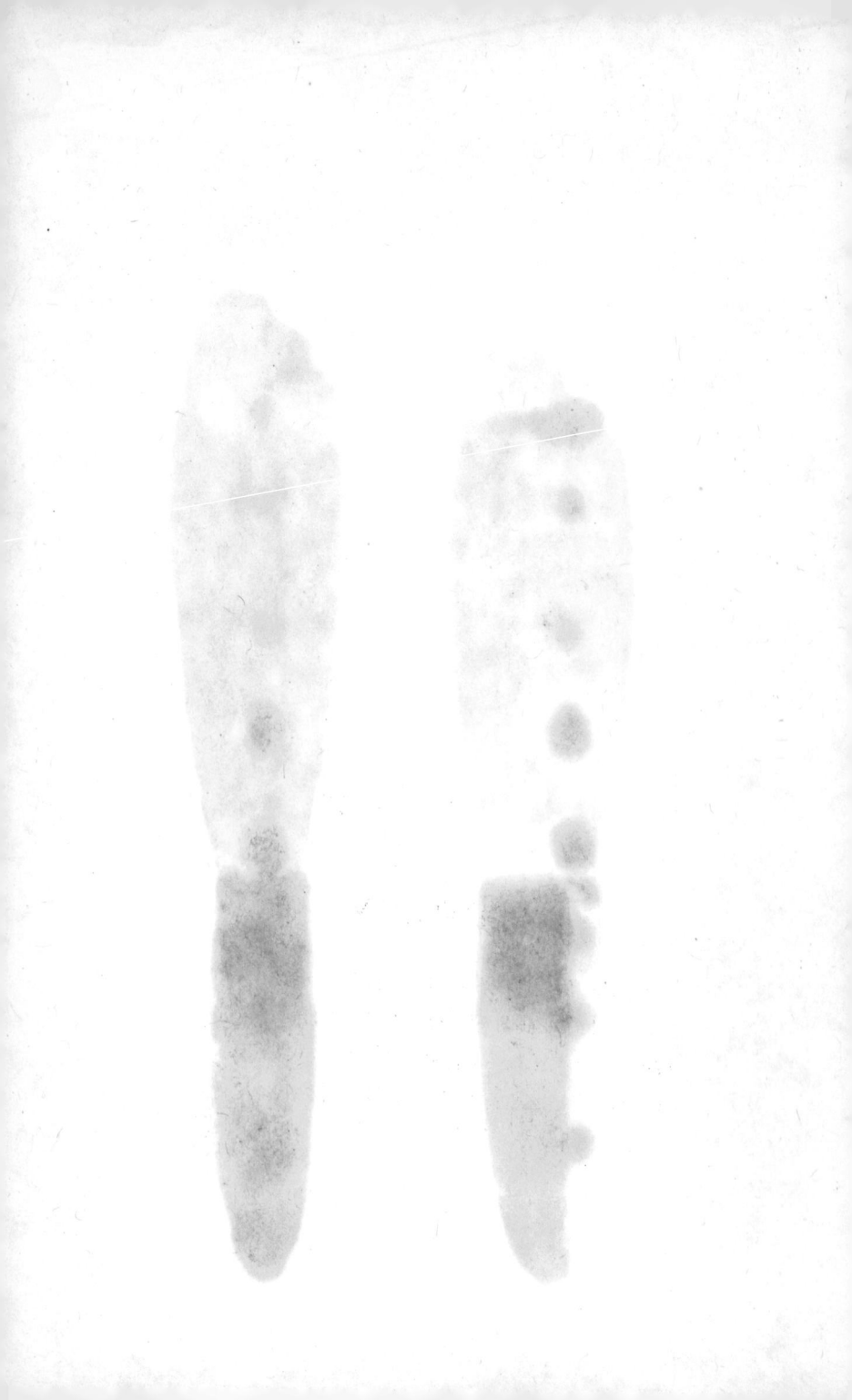

LUKE'S GOSPEL TODAY

**DIMENSION BOOKS
DENVILLE, NEW JERSEY**

"If ever I had to choose to keep one book of the New Testament, and one book only, the book I would choose would be Luke's Gospel, for in it I believe that we have Jesus at his most beautiful and the Gospel at its widest."

William Barclay

"Is the Christ of the Gospels, imagined and loved within the dimensions of the Mediterranean world, capable of still embracing and still forming the center of our prodigiously expanding universe?"

Teilhard de Chardin, Le Milieu Divin, 1926

"Vain is the discourse of philosophy by which no human heart is healed."

Epictetus

"A book must be the axe for the frozen sea inside us."

Franz Kafka

LUKE'S GOSPEL TODAY

"That you may know the Truth"

Luke — 1:4

by John P. Kealy, C.S.Sp.

Dimension Books
Denville, New Jersey

First Edition by Dimension Books, Inc.
Denville, New Jersey 07834

Copyright © 1979 by Sean P. Kealy, C.S.Sp.

All rights reserved

CONTENTS

LUKE'S GOSPEL TODAY

"That you may know the Truth"—Lk 1:4

INTRODUCTION	
The New Look in Luke's Gospel	13
CHAPTER 1—WHY A NEW LOOK IN LUKE'S GOSPEL?	19
1. Modern Gospel Studies	19
A. Source Criticism	19
B. Form Criticism	20
C. Redaction Criticism	22
2. Luke, Historian or Theologian	28
3. The Old Testament Background to Luke	34
4. Infancy Narratives	41
5. The Text of Luke	47
CHAPTER TWO—LUKE'S INTRODUCTION—1:1-4	61
The Author—According to Luke	62
Place and Date of Writing	64
Theophilus?	66
Luke's Research	68
Luke and Mark	70
Luke and Matthew	71
Luke's Special Material	72
Luke and John	73
Luke and Paul	74
Luke's Aim	75
Luke's Community	76
Luke's Structure and Style	78
Themes and Characteristics of Luke's Theology	82
The Way to Jerusalem	83
The Father's Plan	85
Christology	86
Saviour	87
Jesus the King and Saviour	88

Jesus the Prophet Saviour, the Bearer of the Spirit	89
The Spirit and Prayer	92
Good News to the Poor—Joy	93
Jesus' Attitude towards the Poor	96
The Rich and the Poor	97
Women	100
The Universal Saviour	100
The Church and Eschatology	105
A Parenetic Gospel	107
CHAPTER THREE—LUKE'S INFANCY NARRATIVES—1-2	111
John and Especially Jesus are the fulfillment of God's Promises and Hope of Israel	
Contents:	115
A. The Announcement of the Birth of John the Baptist—1:5-25	116
B. The Announcement of the Birth of Jesus—1:26-38	121
C. Mary's Visit to Elizabeth—Mary's Song of Praise—1:39-56	126
Mary's Song of Praise	127
Introduction (v 46b-47)	130
Strophe One (v 48-50)	130
Strophe Two (v 51-53)	131
Conclusion (v 54-6)	133
D. *The Birth, Circumcision and Naming of John the Baptist—Zechariah's Prophecy—1:57-80*	133
The Benedictus—1:67-79	135
Introduction (v 68a)	135
Strophe One (v 68b-71)	136
Strophe Two (v 72-5)	136
Strophe Three (v 76-7)	136
Conclusion (v 78a-79b)	137
E. *The Birth, Circumcision and Naming of Jesus: Shepherds and Angels—2:1-21*	138
The Census—(v 1-5)	139
The Birth, The Swaddling Clothes, The Manger—(v 6-7)	141
The Announcement to the Shepherds—2:8-14	142
Gloria in Excelsis	143
To Bethlehem—(v 15-20)	144
The Circumcision and Naming—(v 21)	144
F. *The Presentation of Jesus in the Temple—Simeon and Anna Prophecy—2:22-40*	145
The Setting—2:22-4	146
Simeon's Greeting—2:25-35	146

Index

Nunc Dimittis—2:29-32	147
Simeon's Second Prophecy—34c-35.	148
Anna's Greeting—2:36-8	149
Conclusion	150
G. The Boy Jesus in the Temple—2:41-52	151
Setting—2:41-5	152
Jesus in the Temple—2:45-50	153
Conclusion—2:51-2	154

CHAPTER FOUR—PREPARATION FOR THE PUBLIC MINISTRY—3:1-4:13

CHAPTER FOUR—PREPARATION FOR THE PUBLIC	156
MINISTRY—3:1-4:13	156
A. John the Baptist—3:1-20	158
Luke's Synchronism—3:1-2a	160
The Call of John—3:2b-3	161
Luke's Quotation from Isaiah—3:4-6	162
Repent—3:7-9	163
What Ought we Do?—3:10-14	164
The Messiah—3:15-18	165
Conclusion: John in Prison—3:19-20	166
B. The Baptism of Jesus—3:21-2	169
C. The Genealogy of Jesus—3:23-7	
D. The Temptation in the Desert—4:1-13	173
Traditional Interpretations	173
Modern Interpretations	174
Luke, Matthew and Mark	177
Setting—4:1-2	177
First Temptation—4:3-4	179
Second Temptation—4:5-8	179
Third Temptation—4:9-12	180
Conclusion—4:13	181

CHAPTER FIVE—MINISTRY IN GALILEE—4:14-9:50

CHAPTER FIVE—MINISTRY IN GALILEE—4:14-9:50	182
A. Jesus' Inaugural Sermon at Nazareth and his Rejection—4:16-30	184
Setting—4:14-16	186
Jesus' Sermon from Isaiah—4:17-21	187
Reactions—4:22	189
Jesus' Reactions—4:23-7	190
Conclusion—4:28-30	191
B. Jesus' Activity around Capernaum, Call of the Disciples, Miracles and Controversies—4:31—6:11	192
1. A Sabbath in Capernaum and a Preaching Tour—4:31-44	192
Teaching with Authority—4:21-2	193

The Healing of the Man with the Unclean Spirit—4:33-7	193
Simon's Mother-in-Law—4:38-9	195
Many Healings—4:40-1	195
A Preaching Tour—4:42-4	196
2. The Call of the Leading Disciples: Healings and Controversies—5:1-6:11	197
(a) The Call of the Three Leading Disciples, Simon, Peter, James and John—5:1-11	198
(b) Two Healings—The Cure of the Leper—5:12-6	201
The Cure of the Paralytic—5:17-26	202
(c) The Call of Levi—a Feast—The Question of Fasting—5:27-39,	205
The Call of Levi—5:27-28	205
Levi's Feast—5:29-32	206
On Fasting—The Radical Newness of the Gospel—5:33-8	207
(d) Two Sabbath Incidents—Controversies—6:1-11	209
Plucking the Grain on the Sabbath—6:1-5	209
Healing on the Sabbath—6:6-11	211
C. The Choice of the Twelve and a Manual of Instruction—The Sermon on teh Level Place—Miracles—6:12-7:50	212
(i) The Choice of the Apostles—6:12-16	213
(ii) The Sermon on the Level Place—6:17-49	
Setting—6:17-19	216
Four Beatitudes and Four Woes—6:20-23	220
Love of Enemies—6:27-36	222
Self-Criticism—not Judging Others—6:37-42	224
Fruit, the Test of Pure Discipleship—6:43-9	225
Be Hearers and Doers—The Parable of the Builders—6:46-9	226
(iii) The Cure of the Centurion's Servant—7:1-11	226
(iv) The Widow's Son at Nain—7:11-17	229
(v) John's Question about Jesus—7:18-34	232
A. John's Question is Answered—7:18-23	233
B. Jesus Praises John—7:24-30	234
C. Jesus Describes his own Generation—7:31-35	235
(vi) The Penitant Woman—7:36-50	236
D. Jesus with the Twelve Proclaims the Kingdom—Move from Capernaum to a wider Tour—Instructions to the Disciples—8:1-9:50	238
(1) Jesus on Tour with the Twelve and some Women—8:1-3	240

Index

(2) The Parable of the Sower—8:4-15	241
The Explanation of the Parable—8:11-15	243
(3) The Parable of the Lamp—8:16-18	244
(4) The True Kindred of Jesus—8:19-21	245
(5) The Calming of the Storm—8:22-25	246
(6) The Gerasene Demoniac—8:26-39	247
(7) Jairus' Daughter and the Woman who Touched Jesus' Garment—8:40-56	249
(8) The Mission of the Twelve—9:1-6	250
(9) Herod's Anxiety—9:7-6	252
(10) The Return of the Twelve—The Feeding of the Five Thousand—9:10-17	252
(11) Peter's Profession of Faith—9:18-21	254
(12) Jesus' First Passion Prediction—9:22	256
(13) The Conditions of Discipleship—9:23-7	256
(14) The Transfiguration—9:28-36	258
(15) The Cure of the Boy with the Unclean Spirit—9:37-43a	261
(16) Jesus' Second Passion Prediction—9:43b-45	262
(17) The Dispute about Greatness—Tolerance—9:46-50	263

CHAPTER SIX—A TEACHING JOURNEY TO JERUSALEM—9:51-19:44

	265
Stage A:—9:51-13:21	269
(1) A Samaritan Village Refuses to Receive Jesus—9:51-6	269
(2) Would-be-Followers of Jesus—9:57-62	271
(3) The Mission of the Seventy Two—10:1-24	273
(4) The Good Samaritan—10;25-37	276
(5) Visiting Martha and Mary—10;38-42	280
(6) Teaching about Prayer—11:1-13	281
(7) Opposition and Temptation for Jesus—11:14-36	286
(8) The Hypocrisy of the Pharisees and Lawyers—11:37-53	291
(9) Courage under Persecution—12:1-12	294
(10) The Rich Fool—12:13-21	298
(11) Trust in Providence—12:22-34	300
(12) Vigilance for the Master's Return—12:25-48	303
(13) The Mission of Jesus—12:49-53	305
(14) Discerning the Signs of the Times—12:54-9	307
(15) A Call to Repentance—The Fig Tree—13:1-9	310
(16) The Bent Woman healed on the Sabbath—13:10-17	312
(17) Ultimate Success—Parables of the Mustard Seed and the Leaven—13:18-21	314

Stage B: 316
(1) The Narrow Door—13:22-30 316
(2) Lament over Jerusalem—13:31-35 318
(3) Four Parables at Dinner with Pharisees—14:1-24 321
(4) The Cost of True Discipleship—14:24-35 325
(5) Three Parables on God's Joyful Mercy—15:1-32 327
    The Lost Sheep—15:1-7 328
    The Lost Coin—15:8-10 330
    The Prodigal Son's Unloving Brother—15:11-32 330
(6) Parables on the Right Use of Money—16:1-31 334
    The Astuteness of the Dishonest Steward—16:1-13 334
    The Law and the Kingdom of God—16:14-18 338
    The Rich Man and Lazarus—16:19-31 340
(7) Four Sayings about the Disciples' Duties—17:1-10 343

Stage C:
(1) The Ten Lepers—Faith and Salvation—17:11-19 345
(2) The Coming of the Kingdom—17:20-37 347
(3) Two Parables on Prayer—18:1-14 350
    The Pharisee and the Tax-Collector—18:9-14 352
(4) Jesus and the Children—18:15-17 353
(5) The Rich Ruler—18:18-30 355
(6) The Third Passion and Resurrection Prediction—18:31-4 358
(7) The Blind Beggar near Jericho—18:15-34 359
(8) Salvation for Zacchaeus, The Tax-Collector—19:1-10 360
(9) The Parables of the Sums of Money—19:11-27 362
(10) The Messiah of Peace Enters the Temple in
    Jerusalem—19:28-44 366

CHAPTER SEVEN—JERUSALEM—19:45-24:53 371

A. Jesus in the Temple—19:45-21:35 371
  (1) The Cleansing of the Temple—19:45-7 373
  (2) The Authority of Jesus is Questioned—20:1-8 376
  (3) The Parable of the Vineyard and its Wicked
     Tenants—20:9-19 377
  (4) Paying Tribute to Caesar—20:20-36 380
  (5) The Saducees and the Resurrection of the
Dead—20:27-40 382
  (6) Jesus, David's Son and Lord—20:41-44 384
  (7) The Scribes are Denounced—20:45-7 385
  (8) The Widow's Mite—21:1-4 386
  (9) The Destruction of the Temple Foretold—21:5-7
     Luke's Eschatology 387
  (10) False Signs and Cosmic Disasters—21:5-7 389
  (11) Persecution of Christians 390

Index

(12) The Siege and Destruction of Jerusalem Foretold—21:20-24	391
(13) The Coming of the Son of Man—21:25-8	393
(14) The Lesson of the Fig Tree—21:29-33	394
(15) Exhortation to Watch—21:34-6	
(16) The Last Days of Jesus—21:37-38	395
B. The Passion of Jesus—22:1-23:56	396
(1) The Plot of the Sanhedrin to Kill Jesus—22:1-6	401
(2) The Preparation of the Passover—22:7-13	404
(3) The Institution of the Lord's Supper—22:14-20	406
(4) The Announcement of the Betrayal—22:23-3	413
(5) The Dispute "Who is the Greatest?"—22:24-30	414
(6) Peter's Denial Foretold—22:31-4	416
(7) The Hour of Testing—22:35-8	417
(8) The Agony in the Garden—22:39-46	419
(9) The Betrayal and Arrest of Jesus—22:47-53	420
(10) Peter's Denials of Jesus—22:54-65	422
(11) The Mockery and Beating of Jesus—22:63-5	424
(12) Jesus before the Sanhedrin—22:66-71	425
(13) Jesus before Pilate—23:1-5	426
(14) Jesus before Herod—23:6-12	428
(15) Jesus is Sentenced to Die by Pilate—23:13-25	429
(16) The Way of the Cross—23:26-32	431
(17) The Crucifixion of Jesus—23:33-8	43
(18) The Penitent Thief—23:39-43	437
(19) The Death of Jesus on the Cross—23:44-9	438
(20) The Burial of Jesus—23:50-56	442
C. After the Resurrection—in Jerusalem—24:1-53	445
(1) The Women at the Empty Tomb—24:1-12	453
(2) The Way to Emmaus—24:13-35	456
(3) Jesus Appears to the Eleven in Jerusalem—24:36-49	461
(4) The Ascension—24:50-53	465
Notes	469
Select English Bibliography	497
A. General Works	497
B. Books and Articles on St. Luke	498

INTRODUCTION

The New Look in Luke's Gospel

All Scripture is relevant (2 Tim 3:16) and while the heresy of selection is always a danger, nevertheless, it is true to say that some books, particularly the gospels, have always formed "a canon within the canon" for Christians. Luke, in particular, has been a popular gospel for a variety of reasons. Dante called him "the scribe of the gentleness of Christ" because the gentleness of Jesus is so emphasized in his gospel. Luke, in fact, has an extraordinary attractive capacity of combining the soft and the hard in Christianity, the homeliness and kindness of Jesus with a no nonsense call to radical discipleship. In an age of easygoing tolerance in Christianity together with its tendency to dilute whatever is uncomfortable, Luke's statement on the absolute renouncement required of a Christian, especially his statements on riches and poverty, are very radical and must have originally shocked his bourgeois audience (e.g. 5:11; 6:20ff; 14:25).

To many he is the "beloved doctor" of the soul who has given us such wonderful songs as the Magnificat, so much Christian imagery, and that most popular of titles, "Saviour." He is the marvellous artist and storyteller who alone has recorded such priceless stories as the Good Samaritan, the Prodigal Son, the Walk to Emmaus. Luke's gospel has been described as providing a rule of life, an invitation to imitate the life and example of Jesus. It is even described as a social gospel, as some would put it, or a gospel whose aim is to create a community of prayer and sharing. Luke faces the problem of history, the ongoing Church in the light of God's plan and purpose, as no other New Testament writer. In particular, he deals calmly with eschatology and the parousia or second coming, an approach which is very relevant in the light of the fervid apocalyptic speculations and predictions which are ever with us.

He is frequently described as the most personal of the evangelists with his psychological interest in, and constant emphasis on people, on the individual, particularly the outcasts and underdogs of society. He has been called an "ardent feminist." He is the writer of forgiveness, peace, prayer, joy and the Holy Spirit.

Today, Luke speaks to many who are wrestling with the difficult and especially the contemporary confusion over what are the essentials of the gospel of Jesus. While he stressed continuity with the life and work of Jesus of Nazareth, he struggled with the universal implications of the gospel for his "community in transition" as it has well been described.

> "The Lucan community's predominantly Gentile Christians faced the challenge of integrating their Hellenistic culture and their existence in the Roman political world with their conversion to Christianity, a religion founded by a Jew from Nazareth."

He presented them

> "with a new understanding of what it meant to be Christians and how they should live in their contemporary world."[1]

Thus, in modern discussions on religion and politics, on living with an antagonistic or at best, neutral government and political system, on distinguishing between religious and merely political salvation, Luke is often seen to have many insights to offer. In recent times it is often

Introduction

said that freedom has become the predominant motif in theology, as revelation was a generation ago. Here again Luke has been a fertile ground for research with his Magnificat, for example, being called the most revolutionary song ever written. In the light of the renewed Christian interest in dialogue with Judaism in modern times, the reflection of Luke, the Gentile, on Judaism, one of his main themes, is very interesting. He especially wants to demonstrate that Christianity came from Judaism at its best, from pious people who kept its laws, whereas many of the Jewish leaders were anything but exemplary.

Again, by many concerned with our cities, who see only Paul as he was of urban origin and exercised his ministry almost exclusively in cities, while Jesus was basically a pastoral and agrarian figure, Luke's "urbanism" deserves careful study. He mentions the word "city" some thirty-eight times in his gospel, the word "village" twelve times and frequently emphasizes Jesus' ministry in cities and villages.[23]

Luke wrote for the Theophiluses of his Church and of every Church to assure them, threatened as they were by savage wolves from outside and by men who distort the truth from inside, with "the facts," by showing them that their faith is well founded on Jesus himself and his way of life.

> "He strives by might and main to build up Theophilus' confidence in the apostolic tradition, a confidence which is being shaken by circumstances all around him, persecution, the trials of missionary work, false teachers, less-than-exemplary church leaders, the problems of rich folk. Underlying all Theophilus' problems, tensions and sleepless nights, are the questions: Is God merciful and gracious? Is he faithful to his promises?"[4]

However, despite his constant attractiveness, it is only since about 1950 that Luke's talent as a creative theological thinker and writer has been adequately recognized and systematically examined even though, in quantity, he is the chief contributor to the New Testament, some 28% in fact As he was the only evangelist to write an Acts, it is easier to distinguish his stylistic, linguistic and theological characteristics. Nevertheless, in 1952 C.H. Dodd could write:

> "Among Christian thinkers of the first age known to us, there are three of genuinely creative power: Paul, the author of Hebrews and the Fourth Evangelist."[5]

Many of the past, incomplete interpretations of Luke were only possible because his gospel was separated from his Acts by the gospel of John and because it was forgotten that together they form a unified two-part work.

Luke at best was considered an accurate historian, confirmed by the investigations of archaelogists and historians. Whenever he departed from the basic and simple gospel of Mark it must have been due to his historical investigations or literary talents but not in any way due to his theological thinking. Today, there is "a new look" in Lucan studies as the personality of this attractive writer has emerged from the twilight, no longer "a somewhat shadowy figure" who assembled stray pieces of more or less reliable information, but as a theologian of no mean stature, who very consciously and deliberately planned and executed his work.[6]

Even more, Luke has become "one of the great storm centers of New Testament scholarship,"[7] whose dust has scarcely settled as yet since there is very little general agreement among scholars on many issues. Witness the title "Shiftin Sands" which a recent and useful survey of Lucan studies bears[8] as modern gospel criticism has progressed from Source Criticism to Form Criticism to Redaction Criticism. Luke has received more than his share of attention from scholars particularly the German critics who have rescued him with justice both from the romantics and the liberal humanitarians who have so often distorted his message. Yet all too often it has been forgotten that the ultimate purpose of studying a gospel is to discover, not how it orginated or what it meant long ago, but rather what it means today for us. Many scholars in the past seemed to assume the genuine gospel lay somewhere behind the present gospel forms. Thus the gospels were considered of secondary importance and the contributions of their authors either a distortion of the message of Jesus or irrelevant at best. Preoccupation with sources, transmission of the text, transformation of previous materials, reconstructions of the original, all of which are important, yet frequently only an unattainable ideal, have too often tended to deflect concern from what is most important, namely, to interpret the text as it is. Today a wholeness of view is coming back into vogue. This wholeness of view means that the whole canonical book should be treated as a literary unit and that any individual line or section should be interpreted in the light of its function in the whole.

Our approach will be to investigate in order, like Luke himself, the background to this new look in Lucan studies. It is obvious that to pursue such an investigation is to enter, like Luke himself, into the labors of so many who have labored in the field of interpretation. The chief debts are indicated in the footnotes and in the select English Bibliography. Those who are familiar with the field will recognize the indebtedness on every page. Many friends such as Fr. Basil de Winton C.S.Sp.and Fr. Frank Commerford C.S.Sp. have contributed some very valuable suggestions. A special word of thanks is due to Sr. Tina Heeran H.R.S. without whom a dreadful manuscript would never have been brought to fruition and many errors would otherwise have been included.

                      Sean P. Kealy, C.S.Sp.
                      Department of Philosophy and
                          Religious Studies,
                      Kenyatta University College,
                      NAIROBI,
                      Kenya,
                      East Africa.

CHAPTER ONE

WHY A NEW LOOK IN LUKE'S GOSPEL?

The answer to this question will be attempted in five sections:

1. Modern Gospel Studies — Source Criticism, Form Criticism, Redaction Criticism.
2. Luke, Historian or Theologian?
3. The Old Testament Background to Luke.
4. The Infancy Narratives in Luke.
5. The Text of Luke's Gospel.

Some readers may find this chapter rather difficult and may tend to skip it or perhaps to read it at the end. The writer's intention here is to give as wide as possible a selection of the tremendous variety of scholars who have contributed to the present position of Lucan gospel studies and as far as it is possible within a limited space, to let the more important ones speak in their own words. To struggle through such a survey is essential if one desires to have any adequate understanding of modern Lucan studies, the many problems involved and a basis for future developments which will of necessity take place.

1. *Modern Gospel Studies:*

A. Source Criticism: Gospel study in modern times has received the major share of Biblical Scholars' attention.

No book in history has been subjected to such prolonged and detailed examination by some of the best minds in the world. Three successive methods have been proposed. The earliest is commonly called *Source Criticism* — an attempt to explain the striking similarities and dissimilarities, the literary interdependence of the first three gospels. The publication of a synopsis of the gospels, in parallel columns in 1774 rendered accurate study of the problem possible for the first time.

B. Form Criticism: The next movement in gospel study which developed after the First World War is commonly known as *Form Criticism,* though a more accurate translation of the German term would be Form History.

Source criticism was only able to examine a developed stage of the gospel tradition. Its widely accepted, though not definitive conclusion, was that Mark was the earliest gospel and that Matthew and Luke had developed Mark's gospel by using a collection of sayings of the Lord (Q -probably the first letter of the German word for source, Quelle), and their own personal sources, M for Matthew and L for Luke. However, the story of the gospel tradition between its beginnings and its developed form in Mark and Q was covered with darkness. Form Criticism was an effort to get behind the written sources of the gospels and study the period of oral tradition. A recent writer, G.B. Caird, while acknowledging that the Form Critics ranged from radical (Bultmann) to rather conservative, by comparison (Dibelius), suggests that they did agree in making five claims.[1] Many of these claims look so evident today like many of the great discoveries of history, that it is only by going back to the older text books on gospel criticism and by trying to project ourselves back into the minds of the Source Critics that we can appreciate the achievements of the Form Critics.

(i) "Before the writing of any of our gospels or their documentary sources there was a period of oral transmission."

(ii) "During this period, sayings of Jesus and stories about him circulated by word of mouth in isolated units (pericopae), not in a continuous account (with possible exception of the Passion Narrative)."

This principle was pushed too far as it neglected the fact that oral tradition (e.g. Luke's version in the Sermons in Acts), contained a summary outline of the public ministry of Jesus.

There is also the key point that much of Jesus' teaching was given in easily remembered structures due to the nature of the Jewish method of teaching in parallelisms, inclusions, etc. Further, the Passion story has always been a stumbling block to the claim that the early Christians had little or no concern for a historical account of Jesus' life.

(iii) "The pericopae can be classified into a limited number of forms," e.g., Pronouncement Stories and Miracle Stories. The work of the Grimm brothers in collecting and analyzing German folk stories in 1810 was very influential on Biblical Studies. They had discovered that illiterate peasant women could repeat the same story many times because of the form in which the story was handed on. Likewise, many of the gospel stories (e.g. miracle stories with their simple structure — a description of the disease, its cure, the visible consequences) had taken on definite forms during the oral period and this helped for a more accurate transmission. However, some scholars tended to jump illogically from classification to a negative opinion of the historicity of the particular pericopae and to over stress the creative faith of the first generation Christians.

(iv) "The process whereby the material was selected, preserved and molded into these forms was controlled by the interests and needs of the early Church," e.g. situations of the early Christians, such as their preaching, apologetics and liturgical activities. However, we have little or no evidence that the early Christians ever invented any sayings of Jesus, or stories about him, as some seem to suggest.

(v) "From a study of this process it is possible to adduce laws which will enable the student to distinguish later accretions from the earliest and most authentic traditions."

Here we come to the most subjective part of the Form Critics' contribution and an area where little or no success can be reported. However, nine "laws of transmission" which altered the parables between utterance and appearance in the gospels according to Jeremias[2] are at least a very useful basis for discussion:

(1) change brought about by translation from Aramaic to Greek;

(2) "translation" of illustrative material in a new context;

(3) embellishment;

(4) change under the influence of the Old Testament or other popular stories;

(5) change of audience (e.g. from opponents to Christians);

(6) change from the eschatological to the hortatory;

(7) adaptation to make the parable refer to the Church's mission or the delay of the Parousia;

(8) allegorization;

(9) collection, and sometimes fusion, of two or more parables.

C. Redaction Criticism: This was a movement since the Second World War which tended to focus on the contribution of the evangelists, who are rightly seen as creative authors and theologians and not just compilers, as some Form Critics suggested. Each evangelist emphasized those aspects of Jesus' life and teaching according to their particular readers and their new needs, problems and situation. Each evangelist is now seen to be a creative writer, bringing imaginative solutions to the problems of their differing churches and cultures, as they strove with the perennial problem of reconciling faithfulness to the past with openness to change and adaptation in the light of new situations, cultures and problems. Thus it was felt that a careful study of the texts as we have them would lead to an understanding of the author's theological presentation and the kind of situation and community he addressed. Of course all the older books on the gospels contained sections on the characteristic interests, theology and editorial activity of the evangelists. Thus Henry J. Cadbury, in the preface of his study, The Making of Luke-Acts, could write in 1927:

> "The third evangelist came to be regarded by tradition as a portrait painter . . . The following pages aim to recover some features of his character, to visualize the other factors which went into his noteworthy undertaking, to illustrate from his contemporaries the methods of composition that he employed and so to give as clear, comprehensive and realistic a picture as possible of the whole literary process that produced Luke and Acts."

But today there is a particular surge of interest in Redaction Criticism since the famous study of Luke by Hans Conzelmann which was published in 1953.[3] Conzelmann was followed by Willi Marxsen, who in his work *Mark the Evangelist*[4] attempted a careful definition of the area of study of the redaction critics, recognizing that the gospels as we have them today and probably also their written sources, represented a third life setting. He described altogether three stages or life settings in the growth of the gospel tradition. The first was that of the historical Jesus and the second was a period of unwritten tradition in the early Church. Both scholars believed that the third setting needed further investigation — the imaginative and creative production of a complete gospel from written and unwritten sources by a particular author for a particular community and situation. The evangelists are seen to be skilled theologians and portrait painters, each giving his own portrait of Jesus of Nazareth by a genuinely artistic process, which it must be admitted, is impossible to analyze scientifically. This artistic process is certainly as removed from the Form Critics' jigsaw-puzzle approach of collecting anonymous pieces of tradition, in a random order, as photography is removed from genuine portrait painting today. One notes also among some modern writers a welcome interest in a particular gospel, seen as a whole, as we have it now, and not just with special sections such as introductions, summaries, interpretative comments, omissions, key words, titles of Jesus, parables, miracles. Luke was a particularly interesting gospel for the redaction critics. In Mark they had something which they considered to be very close to a direct source and in Luke's second volume (Acts), they had a study guide to his methods.

But Conzelmann's work was that of a somewhat one-sided pioneer and his picture of Luke as a radical innovator has run into devastating criticism. For Conzelmann,[5] Luke represents a further stage even from that of Mark and Q, because in Luke "the kerygma is not only transmitted and received but itself becomes the subject of reflection." Luke adopts a "critical attitude to tradition" as well as positively forming a new view of history from those already current, "like stones used as part of a new mosaic." Luke replaces the Markan plan of an imminent end with an indefinite, ongoing church. Conzelmann sees Luke's aim as an attempt to explain the embarrassing delay of the parousia, so that the church could come to terms with its own seemingly indefinitely prolonged existence in the world. He assumed that the first generation of Christians expected the return of Christ to be very soon and that this eschatological fervor was in danger of leading to disillusionment. Luke then was the creative genius who substituted a history of salvation for the eschatological content of the Christian tradition — the parousia would be *sudden, not soon,* and in the indefinite future rather than in the present. The starting point for Conzermann was

Luke's emphasis on God's redemptive plan which earlier scholars had also recognized.[6] Luke saw salvation history unfolding in three distinct stages — one long, one brief and the third one indefinite.

(a) *The period of Israel* and the Jews. "The Law and the Prophets were in force until John; since then the good news of the kingdom of God is preached . . . " (Lk 16:16). John belongs to the prophetic past, the period of preparation. "He is not the precursor, for there is no such thing, but he is the last of the prophets." He speaks of the coming of the Spirit as belonging to the future and not to his own present (Lk 3:16). Luke describes the imprisoning of John the Baptist before the baptism of Jesus, which is described without mention that it was performed by John (3:18-21).

(b) *The brief period of Jesus' Ministry* or "the middle of time," to quote the title of Conzelmann's German edition, a title which expresses more clearly Conzelmann's idea of the period of Jesus as the center-point of history. From Jesus' baptism onwards, the Spirit is active in a new way but only associated with Jesus himself (3:22; 4:1, 14). For his disciples, the Spirit is only a promise for the future (12:12). Curiously, Conzelmann saw this period as a peaceful one, free from Satanic influence (4:13; 22:3), because he seemingly overlooked 11:16 (see also 22:28). Jesus' ministry is also divided into three parts — (i) the time in Galilee (Lk 3:21-9:50), (ii) the travel section (9:51-19:27), (iii) Jesus' entry into Jerusalem up to his death (19:28-23:49).

Two points should be noted in Conzelmann's presentation here. First, he almost ignores the infancy narratives (Lk 1-2). Secondly, he accepts an older interpretation, namely, that Luke's geographical names are to be interpreted as theological symbols rather than as precise geographical information. Thus the journey (9:51-19:27) is not to be taken as a geographical journey but rather as an artistic invention — the mountain is the place of prayer, of communication with the Father, not of temptation (compare Lk 4:5 and Mt 4:8), and cannot be identified on any map. Similarly, the lake (5:1) is a place for manifestation of power.

(c) *The indefinite period of the Church in the world* — Luke's original contribution. Now the Spirit has become available for all believers.

Many criticisms were made of Conzelmann such as his subjective interpretation of geographical names, his rather unconvincing view that Luke's knowledge of Palestinian geography is inaccurate, his ignoring of passages which did not suit his thesis (e.g. Lk 1&2; 11:16); even his threefold division has been severely criticized. Helmut Flender has a more convincing interpretation of Lk 16:16.[7] He agrees that Lk 16:16 heralds a division of periods. Nevertheless, it speaks of only two periods, the new and the old. The new includes both the period of Jesus' ministry and the period of the Church when Jesus is present as exalted Lord. It is divided, from a historical point of view, into two — the Gospel, which describes Jesus' earthly ministry up to the Ascension, and Acts, which marks the period of the Church up to Luke's own day. Luke's most obvious innovations are the writing of Acts and the long travel narrative (9:51ff). Both involve real journeys and not just imaginative movement.

Flender himself has a very interesting, although somewhat over-systematized interpretation of Luke's technique.[8] Following the detailed studies of R. Morgenthaler, he sees a dialectical structure in Luke-Acts and concludes that the "law of two" is the characteristic feature of Lucan style and that Luke's special ability as an editor lies in shaping his material in accordance with this law.

Flender gives many examples of complementary, climactic and antithetic parallelism and suggests that a

Why A New Look In Luke's Gospel?

careful examination helps us to discover the theological concerns of Luke. We can see examples of complementary parallelism in Luke in his frequent habit of paralleling a story about a man with a story about a woman, e.g., Zechariah and Mary (1:55ff), Simeon and Anna (2:25-8), the Widow of Zarephath and Naaman (4:31-9), the Centurion of Capernaum and the Widow of Nain (7:1-17), Simon, the Pharisee and the woman who was a sinner (7:36-50), the man with the mustard seed and the woman with the leaven (13:18-21), the Good Samaritan and Mary and Martha (10:29-42), the man with the hundred sheep and the woman with the ten pieces of silver (15:4-10), the importunate woman and the publican (18:1-14), the women at the tomb and the Emmaus disciples (23:55-24:3). Flender's conclusion is that by this arrangement Luke is expressing that "man and woman stand together and side by side before God. They are equal in honor and grace, they are endowed with the same gifts and have the same responsibilities (cf Gen 1:27; Gal 13:28).''

Flender finds a striking climactic parallelism between the stories of John and Jesus — both are parallel and alike up to a point yet there is a decisive difference and both are poles apart. The superiority of Jesus over John is immediately made obvious — the supernatural birth of Jesus; his names, "Son of the Most High" and "Son of God" (1:32-5). The climax comes in the song of the angels at Jesus' birth (2:13f). Here the parallel breaks down before the unique dignity of Jesus. Antithetical comparison is also frequent as the old world stands in antithesis to the new world, created by God in Christ. Thus the four beatitudes are followed by four woes exactly parallel in content (6:20-6). Jesus is rejected at Nazareth but accepted at Capernaum (4:16-37). At Jericho we find salvation for the son of Abraham who welcomes Jesus (19:19), but judgment on the unrepentant Jews (19:27). For Flender this dialectical pattern is not just a literary technique but is basic to the tradition of Christology not just in Luke but in fact taken for granted throughout the New Testament (e.g. 1 Tim 3:16; Rom 1:3f; Mk 12:35ff). This is Luke's Two Stage Christology (which he says Conzelmann did not notice) — the interplay of the earthly and heavenly modes of Jesus' existence. Although the evangelist knows Jesus now as the exalted, ever-present Kyrios, yet he must describe the man Jesus in the past tense.

Whatever one thinks of Conzelmann, it can be truly said that Lucan studies will never be the same again since his contribution and that subsequent writing must revolve around many of the issues which he raised. Oscar Cullmann has reacted strongly to Conzelmann's idea that Luke's idea of salvation history is secondary and in fact a falsification of the original gospel.[9] He sees salvation history not only solidly based in the teaching of Jesus, but as a consistent characteristic of the whole New Testament (e.g. the realized eschatology of John, whose gospel shows that the paschal events of Jesus' life were the decisive eschatological events in the thinking of the early Christians). He accuses Conzelmann of distorting the eschatological thinking of the early Christians and finds little evidence for the assumption that they considered that the coming of Jesus meant the end of history. In fact, a careful reading shows that in Luke, while there are some passages which suggest or assume a delay of the Parousia,[10] there are other passages which see the Parousia as imminent.[11]

2. *Luke, Historian or Theologian:*

> "All worthwhile historical writing is primarily an artistic exercise, consisting in an attempt to master a large body of facts and to present a small selection of them in the proportion and

form that seem most meaningful at a particular moment in time."[12]

Until Conzelmann (1954), Luke was normally considered to be a historian among the evangelists as the title of C.K. Barrett's book suggests — *Luke the Historian in Recent Studies.*[13] Hitherto, critical study had mainly concentrated on Source Criticism and such historical problems as the date of the Roman census at the time of Jesus' birth. The claim was often made that of the four evangelists, Luke was the nearest to being a historian, that he was interested in Jesus as a historical person — in his antecedents (ch 1,2), his historical and cultural setting (3:1f), his friends (10:38ff), his prayer, and that his gospel was the nearest to a biography of Jesus. Thus E. Kässermann, in discussing the problem of the historical Jesus, states:

> "His gospel is indeed the first 'life of Jesus'. In it, consideration is given to the points of view of causality and theleology, and psychological insight, the comparison of the historian and the particular slant of the writer who aims at edification, are all equally discernable."[14]

Conzelmann's analysis can be said to have swung the pendulum to the opposite corner and today Luke, the theologian, can take his place with such major New Testament theologians as John and Paul. In fact, one of the accepted results of modern study is that the books of the New Testament are primarily theological in character. The new approach however, has tended to see Luke as all theology and to give a very negative view of him as a historian.

History or theology is, of course, a false dichotomy and in any general evaluation of Luke as a historian some important distinctions must be made.

Firstly, Luke's gospel is not to be compared with the works of a modern scientific historian like an Acton or a

Toynbee. His approach and his questions are different from ours. Further, one cannot claim, even for modern historians, the so-called ideal of dispassionate objectivity, but rather what has been aptly described as disciplined subjectivity. Nevertheless, with C.K. Barrett, we can claim that it need not be doubted

> "that he was an honest man, who would not in cold blood distort the truth or say that things had happened when he knew that they had not happened . . . that he admired the great apostles, especially Paul; nor that he was a sincere Christian, who accepted the authority and wished to proclaim the redemptive work of Jesus Christ."[15]

History, of course, is not an exact science. It is useful to remember that no historian, ancient or modern, achieves completeness or objectivity. Ancient writing was, however, often more moralistic than modern history. The first century historian, Dionysius of Halicarnassus, who wrote his History of Rome "in pursuit of truth and honesty" defined history as ' 'philosophy teaching by example." Their approach tended to be narrative, personal and artistic — characteristics which are very evident in Luke himself.

Secondly, we have come to realize in modern times that none of the four gospels is a modern biography of Jesus but rather a unique kind of literature. It is the presentation in narrative form and the expansion of the apostolic preaching. A gospel is a book of faith, the product of at least a generation of theological thinking on the meaning of Jesus and his relevance to very different situations outside Palestine.

Thirdly, one could perhaps classify Luke among the great historians of his time, Josephus, Polybius, Livy Tacitus and Plutarch, and find that he does well in their company. Luke alone of the gospel writers begins his work with a preface, like any other historian of his time (similarly Josephus begins in Wars of the Jews). He describes how he put in a good deal of research as there were many other writers in the field and he himself strove for an accurate and orderly account — writing as he was, for one who had already been instructed in the whole affair. In an age which lacked a universally accepted chronology, he takes great care in his opening chapters to link his account to the rulers and event of the secular history of his time (1:5; 2:1; 3:1f,23) and shows some interest in several of the secular rulers who were important in the gospel times.

Our judgment on Luke's responsibility as a historian is not a purely subjective one. We can compare his tradition with that of the other synoptics, particularly that of Mark who many scholars think was a major source for Luke. In general, one can conclude that he took very few liberties with Mark apart from abbreviating his narrative and polishing his rough style. While Luke shows no hesitancy in making stylistic changes in his introductions and endings, nevertheless, according to Jeremias "he treats the words of Jesus with the greatest reverence and refrains from making greater alterations to them."[16]

A comparison of Luke with the more independent tradition of John's gospel shows remarkable affinities with Luke's special material, e.g., the presence of a second Judas amont the twelve (Lk 6:16; Jn 14:22), Satan's entry into Judas before the betrayal (Lk 22:3; Jn 13:27), the cutting off of the *right* ear in Gethsemane (Lk 22:50; Jn 18:10), the three pronouncements by Pilate of Jesus' innocence (Lk 23:4ff; Jn 18:38; 19:4ff), the presence of two angels at the tomb (Lk 24:4; Jn 20:12), the apparition in Jerusalem which Mark and Matthew place in Galilee.[17] Futher, one can refer to the investigations into the background of Luke's second volume, Acts, of modern scholars like Sir William Ramsey and A.N. Sherwin-White.

Writing in 1895, *St. Paul the Traveller,* the archaeologist, Ramsey, approached Acts with the assumption based on the Tübingen school which denied Lucan authorship and saw Acts as a middle-second century fabrication. Yet he was driven step by step to the conclusion "that it must have been written in the first century and with admirable knowledge." In particular, Ramsey pointed out Luke's care in referring to Roman officials in each case by their correct titles, e.g., the magistrates in Thessalonica are called "politarchs," a fact recently confirmed by inscriptions, some found at Thessalonica itself. A more recent scholar, A.N. Sherwin-White,[18] an Oxford classical historian, criticizes New Testament scholars for failing to recognize what excellent historical sources we have in the gospel. He claims that on points of geography, politics, Roman Law, administration and social practice, Luke was quite accurate in his details. These studies certainly provide a good indication of Luke's accuracy in his gospel presentation.

However, it is with the religious faith historians of the Old Testament that Luke is much more at home. Old Testament writers were definite in their understanding of the development of history as influenced by the divine workings of Yahweh. The Old Testament is content to assert that Yahweh is sovereign lord of history while at the same time insisting that man is free and responsible without any attempt at a speculative resolution of the obvious (to us) problem. Unlike the Greeks, they could rise above the cyclical idea of history and originated the idea that history is a process with a beginning, middle and end, directed by the will and purpose of Yahweh.[19]

The Old Testament gave a theological interpretation of history. In particular, the Deuteronomic historian (Deuteronomy, Joshua, Judges, Samuel and Kings) stresses the prophetic word which pre-ordained history and thus pro-

Why A New Look In Luke's Gospel?

duced a kind of alternating rhythm of prophecy and fulfilment. They used their faith to interpret and even to reconstruct the past. They recounted history, not for its own sake, but in order to better understand the present, to challenge their hearers to a particular response, a conversion, now, today.

Luke took up this Old Testament understanding of history and rethought it in the light of the event of Jesus. If then we consider Luke a historian, we must consider him a historian in the Jewish Biblical tradition and not in the modern or even ancient Greek tradition.[20] He was a religious historian, a minister of the word. He was, in a word, a theologian, but not a theologian dealing with abstractions or pure theological concepts, but with the real concrete historical life of Jesus of Nazareth, whose life he was trying to interpret for Theophilus. He could be described as a pastoral historian, a historian with a message of salvation, a convinced Christian who wrote history with a candidly expressed aim of convincing the intelligent Gentile Theophilus of the soundness, the attractiveness and credibility of the Christian message. He was not dealing with our situation or often with our questions and problems. Despite the many objections and criticisms of some recent scholars, it must be concluded that Luke is in agreement with the central teaching and proclamation of the New Testament (e.g. Jesus, Paul, John). Thus it is often extremely difficult to answer that tormenting modern question: What actually happened? One finds the same problem in dealing with the opening chapters of Genesis. It took the Church a long time to realize that they do not provide the answers to our historical and scientific questions — the "when" and "how" questions about which the Genesis writers had in fact much less information than our scientists today, who still are very much in the dark. It took a long time to realize that the Genesis writers were theologians, preoccupied with the problems of their own day (e.g. star and animal worship, the Caananite fertility cults). Something similar perhaps might be said of Luke's approach. Caird's reflection on the historicity of the Infancy narrative is worth quoting.

> "Luke certainly believed that he was dealing with real events and it would be hypercriticism to doubt that behind these two chapters there is a substratum of the same sort of historical fact as we find described in a more down-to-earth manner in the remainder of the gospel. Equally clearly, Luke does not content himself with that which the television camera and microphone could have recorded. He would not have been a better historian had he done so. All history is an attempt to find pattern and meaning in a section of human experience and every historian worthy of the name raises questions about man's ultimate destiny and the meaning of all history to which, as a historian, he can provide no answers. The answers belong to the realm of theology; and into this realm of metahistory Luke and the other evangelists are concerned to lead us. Whether we like it or not, we must be content to live with a measure of uncertainty as to where fact ends and interpretation begins. Of one thing we may be sure — Luke was no simpleton. We do him a grave injustice if we suppose that, when he wrote in an elevated and imaginative style, he was naive enough to take his own poetry with pedantic literalness."[21]

3. *The Old Testament Background to Luke:*

In common with John, Luke has been situated more firmly against an Old Testament background in recent years. Both the Gospel and Acts are considered to be much more concerned with Judaism and the fulfilment of the Old Testament promises than was previously thought. We have already suggested that Luke was a historian in the Old Testament style and that his books are full of subtle allusions to its historical books. One could perhaps over simplify the question and suggest that previously Luke (apart from the birth narratives which are obviously very Jewish in character) was treated as a Gentile historian, writing for the Gentiles and avoiding Jewish thinking as far as possible. Somewhat surprisingly we can still read the following comment on Luke from a modern Old Testament expert —

" . . . Luke was a Gentile, unacquainted with Palestine, uninformed about Judaism, not understanding it very well and a little afraid of it."[22]

However, today we can say that the pendulum has swung in the opposite direction and scholars are busily researching the Old Testament roots of Luke's thought. According to the commentary by E.J. Tinsley[23] Luke believed that —

"In the life and action of Jesus certain key crises in the history of Israel, when it was faced with acceptance or rejection of the call of God, were being lived over again. What was particularly at stake was whether Israel would recognize and accept as its destiny under God a mission which might involve humiliation by the Gentiles, even if it resulted in universal salvation. It is very likely that Jesus himself saw things in this way. The whole ministry of Jesus faced men with a crisis, the crisis of whether to take him on faith as a sign to be accepted, or to reject him in unbelief, as a 'scandal'. The birth of Jesus is presented alongside that of John the Baptist in such a way as to indicate that John is the last-born of the old Israel and Jesus the first-born of the new, the glory of the people of Israel (2:32) . . .

. . . Luke especially shows how Jesus saw his mission as a way up to Jerusalem which he must pursue in away his Father would indicate. The temptation narratives already show the influence of the book of Deuteronomy on Jesus, and it is quite possible that it was at the back of Luke's mind when he wrote the central section of his gospel (9:51-18:30). Here Luke has so arranged his non-Marcan material as to indicate that the journey of Jesus to Jerusalem was a representation of Israel's journey to the promised land . . . in Jesus, Israel is faced with a perfect image of itself, carrying out in dedicated obedience the age-old mission of the people of God . . . Jesus saw that his chief temptation was like the constant temptation of old Israel — to put God to a test of one's own rather than to trust him (see Exod 17:1-7). And for Luke, the disciples who follow in the 'way' of Jesus will necessarily undergo the same sort of testing. The whole mission of Jesus involves a temptation to disobey. It is Luke who goes out of his way in the account of the temptation to say that the devil left Jesus, not finally, but only momentarily 'biding his time' (4:13); later on the disciples are characterized by Jesus as those 'who have stood firmly by me in my times of trial' (22:28). For those with eyes to see and ears to hear, suggests Luke, here is the new Moses bringing about a new and final Exodus, and here is a new Elijah bringing to completion the whole movement of Old Testament prophecy. This latter suggestion is a feature of the Gospels of Luke and John; in Mark and Matthew, John the Baptist is thought of as a new-born Elijah . . .".

Tinsley emphasizes that all the titles which relate to Jesus were in common use both for Israel as a community and for Israel as personified in an individual human figure (see "Son of God" in Hosea 11:1 and Ps 2:7; "Servant" in Isaiah 40-55 and 42:1-4; Christ or Messiah in Hab 3:13 and 1 Sam 24:10; "Son of Man" in Dan 7 and 1 Enoch). He sees the special emphasis which Luke gives to the significance of Jesus' mission in the fact that the new Israel (the nucleus of which was Jesus and the twelve) will include both Jews and non-Jews, whereas the old Israel included only those who were Jews by birth or adoption.

A more recent study of Luke by Eric Franklin[24] suggests that Luke's theology can only be undertood when the full influence of the Old Testament, which provided the background, ideas and beliefs to his work, is allowed.

> "Luke's theology is best understood if he is accepted as having come to Jesus by way of the Old Testament. But equally, his theological use of that book is of such a kind that makes it likely that he came into the Jewish faith rather than that he was born into it. Luke's embrace of the Jewish religion is almost completely without tensions. The only point at which he shows a dissatisfaction with it or a shrinking from its demands, is on the question of circumcision which, for him, is that part of the Law which is superseded by Christ, but which even then, is not abrogated for the Jew. Christ represents a freedom from the requirement of circumcision rather than a negation of it or a denial of its value. Luke reveals an intellectual conversion to Judaism which accepts its promises, which he sees fulfilled in Jesus. He was a student of the Old Testament, but he was himself numbered among the Gentiles and it is this which determines his interest in the poor, the outcast, the Samaritan, and ultimately, in the Gentiles themselves. Luke's Jewishness must be emphasized, but it is the Jewishness of one who has come into Judaism by conviction."

Franklin argues that history was the servant of Luke's theology. Luke was a creative, pastoral theologian, a historian in the tradition of the Old Testament. He could allow his theology to portray as events of history things which did not necessarily take place, e.g., his account of Paul and possibly his account of the ascension as a separate event in time and space. Luke-Acts is "a tract for the times" which resulted from a threefold threat to the faith: (a) the failure of the parousia to occur — Luke shifted the emphasis from the parousia to the ascension as the pivoted eschatological event, (b) the nature of Jesus' life as characterized by rejection and crucifixion, the very opposite of the glorified life of the ascended Jesus — Luke shows that Jesus' life is one with the Old Testament expectations, (c) the refusal of the Jews to acknowledge Jesus as Christ although he fulfilled the Old Testament expectations. There is still hope for Israel as God has not abandoned Israel. Thus, according to Franklin, Luke was deeply attached to Judaism. He hoped for the restoration of Israel and possibly in his two volumes was speaking primarily to Jewish Christians.

A fascinating, though rather extreme theory, has recently been profounded by John Drury in his *Tradition and Design in Luke's Gospel.*[25] He concludes that the Old Testament has much more influence on Luke than was traditionally supposed. He is clearly influenced by M. Goulder,[26] who expounded "*midrash* as the imaginative literary discipline by which the writers of the New Testament time and milieu did their work." Drury tells us that he himself was "fond of poetry and fiction, which are not universally popular amongst New Testament critics." Further, he was dissatisfied at the way history was practiced in New Testament Studies and in particular with the way that "the gospels were studied with painstaking scholarship, but in relative isolation and with little more than the occasional glance at similar and contemporary literature." Goulder's original thesis was that Matthew had no source for his gospel other than Mark and that what he had in Mark provided him with enough material for the composition of the non-Marcan sections. Thus he dispensed with the hypothesis Q, so beloved of the source-critics.[27] Drury likewise discovered that he could do without Q. His thesis is that Luke's Gospel is sufficiently explained by three principal sources, Mark, Matthew and (much more that was generally supposed) the Old Testament. Drury attempts to show how Luke wove all three together with "the exact and leisurely skill of one of the greatest narrative

Midrashists." He eliminates at one blow the access to oral or early written traditions (e.g. Mary), which many scholars have claimed for Luke. Thus for the infancy narratives he indicates what Luke drew from the Old Testament (e.g. the vocabulary and phraseology of the Septuagint), and from Matthew.

Luke repeats Matthew's "ornate irrelevance of a genealogy (with differences and similarities) which traces Jesus' descent through a man, who was not, on his own evidence, his father." Although a gentile gospel, Luke omits the Magi, as he omits Mark's Syro-Phoenican woman, and instead introduces the homage of the poor shepherds and Simeon and Anna, "ideal types of Old Testament piety and expectation." Like Tinsley, he takes over the suggestion of C.F. Evans[28] that the central section of Luke is not a fairly random collection of teachings, but a deliberate attempt to follow the order of Deuteronomy while still using Matthew, to produce

> "a handbook on the Christian life in the historical setting of a journey to Jerusalem, just as Deuteronomy is a guide for the devout Jew, set in the historical perspective of the journey into the promised land, with Jerusalem, the place where God will cause his name to dwell, as its center."

He does admit, however, that Luke's energies flag towards the end. With regard to the parables which are peculiar to Luke, he hesitates about attributing them to Jesus without a careful analysis of Lucan characteristics which proliferate in them. Even if they are attributed to Jesus they need not be seen as a total creation ex nihilo, but spun "out of ideas known to him as a scripture learned Jew."

Drury has received several favorable reviews from other scholars, yet it is doubtful if many would go as far as he in eliminating other sources, Q in particular or some tradition close to it. The theory that Luke both knew and adapted Matthew seems highly questionable (e.g. the genealogies). Drury's ingenious argument is cumulative and can be questioned at many points. He has done much to elaborate the Jewish background to Luke and his emphasis on midrash is quite important, though extreme. He stresses that midrash is

> "the method by which in historical fact rather than scholarly conjecture, Jews of various colors from the most chauvinistic Pharisee to the most liberal Hellenist, did their history writing."

He points out the "mixture of freedom and conservatism by which *midrash* grafts new contingencies to the stock of ancient authoritative truth," e.g.

> "when the chronicler flattens the Books of Kings to suit his own puritan and pedestrian morality, when Ezekiel in his sixteenth chapter tells the whole Hebrew history concisely and powerfully in terms of the prophetic stock-in-trade of the love story, or when Luke at Acts 7 has Stephen do the same as a prophetic polemic against national disobedience."

Drury sees John's gospel as a free midrash of the gospel tradition, as Matthew on Mark or Luke on both, with the Old Testament reinstated as a source despite the source critics. He quotes with approval the opinion of the Jewish scholar, Vermes, that in midrash

> "lies the answer to a great many problems confronting the New Testament scholar. Since the Christian '*kerygma*' was first formulated by Jews for Jews, using Jewish arguments and methods of exposition, it goes without saying that a thorough knowledge of contemporary Jewish exegesis is essential to the understanding and not just a better understanding, of the message of the New Testament, and, even more, of Jesus."[29]

Strictly speaking, it should be pointed out that to characterize Luke's approach, especially as regards his Infancy Narratives, as *midrash*, (lit "to speak out"), is an oversimplification.[29a] The characteristic point of midrash is that it begins from an ancient biblical text. Then it proceeds to meditate on the particular text, to actualize it and discover its relevance for the present. The result could often be a free and imaginative retelling of the original story, e.g., the narrative parts of Daniel or the praise of famous men in Sirach 45-50. Both Matthew and Luke seem to proceed in the opposite direction by beginning with the person of Jesus and other historical persons and events connected with him. Then they proceed by meditation to express their full meaning and significance with the aid of ancient texts and prophecies. However, this is not to deny that the infancy narratives are continually influenced by midrashic techniques — the imaginative use of parallel and related Old Testament texts.[30]

4. *The Infancy Narratives:*

The infancy narratives (Lk 1-2) have become a storm center of Lucan Studies especially with regard to their historicity.[31] Opinions on them have varied considerably from strict historical accounts to what a friend of mine has called "the first Christian nativity play," a kind of theological comment on the person of Jesus in the light of such texts as Acts 2 :36. In particular, the rediscovery of the literary technique of midrash has been the most important contribution to an understanding of these chapters.

A brief and highly selective historical summary from the many modern contributions towards an understanding of the infancy narratives and their place in Luke's theology is all that can be attempted here. Our brief summary is based on the excellent article published in 1964 by H.H.

Oliver,[32] but adds more recent contributions to the problem.

1921: R. Bultmann claimed that such ideas as "virginal conception," "savior," "good news," "shepherds," are ultimately derived from Hellenistic myths, as the evangelist is speaking to a Hellenistic audience and attempting to show that Jesus was superior to their own heroes and demigods.

1927: Henry J. Cadbury's *The Making of Luke — Acts,* has become a classic in Lucan studies and is full of value even today on the sources of Luke and for example, whether Luke is using written material from Mark of Q (and we can add the Infancy Narratives). Cadbury's words are worth quoting (p. 67f) —

> "His own style is more obvious sometimes than at others, but it is never so totally wanting as to prove alien origin for a passage, and it is never so persuasive as to exclude the possibility that a written source existed, although the source be no longer capable of detection by any residual difference of style. Unlike the process of composition attributed by modern scholars to the writing of the Pentateuch, by which older writings are woven together in truly Semitic fashion without altering the distinctive language of the originals, Luke's method was to recast his material, paraphrasing into his own style. This habit which he shares with Greek and Latin writers generally prevents the determination of his sources by the criterion of vocabulary."[33]

1930: B.H. Streeter in a study of the origins of the gospels claimed that while Matthew's infancy narrative came from oral sources Luke's came from a document which originally may have been composed in Hebrew.

1931: A von Harnack claimed that the first two chapters of Luke existed from the beginning only in Greek. In particular, he claimed that the two songs, The Magnificat and the Benedictus, were composed by the same author

Why A New Look In Luke's Gospel?

who wrote Luke-Acts. Since they contain many Semitic expressions the author must have consciously imitated the Greek Old Testament (the Septuagint). He thought that in Luke's original manuscript The Magnificat was ascribed to Elizabeth and not to Mary. Further, he would delete the word "virgin" in 1:27, also in 1:34-5, and the phrase "as was thought" in 3:23. He believed that the remarkable role of Mary described by Luke is the result of the impression she made on the community where the narratives were collected.

1932: M. Dibelius sees in Luke 1-2, a collection of early Christian traditions. In particular, 1:26-37 and 2:1-10 are two different traditions about the birth of Jesus which the evangelist is content to place side by side. 1:26-37 stressed Mary; the Virgin's Son; the virginal conception by the Spirit. In 2:1-10, Joseph and Mary are Jesus' parents; the signs and wonders center on the child rather than on the mother, and there is no reference to the Spirit. Luke 2 also stresses the savior-child "in the manger," a phrase repeated in v 7, 12, 16. In the present form of Luke's text he finds John shown to be the forerunner of a Jesus, whose superiority is emphasized.

The Visitation is Luke's creation. The Magnificat was originally attributed to Mary but was later attributed to Elizabeth when the "tapeinosis" (lowliness), v 48, was understood as barrenness by comparison with 1 Sa, 1:11. Dibelius' comment on the problem of criteria for deciding the historicity of the account of the origins of John the Baptist, is interesting.

> "It is impossible and also unimportant to determine how much historically reliable information is contained in this legend. For in the face of such a legend, every attempt in that direction seems to be equally devoid of objective criteria: whether one reduces the legend, on critical grounds, to those parts which remain when the miracles have been excised, or

whether one uncritically assigns everything narrated to the field of history, or (finally), whether one simply denies the possibility that particular information about the origins of the Baptist could be reliable."

Dibelius further suggests that

"reflection upon the heavenly origin of Jesus led to the affirmation that he was born, not according to the flesh but *according to the* Spirit (of Gal 4:29), and thus is the distinctive contribution of Hellenistic Judaism to the doctrine; this in turn led to the affirmation that he was conceived by the power of the Holy Spirit *in the womb of a virgin,* and this is an idea which stems ultimately, from Pagan Egypt."

1945: The Swedish Lutheran, H. Sahlin, developed an Aramaic source theory ("Proto-Luke"), proposed by C.C. Torrey. "Proto-Luke" was composed in Hebrew, by an unknown Christian Jew, perhaps from Antioch. He imitated the biblical style as he sought to write the concluding book of the Old Testament. He denied that there was a conscious parallelism between the births of John and Jesus in Proto-Luke. The Magnificat originally followed 1:64 and was a hymn of Zechariah. Sahlin also developed an idea first proposed by the Jesuit, S. Lyonnet in 1939, and argued that in "Proto-Luke" Mary was seen almost as an allegorical figure, as a symbol of the daughter of Zion (see Zeph 3:14; Joel 2:21; Zech 9:9) where the present imperative (chaire, rejoice) is applied to Israel, symbolized as Daughter of Zion and mother and Israel is invited to rejoice because "the Lord is with her" as king and savior. Many recent scholars have agreed that Luke is presenting Mary as the historical embodiment of the "corporate personality" of Israel in the day of eschatological salvation.[35] Luke's choice of the verb "overshadow" is also seen to indicate that the divine presence descended on Mary as long ago on the Ark of the Covenant (Ex 40:34-5). Sahlin also suggested that Simeon's prediction of a sword piercing Mary (2:35) is addressed to Mary as the representative of the people of Israel.

1952: P. Vielhauer in his study of Luke's theology lays the foundation which Conzelmann will develop, e.g., his statement "How uneschatological Luke's thinking is is proved not only by the contents but by the very fact of the Acts of the Apostles."[36] He sees Luke as a theologian whose infancy stories, especially his presentation of the Baptist, express his basic theology of salvation history. But his stress on the infancy stories was neglected by Conzelmann as we shall see.

1954: For P. Winter the Lucan birth stories originally came from a Hebrew text (Luke used a Greek translation) which —

> "could not have been written by anyone but a person or persons rooted in Jewish social tradition, religious custom and general folklore, and acquainted with the topographic features of the surroundings in which the story is set . . . Jews were living in Palestine in a Jewish community well before the start of the armed conflict with Rome, and who share in that community's conventions and held its general outlook on life."

Originally there were two written sources —

(a) a document from Baptist circles (1:5-80) which incorporated (by addition of 1:76-9) two Maccabaean battle hymns, sung before and after the battle.

(b) a Temple document which described a disputation in the Temple — this originated with people around James the Just, people who retained memories of Jesus' parents and their acquaintances. The two sources were joined by someone before Luke by changing the annunciation to Elizabeth into an annunciation to Mary, by composing 2:4-21 and creating the account of the Visitation.

Several scholars quickly reacted to Winter and argued persuasively that the theory of a written Hebrew source was neither proved nor necessary and that the style of the writer was consistent with the rest of his writing, when he is probably not translating Semitic sources.

1954: For Conzelmann

> "the introductory chapters present a special problem. It is strange that the characteristic features they contain do not occur again either in the Gospel or in Acts. In certain passages there is a direct contradiction, as for example, in the analogy between the Baptist and Jesus, which is emphasized in the early chapters, but deliberately avoided in the rest of the Gospel . . . Mary disappears to a greater extent in Luke than in Mark and Matthew."[37]

Since then he has found the first two chapters as questionable and not integral to the Gospel; Conzelmann proceeds to ignore them in his presentation of Lucan theology. The response to Conzelmann's position here has been unanimously negative with some scholars trying to fit the birth narratives into Conzelmann's scheme, while others use them to challenge his theology.[38]

1956-7: R. Laurentin describes the character of Luke 1-2 as archaic and Jewish Old Testament, both in theology and in style. He sees a strong relationship with the rest of Luke's Gospel — the relation between John and Jesus prepares one ('amorce') for the preaching of the Precursor (Lk 3); the episode of Jesus in the middle of the teachers (2:41-53) prepares us for Jesus' public life and his role as a teacher; the words of Simeon (2:35) and the "three days" of his parents anxious search (2:49) prepares us for the Passion. John is the forerunner of the Messiah and his ministry is preparatory (in the role of Elijah 1:16-17); his parents are related to Israel (dikaioi 1:6). Jesus' ministry is eternal and eschatological (1:32-3) and with Mary the new time of grace has begun (charis 1:28). These stories of Luke are no fabrication of him but are a substantially faithful yet stylized treatment of real events handed on by witnesses.

1957: P. Benoit believes that Luke 1:2 is composed originally in a consciously biblical (septuagint) style and inspired by Old Testament models. He finds that the examples which resist the hypothesis of a Hebrew document are more numerous than the opposite examples. In particular, he maintains that the portrait of John as forerunner of Jesus (kyrios) does not come from a circle of John's followers but that it was composed by Luke from the synoptic tradition. Luke clearly regarded John as inferior to Jesus (compare 1:32 and 1:76). Luke used Old Testament models because *the facts* of John's and Jesus' births which are received in the tradition suggested the parallels.

1957: M.D. Goulder and M.L. Sanderson attempted to show that Luke 1-2 is

> "a pious meditation by St. Luke himself; a piece of Haggadah, in which the evangelist has superimposed upon such historical knowledge as he thought he possessed, a pattern from the book of Genesis embroidered upon from the prophets, after the Rabbinic manner."

and the main strand is the

> "theme of the fulfilment of Abraham-Isaac-Jacob in Jesus and his forerunners."

Thus they see the New Israel as beginning with a new Abraham (Zechariah) and a new Sarah (Elizabeth). Zechariah's successor in the biblical canon is Malachi and in Luke it is John, the new Malachi. Elizabeth and Mary correspond to Aaron's wife, Elisheba and her sister-in-law, Miriam. Mary is also seen to be a new Hannah (1 Sam 1:11

and Lk 1:47 have the same word "servant") — this, according to the writers, ends the textual problem as to whether to attribute The Magnificat to Elizabeth or to Mary. Thus they see in Luke

> "a devout and learned man's meditation on the beginning of our redemption in the light of ancient prophecy, written either in an enlightened reverence for the reality behind the symbol, or a conviction that God must have, and had fulfilled the Scripture."

If one believed in Jesus as Messiah, therefore, he must have been born in Bethlehem as the prophet Micah had foretold.

1964: H.H. Oliver believes that Luke deliberately included the birth narratives into his well ordered work "so as to contribute to the overall theological plan of the work." He tries to fit them into Luke's general plan of salvation history and discusses the following themes which reflect Luke's theology: John and the Period of Israel to which he is clearly linked (1:27,73,74f,77,80); John and the Middle of Time (Jesus) — there is a contrast between the prophet and the Son of the Most High (a frequent phrase of Luke 1:31,76); Jesus and World history (2:1-2; 3:1-2); Jesus and Jerusalem — Jerusalem is used six times in 1-2, 24 times in the rest of Luke and 64 times in Acts (according to Laurentin); Jesus and the salvation of the Gentiles; Jesus and his identity (Christ the Lord 2:9-11); The Power of the Most High, i.e., the Holy Spirit. One should mention here that since Oliver the infancy stories are generally considered to be integral to Luke's work and treated as such.

1966: P.S. Minear, building on previous studies, makes a study of Luke's vocabulary and stylistic patterns. He shows that of sixty-two of Luke's favorite words, forty-six are found in the infancy stories, and further, that

Why A New Look In Luke's Gospel?

fifty-five significant words and phrases, which are found in the infancy stories, are found more frequently in the rest of Luke's two volumes than in the other books of the New Testament.[39]

1969: P. Grech gives a brief presentation of the modern approach.[40] He sees the purpose of the infancy stories "as not the satisfaction of the reader's curiosity" by Luke but rather as "deeply theological and apologetical in character," e.g., dealing with a Jewish objection that while Jesus came from Nazareth he should have come from Bethlehem, being a descendant of David (Jn 7:41) — therefore the early Christians collected information about the infancy of Jesus especially by examining the Old Testament. Luke's two chapters, despite their

> "apparent lucidity, are a composition of the most sophisticated nature. The annunciation-birth-narratives about John and Jesus form a diptych in LXX style, which immediately transports the reader into the remote past when judges and prophets were born. The time sequence in Luke however, is not fixed according to Jewish dynasties alone, it is incorporated into general world history to signify its universal value (Lk 1:5,2:1,3:1f). The narrative has a double purpose; that of introducing the reader to the narratives which follow, and the more important one of providing a commentary on that great moment which proved to be such a turning point in history. The theological thought in those two chapters runs parallel with Gal 4:4 and can be summarized thus. A joyful moment has arrived in history (1:5,13). The salvation and redemption which God had provided for the whole world and his special promises to Israel are now finding their fulfilment, through God's faithfulness in sending his Son Jesus, born of Mary the Virgin, the Daughter of Sion, into the world. That Jesus is the Messiah is testified by John and by the Spirit, who moves all these events and presses world history into the service of redemptive history (2:1). The days foretold by the prophets are here; Jew and Gentile alike — the poor especial-

ly — are called to believe in the Christ and render thanks to God for the salvation he has provided."

In the same commentary[41] W.J. Harrington emphasizes the two references to Mary's meditation on the things that concerned her Son (2:19,51) and suggests that "most of the information must have come from her ultimately." As Luke's Gospel is written for the Gentiles he finds the universal aspect of the gospel already stressed in the infancy narratives "despite their marked semitic character," e.g., 2:14 "peace among men"; 2:32 "a light to the Gentiles"; 3:6,38. He finds these chapters dominated by the idea of messianic fulfilment with the different scenes building up to a climax, the formal manifestation of the Messiah in the entry into the Temple. Luke's effect is achieved especially by the use of Daniel 9-10 in the annunciation to Zechariah, the Benedictus and the Presentation, and the use of ephlesthesan (1:23,57); 2:6,21f) and a constant echoing of SCripture or an "allusive theology" to underline the arrival of the messianic age. In summary, his position is that Luke "while leaning on a Greek form of originally Aramaic traditions, has himself written chapters 1-2 of his gospel, and in a style redolent of the LXX."

1976: J. Drury,[42] whose general approach we have already discussed when describing the Old Testament influence on Luke, points out that substantial parts of Luke 1-2 are in verse and that to suggest that Luke composed them in the Old Testament manner "is not to posit any very exalted skill on his part" — "the metrics are so tolerant that the form is virtually a rhythmic and antiphonal prose." He concludes that

> "They are certainly from the same hand which wrote the whole of the first two chapters, for like the prose in them they are so packed with Old Testament references as to be collages

or mosaics or scriptural texts. To find a man with a head full of the Septuagint we need look no further than Luke himself. His claim to authorship is vindicated by the fact that these songs express themes which are integral to his whole work: God's classical action in raising the low and bringing down the lofty; his visiting his people in fulfilment of ancient prophecy; the joy which this evokes; the use of 'soter' (savior) and 'soteria' (salvation), which is peculiar to Luke among the synoptics; the two references to Abraham; and the glimpse of revelation to the gentiles which foreshadows Acts."

He points out that psalms are not only found in the book of Psalms; many oracles of the prophets and sayings of the wise are in the same form and in particular the books of history (Luke's models and tutors) have "bursts of song" which "make explicit the theology latent in the narrative (e.g. Ex 15; Num 23 and 35; Deut 33; 2 Sam 22 and 23 and such books as Daniel, Jonah, Jubilees).

1977: R.E. Brown, S.S., who in a study on the Virginal Conception of Jesus, published in 1973,[43] pointed out that

"Although modern Protestant and Catholic scholars are in surprising agreement on the generally figurative and non-historical character of the infancy narratives, there really is no adequate commentary on these Gospel chapters in English,"

has himself made good the lacuna with the publication of a magnum opus entitled *The Birth of the Messiah.*[44] Here he tries to show how each of the two narratives "fits into the theology of its respective gospel and thus offer some reasons for differences between the infancy narratives." His central contention is that they are "worthy vehicles of the Gospel message; indeed each is essential Gospel story in miniature."

"The appreciation for them among ordinary Christians may in part reflect sentimentality as well as the fact that they are stories well told. But on a much deeper level it reflects a true instinct recognizing in the infancy narrative the essence of the Good News, namely, that God has made Himself present to us in the life of His Messiah who walked on this earth, so truly present that the birth of the Messiah was the birth of God's Son. I maintain that genuine biblical criticism, for all the historical problems that it raises, sets this claim in clear perspective."[45]

Brown distinguishes[46] "three stages in a deepening scholarly penetration of the infancy narratives" —

A. *"The perception that the infancy narratives differ significantly from the main body of the Gospel material."* He sees Gospels as "developing backwards," with no reference at all to the birth at the earliest stage in the sermons of Acts and only one clear reference in the main Pauline letters.[47] Then remembering that biographical interest was not primary, we can see how our written gospels emerged from the prefixing of the ministry accounts (in logical rather than chronological order) to the passion accounts (e.g. Mark, who tells nothing about Jesus' birth, youth or even Joseph's name). Finally, the infancy accounts were composed and brought into the gospel account from Christian curiosity about their master, his family ancestors and birthplace, from a need to reply to Jewish skepticism about a Galilean Messiah (Jn 7:41f,52), who was illegitimate. Matthew and Luke saw the christological implications of such stories and the advantage of weaving such stories into their own narratives and prefixing them to their gospels as a "vehicle of the message that Jesus was the Son of God, acting for the salvation of mankind."

One must remember the development of Christology,

(i) the pre-gospel period (e.g. Acts 2:32,6; 5:31; 13:32f; Rom 1:3-4; Philip 2:8-9), where it is stressed that Jesus had become greater through the resurrection than during his ministry of lowliness.

(ii) Further reflection led to the view by the time the Gospels were written (beginning in the 60s) that what the resurrection simply revealed more publicly was there all during Jesus' ministry (e.g. Mark tells the reader that already at the *baptism* Jesus was the Son of God (Mk 1:11), but Jesus did not openly reveal it as the disciples were unable to comprehend (e.g. the select disciples at the transfiguration scene are *afraid and do not understand,* Mk 8:29). In John, Jesus speaks openly as a pre-existent, divine figure (Jn 8:58; 10:30; 14:9; 17:5). John goes further back to pre-existence before creation, while Matthew and Luke press the mystery of Jesus' identity back to his conception. In Matthew, writing later, the mystery of Jesus' identity becomes more apparent (compare Mt 14:32 and Mk 6:51-2, also Mt 16:16 and Mk 8:29). This process explains such puzzling features as why later during Jesus' ministry no one seems to know Jesus' marvellous origins (Mt 13:54-5; 14:1-2; Lk 7:19) and why accounts of Jesus' ministry were formed without a knowledge of the infancy material.

B. "The problem of historicity becomes more acute through the perception of the degree to which the two canonical infancy narratives differ from one another." Brown finds eleven points shared by the two infancy narratives —

(a) The parents to be are Mary and Joseph, who are legally engaged or married, but have not yet come to live together or have sexual relations.

(b) Joseph's Davidic descent (Mt 1:16,20; Lk 1:27,32; 2:4).

(c) The angelic announcement of the birth (Mt 1:20-3; Lk 1:30-5).

(d) Mary's son is not conceived through intercourse with her husband (Mt 1:29,23,25; Lk 1:34).

(e) The conception is through the Holy Spirit (Mt 1:18,20; Lk 1:31).

(f) The angel's directive that he is to be named Jesus (Mt 1:21; Lk 1:31).

(g) An angel states that Jesus is to be Savior (Mt 1:21; Lk 2:11).

(h) The birth takes place after the parents have come to live together (Mt 1:24-5; Lk 2:5-6).

(i) The birth takes place at Bethlehem (Mt 2:1; Lk 2:4-6).

(j) It is chronologically related to the reign (days of Herod the Great (Mt 2:1; Lk 1:5).

(k) The child is reared at Nazareth (Mt 2:23; Lk 2:39).

All (he notes) are found in one section of Matthew (Mt 1:18-21) except the last one which both writers could have known from the public ministry. For the rest, both are quite different (compare Mt's genealogy 1:1-17 and Luke's, which is outside the infancy story 3:23-38). Luke alone has the story of Elizabeth, Zechariah and the birth of John, the census which brings Joseph to Bethlehem, the shepherds, the presentation in the temple and the loss and finding episodes. Matthew has the star, the magi, Herod's plot, the masacre of the Bethlehem children and the flight into Egypt. How do we explain the agreements, and disagreements, the *concordia discors* which is the synoptic problem in miniature?

Christians have little difficulty in practice in joining the Lucan shepherds and the Matthew magi. Is Joseph the source of Matthew, and Mary that of Luke? How then could Joseph have omitted the annunciation to Mary or Mary omitted the magi and the flight into Egypt? Brown concludes that a close analysis makes it unlikely that either account is completely historical — some of Matthew's extraordinary events should have left traces in Jewish records or elsewhere in the New Testament (e.g. Mt 2:3). Luke's census is "almost certainly wrong" as is his understanding of Jewish customs at the presentation and purification. He sees some of the scenes as a rewriting of Old Testament scenes or themes.

Why A New Look In Luke's Gospel?

C. "The historicity problem is somewhat relativized by the perception that the infancy narratives are primarily vehicles of the evangelist's theology and christology." He points out that in the last twenty years, attention has shifted from the pre-Gospel history of the narratives and sayings to their role in the finished Gospels and that the primary (but not the only) "task of exegesis is to make sense of the existing text."

In the infancy narratives the evangelists had greater freedom to be truly creative authors because the material was less fixed in the course of apostolic preaching. They are "not an embarrassment but a masterpiece," which Matthew and Luke thought were "appropriate introductions to the career and significance of Jesus," and "as profoundly Christian and as dramatically persuasive as the last two chapters, the story of the passion and resurrection."

Perhaps Luke's original opening was at 3:1ff. Parallels in Greek writing suggest this, also the placing of the genealogy in chapter three, and Mark's gospel which begins at this point (see also Acts 1:22). However, even though the opening chapters 1 and 2 may have been composed last, there seems to be no doubt that Luke himself prefixed them. Further, Brown reacts strongly against Conzelmann, for whom the Lucan Baptist was not a precursor of Jesus, who knew nothing of the Kingdom of God but belonged to the last of the prophets of the period of Israel. He thinks Conzelmann's analysis is wrong (e.g. John is closely part of the good news of salvation, fulfilling the prophets in 1:19,70,76) and sees the infancy narrative as a true introduction to some of the main themes of the Gospel proper.

He makes a very interesting comparison between the relation of Acts 1-2 to the rest of Acts (they supply a transition from the story of Jesus to the story of the Church — the apostles who accompanied Jesus are instructed by the risen Christ and receive the Holy Spirit so that the continuity with what follows will be clear). Similarly, Luke 1-2, representatives from the Old Testament, Zechariah and Elizabeth, Simeon and Anna, provide a transition from the story of Israel to the story of John the Baptist and Jesus. If Luke composed 1-2 last of all (i.e. after Acts)

> "it is not surprising that in many ways the infancy narrative is closer in spirit to the stories in Acts than the gospel material which Luke took from Mark and Q" e.g. the outpouring of the spirit (Acts 2:17; Lk 1:15,41,67,80; 2:25-7; in the ministry it is not poured out on others); the angelic appearances (Lk 1:11,26; 2:9; Ac 5:19; 8:26; 10:3; 12:7; 27:23); the title "Messiah, Lord" (Lk 2:11 and Ac 2:36); the parallelism between the Baptist and Jesus and the parallelism in Acts between the careers of Peter and Paul.

Because of the notorious disagreement among scholars, Brown does not use the linguistic criterion to establish the pre-gospel materials but rather the criteria of content and theology. He rejects the possibility of Mary or John the Baptist as sources and suggests that there were pre-Lucan items of an allegedly factual character such as are also found in the pre-Matthean traditions, e.g., the dating of Jesus' birth before Herod's death (B.C. 4), its location at Bethlehem, the names of Mary and Joseph, the tendency to describe Jesus' conception in terms of the Old Testament annunciation pattern, the conception by the Holy Spirit before the marriage was completed by cohabitation. These bare items were fleshed out by Luke the artist with the following materials: the portraits of John the Baptist and Mary in his own description of the public ministry, the descriptions of Abraham and Sarah in the Old Testament for John. After his parallel narrative was completed, Luke added the two major canticles (Magnificat and Benedictus) drawn from "anawim" circles in the Jerusalem community.

5. *The Text of Luke:* The basic fact is that we do not have the original manuscript which Luke wrote. Until the invention of printing (due to the technical innovations of Gutenberg in the fifteenth century) all books were handwritten (manu-script) and copied from other manuscripts. A variety of changes (deliberate or otherwise), errors of eye (misreading, skipping to a similar letter, word or phrase), and errors of ear (dictation was often used), obviously crept in. A rough calculation indicates some 150,000 places in the New Testament where variant readings are possible—with only some 50 of any importance. The fact of variants should not surprise us, as in our daily reading of printed books and articles we often note errors. In fact, a study of some six different printed editions of the Authorized Version by a committee of the American Bible Society, showed nearly 24,000 differences. Thus it is not surprising to find variants in all the more than 5,000 manuscripts of the New Testament, which antedate the invention of printing, not to speak of the early translations of the Bible and the quotations found in the writings of the Fathers, which are studied to produce the nearest text to the originals that we can reconstruct.

The first printed Greek New Testament was in Spain in 1514, by the University of Complutum (Alcala). However, it was the 1516 text published by Erasmus in Basel which was widely used, particularly for such translations as the Authorized Version of 1611. Erasmus had worked, it must be recognized, somewhat carelessly, from not more than ten Greek manuscripts, none earlier than the tenth century. Today we have some seventy bits of New

Testament manuscripts which go back to about A.D. 150-200. Erasmus could find no single manuscript which contained the whole New Testament. He used mainly two Twelfth Century Manuscripts, one for the gospels and one for Acts and Epistles, both of which are in the University of Basel Library today. Thus a late and rather corrupt text became the basis for almost all translations up to the nineteenth century.

In the centuries since Richard Simon published his *Critical History of the New Testament,* 1689, the comparative study of manuscripts has developed into the science of textual criticism, in an attempt to classify the many variants to be found in the textual tradition, and restore as far as possible, the text which the original authors wrote. It is estimated that some seven-eighths of the Greek text used in modern translation is above suspicion. The year 1966 saw the publication of the first new critical edition of the Greek New Testament after many years of scholarly skepticism about the New Testament text.[48]

A commentary was published by Bruce M. Metzger in 1971 to expound the reasons which led the committee to adopt certain readings and relegate others to the critical apparatus. An identifying letter (ABCD) was prefaced to each set of textual variants — "A" to indicate that the text is virtually certain, "B" to indicate some degree of doubt, "C" a considerable degree of doubt, and "D" a very high degree of doubt concerning the selected reading, where the only recourse was to print the least unsatisfactory variant. Their conclusion was that by far the greatest proportion of the text represented the "A" degree of certainty. This text, which was not available to Conzelmann writing in 1953, has provided a very useful basis for modern discussion, translation and commentary. It should be obvious, even from a rapid survey, that while the text of the New Testament is better preserved than any other work of ancient literature, the problem is the mass of evidence which needs to be collated rather than the deficiency of material available for a sound judgement about the original text.

Luke's text has been a most vexed problem to scholars.[49] To simplify, one can say that almost all the sources used to reconstruct the original text (i.e. the Greek Manuscripts, the early translations into such languages as Latin and Syriac, and the many quotations in such early Church Fathers as Ignatius and Irenaeus) fall into one of two groups. The Alexandrian tradition is represented especially by the mid-fourth century Codex Vaticanus (known as B) and the fourth century, Codex Sinaiticus (S), also written on vellum. The other tradition commonly called the Western text is represented by the fifth century Codex Bezae (D); two fifth century Old Syrian Manuscripts and quotations found in the early Latin Fathers. In Acts, for example, the Western text is nearly one tenth longer than the Alexandrian tradition.

Since the end of the nineteenth century the theory of Hort, that B and S represented the best and earliest textual tradition, can be said to have prevailed and to have been accepted as the basic principle in the establishment of the critical editions as we have them.[50] Nevertheless, as we shall note in more detail in Luke chapter 24, with its peculiar problem of the so-called "Western Non-Interpolations," Westcott and Hort ruled, somewhat arbitrarily, against such excellent manuscripts as B and S in favor of much inferior manuscripts.

Opposition to their general theory came from such scholars as Bousset, Kenyon and Kilpatrick. Kenyon suggested that at the beginning of the fourth century some scholar set himself to compare the best texts which he found, to produce a text of which B is an early descendant.[51] But the publication in 1961 of an Egyptian papyrus (P 75) dealt a severe blow to these criticisms.

Papyrus 75, which contains the oldest copy of Luke, contains, with some gaps, Luke 3:18-18:18 and Luke 22:4 — John, 15:8 reads surprisingly closer to B than any other manuscript and is dated almost unanimously, by experts to the beginning of the third century, or even to the end of the second century, thus demonstrating the antiquity of the text type of B — going back to the early second century. Both B and P 75 omit, for example, the fuller text of 9:55; 11:2-4 and 22:43-44 (on the bloody sweat of Jesus), all three of which are found in D. On the other hand, they agree with D in omitting in 23:34, the prayer of Jesus for the forgiveness of his executioners. Further, P 75 and B have eight longer readings which are omitted in D (22:19b-20; 23:3 "of the Lord Jesus"; 24:6 "He is not here but is risen"; 24:12,36 "and he said to them, Peace to you"; 24:40,51 "And he was carried up to heaven"; 24:52 "worshipping him."

However, the evident supremacy of B in evaluating the textual problems of Luke does not absolve the scholar from a careful examination and weighing of the evidence, not just the textual, but also theological, in each case. It should be insisted that there is *no* completely perfect manuscript or textual tradition and also that the Western text type has roots which can be traced to the second century. Thus it is easy to imagine an anti-Jewish scribe excising Luke's prayer for forgiveness from the text. Again the text about the bloody sweat of Jesus could have been deleted by those who felt that this display of human weakness was incompatible with the divinity of Jesus. In fact, many somewhat conflicting criteria can be used, e.g., the greatest number of surviving manuscripts, the oldest manuscripts, those with the widest geographical circulation, conformity to the writers style and doctrine, the shortest reading, the most difficult reading, the one that explains the other scribal mistakes. Here we will follow the readings of the United Bible Societies' 1976 Text.

CHAPTER TWO

LUKE'S INTRODUCTION 1:1-4

Luke's courteous and solemn opening is in marked contrast to the other gospels because it is in the manner of the literary writers of his time (e.g. the Jewish historian, Josephus, Against Apion, the medical writer Dioscurides, on Medicine, or such Old Testament books as Ecclesiasticus, which begins with a justification of its writing and Second Maccabees). Drury sees a striking parallel in the preface to the Letter of Aristeas, which contains the legend describing the miraculous origin of the Septuagint —

> "Since I have collected material for a memorable history of my visit to Eleazor the High Priest of the Jews, and because you, Philocrates, as you lost no opportunity of reminding me, have set great-store upon receiving an account of the motives and object of my mission, I have attempted to draw up a clear exposition of the matter for you, for I perceive that you possess a natural love of learning, a quality which is the highest possession of man — to be constantly attempting to add to his stock of knowledge and acquirements, whether through the study of history or by actually participating in the events themselves."

Drury comments that despite such protestations "it is worth remembering that the work which follows is an elaborate fiction."[1]

These four verses of Luke's prologue are written in an excellent, though dense Greek classical style. Yet they fairly bristle with questions for us twentieth century people, who are so removed from Luke's world and presuppositions. "It seemed good to me also." Who is the writer? The text does not tell us. When and where was he writing? Who is Theophilus? What kind of audience did the author have in mind for his necessarily selective work? What was their situation, their problems, their previous knowledge? Who were the many who preceded Luke? What kind of research did the writer undertake? What kind of purpose did he have in mind in writing? Luke exposes his own thinking in his preface and provides a valuable basis for an analysis of his work. However, we are not his original audience, who we may presume, could rather easily tune in to the wave length of his writing. Some kind of systematic study of his preface and the questions which it raises for us is essential if we are to read with depth and appreciation. A prologue is perhaps the last part of a work to be written and an opportunity for the author to clarify the aims which guided his work.

The Author — According to Luke:

Irenaeus (c 180) gives us the earliest discussion of the problem in his writing against heresies (3, 14, 1). He begins with the "we" sections of Acts, part two of Luke's work, which seems to show how the author travelled with Paul to Troas and Macedonia (Ac 16:8-17), back to Troas (20:5-15) and then on to Jerusalem and Rome (21:1-18; 27:1ff). By a process of elimination among Paul's companions (Luke or Demas or Crescens), the authorship can be narrowed down to Luke, to whom there are three references by name in the New Testament. The Epistle to the Colossians (4:10-14) describes him with Paul in his Roman prison, as the "beloved doctor," a fact which seems to agree with his frequent medical emphasis (e.g. 4:38; 5:12 and his omission of Mark 8:43). It places him among the Gentiles thus making him the only Gentile writer in the New Testament. From 2 Timothy 4:11 (also Philemon) we learn that he was the faithful companion alone with Paul. It can be added that Origen (early third century) identified him with the Lucius in Romans (16:21) and the fourth century Ephraim Syrus identified him with the Lucius of Cyrene (Ac 13:1).

The testimony of tradition since Irenaeus has been unanimous on the authorship of the third gospel and modern scholarship in general has agreed. Luke was not an important or famous figure in the early church and it is difficult to understand the attribution of the composition of the third gospel to him if he did not actually write it. However, we have comparatively little direct information about Luke. The text of the gospel itself is anonymous and gives no information which would actually enable us to identify the author. An introduction to the gospel from the time of Irenaeus written to counteract the influence of Marcion, tells us that he was from Antioch in Syria, a doctor by profession, a companion of St. Paul till his martyrdom, unmarried, that he died aged 84 in Boeotia, that he composed "all of his gospel in the districts around Achaia, although there were already gospels in existence — one according to Matthew in Judea and one according to Mark written in Italy."

The prologue tells us that the author was not an "eyewitness from the beginning," but this does not exclude such conjecture as that he was the companion of Cleopas on the road to Emmaus (Lk 24) or that he was one of the seventy (Lk 10). The gospel seems to show that he was an educated man, familiar with the other historians of his time (e.g. the excellent Greek of the prologue), with time for writing and research. His own words "a noble and generous heart" are a good description of himself. It is interesting to note how concerned he is about reputation and public opinion (e.g. 14:7ff; 16:3; Ac 5:34; 6:3; 10:22; 16:2).

A further examination reveals his familiarity with the Greek Old Testament (e.g. the infancy stories) and that as Caird put it:

> "He had something of the poet in his make-up and an artist's ability to depict in vivid pen-portraits, the men and women who inhabit his pages. He delighted in marvels and was a little inclined to emphasize the miraculous element in his story. He was more interested in people than in ideas. He had a lively social conscience and an inexhaustible sympathy for other people's troubles."[2]

Place and Date of Writing:

Greece (Achaia) has the best support in the tradition concerning the place of Luke's writing, although Rome and Caesaria have some advocates. However, it obviously comes from a place where Greek was the primary language and a cultured man like Theophilus would feel at home.

The date is difficult to decide even though Luke in fact is the only one of the gospels which has incorporated into his text references to historical events (e.g. 13:1-5). Irenaeus put the date of his gospel before the death of Paul (approximately A.D. 67), whereas Jerome, depending on Eusebius, puts it after Paul's death. Today most scholars agree that Luke's composition presupposes that of Mark, but ultimately, the dating of Luke depends on the interpretation of the texts in his work which refer to the destruction of Jerusalem (A.D. 70) —

19:43f which predicts a siege, ramparts, attack on every side, not a stone left on a stone.

21:20ff a prediction that "Jerusalem will be encircled by soldiers"; and the advice to flee which it seems the Christians took *before* the siege and not during it as Luke suggests.

"The people will fall by the sword, will be led captive in the middle of the Gentiles, Jerusalem will be trampled down by the Gentiles . . . "

This description is often compared with Mark's vague quotation from the Book of Daniel (Mk 13:14; Dn 9:27).

The crucial question is whether Luke is writing before or after the destruction of Jerusalem. Are the details of his account based on what actually happened? If so, why did Luke not actually describe the destruction of Jerusalem, a city which was so important to him? Is Luke being dramatically silent about an unforgettable disaster which everybody knew about? He has in fact described the fulfilment of all the prophecies included in his work except the destruction of Jerusalem and the return of Christ. Most scholars until recently would have accepted for Luke a date as late as 80-90, before the collection of Paul's letters, which are not mentioned, but when the Jewish debate had lost much of its bitterness. However, recently a re-evaluation of the evidence has been taking place. No convincing reason is given why Luke omits a clear reference to the destruction of Jerusalem and in particular of the temple itself. Luke's prediction is at most quite vague and can be seen to have been derived from the Old Testament (Greek) description of the previous siege and destruction of Jerusalem in B.C. 586, by the Babylonians. Therefore a date after Mark's gospel in the late sixties cannot be ruled out for Luke's gospel.

Theophilus?:

Many suggestions have been made as to his identity. Thus Streeter suggested that it was a pseudonym (Theophilus means "beloved of God" and is perhaps a translation of the Hebrew Yedidyah, the name conferred on Solomon by Nathan 2 Sam 12:25; 2 K 2:21) for the Emperor Domitian's cousin, T. Flavius Clemens, who was interested in Christianity. In Jerome's translation of Origen we read —

> "You all, who hear us speaking, if you are such as to be loved by God, are Theophiluses, and to you the gospel is written. If anyone is a Theophilus he is best and strongest. That is what is clearly meant by the Greek word 'kratistos'."

The Greek name Theophilus has been found in Jewish inscriptions and papyri since the third century B.C. The title "most Excellent" has been applied by Luke three times — to governors, to Felix (Ac 23:26; 24:3) and to Festus (Ac 26:25). While in theory Theophilus could be almost any concrete Jew, Greek or Roman or even just a symbol of the Gentiles, attracted to Christianity, it is quite likely that he is some prominent person of high rank, who perhaps helped Luke with the cost of publishing his book. Perhaps he was even a catechumen (catechetes v 4, see also its use in Ac 18:25; 21:21,24; Rom 2:18; 1 Cor 14:19; Gal 6:6). Certainly Luke was not giving him his first knowledge of Christianity[3] as he already had received some information and Luke was writing to develop, to confirm and possibly to correct it (aspheleia).

Possibly, the correct translation is not "informed" but "misinformed" and thus Luke is writing to give Theophilus the correct facts about Jesus and Christianity. The word "asphaleia" means firmness (Ac 5:23), safety (1 Thess 5:3), reliability (Ac 2:36; 21:34; 22:30; 25:26). Fur-

Luke's Introduction

ther, it is evident from even a superficial reading that Luke presupposed in his audience some knowledge of the Jewish background to the gospel, its literature, its Temple, synagogue, customs, beliefs (angels, genealogies, etc.), with some knowledge of the secular history of his time (1:5; 3:1). Nevertheless, Luke writing in Greek seems to have primarily a Gentile readership in mind. Origen had written that it was "for converts from the Gentiles," and the (late second or perhaps the fourth century) Monarchian Prologue said that its object was to keep Greek believers steadfast in the faith. Jerome suggested that because Luke was unable to translate "hosanna" properly into Greek he thought it better to omit it rather than disturb his Greek readers with a strange word. His Gentile stress can be seen from a careful reading of his gospel and a comparison with other gospels, especially the synoptics.

(1) One notes that Luke seldom gives quotations from the Old Testament.

(2) He omits the many Semitic words which we find in the other gospels (e.g. ephphatha in Mk 7:34; Abba in Mk 14:36). He regularly substitutes a good Greek word for a Hebrew word (instead of Rabbi we get epistata or didaskale or kyrie, compare Lk 9:33; 18:41 and Mk 9:5; 10:51; instead of Golgotha we get Kranion, Simon the Cananaean becomes Simon Zealot) or even for a Latin word (compare Lk 23:47 and Mk 15:39; Lk 20:22 and Mk 12:14).

(3) He omits many Jewish controversies which might not be of interest to a Gentile audience (e.g. Mk 7:1-23; or the controversy about clean or unclean Mk 9:11-13; or the return of Elijah; the antitheses in Mt 5:21). He explains some customs very familiar to a Jewish audience (Lk 22:17).

(4) He tends to omit whatever might seem harsh or uncomplimentary to a Gentile audience (e.g. 10:5; and 15:21ff — the Canaanite woman; also Mt 5L47 is toned down in Luke 6:33).

(5) One notes that Luke tends to omit difficult sayings which might be easily misunderstood or even shock his Gentile converts (e.g. Mk 13:32 — not even the Son knows the exact day; Mk 15:34 — the cry My God, My God, why have you forsaken me?). Luke never attributes the external expression of strong feelings like anger, indignation, sorrow, to Jesus (compare Lk 6:10 and Mk 3:5; Lk 19:45f and Mk 11:15f; Lk 22:39-46 and Mk 14:32-42). He omits sayings which apparently deny the omnipotence of Jesus (compare Mk 6:5f "he could do no mighty work . . ." with Lk 4:25-30; Mk 1:45 with Lk 5:15). Luke also omits or changes details which are not to the credit of the Apostles in accordance with his own obviously kindly nature and perhaps also as he was addressing "Greeks prone to discussions and criticisms," as Lagrange put it (thus he omits sayings like Mk 4:13; 8:23f; 9:10,28ff — compare Lk 8:24f with Mk 4:38; Lk 18:25f with Mk 10:24-6; Lk 22:31-4 with Mk 14:27-31).

(6) There is a stress on episodes which redound to the praise of non Jews, whether Samaritans or Gentiles (e.g. the centurion in 7:1-10; the Samaritan in 10:28ff and 17:16).

(7) Luke stresses the universality of salvation, e.g., he traces the descent of Jesus to Adam, the founder of the human race (compare Mt 1:2 and Lk 3:38).[5] Many scholars think that the prologue was intended to introduce Theophilus to the *two* volumes of the one work. Whereas, in the gospel, he never shows Jesus preaching directly to the Gentiles, nevertheless, in Part 11 (Acts) he alone of the evangelists explains how the gospel spread even to Rome itself.

Luke's Research:

"Since *many* have set their hands to draw up an account (diegesis) of the *events* (pragmaton) which have been fulfilled among us following the tradition handed down to us by those who were *eyewitnesses* from the beginning and became servants of the word, I too made up my mind to go over carefully the whole sequence of events from the beginning and to write an orderly (Kathexes) account for you . . . "

In a carefully constructed sentence, Luke makes valuable distinctions which must be kept in mind for a proper appreciation of the production of a gospel, and it should be added, any theory of its inspiration. Luke carefully distinguishes four stages in the production of his own gospel —

(a) The eyewitnesses of the events from the beginning, who accompanied Jesus in his historical career (Ac 1:21b). These, Luke tells us, are fulfilled events which were foretold in the Old Testament already (Lk 4:21). The passive form of the verb fulfilled suggests God as the subject. Thus he is not just describing event or bare facts, but events in the light of the Old Testament.

(b) These eyewitnesses did not disappear but became servants of the word, i.e. the gospel[6] — the period of oral tradition from A.D. 30-50 in particular.

(c) The many writers whose products we may assume Luke both read and used.

(d) Luke's own further research (as he obviously was not satisfied with his predecessors) and his own aim and method of production. He believed that his story could be verified for "it did not take place in a dark corner" (Ac 26:26).

Many:

This is one of the tantalizing words thrown out casually by Luke about which we would like to know more. There is no doubt that Luke was influenced by the Old Testament and by the common Christian oral tradition which in particular provided an artificial yet simple fourfold sequence for describing the public ministry of Jesus—the preaching of John; the ministry of Jesus in Galilee; the ministry outside Galilee and the journey to Jerusalem; the events in Jerusalem—passion, death and resurrection. Even though the reference to "many" is a frequent literary expression found in such contemporary prologues as the prologue to Josephus' War (1:17), nevertheless, it seems certain that Luke has used written Christian sources we can identify to varying degrees.

Luke and Mark:

The similarity of material found in both Luke and Mark is undeniable — to quote statistics: about 33-1/3% of Luke's total of 1,150 verses are very similar to about 60% of Mark's 677 verses. From Luke 3:1 — 9:50 and 19:28-24:9, Luke's order is that of Mark and often the actual wording is quite identical. Scholars almost unanimously conclude that Luke had before him when writing, a source very similar to Mark as we see it, even though twice Luke departs from Mark's order to insert sections which are only found in his gospel.[7]

Luke		*Mark*
1:1 - 2:52	=	----------
3:1 - 6:19	=	1:1 - 3:19
6:20 - 8:3	=	----------
----------	=	3:20 - 35
8:4 - 9:50	=	4:1 - 9:50 (except 6:45 - 8:26)
9:51 - 18:14	=	----------
18:15 - 19:27	=	10:13 - 52
19:28 - 24:53	=	11:1 - 16:8

Luke's Introduction

Thus Luke twice interrupts the Marcan order to insert a section of his own (Lk 6:20-8:3 and 9:51-18:14) and only once changes it. He relates Mk 3:20-35 in Lk 11:14-23; 12:10 and 8:19-21. Luke in general reproduces Mark faithfully although he evidently had little hesitation in adding material from other sources, omitting Mark's repetition (whether phrases or words or even such a section as Mk 6:45-8:26), abridging such accounts as the cleansing of the Temple, improving Mark's Greek style, omitting Mark's descriptions of Jesus' human emotions and the intricacies of Judaism or embarrassing statements such as the running away of the "now revered" disciples (Mk 14:52; 9:32-3) — much of which can be explained due to his sensitivity to his gentle audience.

Luke and Matthew:

About 235 verses are common to Matthew and Luke but are not found in Mark. These begin with the Baptist's preaching (Mt 3:7-10 and Lk 3:7-9) and include the baptism and temptation of Jesus and especially a large amount of Jesus' teaching such as is common to both versions of the Sermon on the Mount and the healing of the centurion's servant which follows the sermon in each (Mt 8:5-13; Lk 7:2-10). Three interpretations are possible — either that both used a common source or that one used the other — unless one thinks of both as exposed to a fluctuating tradition partly oral and partly written. No satisfactory case has been argued for Matthew's dependence on Luke and most scholars side with the theory of a common source whether it be the lost source referred to as Q or an early Aramaic version of Matthew. If Luke used Matthew he used it in a very different way from Mark whom he reproduced in blocks as we have seen. Thus Luke 11 is composed in the following way: Lk 11:1-4 (= Mt 6:9-13); 11:5-8 (special to Luke, L); 11:9-13 (= Mt 7:7-11); 11:14-32 (= Mt 12:22-30,43-45,38-42).

It is better to compare Luke passage by passage with the other evangelists without any Procrustean solution in advance even though one must admit that the weight of evidence inclines towards Q and that it is at least a good working hypothesis. We can, for instance, account quite reasonably for many of the minor differences between Matthew and Luke in their use of the same material by reflecting on their different cultural audiences, aims and habits of selection and approach — Matthew writing mainly for a Jewish audience and Luke with Gentiles in mind. Thus in recounting the Baptist's speech Luke can omit that he was attacking Pharisees and Sadducees.[8]

Luke's Special Material (L):

520 verses (almost 50% of Luke) which has no parallel in any other of the gospels. Here we can perhaps more easily discern the special emphasis and interests of the author and his distinctive style and phrases. This material can conveniently be divided into three —

(a) The Infancy Narratives (Lk 1-2).

(b) During the public ministry of Jesus (3-21) — fourteen parables, e.g., some of the most beautiful and famous, the Good Samaritan, the Prodigal Son, the Pharisee and the Publican and some thirty narratives, e.g., the Sermon at Nazareth, the Widow's Son at Nain, the Samaritan Village (9:51-6), Zacchaeus (19:1-10), such miracles as the catch of fishes (5:1-11), the bent woman (13:10-17), the man with the dropsy (14:1-6), the ten lepers (17:11-16).[9] Here we find in particular the long travel section from Galilee to Jerusalem (9:51-18:14).

(c) Elements in the Passion and Resurrection story, e.g.,

Luke's Introduction

Jesus before Herod, the Good Thief, the Emmaus Story, the Resurrection appearances near Jerusalem.

Did Luke find all this material from his reading of the Old Testament or in one of the "many" documents or in several documents from the oral traditions of several churches or from the personal accounts of eyewitnesses, or did he have a combination of all these? The last alternative seems to be most likely. The story of Jesus' birth is told from the viewpoint of Mary and may even have come from her directly. Luke, from what we know of him, had travelled extensively and had plenty of opportunity to interview a variety of people as we can see from Acts. In particular, he could have interviewed the disciples of John the Baptist at Ephesus (Ac 19:1ff), Philip on Samaritan affairs,[10] Manaen, who was brought up with Herod, on Herod's affairs in which Luke shows some interest (Ac 13:1ff), also the women who followed Jesus,[11] Joanna, the wife of Herod's steward, Chuza (Lk 8:3), Cleophas (Lk 24:18), Manson (Ac 21:16), Martha and Mary. When Paul spent two years as a prisoner at Caesarea in Palestine (Ac 24:27; A.D. 58-60), Luke had plenty of opportunities for his researches. It seems he accompanied Paul to Rome and could have met Mark and others there. One can only conclude in the absence of firm evidence that Luke had a number of oral and written sources at his disposal from his journeys to various Christian communities.

Luke and John:

Scholars have noted the remarkable parallels between Luke's special material and John's gospel, not only in their narrative arrangements[12] but in the minutest details especially in the last three chapters, e.g. both alone mention Lazarus, Martha and Mary, the second Judas among the twelve (Lk 6:16; Jn 14:22); Satan's entry into Judas (Lk 22:3; Jn 13:2,27); the denunciation of the traitor (Lk 22:21; Jn 13:18); Jesus' custom to visit the Mount of Olives (Lk 22:39; Jn 18:2); that the High Priest's slave lost his *right* ear (Lk 22:50; Jn 18:10); Annas as High Priest (Lk 3:2; Jn 18:13); no night trial before Caiaphas; the double question to Jesus (Lk 22:67,70; Jn 10:24-5,33); three statements of innocence from Pilate (Lk 23:4ff; Jn 18:38ff); that Joseph's tomb had never been used (Lk 23:53; Jn 19:41); the *two* angels (Lk 24:4; Jn 20:12); the appearances of Jesus in Jerusalem; the story of Peter and a miraculous catch of fish (Lk 5:4-9; Jn 21:5-11). Both show an interest in Samaria and in Jerusalem and its temple which is much greater than that of either Matthew or Mark. In Luke's accounts of the transfiguration (9:28) and the raising of Jairus' daughter, the order of the inner group of Apostles is Peter, John and James. All these indicate that where Luke collected his material, possibly Achaea, there was a strong Johannine tradition and John was particularly remembered.

Luke and Paul:

A strong early tradition (Muratorian Canon, Irenaeus, Origen, Tertullian Jerome, Eusebius) so closely associates Luke and Paul that some suggest that whenever Paul uses the words "my gospel"[13] he means Luke's book.[14] There is no reason to doubt the essentials of this tradition when one takes the two differing characters into consideration, the different kind of literature involved (letter and gospel), their different aims in writing — the one concentrating more on the life of Jesus, the other a more systematic presentation of ideas, and also that it is quite probable that Paul's letters were not available to Luke when he wrote his two volumes but were collected only much later.

One can work closely with another without sharing all his enthusiasm or sides in disputes. One in fact can detect a Pauline influence not only in Luke's vocabulary (Lk 18:14

Luke's Introduction

"justified"; one notes that Luke is the only synoptic to give Jesus the title Kyrios — Lk 7:12,19 etc., Rom 10:9; Phil 2:11); style and traditions e.g. the institution of the Eucharist (Lk 22:19ff; 1 Cor 11:23-5),[15] but especially in the theme of Luke, e.g., the universality of salvation, attitude to the Law — such stories as the "good thief" are perfect examples of justification by faith; and in their common atmosphere and sentiment, e.g., the atmosphere of joy, emphasis on prayer and the Holy Spirit.

Luke's Aim:

In speaking of Luke's purpose one can perhaps speak of his over-all purpose in writing his two volumes (Gospel and Acts) and his more precise purpose in writing volume one with which we shall be specially concerned in this work. One can see that Luke's over-all purpose is to describe the fulfilling of God's plan from the annunciation to the Baptist's father in the holy place of the Jews to the proclamation of the gospel at Rome, the ends of the earth. His theme is the Spirit guided progress from Jerusalem (perhaps by now destroyed) to Rome. Luke wrote at a time when writings were mainly heard and therefore his final words are an important clue to his aim. We can see Luke's end stress on the last words put into Paul's mouth as he addresses the leading Roman Jews — first a quotation from Isaiah about the Holy Spirit's apt words about the Jewish blindness and finally Paul's words—

> "Understand then that this salvation of God has been sent to the Gentiles — they will listen to it."

Next, in assessing Luke's aim in writing his gospel, Luke's own preface must be taken seriously — many scholars have neglected to do so. "Others," Luke says, "have written a narrative" (diegesis). This word is found twice in 2 Maccabees — 2:32, "let us begin our narrative," i.e., history; 6:17, "we must return to our story." We have noticed already the close similarity between Luke and Mark's work. Further Luke gives us four Greek words to describe how he went about his work — "all things"; "carefully"; "from the beginning"; "in order." What these mean for Luke is, to put it simply, the actual text of the third gospel as we have it. His intention is to give serious information in an orderly fashion. But what kind of order? Is it chronological or theological? His "order" was that of Mark except for his own material and comments as he went over the story already known to Theophilus. He tried to show from his research that Theophilus' own information was no different from what the eyewitnesses had originally preached.

Unfortunately we do not know the content of Theophilus' information and so find it almost impossible to appreciate adequately what Luke was trying to do as he tries to show him the security (solidity or credibility) of what he already knew and what he had seen happening around him in the early Church — that it was solidly based on Jesus of Nazareth. He gives synchronisms so that Theophilus can relate the events of Jesus to secular historical events (2:1-3; 3:1f), also he gives the approximate age of Jesus (3:23). However, we can analyze the text as we have it to see what order Luke actually presents and also to try and understand how his mind worked and what he emphasized.

Luke's Community:

A careful reading of the text provides many indications of the communities and their problems which Luke had in mind when writing — the communities within which the third gospel grew and for which it was written. Some indications will help for a fruitful reading of Luke in this aspect. His community is evidently an urban Christian community in one of the Greek-speaking parts of the Roman Empire. Note for instance how the highly domesticated Luke points out that the Gerasene Demoniac did not live in a house (8:27). Repeatedly, Jesus is a guest in people's homes (7:36; 10:38; 19:5). He mentions the word city 38 times and frequently emphasizes Jesus' ministry in cities and villages.

He wrote for people outside Palestine who were at some distance from the ministry of Jesus. They obviously had some knowledge of Jesus' life and ministry and his aim is to give them the true facts about Jesus so that they will remain in continuity with Jesus and the early eyewitnesses. There are problems in his community such as the delay of the parousia with which he deals. Many ideas and even rumors were probably circulating and Luke's intention is to help his community to distinguish the true from the false. Some sections (e.g. 12:1-12) read like a warning to a persecuted community tempted to apostasy, to deny Jesus or even to withdraw into a ghetto rather than to confess Jesus publicly and "launch out into the deep" to spread the word. It is a missionary center for the world around them.

His frequent remarks about wealth indicate that there were many poor in his communities as in Paul's (2 Thess 3:12; 1 Cor 26-8). The emphasis on Paul in the second half of Acts suggests that his community was a product of Paul's missionary activity. Evidently too, from his emphasis, the role of women was important in his community.

There was a particular problem of culture, of reconciling the gospel with their Hellenistic culture, not to mention the problem of reconciling loyalty to Jesus with citizenship in the Roman world. In the Hellenistic world the position of woman was much higher than in Judaism. Luke takes great pain to show that the attitude of Jesus and his gospel is quite different from that of the Jews.

As his community lived at a time when the Christian Church had separated definitely from Judaism, Luke is at special pains to explain the uniqueness of the Christian Church and what must have been a difficult problem, the refusal of so many Jews to accept Jesus.

Luke's Structure and Style:

Ancient books did not have a table of contents and chapter headings. In fact, our present chapter divisions were introduced by Stephen Langton who died in 1228 and are little more than convenient reference points today (he missed such important divisions as 9:51 and 19:28). One notes also that modern Bibles are arranged in sense paragraphs and not as in the King James Version which was broken up into equal single verse units which tended to be interpreted without reference to connection and context.

A survey of recent commentaries (New Catholic, Jerome, Interpreter's, New Bible) and Bibles (Jerusalem, New American) show more or less common agreement on Luke's basic structures of seven divisions with a preface as follows —

Preface: 1:1-4.
(1) Infancy Narratives 1:5-2:52.
(2) Preparation for Public Ministry 3:1-4:13.
(3) Ministry in Galilee 4:14-9:50.
(4) Journey to Jerusalem 9:51-19:27.
(5) Jerusalem Ministry 19:28-21:38.
(6) Passion 22:1-23:56.
(7) After the Resurrection 24:1-53.

Luke's Introduction

Luke, as he goes over the story in order from the beginning (Adam, the Infancy stories), adds sections (1), (4) and (7) to Mark to produce a much fuller and more rounded presentation of the gospel message. Granted Luke's basic structure, one must ask what Luke, the theologian, does with it, what was his mind and how did it work as he went over the basic form of the Christian story for Theophilus? What were the characteristics, the themes which he stressed? Frequently the amount of actual text devoted to a particular subject shows the authors actual interest. Thus it is estimated that one quarter each of Luke and Matthew, one third of Mark and nearly one half of John are devoted to the immediate events leading up to the Crucifixion and Resurrection.

To penetrate Luke's mind one must not only examine carefully the prologue, but also such redactional notes as Lk 3:15; 9:51; 19:28; 19:45. It is evident that Luke carefully organizes his narrative structure. Matthew places much more emphasis on carefully arranged discourses. In comparison with the abruptness of Mark, his perpetual "and" and his "Immediately" connections, it is evident that Luke aims at continuity and flow between his sections or periscopes, e.g., 4:1-12 which connects the baptism and temptation of Jesus. Many of his sections have a bridge function and both flow from what precedes and into what follows. His method however is not that of closely reasoned arguments but rather of associated pictures and ideas often joined together by catchwords. Luke often gives us a psychological insight into the characters in history.[16] He often connects up events and prepares his reader for later events.[17] We have already noticed Luke's consistent use of contrasting doubles, e.g., the unwilling Zechariah and the willing Mary (1:18,39); the humble tax-collector and the proud Pharisee (18:9-14); the cold contemptuous Pharisee and the loving sinful woman (7:36-50);

the thankful and thankless lepers (17:11-19); the active Good Samaritan and the contemplative Mary (10:38-42).

Many writers have commented on the excellence of the narrative art and literary style of Luke especially the cameo-like quality of such stories as the widow's son at Nain (7:11-17); the incident of the sinful woman in Simon the Pharisee's house (7:36-50); the walk to Emmaus, which has been called "the greatest recognition scene in literature" (24:13-35); also Luke's technique, in common with many of the ancient writers, of using a banquet scene as a background for recording a great man's reflections (7:36-50; 11:37-52; 14:1ff; 22:1-38), all of which can so easily be visualized. Stephen Neill analyzes the two well-known parables, the Prodigal Son and the Good Samaritan.[18]

> "Not a word is excessive or out of place. Great skill is shown in the choice of just the most expressive phrase. Each works up to a climax in the enumeration of all the things that the father did for the returning son and that the kind Samaritan did for the victim of robbery with violence:
> had compassion,
> and ran
> and embraced him and kissed him
> . . . and said 'Bring quickly the best robe . . .
> and put a ring on his hands,
> and shoes on his feet
> and bring the fatted calf and kill it'. (15:20-22).
>
> he had compassion, and
> went to him and
> bound up his wounds . . .
> set him on his own beast and
> brought him to an inn and
> took care of him . . .
> took out two denarii and gave them to the host . . .

Luke's Introduction

> It is possible that the number seven in each case is due only to coincidence; it may be, however, that Luke is reproducing a remembered characteristic of the speech of Jesus himself."

We have already noticed when comparing Luke and Mark that Luke tended to produce an ordered text and thus avoid some of Mark's repetitions. There is also evident a tendency to complete a story (e.g. 1:56 does not mean Mary left before the birth 1:57) and to describe events in a more logical order even by transposing some material from the Markan order. Thus Luke combines the preaching and imprisonment of the Baptist.[19] John is then in prison (3:20) somewhat illogically before the baptism of Jesus — however Luke is clearing the way as it were to concentrate on Jesus. The call and immediate response of the disciples is placed, more logically than in Mark, after several miracles (5:1-11). Luke seems to have combined three visits of Jesus to Nazareth into one dramatic encounter, which is symbolic of Jesus' ministry — (1) Lk 14:16-22 and Mt 4:13 where Jesus is praised; (2) Lk 4:23-4; Mt 13:53-8 and Mk 6:1-6. "Is not this the son of Joseph?" (3) in Luke alone where they try to kill Jesus — 4:25-30. His version of the Last Supper is more logical as we shall see.

Scholars from Jerome onwards have commented on the fact that Luke has the best Greek (popular or Koine Greek) among the evangelists — "more eloquent and smacking of secular eloquence" as Jerome put it in his commentary on Isaiah. Luke has a very rich vocabulary and a mastery of Greek tenses, moods of verbs and connecting particles. Nevertheless, it is surprising to note that true "hebraisms" or Hebrew idioms are found almost exclusively in Luke, who it seems often deliberately imitated the style of the Greek (Septuagint) Bible, e.g., the verb construction "it came to pass" plus a finite verb used some

22 times — 5:12,17; 8:1; 9:51; "and behold" 23:25; 5:12; 8:41; "the day will come" 5:35; 17:22; 21:6; "in the presence of" 1:15,19,76; 12:6,9; 15:6, "he set his face" 9:51; 2 K 12:17. He usually uses the septuagintal *Hierousalem* (Lk 26 times, Ac 39 times) instead of the grecized form *Hierosolyma* (Lk 3 times, Ac 23 times) preferred by Matthew and Mark. Some would suggest that when Luke uses Hierosolyma (13:22; 19:28) it signifies merely a geographic place whereas Hierusalem, the semitic form (4:9; 13:33) means the city of salvation, the city foretold by the prohpets, who like Jesus are rejected.

Luke's vocabulary consists of about 2,055 words of which 266 are not found in the rest of the New Testament. He has 1,150 verses and 19,400 words, to make his the biggest gospel, whereas Acts has 13,380 words.

Themes and Characteristics of Luke's Theology:

Luke is the most comprehensive writer of the New Testament and its biggest contributor. His gospel and Acts together comprise about 27% of the New Testament. It is not surprising therefore that since he was reflecting on the traditional teaching of the early Christians on "all that Jesus did and taught," as he summarized his gospel himself (Ac 1:1), his work contains no new doctrines but rather differs from the other writers in his emphasis on particular aspects of the Jesus event and mystery. Thus, one should not seek one theme in Luke but rather, many. With the complexity of a human mind which so often defies mathematical analysis, he unfolds the story of Jesus already familiar to his audience. He touches on many aspects but is no more a systematic theologian than the other biblical writers. The following themes are not intended to be complete but to be a help towards a synthetic reading of Luke, to give a sense of the whole which is fundamental for any proper understanding of particular verses or sections.

Main Theme:

"All that Jesus did and taught." More precisely for Luke, Jesus the Lord is the kingly and prophetic man of the Spirit and of prayer who fulfills God's plan which was revealed in the Old Testament. He is the universal benefactor who brings joy to the poor who are rejected by men. Luke sees Jesus' life as symbolically a journey to Jerusalem where the central events of salvation take place — the death, resurrection and ascension of Jesus, the outpouring of the Spirit and the beginning of the Church.

The Way to Jerusalem:

Acts is dominated by a Journey from Jerusalem to Rome, the ends of the earth, so likewise, a journey or journeys to Jerusalem dominate in symmetrical fashion Luke's Gospel.

Gospel: Galilee to Jerusalem.
Acts: Jerusalem to Rome.

While Luke keeps the simple fourfold structure of the gospel tradition (the Baptist, Galilee, a journey, Jerusalem), nevertheless, a careful examination of his gospel shows that he pictures the life of Jesus as a solemn going up to Jerusalem with the climax not the crucifixion, but the ascension.[20] Jerusalem is for Luke much more than a mere geographic place. Rather, Jerusalem and especially its temple is the holy city where according to Deuteronomy God causes his name (person) to dwell. It is especially the place where salvation and judgment (13:33f) are accomplished and Jesus ascends (9:51). Luke mentions Jerusalem some 30 times in his gospels (Ac 64; Mt 13; Mk 10; Jn 12). Luke centers his gospel on Jerusalem from its first announcement to Zachary to its conclusion when the apostles return to Jerusalem with joy and are found constantly in the temple praising God (1:5; 24:63). In the infancy stories we are given two journeys to Jerusalem, the presentation of Jesus in the temple and the climax when Jesus is found in his Father's house (2:22-38,41-50).

In the preparation for Jesus' public ministry his temptations culminate not as in Matthew on the mountain, but in Jerusalem (4:9-12). After the Galilean ministry Jesus is solemnly described (9:51) as journeying (a phrase found some 88 times in Luke) as a prophet to die in Jerusalem (13:1,33). In this section it is conspicuous that precise topographical information is not given except with relation to Jerusalem. Such names as Tyre and Sidon (Mk 6:45-8:26), Caesarea Philippi (Mk. 8:27) are omitted.[21] Luke stresses that Jesus was nearing Jerusalem (18:31), nearing and entering Jericho (18:35; 19:1), near Jerusalem (19:11), Bethany (19:28ff), weeping at the sight of his city (19:41), entering the temple (19:45). Jesus purifies the temple and gives some of his most important teaching there on the Law, his authority and their responsibility (the parable of the tenants), tribute to Caesar, Resurrection and the last things and the future of Jerusalem. Here Jesus rises, appears (compare Mk 14:28; 16:7 and Lk 24:6ff) and ascends. In Jerusalem the Spirit descends on the assembled community;[22] here Paul receives his authorization[23] and the witnesses go forth (24:47; Ac 1:8). Jesus thus goes his way.[24] It is the way of salvation, a new exodus of Israel from sin and death (1:77; 9:31). It is not a mere sect as it has been called but a new way yet the true way to worship the God of the patriarchs (Ac 24:14). Thus Luke's understanding of discipleship takes the form of a journey. He determines the way and a disciple is invited to follow. His symbol of the Christian life is a journey through anxieties, fears, dangers of apostasy. It is a pilgrimage to paradise.

Luke's Introduction

John had prepared this way and Jesus is led by the Spirit on the way (1:76; 4:1,14,16), which begins in Nazareth (4:16), extends to Capernaum (4:16) and throughout all Judea (4:44,23:5) to Jerusalem (22:22). The way of Jesus is the way of the Lord (3:4; 7:27). To decide to follow Jesus (9:57,59,61; 10:18-25) is to be a disciple. Perseverance, apostasy and rejection of faith are symbolized by "standing by" Jesus or turning aside or by refusing to welcome Jesus or to grant him hospitality (9:53; 19:37f).

The Father's Plan:

For Luke, Jesus' way is the working out of God's plan of salvation (22:22; Ac 2:23), which cannot be resisted (Ac 5:39; 11:17; 26:15,19). God's purpose and providence underlie everything especially the crucifixion of Jesus.[25] Paul has the same term "boule" in Eph 1:11 (see Rom 8:28f). There is a divine necessity about this plan — it *must* be fulfilled.[26] Such an expression is found but once in Mark (8:31), whereas, Luke, perhaps influenced by the Septuagint, uses it some 44 times, e.g., 12 times with regard to Jesus' ministry[27] (102 times in the New Testament). This plan was "according to the Scripture" (1 Cor 15:3-4) as Luke learned from the early tradition. In Luke, much more than in Mark (Lk 18:31; Mk 10:33), Jesus himself is portrayed not only as interpreting his own ministry's pattern from the Old Testament (4:21; 7:22f; 10:23f), but as also teaching his disciples to do likewise.[28] This divine necessity does not lead Luke into any fatalism or denial of freedom to the people involved in his story or to any speculative answer to the problem involved. Rather like the writers of the Old Testament he is content to affirm both the sovereignty of Yahweh as Lord of history and at the same time freedom and responsibility of the human characters involved whether they be Pharisees, or a Judas or the disciples.

For Luke the God of history is Father and in Luke all Jesus' prayers begin with Father. Only Jesus says "my Father" in the New Testament (4 times in Luke), but all the evangelists and Paul agree that Jesus' mission is to share his sonship with others, a mission which is summed up in the disciples' prayer (11:2). The Father is no cold, aloof or capricious and cruel God but a merciful God (6:26) who knows the disciples' needs (12:30), who wishes to give them the best of gifts, the Holy Spirit (11:13; 24:49) and to share in his own kingship (22:29), thus taking fear out of their lives (12:32) and anxiety about food and drink (22:29-31). He is a wise God (7:35; 11:49). He is wonderfully described as the father of the Prodigal Son (15:11ff). God's love is the source of salvation in Luke. Mark rather emphasizes power and Matthew kingly authority.

Christology:

For Luke Jesus was no mere figure of past history but just as for Paul (Rom 10:9; Phil 2:11), Jesus is the risen Lord of the present. Lord was the Septuagint and early Christian translation of the Hebrew Yahweh. Luke then sees the historical Jesus in the light of the resurrection and in his gospel the activity of God and Jesus is to a large extent identical. Alone among the synoptics (except Mt 28:6) Luke gives Jesus the title Kyrios in the full post-resurrection sense and not just a word meaning Sir or Master, already in the infancy narrative (1:43; 2:11,26), at Peter's confession (5:8) and especially from 7:13 onwards.[29] Here Luke is anachronistically reading back into the life of Jesus a title which was scarcely ever used until the resurrection showed the full glory of Jesus to the believers. In fact, Luke describes four times the ministry of Jesus as God visiting and redeeming his people — a divine savior (1:68,78; 7:16; 19:44).

Luke's Introduction

Savior:

All the synoptics share certain titles for Jesus. Luke uses Messiah some 12 times; teacher, the common title for Jesus when he was alive 15 times; Son of David 3 times; Son of Man 25 times, but his special presentation of Jesus is summed up in a title which he alone uses (and only once in the angels' words) Savior (2:11; Ac 5:31; 13:23; Jn 4:42). He uses the verb "to save" 13 times in his gospel. Luke avoids the normal word "to save" when describing physical cures and uses "diasozein" (7:3; compare Mt 8:25 and Lk 8:24). He keeps it normally for a context of faith, e.g., the four times he says "your faith" has saved you (4:48; 7:50; 17:19; 18:42). In Paul it usually refers to final salvation (Rom 5:9f), in Luke it generally applies to the present and includes forgiveness as well as healing. For Luke, salvation is achieved, not only in the cross, resurrection and ascension of Jesus, but it also includes evangelization, the preaching of the gospel (Ac 13:46f; 28:28; 2:23; 4:28; 20:27). Jesus had come to save the lost (19:10) but faith is the necessary condition if one wants to pass through suffering and death to enter Jesus' kingdom and share his life (Ac 33:15; 5:31). This salvation in its negative and positive aspects is well summed up in the Benedictus as "from fear of our foes to serve him in holiness and justice all the days of our life in his presence" (1:74f). It includes both physical as well as spiritual healing or forgiveness. It is peace based on faith which comes through hearing the Word and sometimes seeing the miracles.

Jesus the King and Savior:

In common with Matthew's gospel, Luke's work can be called "a kingly gospel."[30] The kingship of Jesus, the Messiah, is found in all gospels, e.g., the synoptic accounts of the baptism and transfiguration of Jesus use the royal coronation psalm (2:7). Jesus is the Son of King David (3:23-31). Peter confesses him as King Messiah (9:20) and Jesus enters Jerusalem as a king of peace (13:35). But Luke has his own special texts — he introduces God's kingdom in texts where Mark does not mention it (Lk 4:43; Mk 1:38; Lk 9:2; Mk 6:7?. He also emphasizes that the kingdom is the content of the gospel which Jesus preached (8:1; 16:16; Ac 8:12). In addition there are six special texts proper to Luke alone:

(1) In the infancy narratives which contain the main themes of Luke we find the annunciation to Mary "He will be great and will be called the Son of the Most High. The Lord will give him *the throne* of David his ancestor. He will rule over the house of Jacob for ever and *his reign will have no end.*" (1:32-3; 2 Sam 7:14-16; 1 K 1:31; Dn 2:4).

(2) As he nears Jerusalem having thrice predicted his death, he tells a parable of a man who similarly went on a journey so as to be appointed *king*, an appointment which his compatriots similarly rejected (19:12ff) and were consequently punished (19:27,41-4).

(3) Luke deliberately shows Jesus entering Jerusalem as a king Messiah in terms which recall the coronation of Solomon (compare 19:35-42 with 1 K 1:33-40).

(4) At the Last Supper Jesus explicitly confers a kingdom on the disciples which the Father had conferred on him (22:28-30).

(5) Before the Sanhedrin, Jesus proclaims that "He will sit at the right hand of the Power of God" (22:69).

(6) The good thief believes in Jesus' kingdom and is rewarded for his faith (23:40-43, 35-9).[31]

Luke's Introduction

In Luke the ascension is the historical actual enthronement of Jesus as king. He omits the future coming in glory envisaged by Mark and Matthew (Dn 7:13). Jesus' suffering service was necessary for him to enter into this glory. For Luke then Jesus is a king who walks through angry crowds unharmed, excited awe, but unlike earthly kings is the compassionate servant of man, the sick and the dead, yet is greater than Solomon or Moses.

Jesus Prophet Savior, the Bearer of the Spirit:

Matthew presents Jesus as a new Moses legislating a new law and John shows Jesus as the Son of God offering eternal life. Luke, although he uses the post-resurrection title of Lord, presents Jesus especially as the prophet, the unique bearer of the power of the Spirit, either in his own words or those of the crowd (7:16; 24:19). In all Luke gives 17 references to the Holy Spirit ("the Holy Spirit" 13 times, "the Spirit" 3 times, "the Spirit of the Lord" once),—57 in Acts, 5 in Matthew and 4 in Mark. There are 7 in Luke's introductory chapters, where we find a veritable outburst of the Holy Spirit in the preparation for Jesus' ministry. He often substitutes "demon" for "unclean spirit" in Mark's material so as to reserve the word spirit as much as possible for the Holy Spirit (4:33ff; 8:27ff; 9:42). One should recall how the rabbis insisted that the Holy Spirit had departed from Israel with the last of the prophets (Haggai, Zechariah and Malachi) and further that neither the presence nor the glory of the Spirit of God was to be found in the second Temple. Almost everybody in Lk 1-2 is said to be either moved by or filled with the prophetic Spirit—the Baptist (unlike Jesus) from his mother's womb is said to grow in the Spirit (1:80 and 2:40; also 1:15, 18); his parents Zechariah (1:67ff) and Elizabeth (1:4ff) also Simeon (2:27ff) and Anna (2:36). With Mary the Holy Spirit's coming is the activity or power of God (1:35 and 4:14 where Jesus is the power of the Spirit). Luke's characteristic expression "full of" or "filled with" the Spirit is found 4 times in the gospel and 10 times in Acts.

Then we find John the last and greatest of Israel's prophets, proclaiming that Jesus is the climax of all that has gone before (3:15-18). At his baptism Jesus is anointed (Messiah) by the Spirit for his mission which is described in similar words to Isaiah's description of the mission of the servant of Yahweh. (Is 42:1). Jesus, the only bearer of the Spirit, during his ministry is led into the desert by the Spirit and in the power of the Spirit returns to Galilee to begin his public ministry (4:14). In his inaugural address at Nazareth Luke shows that all Jesus' teachings and works are from the Spirit which rests on him especially. Having thus set the keynote for Jesus' ministry as prophet and Messiah, anointed by the Spirit and as Isaiah's servant (Is 61:1-2), it is not surprising that the number of references to the Spirit become fewer. In 11:13 he is the "good thing," *the* gift of the Father. An ancient variant of the Our Father from at least the second century, replaces "Thy Kingdom come" and reads perhaps its equivalent "May your Spirit come upon us and cleanse us." Finally, the risen Jesus sends "the promise of the Father," "power from on high" (24:49; Ac 1:8) and the result is Pentecost and the story of Acts. It is the Spirit which is the source of continuity between the life of Jesus and that of the early Christians particularly that of Luke's own community. It is through his understanding of the presence of the Spirit that Luke explains and justifies the mission to the Gentiles. "Witness" which is one of Luke's favorite words (45 times) is closely linked with the Spirit and his power (e.g. 24:48; Ac 1:8).

Jesus is not only called the prophet (4:24; 7:16,39; 9:19; 13:33; 24:19), but Luke interprets him in terms of Elijah (4:26; 7:12, 15; 9:42,51,54,57,61-2; 22:43-5), who was sent to a Gentile land to be fed there and who also ascended to heaven.[32] Although Luke mentions the Baptist as a forerunner "in the spirit and power of Elijah" (1:17), or rather as secondary like Elisha, he avoids Mark's and Matthew's identification of John and the returned Elijah (Mt 3:4; 11:12ff; Mk 9:13). Jesus carries out his work by the power of the Spirit (1 K 18:12; 2 K 2:9-16) just like Elijah and his disciple Elisha, two of the most familiar miracle workers in the Old Testament.

A comparison between Elijah's raising of the widow's son and Jesus' raising of the widow's son at Nain (Lk 7:15; 1 K 17:22-3; 7:16:1 K 17:24), shows both Elijah and Jesus acclaimed by the crowd as a prophet. The expression "has been raised up" is used of God raising up the spirit filled judges and also Isaiah's description of God raising up Cyrus to be his agent (Is 41:25; 45:13). The disciples expect Jesus to call down fire from heaven like Elijah (2 K 1:10 and Lk 9:54). But Jesus has come "to cast fire on the earth"(12:49), recalling the description of Elijah (Ecclesiasticus 48:1), who "arose like a fire" and whose word could both bring disaster as well as life—see Simeon's prophecy 2:34-5 and the Baptist's prophecy that Jesus would baptise with the Spirit, with fire (3:16).

Some people think Jesus is Elijah (9:8) and significantly, Elijah appears at the Transfiguration which prefigures the Ascension. The same word is used by Luke to describe Jesus Ascension as was used to describe the Ascension of Isaiah (2 K 2:9-11; Ecclus 48:9; 1 Mac 2:58; Lk 9:51). The Ascension and Pentecost show Jesus as the new Elijah who endows his disciples as Elijah had done, so that they can continue his work. Elisha raises the son of the woman of Shunem and Peter will raise Tabitha (2 K 4:8ff; Ac 9:36f).

In brief, we can say that in Luke the Spirit in Jesus is a power (1:35; 4:14; 24:49; Ac 10:38) for preaching the good news to the poor, for teaching and doing—preaching the good news is a characteristic word of Luke (10 times; once in Mt and never in Mk). It recalls the prophet's mission in Isaiah (40:9; 52:7; 60:6) and Joel (2:32). This word distinguishes the period of Jesus from that of John, the last of the Old Testament prophets (16:16). However, in Luke as in Matthew, the idea of the Holy Spirit as a person is not as developed as in John's Paraclete references. Rather for Luke the Spirit is the action of God and according to Brown (p. 125) "the broader category of divine agent best covers the evaluation of the Spirit throughout most of New Testament Christian thought."

The activity of the Spirit is the characteristic of the new age. It unites the Church of Jesus and his mission. It directs both the mission of Jesus and of the early Christians (4:14; Ac 1:8; 10:38). Also in Luke's presentation of the Spirit there is an emphasis on the fruits of the Spirit especially joy and prayer.[33]

The Spirit and Prayer:

For Luke there is a close connection between the Spirit and prayer. Thus both Jesus and the early Christians are praying when the Spirit descends (3:22; Ac 1:14; 2:1). Luke calls special attention to Jesus as a man of prayer in his gospel. Matthew and Mark have Jesus praying in Gethsemane (Luke more earnestly), and after the first multiplication of loaves; Mark also has Jesus praying after he cured many (Mk 1:35). Luke gives eight further instances of Jesus at prayer. Only Luke mentions Jesus at prayer when the Spirit descended at his baptism (3:21). According to Lampe, prayer is "the means by which the dynamic energy of the spirit is apprehended."[34]

At crucial points in his career Jesus often retired to desert places to pray (5:16); before choosing the Twelve he

Luke's Introduction

prayed all night (6:12); before Peter's confession (9:18; 22:32); at the Transfiguration (9:28) and on the cross for his executioners (23:34 and see 46). Thus one can say that Jesus' whole mission is accomplished in a spirit of prayer, of dependence on the Father which is expressed in prayer. For Luke it was the sight of Jesus at prayer that occasioned Jesus' teaching the Our Father (11:1). Jesus often recommended prayer to his disciples — like the insistent friend (11:5-13) or like the widow before the unjust judge — "always to pray and never to lose heart" (18:1-8) — at all times (21:36). Prayer should be like that of the publican (18:13) and especially to obtain the Holy Spirit (11:13). One can say that Luke's gospel begins (1:10) and ends in prayer.[35] Luke's gospel has contributed some of the finest prayers to the Church — Benedictus, Magnificat, Nunc Dimittis, Gloria in Excelsis, all of which are inspired by the Spirit. In Acts Luke has 25 references to prayer and praying.

Good News[35] to the Poor—Joy:

This is in summary form the joyful salvation brought by Jesus as he explained his program at Nazareth. Jesus is the savior, the compassionate Good Samaritan who came (Ac 13:24 "eisodos") to search out and save the lost and to invite them into a banquet fellowship of joy with himself (1:45; 2:11; 8:12; 19:10; 21:28).

Joy:

A note of joy and the peace which Jesus alone gives[36] runs right through Luke's gospel from the promise of joy at the annunciation of the birth of John (1:14,41,44,58) and the angel bidding Mary to rejoice, to the final scene of the gospel of thanksgiving in the temple (24:52). The coming of Jesus was the good news that God had arrived as savior once again among his people to rule as Isaiah had foretold in joyful words (Is 40:9f; 52:7). This is the striking contrast to Mark and Matthew who scarcely ever mention "joy." Mark is more bleak and intense as he faces the problem of suffering and persecution, whereas Matthew is stressing the coming judgement and the need to bear fruit, unlike the Jews. Luke tells us that Jesus himself rejoiced in the Holy Spirit, using a word which means a deep and intense joy, almost exhilaration (10:21). This joy is shared in heaven (15:7) and on earth. In a very useful collection of Lucan Themes, John Navone, in discussing the theme joy, finds 20 references to joy and 10 pericopes in which this theme is basic in Luke's travel story. He lists 10 characteristics of Lucan joy.[37]

> 1. *Willingness to accept a mission* conditioned the joy of the seventy at the signs that the kingdom of God has wrought (10,17). The disciples rejoice that even the demons are subject to them.
> 2. *Belonging to God,* Jesus tells his disciples, is a deeper motive for their rejoicing rather than their power over demons. The joy of participation in the divine mission ultimately derives from the fact that the disciples belong to God, " . . . rejoice that your names are written in heaven" (10,20).
> 3. Mission is intimately connected with *eschatological joy.* The disciples rejoice over the signs of the coming consummation. Their joy is based on the conviction that salvation is a present reality and will be such even more in the future. Theirs is the joy of rising hopes and deepening faith in the fulfilment of the divine promises based on the growing evidence which is recognized by those who actively participate in their realization. Reicke writes that the Travel Narrative is sustained by a genuine ecstasy of eschatological joy which intensifies with the progressive realization of the divine plan of salvation.

4. *The Father's effective salvation of the Anawim* brings joy to Jesus (10,21). The Father's plan and action of salvation delight Jesus. He rejoices at the revelation of grace to the poor and humble faithful. (The second half of the Parable of the Prodigal Son relates Christian joy to that of Christ. The Christian is called to participate in Christ's joy in the Father's work of salvation in ourselves and others.)

5. *The joy of Jesus is in the Holy Spirit.* It is only Luke who refers here to Jesus' joy in the Holy Spirit:

> "At that time Jesus was filled with joy by the Holy Spirit and said, O Father, who art Lord of heaven and earth . . ."

Matthew gives the same prayer (11:25-27) but not the opening phrase, which is Luke's own, and characteristic in bringing together three of his favorite themes: Joy, prayer and the Holy Spirit. In prayer Jesus is closest to the Holy Spirit and to his Father in a union of ecstatic joy.

6. *Hearing and keeping the word of God* is a source of blessedness:

> "Blessed are they who hear the word of God and keep it!" (10;38-41).

Christian joy is based on sharing the same spirit that was in Christ and not on physical ties.

7. *Joy is enduring,* because the word of God from which it originates is enduring. Mary sat at the feet of Christ, listening to his words. The joy of those who hear the word of God and keep it is *theirs.* She is wiser than Martha, because what she has "shall not be taken from her" (10:38-41); his words "will never pass away" (21,33).

8. *The work of Jesus* in healing the crippled woman is a sign of the presence of the kingdom of God and of the joy of God's benevolent reign. "All the people rejoiced" because a daughter of Abraham had been saved from the bond of Satan (13,16). Thus, the kingdom of God in the words and saving work of Jesus brings joy to the multitudes.

9. *Preparedness for the Lord's visitation* is a preparation for joy:

"Blessed are those servants whom the master finds awake when he comes; truly, I say that he will gird himself and have them sit at table, and he will come and serve them" (12,37).

The Father has given Christians a kingdom (12,32) in which they may rejoice, provided that they are ready for it. Preparedness is maintained through participation in Christian life and worship (12,35; 17,26; 21,34).

10. *Poverty and renunciation* are preconditions for Christian joy, which indicate its trans-temporal origins. Christian joy does not derive from the wealth, pleasures and esteem of this world; in poverty and renunciation is an invitation to free one's spirit from these bonds for a joyous participation in the benevolent reign of God within his kingdom. Jesus advises the rich ruler to sell all that he possesses and give it to the poor that he might have treasure in heaven (18,22); he adds that it is hard for the rich to enter the kingdom of God (18,24). Luke's first beatitude (6,20) promises the kingdom of heaven, and implicitly its joy to the poor.

True joy for Luke flows into thankfulness to God which he stresses — the parable of the ten lepers (17:15). There is a constant theme of thankfulness to God in Luke.[38]

Jesus' attitude towards the Poor:

At the beginning of Jesus' public ministry he invites his disciples to *become* merciful in imitation of the heavenly Father who is always merciful and compassionate towards the lost and the poor—see also the parable of the Prodigal Son (15:11ff) and the parable of the lost sheep (15:4-7) which is addressed to critics of Jesus' friendship with outcasts of society. Particularly in his mercy parables, Luke brings out Jesus' and God's concern for those whom man rejects in unique fashion among the gospels. Such parables as the famous three in chapter 15 — the lost

Luke's Introduction

sheep, the lost coin and the lost son are polemical against the unfeeling and unsympathetic pharisaical mentality which cannot understand what God is really like, how there is more joy in heaven when a sinner returns than over the so-called virtuous who are like the brother of the prodigal son. This is why Jesus is imitating God in being friendly with the outcasts of society who are helpless so often — like the victim helped by the Good Samaritan (i.e. Jesus).

The Pharisee mentality does not recognize its own guilt — the parable of Dives and Lazarus (18:9-14). There is so much of Jesus' teaching addressed to this hostile audience that it must be seen as his "loving his enemies," making every effort to open their blind eyes and deaf ears to what God was really like. Jesus' kindness to sinners and outcasts is frequently emphasized in Luke's narrative, e.g., Zacchaeus, the hated tax collector (19:5ff); the contrast between the forgiveness of Jesus to the woman and the self-righteousness of his host Zacchaeus (19:1-10). Jesus is the one who brings joy and comfort by his teaching, his forgiveness, his healing and his other miracles. Not only does Jesus forgive sinners but he also defends them (7:36-50; 19:1-9). He forgives and heals the paralyzed man (5:17ff), the sinful woman (7:367-50) and even those who crucified him "for they know not what they are doing" (23:34), "love your enemies, do good . . . " (6:27). Even the Baptist has time for tax-collectors and soldiers in Luke (3:12ff). Yet Jesus does not condone sin; twice in Mark's and Matthew's text he adds the phrase "to repentance."[39]

The Rich and the Poor:

Luke especially stresses Jesus' attitude to riches and his special compassion for the poor. He has 21 references to riches and rich men in his gospel and all are disparaging

(Mark has 5 and Matthew has 1). Luke has 8 references to poverty and the poor (Mark has 4 and Matthew 5).[40] Jesus is born in poverty and laid in a manger and his birth is announced to poor, despised shepherds. When he is presented in the temple his parents make the offering of the poor (2:24; Lv 12:8). He is recognized by Simeon and Anna, symbolic of the humble poor (anawim) who trust in God and await his redemption. Mary too is symbolic of the poor and her song announces a great social reversal. John demands a sharing of goods among the needy.

Jesus lives in the obscurity of Nazareth and during his ministry can say "foxes have holes . . . but the Son of Man has no where to lay his head" (9:58). In his inaugural sermon Jesus sees himself as good news to the poor. The same word is used in the Beatitudes and in 7:23; for the poor invited unexpectedly (14:21); for Lazarus (16:20,21) and for the poor widow (21:3; also Mk 12:42,43; Mt 5:3; Jas 2:23) — it means the downtrodden who do not trust in their own resources but in Jesus. Here the poor are Isaiah's captives, blind and prisoners for whom the Hebrews celebrated their jubilee year (Lv 25:8-17,29-31; Is 5:8-10).

Later Jesus identifies these needy to John's disciples (7:23). In the Sermon on the Plain the poor are the disciples who put their trust in God (not the *mere* materially poor who often do not trust God). Here Jesus contrasts them with the rich and even feels sorry for the rich, who are already satisfied with wealth, enjoyment, honor and esteem.

He even seems to condemn riches in themselves and not just excessive attachment — "it is easier for a camel . . ." (18:25f). The rich fool in his self-centered living sees riches as a means to perfect happiness (12:13-21). " . . . sell your possessions . . . treasure in heaven . . . whoever

Luke's Introduction

does not renounce all . . . '' (14:33). The rich man (Dives) is condemned precisely because he has done nothing for poor Lazarus (16:19-31) — you cannot be the servant of God and money (16:13) i.e., the Pharisees who loved money laughed at him (16:14). But it is evident that Jesus did not expect every Christian to divest himself of all his possessions and to give up their jobs, to sever all family ties.

Luke has two types of passages about wealth. One kind demands the complete renunciation of earthly possessions. The other teaches a right attitude towards the continuing possession of wealth. Martha and Mary obviously did not leave all to follow Jesus (10:38-42). After it is said that Levi left all he made a great feast in his house (5:28f). The women who ministered to Jesus had their own means (8:2f). Neither did Zacchaeus give all away. What was asked of the inner group of disciples who followed Jesus (a technical word) was not asked of everybody (Ac 4:37; 5:1ff; 10:1; 16:14f). Yet both would inherit the kingdom.

Lazarus' story, also the counsel to sell possessions (which the disciples did 5:11) and to invite the poor to dinner are found in Luke alone (12:33; 14:13). This is the fulfilment of Mary's revolutionary song — he has filled the hungry and invited them to the messianic banquet in Abraham's bosom and sent the rich away empty (1:53). Luke's gospel is a message of hope for the poor here and now and is a warning to the rich to repent like Zacchaeus and recompense the poor and break down the class distinctions resulting from different economic status (see chapter 14). What is recommended is the right use of this world's goods (16:9) and a readiness to leave all things (even one's wife is added by Luke alone 14:26).

Women:

Women in general occupied a lower position in the ancient world. The normal Jewish man thanked God in his daily prayer "that he was not born a Gentile, a slave or a woman." Not surprisingly, Luke gives a very sympathetic portrayal of women in his gospel. For him, women are just as capable as men of faith, spirituality and responsibility before God.[41] Scholars have noted his tendency to parallel stories about a man with a story about a woman to show them equally in honor, grace and gifts before God as in Genesis — "no more male nor female" (Gal 3:28; Gen 1:27). In fact several of Luke's examples show greater faith and love on the part of the woman — Mary's faith is superior to Zachery's, the sinful woman has greater love than Simon the Pharisee, Simon of Cyrene is forced to help Jesus carry his cross whereas the women of Jerusalem weep for Jesus. Matthew tells the birth story from Joseph's point of view whereas Luke stresses Mary. Luke tells us of Elizabeth and Anna (2:36-8); the sinful woman (7:36-50); Mary Magdalen, Joanna and Susanna (8:2f); Mary and Martha (10:38-42); the woman who declared Jesus' mother blessed (11:27f); the Galilean women who accompanied Jesus on his ministry; the woman with the eighteen year infirmity (13:11-13); the women who were with him at the end (23:55f). Luke has two parables in which women are principal characters — the lost coin (15:8-10) and the Unjust Judge (18:1-8). One can read the parable of the lost coin as Jesus projecting God in the image of a woman — God can be pictured as much female as male.

The Universal Savior:

Commentaries on Luke's gospel have a tendency to draw attention to the theme of the universalism of salva-

Luke's Introduction

tion without a careful analysis of how Luke presents it. Although recent scholars have concluded that it is not the dominant Lucan theme, nevertheless, it is found in his gospel far more than in Matthew and Mark. Luke has various ways of presenting this theme, sometimes explicitly by his use of prophetic texts especially from the Old Testament (2:1,32; 3:1f,38), sometimes it is suggested as in 10:1 where the number 70 (72) is the number of the nations of the world (Gn 10:1-32; see Num 11:16). Jesus' universality can be inferred from the variety of people to whom he appeals in his opposition to Jewish narrowmindedness and exclusiveness, the poor, sinners and outcasts, women and particularly the Samaritans, perhaps also the lessons for Peter that he should put out into the deep (5:4 — the people on the shore can be understood as the Jewish people).[42]

It is easy to see how Jesus' message showed a more universal concern than any of the groups in Palestine such as the Pharisees or the Zealots. Taking the gospel and Acts together it is possible to see how Luke sees God working through Jesus in breaking down the division between Jew and Gentile and making his salvation available to all. But here our concern is particularly with the gospel which in its introductory chapter sees the birth of Jesus against the background of "a census of the whole world" (2:1) and the child Jesus proclaimed as both the glory of Israel and light of revelation to the Gentiles (2:32; Is42:6-7). He dates his events with reference to the Roman Empire and puts the Roman dates first (3:1).

In his account of the preparation of the public ministry, Isaiah's universaliam is used again and only Luke among the synoptics extends the text of Isaiah to show that the "Way of the Lord" leads to the Gentiles (compare Mk 1:1-6, Mt 3:1-6 and Lk 3:1-6). Next when Luke is tracing Jesus' ancestry he begins not from Abraham downwards but goes backwards all the way to Adam (a favorite topic of Paul), to show that Jesus is related to every man who is born (3:23-38).

Abraham is mentioned 15 times in the gospel text and 7 times in Acts. In Acts 3:25 (Gal 3:8,16) Luke gives the Christian understanding of the theme of the universal blessing through Abraham's seed which is mentioned some 19 times in Genesis. He follows the Septuagint reading "In your seed shall all the nations of the earth be blessed" (Gn 22:18). The Hebrew version can be translated as "all the peoples of the earth will bless themselves" or "with to be blessed as Abraham was."[42]

In Jesus' sermon at Nazareth, when quoting Isaiah again he seems to stop short of Isaiah's condemnation of the Gentiles and he deliberately speaks of the Sidonian Widow and the Syrian Naaman both of whom were non-Israelites who were blessed of old through the prophets Elijah and Elisha in preference to many needy Israelites.

A large place in Luke is given to the Samaritans who were considered heretics by the Jews on both religious and political grounds, rated perhaps even worse than the Gentiles. There was a Jewish saying that "a pig's blood is cleaner than the blood of a Samaritan." The Good Samaritan is shown to be superior to the priest and the levite and the Samaritan leper to the Jewish lepers (10:13,18). We do not find in Luke such instructions as "to go nowhere among the Gentiles and enter no town of the Samaritans but go rather to the lost sheep of the house of Israel" (Mt 10:5-6; 15:24). The desire of James and John to destroy the Samaritan town which refused to welcome Jesus is firmly resisted (9:52ff). Luke is obviously preparing the way for the Samaritan mission (which he describes in Acts 8) and the controversy which it must have aroused.

Luke's Introduction

These references are quite significant when we observe that Mark never mentions either Samaria or the Samaritans, whereas Matthew only mentions the Samaritans once in the text just quoted (Mt 10:5). John uses the Samaritans like Luke as an example of ethnic universalism (Jn 4).

Luke's approach to the Gentiles and pagans is interesting. He only tells of one miracle for them, the cure of the Roman centurion's servant (7:1-10) — he omits the Syrophenician woman (Mk 7:24-30) which though in reality an example of Palestinian repartee, might perhaps offend his Gentile audience. However, in the cure of the centurion's servant it is evident that Luke stresses more than Matthew the merits of the centurion and hints that he is every bit as good as a Jew (Lk 7:2-9). It should be noted however that in Luke the centurion never meets Jesus personally but through the Jewish elders and friends (7:1ff). Luke however notes the cure of the Gerasene demoniac (8:26-39). It is correct to say[43] that in Luke Jesus does not evangelize the Gentiles and that their presence is not a reality during his life time.

In Luke the first section of Jesus' public ministry (4:31-9:50) is strictly limited to Galilee apart from a reference in (6:17) to a large crowd who had come to Galilee from Tyre and Sidon to hear Jesus and be cured of their diseases. Luke omits Jesus' actual journey to Tyre and Sidon (Mk 6:45-8:26) and takes up Mark's narrative when Jesus returns to Caesarea Philippi (9:18) but he omits this name of a Gentile region. Thus Luke has streamlined Jesus' way from Galilee to Jerusalem and thence in Acts to the Gentiles. On the journey (10:13-14) during the mission of the seventy-two Jesus stresses that the ultimate fate of Sodom, Tyre and Sidon will be less severe than that of Corozin, Bethsaida and Capernaum (10:12-15). To the question as to whether the saved will be few Jesus answers that "people will come from the east to the west, from *north to south*" (a Lucan expression), "to take their place at the feast in the kingdom of God," while the first (the Jews) will be last and the last (the Gentiles) first (13:22-30).[44] Thus for Luke, Jesus possessed a universal vision which the Spirit would *gradually* work out in Acts as he led the way from Jerusalem to Rome — the universal church, but not in Jesus' lifetime. The emphasis of an ancient work which was intended to be read aloud is often found at the end. There Luke shows the risen Jesus as saying that "in his name penance for the remission of sins is to be preached to all the nations, beginning at Jerusalem" (24:46f) — the story of Acts.

It is important to note that Luke, in emphasizing the universality of the gospel, can in no way be labelled anti-semitic even though he points out clearly the rejection which Jesus suffered — e.g., in his program (4:16ff) and in his prediction of the Passion (9:22ff). Luke is less hostile to the Jews than any of the other evangelists. Yet he frequently seems to make the subtle point that the response of some Gentiles is at least as good as that of the best Jews (7:1ff; Ac 10:1ff; 17:1ff).

Luke's Jesus is a solid Jew. Only Luke tells of his circumcision and dedication (2:21-4), his Bar Mitzvah visit to the Temple (2:41-52), how he was accepted by the pious Jews like Simeon and Anna who looked forward to the consolation of Israel (2:25), how right through the gospel Jesus is the fulfillment of the hopes of Israel and how his career can only be rightly undertood in the light of the Law, the Prophets and the Psalms (24:25-7,44-7). Luke here is less anti-Jewish than Matthew, Mark or John. While Matthew seems to see the universality of salvation almost as a consequence of the failure of the Jews to bear fruit, Luke sees the universality of the gospel and the tragedy of Jesus as part of God's plan from the beginning. In

Luke's Introduction

Acts Luke frequently describes mass conversions of the Jews.[45] Twelve Jews become leaders of the new Israel (Lk 22:30). Luke's contribution is to base the Gentile mission in the Old Testament or God's will and to place it in the context of ongoing history.

The Church and Eschatology:

Luke's two volume work is written for a community of Christians living in an area which was becoming post-apostolic. Already the church was well expanded and evidently facing a long period of pilgrimage in the world. His church is the "people of God" rather than the "body of Christ." They had accepted the gospel message and were walking in the "Way."

Jesus the expected one had definitely come and Luke is at pains as we saw in his preface to check out for Theophilus the solidity and credibility and legitimacy of the Jesus story and set it against a background of world history. But the coming of Jesus, as the important text (Lk 16:16) shows, signals a division of epochs, the old from the new, the period of the church were the ascended Jesus is reigning in glory and guiding the Church through his spirit. This period is the end-time, or the period between the two comings of Jesus who will reappear in judgment to fulfill thre expectations of the Son of Man, about whom Luke has numerous references not found in Mark or Matthew.

The kingdom, or rule of the Son of Man, is "present among you" (17:21) in the activity of Jesus (the reign of God is yours 6:21). Yet, the final event will happen with a suddenness that none can calculate or tell by careful watching (17:21,28; 12:28-40ff; 12:54ff). The question is will he find faith anywhere (18:8). One can note a double thrust in Luke for whom the decisive event had already happened in the life and death and ascension of Jesus. On the one hand some of his audience are morbidly excited about the immanent parousia such as Paul countered at Thessalonica (1 Th 5:4-10) while for others the parousia seemed to be a never, never event. To the one, texts like Ac 1:6-8 were a reminder that there was a mission to be carried out. To the other a text like Ac 1:11 was a firm warning that Jesus would come back.

Not unlike Matthew, there are several texts in Luke where the idea of eschatology, which basically means that history will end[46] becomes more remote than in Mark and the expectation of an imminent end does not dominate (but see Mk 13:10,32). All three synoptics begin their gospel accounts of Jesus' public ministry on the same note: Jesus began to preach, but each adds its own individual development. Thus for Mark when Jesus appears from the desert to proclaim "The time is fulfilled and the reign of God is at hand, repent and believe in the gospel" (Mk 1:5),[47] one tends to expect the final consummation at once. Luke omits the saying completely and substitutes the episode of Jesus explaining that Isaiah's text is fulfilled — the kingdom is here (17:21).

Jesus' message before the events of his death and resurrection is different from that of the early Christian (i.e. Luke) on the other side of the resurrection which gives a newness to their message. Matthew stresses the continuity between Jesus and John the Baptist so much that he has both proclaim the same message (Mt 3:2 and 4:17). But Luke stresses the newness of Jesus' message about the kingdom so much that he never has John even refer to the kingdom (compare Lk 3:3 and 4:3).[48]

With Mark and Matthew Luke warns about the last judgment when the Son of Man will come in his glory and the glory of the Father and of the holy angels in judgment on whoever is ashamed of him and his words (Mt 16:27-8; Mk 8:38-9:1; Lk 9:26-7). Mark and Matthew continue with

Luke's Introduction

the prediction that some who are standing there will not taste death before they see God's kingdom *come* with power (Mk 9:1; Mt 16:28). Luke leaves out the expression *come* thus separating the present vision and presence of the kingdom from the future parousia. One can also note the dominant presentation of a settled church community which is not feverishly expecting the end in the way Luke — as compared with the somewhat confused version of the "Apocalypse" to be found in Matthew (24) and Mark (13) — tries to separate as far as possible the fall of Jerusalem (21:20-4) from the Parousia (21:25-8). One could also get the impression from the other gospels that the glorification of Jesus is not distinguished from the Parousia whereas Luke alone shows that Jesus, through the ascension, is already glorified and that eschatological salvation is already available through Christ living in the Christian community with his new life poured out through his Holy Spirit. Luke has a tendency to separate for a better understanding. In Paul, the resurrection and exaltation seem to coincide (Rom 8:34). In John the resurrection and Pentecost take place on the same day. But Luke, in whose gospel (ch 24) the ascension takes place on Easter Sunday (Mk 16:19) has separated in Acts the resurrection, ascension and pentecost in historical succession.

A Parenetic Gospel:

It is true to say then that Luke is not so much interested in the remoter aspects of eschatology as in the application of the gospel's eschatological message to the here and now, to the between period of the contemporary church in which he lived. While he goes out of his way to emphasize the basic historicity of the Jesus story (e.g. 2:1-2; 3:1-2), that they were verifiable facts "which did not take place in a dark corner" (Ac 26:26), nevertheless, one notes a very emphatic parenetic emphasis in his gospel which shifts the focus from the second coming to seeking the relevance of the gospel to daily Christian life. That there is work to be done here and now is the theme of the introduction to Acts — "Men of Galilee why do you stand here looking up at the skies?" (Ac 1:7ff). In Acts the work to be done is one of witness,[49] which he portrays the early Christians as carrying out by their words, deeds and community life.[50]

In Luke's first volume there is a strong emphasis on discipleship. Thus Luke's insertion of a long journey narrative (9:51-18:14) can be seen as a study in the following of Jesus along his designated way. Beginning with three vocation stories, at 9:57 we get a story of a man who says he will *follow* Jesus wherever he goes (9:57), then a man to whom Jesus says "Follow me" (9:59), thirdly, another man who said he would follow Jesus (9:61), then a scribe asking what he must do to inherit eternal life (10:25). The theme continues, "with Jesus challenging one man to more decisive action, cautioning another by asking had he really counted the cost and always teaching crowds and his disciples what following him would mean." We "get three sayings about privileges of discipleship (10:18-24), three instructions about prayer (11:1-3), three parables about God's mercy to sinners (15:1-32), three sayings about the Law (16:16-18 and so on."[51]

Luke spends much effort in painting a portrait of the life of a disciple; his conversion;[52] his faith;[53] his fraternal charity;[54] which is manifested by "giving to all who beg";[55] his *prayer*;[56] his perseverance and his absolute and radical *renouncement* of anything which would lead a disciple from following Jesus, which is far from the soft and easy going popular image of Luke;[57] he describes the *joy of the believer,* before the annunciation of salvation,[58] before miracles,[59] before the great pardons (15; 19:6), in the Holy

Luke's Introduction

Spirit at the Father's revelation (10:21). It results from the Easter mystery (24:52-3) and *replaces anxiety* about worldly cares, riches and pleasures[60] and therefore should pervade the life of the disciple.[61]

The word "Today" has a remarkable place in Luke's gospel — almost everywhere the word "salvation" occurs it is accompanied by "Today."[62] It occurs 11 times in Luke and 8 times in Acts (in Mt 8 times, Mk once). It is used in the Old Testament to point out important occasions and is found repeatedly and solemnly in Deuteronomy, a book which is an artificial invitation to Israel to stand once again with Moses in the presence of Yahweh and commit itself wholeheartedly to the covenant. Luke does not treat the gospel as pure history or as an archaeological study of the past, but as an existential gospel in which one hears and responds to a God speaking today. Thus he actualizes the gospel. His God is neither merely of the past or of the future but one who calls and saves us today. In Jesus salvation is inserted into the now of history.

Some of Luke's eleven "Today" texts which he alone has (Mt 8, Mk 1).

2:11 *Today* in the town of David a Savior has been born to *you*.

4:21 *Today* this scripture passage is fulfilled in *your* hearing.

5:26 We have seen strange things *today*.

13:32f I cast out devils and perform cures *today* and tomorrow . . .

19:5 *Today* I must stay at your house.

19:9 *Today* salvation has come to this house.

22:61 Before the cock crows this day.

23:43 *Today* you will be with me in paradise (see also 3:22; 24:21).

Today with the coming of Jesus to the believer salvation has come, eschatology has begun even though the parousia is far distant. According to Flender, Luke puts so much emphasis on the today of his inaugural sermon (4:18) for three reasons —

>   1. It rivets the Christ event to the historic past, the Old Testament prophecies which are being fulfilled.
>   2. But it is not just past history, it remains a continuing today which is constantly given anew as the exalted Christ speaks through his Spirit.
>   3. It is offered to the reader of Luke no less than to the people of Nazareth or the shepherds or Zacchaeus.[63]

Luke focuses his salvation on the *NOW* of Christian living today — an expression which occurs 14 times in the gospel and 25 times in Acts (Matthew 4 times and Mark 3) —

>   6:21ff Happy are you who are *now* hungry . . . Alas for you who are *now* full . . . *Now* is repeated some 4 times.
>   6:35ff Love your enemies . . be compassionate.
>   9:23 "Whoever wishes to be my follower . . . take up his cross *each day* (an expression found in Luke alone).
>   14:17 "everything is *now* ready" (for the feast).
>   21:19 "By patient endurance you will save your lives" — an appeal for Christian patience now, whereas in Matthew 10:22 and Mark 13:13 the emphasis is on *final* perseverance — "the man who stands firm to the end will be saved."

CHAPTER THREE

LUKE'S INFANCY NARRATIVES — LK 1-2

John and especially Jesus are the Fulfillment of God's Promises and the Hope of Israel:

In addition to what we have already said about the Infancy Narratives in Luke, some introductory points must be made here before we reflect in more orderly detail on his actual text.

1. These chapters are not the first part of the gospel message to be composed nor are they in any way reporter's accounts or T.V. accounts of what actually happened.

2. We do not find them in the early preaching of the Church as given in Acts or Paul. Mark, probably our oldest gospel, does not have them and John seems to jump over this period in Jesus' life to a reflection on the "beginning."

3. Many romantic notions have crept into our thinking and even such well-established habits as celebrating December 25, originally a day of the sun god which the early Christians adapted into a Christian celebration. Careful attention should be paid to what the text of the gospel actually says.

4. These chapters must be read as a part of Luke's whole work and in particular as his introduction to a number of people, problems and themes which will fill the main part of his gospel. Luke, and this helps to explain his differences from Matthew, is giving, not just a chronicle of cold facts but is giving, like Matthew also, an interpretation, his own theological reflection which will both show

Jesus as the fulfillment of the past, the hopes of the Old Testament, and lay a basis for the great events of Jesus' public ministry.

5. It is essential to remember that these stories are written with the benefit of hindsight in the light of the developing post-resurrection insights of the early Christian Church and their faith as to who Jesus really was. They are best seen as a prologue written after Jesus' public career. They tend to telescope the whole career and ascension of Jesus. They apply to Jesus from his birth such titles and understanding of his mystery which only gradually becomes evident during his career particularly at its climax. They are a study in the uniqueness of Jesus in evidence of which many witnesses are brought forward — God himself through his angel Gabriel, the faith of Mary, the prophetic testimonies of Elizabeth, Zechariah, Simeon and Anna — all building up to a climax as the twelve-year old Jesus recognizes his unique commitment to his Father's business.

His language can be understood as the language of dramatic creation. Thus his characters speak words which proclaim the faith of the first Christians. It is almost as if he said "This is what really happened and this is what we would have seen and heard if we had known what we know now and if we had had eyes to see." This is faith illuminating the real and hidden meaning of the event as understood when we look back at it in the light of the faith of the early church.

However, the development of understanding of Jesus by the early church should not be seen as the creation or evolution of someone who became something which he was not. Rather, it should be seen as a developing attempt to describe what was there essentially from the beginning in Jesus, but which was only gradually realized by the early followers of Jesus and which put incredible strains on their monotheistic concepts and beliefs. Mark especially em-

Luke's Infancy Narratives

phasizes the lack of understanding and the hardness of heart of the disciples during Jesus' public ministry. Luke and John make it clear that it was not until the resurrection that the disciples really penetrated the mystery of the person and ministry of Jesus (Lk 18:34; 24:1ff; Jn 2:22; 12:16; 16:4). Matthew is different as he consistently endows the disciples with post resurrection insight during the ministry of Jesus.

6. All modern commentators agree that these chapters of Luke are strongly influenced by the Old Testament (Greek) both as to language, themes, prophecies and even construction of such events as the two annunciations (1:5-25 and 26-38) and the two psalms (1:46-55 and 68-79) which are veritable mosaics of Old Testament references. The Semitic density is unique in Luke-Acts.

7. All modern commentators comment on Luke's artistry and use of parallelism — called a "diptych" when the parallel episodes are consecutive to each other as the two annunciations and the two birth narratives. This is an interesting example of Luke's claim (1:3) to write an orderly account. Here Luke is evidently stressing the superiority of Jesus over John in his origin, person and mission. He is expanding on the statement which John will make in the main section of the gospel: "There is one to come who is mightier than I. I am not fit to loosen his sandal strap." (3:16ff). John's gospel also felt the need to stress the comparison between Jesus and the Baptist as it was evidently a problem among some members or acquaintances of his community and it was felt necessary to clarify the relationship between the two great martyrs, Jesus and John whose followers continued to follow his way of life after his death (Ac 19:1ff).

However, as in any interpretation of a work of art, it is difficult to decide exactly how far to go and how much parallelism Luke actually intended us to see in his subtle placing of scenes and pictures side by side. It seems best then not only to analyze Luke's pictures but to stand back from them, see them as continuing tableaux as it were and let the full impact of them strike one. When the analysis is complete and the necesary information for an interpretation of an ancient writing achieved, one should re-read Luke's scene afresh and let it come alive and speak for itself.

8. As most modern translators show at a glance, quite a number of sections in these chapters are in poetic verse in the Hebrew style of antiphonal or parallel verses such as we find in the Psalms. These psalms are not composed of rhyming poetry but have a rather loose rhythm like some modern blank verse, such as that of T.S. Eliot. The striking characteristic of Hebrew poetry is its parallelism. This means that its basic unit, a line is followed by a second (and sometimes a third) which restates it in synonyms ("synonymous parallelism") or contrasts with it (antithetic parallelism) or further develops or completes it (climactic or step or synthetic parallelism).

Many of the Old Testament books which Luke must have known[1] provided examples of a prose text "bursting into song" to interpret the meaning of the particular event. Luke not only gives us the songs of Mary (1:46-55), Zechariah (1:68-79), Simeon (2:29-32), which are constructed in the manner of Old Testament psalms, but other sections such as the angel's words to Zechariah and Mary, and their song to the shepherds are clearly in verse form. The discoveries at Qumran show us that psalm composition was still alive in Israel in the time of Jesus.

Lastly, in discussing R.E. Brown's masterly study we noted the differences and similarities between Matthew's presentation and that of Luke. His summary of a broad range of recent scholarship will strongly influence the presentation here and those anxious for a fuller treatment should consult his excellent work. For Brown, Luke, unlike Matthew, does not draw upon already composed sources either oral or written for the main part of his narrative, which he composed "from beginning to end himself on some items of historical information and popular tradition" such as the names of the Baptist's parents. However, he posits that

> "Luke drew upon sources in a second stage of composition when he added four canticles to the main infancy narrative along with a story of the boy Jesus in the Temple."

Where Matthew emphasizes Joseph, Luke chooses Mary and John the Baptist,

> "using what is said of them in the gospel accounts of the ministry as a guide to depicting them in the infancy narrative."

In referring to the Old Testament his method is by way of atmosphere and subtle allusion, especially to "the patriarchal couples (Abraham and Sarah), the births of Samson and Samuel and the post-exilic piety of the Anawin."

He paints in Old Testament colors especially those who do not figure in the main part of his gospel (Zechariah, Elizabeth, the shepherds, Simeon and Anna). Whereas Matthew introduces his Old Testament quotations with solemn formulas, Luke absorbs the Old Testament texts, words and allusions into his own text itself.

Contents:

Luke, in seven episodes, presents to our eyes the mystery of Jesus and the mission of the Baptist through a series of angelic messages, inspired pronouncements and finally through the words of Jesus himself (2:49). In addition, Luke points out the joyful response which his audience should make —

A. The Announcement of the Birth of John the Baptist 1:5-25.

B. The Announcement of the Birth of Jesus 1:26-38.

C. Mary visits Elizabeth — Mary's Song of Praise 1:39-56.

D. The Birth, Circumcision and Naming of John the Baptist, Zechariah's Prophecy 1:57-80.

E. The Birth, Circumcision and Naming of Jesus: Shepherds and Angels 2:1-21.

F. The Presentation of Jesus in the Temple: Simeon and Anna 2:22-40.

G. The Boy Jesus in the Temple 2:41-52.

A. *The Announcement of the Birth of John the Baptist — 1:5-25.*

Luke's beginning is in striking contrast to that of Mark, who with a brief Old Testament summary which combines Ex 23:20, Mal 3:1 and Is 40:3, takes us straight into the adult careers of John and Jesus. (Only after eighty five verses will Luke's main character, Jesus, be born.) After his preface to the reader he carefully gives us a historical note "in the days of Herod" (Mt 2:1), the cruel half-Jewish king who ruled over all Palestine (see Lk 7:17 and Ac 10:37, where "Judaea" includes Galilee), from B.C. 37-4. This, incidentally is the only reference to Herod in the gospel.

The custom of beginning with a date is frequent in Old Testament books (Joshua, Judges, Ruth, Samuel, 1 Maccabees, Hosea, Amos and Jeremiah) and Luke's history can be seen against such a background of prophetic history which attempts to describe the activity of a transcendent God in human affairs, unlike the modern empirical historians who tend to leave God out of consideration. The pre-

Luke's Infancy Narratives

cise date of Jesus' birth is not given by Luke and probably was unknown to him. His lack of precision here is in contrast with his later dating in 3:1-2. However, as Herod died in B.C. 4 we can easily see how the Scythian monk called Dionysius who introduced the custom of reckoning time from the birth of Jesus (A.D. = anno Domini) erred in placing the birth of Jesus after the death of Herod. One easily notes the very different style and grammar of these two chapters in contrast with that of the prologue which would be almost impossible to translate into a Semitic language.

The childless country priest and his wife to which Luke first introduces us can be seen to represent the best of Judaism (2:33) with the other characters who will follow, such as Mary, Joseph, Simeon and Anna. These people are righteous and devout (1:6; 2:25), given to prayer (1:13; 2:37), receptive to God's word and will (1:38.60.63; 2:25,36f; 3:2), prompt (and on occasion filled with the Holy Spirit), to articulate joy and praise (1:41,67; 2:20,27-32,38), looking for the time when God will bring about repentance and salvation to Israel (1:16f,47-55, 68-79; 2:30,38), obedient to the law of the Lord (1:6,9; 2:21,22-4,39), and of notable family heritage (1:5,27; 3:23-38).[2]

Many of Luke's themes are here. In particular, Luke emphasizes the lowly as God's concern in a land dominated by the powerful Roman, Herod and his following, the Pharisees, Scribes and Sadducees. Zechariah was just one of an estimated 18,000 priests and Levites who had minor roles in the Temple (1 Chron 24:1ff). Yet with Elizabeth he was upright "in God's sight" even though many would have interpreted their childlessness as a sign of the opposite, a disgrace (1:25) and even a punishment for serious sin (Lv 20:30f).[3] The barrenness of Elizabeth reminds one familiar with the Old Testament of the barren women of the Old Testament such as Sarah (Gn 16:1ff), Rebekah (Gn 25:21), Rachel (Gn 29:31), the mother of Samson (Jg 13:2) and especially Hannah, the mother of Samuel, likewise a Nazarite (1 S 1:2f), who received an answer to her prayer during the annual pilgrimage to the sanctuary at Shiloh. These women gave birth to some of the great leaders of Israel. But Luke's description alludes in particular to Abraham and Sarah (Gn 18:11) who were likewise elderly and likely to remain childless.[4]

Having introduced his first two characters both of whom were of priestly lineage and having stressed their "impossible" problem of having no children, Luke places his opening at prayer time in Jerusalem (the city that the Lord has chosen as Deuteronomy says), in the Temple, the house for God's name, his special presence. There too his gospel will end (24:63). It was Zechariah's moment of a lifetime when he won the lot, a method of discovering God's choice (Ac 1:26), to burn the afternoon (Ac 9:1) incense (Ex 30:7-8; Sir 50:12), which was symbolic of the prayers of the people of God. Luke uses a technical phrase (laos) for the "people of God" from the Septuagint some 37 times, Matthew 14 times and Mark 3 times. It was a once in a lifetime event for a priest, a member of Aaron's tribe thus to enter the sanctuary which was distinct from the general Temple courts and next to the Holy of Holies, which only the High Priest entered on the Day of Atonement (Heb 9:1-7). He would not be eligible again until all the other priests of his section had had their chance. In this moment was Zechariah (1:13) praying for the seeming impossible, a child, or rather, as Israel's representative, for the blessing and redemption of his people? Certainly, the answer solves both problems as the child is destined to play a part in the redemption of Israel.

In describing Zechariah's vision, Luke seems to follow a set biblical pattern which he will also use to describe the announcement to Mary (1:26ff).[5] This pattern which describes the births and commission of famous figures in the Jewish salvation history consists in five basic steps. A close comparison shows that almost all Luke's details can be found in one or other of the Old Testament patterns which must therefore have influenced his reconstruction of the scene:

1. The appearance of an angel of the Lord himself (Lk 1:11,26).
2. The fear, troubling or prostration of the recipient (Lk 1:12,29).
3. A message is given to the visionary who is addressed by name and urged not to be afraid — a birth is announced giving the name of the child and his future accomplishments (Lk 1:13ff,30f).
4. The recipient raises an objection or asks for a sign (1:18,34).
5. A sign is given to reassure the visionary (1:19f,36f).

One should be cautious about jumping from a literary resemblance or influence to a judgement (negative) about the subjectivity and basic historicity of such an episode as Luke relates.[6] It is however evident that the infancy narratives do not give us any simple reporting of actual events. What Luke does is to look back and draw out the significance which he describes in biblical language. Nevertheless, to make a definitive judgement on many points in the text we would need much more historical information than we possess or Luke gives. Some further notes on each of the five steps will help deepen our understanding of Luke's presentation of this unusual and mysterious episode.

1. The angel Gabriel's only previous appearance is in Daniel (8:16-26; 9:21-7; see Job 12:15; Rev 8:2), one of the last books of the Old Testament to be written. There he appears likewise to a man praying in distress and tells him not to fear, but like Zechariah, Daniel is struck mute. He announces to Daniel the final eschatological struggle, the

period of seventy weeks of years,[7] which will lead to the introduction of everlasting justice and the fulfillment of visions and prophecies and the anointing of the Temple which had been profaned. Frequently in the Bible an angel is simply another way of saying God (see Ac 11:15). The meaning of the name Gabiel is "El (God) is strong" or "Man of God."

2. This fear correspondents to what the philosophers call the *numinous,* the feeling of awe before the presence of the "wholly other," the mysterious which seems to come from beyond the world. It is not a servile or cowardly fear but rather awe and reverence which attracts rather than repels.

3. The message to Zechariah shows that this expectation is now being accomplished through the special role of his son John ("Yahweh has given grace"). We hear also about the future career of John, his greatness and his Nazirite-like asceticism,[8] his prophetic-like filling with the Holy Spirit in words which are similar to what is said about John in the body of the gospel (7:27ff). His role will be to call many in Israel to repentance.[9] Malachi (3:24 also Sir 48:10) had foreseen the role of Elijah as one of reconciliation before "the great and terrible day of the Lord." Mark also had opened his gospel as we have seen with a reference to Malachi. Elijah was famous for his miracles (unlike John), and his prophetic spirit and for his confrontation with King Ahab (like John). But who are the fathers whose hearts John will turn to the children, and the disobedient unto the wisdom of the just? (see Mal 3:24). Brown suggests an interpreation from a combination of Lk 3:8 "We have Abraham as our father . . ." and Lk 7:21-5 ". . . Yet wisdom is justified by all her children," to mean that

"an acceptance of John the Baptist's challenge (which is reinforced by Jesus) produces a new generation of children who possess the wisdom of the just, while those who think of the patriarchs as their fathers are disobedient and not justified in their wisdom."

The gospel or good news (1:19) is too good to be true for Zechariah—the sign of the angel's appearance and the promise of the birth of a son are not sufficient for him. In words similar to Abraham's reaction (Gn 15:8; also Gideon, Jdg 6:36ff and Hezekiah 2 K 20:8), he asks for a further sign (a Jewish failing 11:29; 1 Cor 1:22). It should be noted that Abraham's question is different from Zechariah's and is not treated as lacking in faith.

5. Zechariah receives an unexpectedly punitive sign of dumbness like Daniel (Dn 10:15—Paul became blind Ac 9:9). However, the fact that the people need signs to communicate with him in 1:62 suggests that he was also deaf. That "he was unable to speak to them" when he came out probably means that he could not pronounce the blessing of Aaron (Num 6:24-6) from the steps of the sanctuary as Jewish tradition prescribes. It is Jesus himself who at the end of the gospel (24:50-52) will pronounce the blessing.

The episode finishes with the return home of Zechariah—the departure theme is almost a refrain in these chapters (1:23,38; 2:20,39,51). Then he gives a brief mention of Elizabeth's conception and of her seclusion, a curious fact which perhaps highlights the coming revelation to Mary that Elizabeth has conceived (see the instructions to Samson's mother Jdg 13:6ff). We do not know of any custom of seclusion but it meant that no outsider would know of it.

B. The Announcement of the Birth of Jesus—1:26-38:

In giving us the annunciation to the *mother* of Jesus, Luke follows the same basic announcement pattern which we have seen in his previous description of the announcement to the *father* of the Baptist. But there are evident similarities and differences in both which are a calm assertion of the differing roles of John and Jesus and especially of the superiority of Jesus over John (and the faith of Mary 1:45 in comparison with the lack of faith of Zechariah). It is the same angel Gabriel in both. However, John "will be great before the Lord" while Jesus "will be great" without qualification, i.e., not just one of God's great men. (God was called great in the psalms.) John will "be filled with the Holy Spirit from his mother's womb" while the Holy Spirit will come upon Jesus' mother so that her "holy child will be called Son of God."

In the conception of John the age and barrenness of his parents are overcome. The virginity of Mary leads to a still more wonderful intervention of God. John's role is preparatory "to prepare a well disposed people" while Jesus will have the throne of David his father and rule forever. Elizabeth will praise Mary as the mother of *my* Lord and even John will testify by leaping for joy in Elizabeth's womb. One should note in particular, Luke's expansions of the basic pattern especially in verses 32-33,34,35,38, where he stresses the unique virginal conception, the future achievement of the child, and also gives us a description of Mary herself which resembles the Old Testament description of Samuel's mother, Hannah, just as Mary's song also resembles that of Hannah (1 S 2). We note also Luke's threefold construction—the angel speaks three times to Mary and her reaction is also told three times.

The setting is simply told; the time is six months later, Elizabeth has secluded herself for *five* months (1:24,36); the place, Nazareth which Luke identifies as in Galilee for his Gentile readers. Here in contrast to the opening scene, which takes place in the solemn Temple in Jerusalem at a solemn hour to a priest, we are switched to the other end of the country, Galilee of the Gentiles (Mt 4:15; Jn 7:52), to insignificant Nazareth which is not mentioned in any pre-

Luke's Infancy Narratives

Christian Jewish writing (Jn 1:46). Here we meet "a nobody," Mary, a young girl on the threshold of married life. Her name perhaps means "beloved by Yahweh." Betrothal in Jewish law was a binding contract of consent before witnesses (Mal 2:14), but the wife did not live in her husband's house for about another year (Mt 25:1-13). Joseph (or perhaps Mary!) was of the house of David,[10] an important point as (1:32) the child is to receive the throne of his father David.

1. The angel who is *sent from God* has a highly respected greeting for Mary—there is no such greeting recorded for Zechariah. In fact, the greeting is in two forms — (a) a Greek pun (chaire checharitômene), which is best translated perhaps[11] as "Hail" (the ordinary Hello of Luke's readers as in the Latin Ave), "O favored one." This probably causes Mary's wonder so that the angel had to explain that the favor is the conception of Jesus; (b) the Old Testament greeting which the angel used to Gideon (Jd 6:12) to assure him of God's support (also Moses in Ex 3:2). In Ruth (2:4) it is an ordinary greeting of Boaz to the reapers.

2. Mary's response (as in typical pattern) is to be startled (deeply troubled—it is a strange form of the verb used in 1:12f of Zechariah's reaction) at the *words* of the angel, not, like Zechariah at the *sight* of the angel. She wonders about the favor and is enlightened by the angel. In Genesis 6:8 we are told in the same Semitism that Noah also found favor with God.

3. Like many before her,[12] Mary is reassured and receives a message about the conception of a son to be named Jesus[13] with a description of his future accomplishments. As in Matthew, the message describes not only the identity of Mary's child as God's son yet David's son, but also the extraordinary manner of his conception through the Holy Spirit. This message is in poetry and

verses 32-3 are a commentary on Old Testament messianic expectations, particularly 2 S 7:9-16—the promise of the prophet Nathan to David which became the basis of the Jewish hope of the re-establishment of the Davidic reign forever.[14] The "house of Jacob" clearly means all Israel. However, as Jacob was the name of the Northern Kingdom which became separated from the Southern Kingdom in the great schism which led to the destruction of both, its mention would call to mind the expected reunion of the Hebrew people which the coming Messiah was expected to achieve (Ezech 37:16-28). The title "Son of the Most High"[15] should be interpreted in the light of the faith of the early Christians with a fullness which it did not possess in the Old Testament applications to the Hebrew kings.[16]

4. "How can this be since I have had no relations with a man?"—this is a Semitism for sexual relations (Mt 1:25). This is a verse that has fascinated commentators down through the ages. Mary's questions, unlike Zechariah's is not a request for a sign—yet a sign is given. It is not a comment on the depressing political situation like Gideon's (Jdg 6:11-16). Rather it is like Abraham's how (Gn 15:8) which is not treated as a doubting question. Any solution should keep in mind Mary's intended marriage, the twice mentioned fact that she was a virgin and, thirdly, that Mary's (wondering) faith is not in doubt (1:29,45). Luke is probably dealing with a difficulty in his own community for whom such a virginal conception is without parallel in their Gentile traditions. The question is a literary technique so that he can explain that the Davidic Messiah whom he has proclaimed in v 31-33 is the Son of God in an unique sense because he is begotten through the Holy Spirit. Later he will describe Jesus as the supposed son of Joseph in his genalogy (3:23).

Luke's Infancy Narratives

The insistence on the virginity of Mary and the idea of Spirit as "the power of the Most High" (the view of the Spirit in the Old Testament) suggests that the child is God's work, a new creation, that here God is beginning again a new man (Adam). The same verb "overshadow" is used in the Old Testament to describe God's presence in the tabernacle (Ex 40:35; 1 K 8:10; Hg 2:7), at the transfiguration (the cloud) and of the coming of the Holy Spirit at Pentecost—thus the sense is not sexual (1 S 16:13; Is 32:15). The Holy Spirit gives a basic unity to Luke's early chapters. We will hear of him again at the baptism (3:22), the temptations (4:1,14) and at the beginning of Jesus' ministry (4:18). The child will be called holy, an expression found in Isaiah 4:3 but normally associated with God, Son of God (10:21f; 22:70). This revelation of the mystery of Jesus will not be found as fully again before the post paschal events when we find Jesus confessed by Paul as the Son of God.[17]

5. Mary is given a sign and told of God's favor to her relative (syggenis) Elizabeth—this joins the two stories together. The degree of relationship is not specified. It was Wycliffe who popularized the "cousin" idea. Thus perhaps Mary was of the tribe of Aaron like Elizabeth, or perhaps of David (1:27). The Semitic statement "Because not impossible with God will be every word (rhema)" is a quotation from Genesis 18:14—in fact is one of the questions which Yahweh himself asked Abraham when Sarah laughed at God's promise of a wondrous conception. This is perhaps a subtle reminder of Luke that Jesus is the fulfillment of the promise of the blessing of all man made to Abraham (Gn 12:3).

Mary's final response is not part of the typical announcement pattern and so is emphasized by Luke. She is presented as the true, enthusiastic, obedient disciple (see 8:19,21; Ac 1:14), not unlike Hannah's reaction to the news of a son. "Let your handmaid find favor in your eyes" (1 S 1:18). "Be it unto me according to your word (rhema)" ia a common Septuagint phrase (Josh 2:21; Jdg 11:10; 2 K 14:25).

C. Mary's Visit to Elizabeth — Mary's Song of Praise — 1:39-56:

The visitation scene brings together the characters from the two announcement scenes before dividing them again for two separate birth scenes. Again it shows the subordinate role of John, making him a joyful witness to Jesus while still in his mother's womb. Mary evidently takes the angel's revelation about Elizabeth as a command and hastens to witness the sign. The journey is estimated at about three days distant "to a city Judah" which pilgrim tradition, dating at least from the sixth century, has identified with the modern Ain Karim, some five miles west of Jerusalem in the hill country which lay between the flat western coastal plain and the Jordan valley.

At Mary's greeting, Elizabeth's child begins to jump with joy in her womb, i.e., to prophecy. The angel had told us that he would be filled with the Holy Spirit (i.e., be a prophet) from his mother's womb. The word used ("skirtao") is not frequent in the Septuagint. In Psalm 113:4-6 it describes the reaction of the mountains at the presence of God during the Exodus. In Mal 4:2, a messianic text, it describes the triumph of those who fear Yahweh on the great day of Yahweh.[18]

Elizabeth has a sudden gift of prophecy.[19] Through the joy of her unborn child it is revealed to her that Mary's child is the Messiah. Both Elizabeth and Mary now proclaim songs of praise. Elizabeth praises Mary with words that are later echoed by the woman in the crowd (11:27-8). She recognizes the divine favor which Mary has received (see Judith 13:18; Jdg 5:24) and also blesses the child-to-be (Gn 30:2; Lm 2:20). Her protestation of unworthiness to receive a visit from "the mother of my Lord"[20] is an allusion perhaps to David's greeting of the ark (2 S 6:9), or rather the greeting which David himself received at what would become the site of the Temple (2 S 24:21). Some go even further and suggest that Mary is the new ark of the covenant which contains the special presence of Yahweh, and which is welcomed with joy, the response which Luke would like to emphasize for his community.

Mary's Song of Praise:

Mary responds to the blessing of Elizabeth with a song like that of Judith of old (Jdt 16:1ff). Most scholars hold that the canticles, Magnificat, Benedictus and Nunc Dimittis were taken over by Luke from a source such as the Jewish Christian poor (Anawim) which he describes in Acts (2:43-7; 4:32-7). The title "Magnificat" comes from the first word of the Latin version. Scarcely any scholar would hold that Mary herself composed the Magnificat as an on the spot response to Elizabeth's praise. It has little direct reference to the visitation context apart from v 48 which Luke may have added, but rather describes the more general situation of the poor, downtrodden remnant of Israel. In general, there is a lack of christology in these canticles as compared with the context, and they reflect Old Testament understanding of salvation which is both personal and spiritual, material and also political. In fact, the canticle is so general that some have argued with some support from a few, mainly Latin, manuscripts, that it was spoken by Elizabeth.

However, v 48 suits Mary (the same word, handmaid is used in v 38) rather than Elizabeth and the overwhelming manuscript evidence, including all Greek witnesses and almost all the early translations and quotations, attribute the Magnificat to Mary. It is interesting to note that Hannah's song to which the resemblance is so close that it cannot be accidental (1 S 2:1,4,5,7,8), has scarcely anything to say about Hannah's personal situation but concentrates on such similar themes as God's concern for the vindication of the poor, his faithfulness to Israel (the poor, oppressed, faithful), and his judgment on the rich; themes quite frequent in the psalms and later Hebrew poetry.[21]

Like Hannah, Mary's song emphasizes a merciful God's vindication of the faithful weak against the strong, his rejection of human pride in power, prestige and possessions. Luke will often stress this theme in his gospel—in the Beatitudes, the story of the Rich Man and Lazarus, the poor widow whose contribution was of much greater value than that of the rich.[22] Some would go so far as to call the Magnificat one of the most revolutionary statements in all literature, advocating *now* the scattering of the proud (a moral revolution), putting down the mighty from their thrones and exalting the lowly (a social revolution), filling the hungry and sending away empty the rich (an economic revolution)—a much more profound revolution than many contemporary Jews with their narrow, fanatical nationalism ever hoped for or were prepared to accept.

The values of Judaism itself from the rich and indifferent Sadducees (10:31) to the proud Pharisee (11:37ff; 18:9ff), to the rich tax-collector (19:1ff) and even the vast majority of the people who experience shocking poverty, would receive in Jesus a tremendous upending. Yet the coming of Jesus did not mean any revolutionary overthrow in the modern meaning of the term. One must interpret the Magnificat in terms of what Luke's audience would have experienced and understood. What it proclaims is the double edged judgment and mercy theme so basic to the prophetic message in Israel and right through the Bible from the early chapters of Genesis, e.g., the scattering of the proud in the Tower of Babel incident which is balanced by the call of Abraham which follows it in Genesis and to which reference is also made here in v 55.

However, the Magnificat must be basically seen as a hymn of praise to God for *his* revolution. Mary reacts to Elizabeth's praise of herself by turning to praise God himself. It is similar in structure to many Psalms from the Old Testament[23] and Qumran. It has an introduction (46b-47) which expresses Mary's personal, joyful thanks for her favor, to her saving God; next a listing of God's qualities—mighty, holy, merciful (v 49-50) and his deeds (51-3) both for Mary and then the poor whom Mary represents; finally a summarizing conclusion (54-5) which takes us way back in history to the promises to our fathers, and Abraham in particular, who was to be a source of blessing for all the nations—this shows the unity of God's plan and action down through the ages.

The Magnificat is in fact a very profound meditation of God's power and activity in the world. Interestingly, Martin Luther, who always kept a picture of the Virgin Mary in his room, pondered carefully on it as he journeyed to meet the political powers of his world at the Diet of Worms, a time when it seemed that he was a lone, weak human with such mighty powers ranged against him. His meditation on the Magnificat is one of his best writings. He did not attack political power or human politicians as such directly. In fact he emphasized that good government, good rulers and order and peace are God's good gifts. However, he found in Mary's song the clue to an understanding of world history. He described how one great empire after the other rose in bubble-like quality, swelling and inflating. Yet he saw how eventually God brought to nothing the proud people who abused his gifts and his people so that they collapsed when God stretched out his hand and touched them. These schemers, hard faced men, were fools for Luther, people who lived in an unreal world, dreamed foolish dreams and in the end were seen to be the real dupes, which they were.

Introduction (46b-47):

Here we find the joyful, personal thanksgiving and praise from the whole being of Mary. "God my Savior." This phrase is used of God some 35 times in the Greek Bible in contrast to 5 applications to men. It reminds us of Jewish history of the God who so often came to Israel's help in time of danger. It echoes Habakkuk's song (Hab 3:18; Ps 106:21) and indicates that his longing for salvation is now being realized. This expected salvation is now becoming a reality with the pregnant Mary and her future child, the Savior (1:69; 2:11,30). Luke thus associates salvation with the whole life of Jesus from his birth.

Other New Testament writers would stress in particular the climactic events of his life, his crucifixion and resurrection.

Strophe One (v 48-50):

This gives us Yahweh's qualities which explain his favor to Mary, a favor which all ages will recognize (Gn 30:13; Lk 11:27). She is of "low estate" and a handmaid or female slave. Such terms associate her with the faithful poor of Israel whom God has helped in the past. Some were barren women desiring children. Others were persecuted or oppressed.[24] Mighty,[25] Holy[26] and Mercy[27] are the outstanding characteristics in the Old Testament description of the transcendent powerful Yahweh who is a merciful savior to those who fear him. This is not a servile fear but a decription of the pious, who recognize his sovereignty and worship him alone (Ps 103:17).

It is interesting to note how Luke uses six verbs in the past (Greek aorist) tense to describe God's activity. They are best explained as gnomic aorists pointing out God's customary way of acting towards the poor who trust in him; past, e.g. his salvation from the mighty Egyptian and Babylonian kings: present—his favor to Mary, the coming of Jesus: and future—God will act consistently as in the past and his promises will be fulfilled and already are as it were accomplished in Jesus' coming. But when Luke is writing, the lowly, crucified Jesus, the stone which the builders rejected (20:17), had already been exalted (Ac 2:33; 4:24ff; 5:31) and the wisdom of the proud and mighty rulers rejected (Ac 4:24-7). One can easily see a pattern of reversal in Luke—a barren woman and an unmarried woman becoming mothers, lowly Zechariah (not the important priests), obscure Nazareth, the poor shepherds (Matthew's Magi are more impressive).

Strophe Two (v 51-3):

Through a chiastic (a b b a) series of antitheses the proud and mighty and the lowly, the hungry and the rich, Luke describes the mighty deeds of reversal, by Yahweh, of the situation of the world.[28] It should be remembered that for Luke *the* gift of the Father, *the* example of "good things" is the Holy Spirit (11:13). For Luke, the truly great people are the least (9:48; 10:21). He was well aware of the corrupt pseudo great in his society, those motivated by self-interest (Ac 19:32), the greedy politicians (Ac 24:26f; Lk 23:12). He stresses the necessity of suffering which is basic to true glory (24:26).

"The poverty and hunger of the oppressed in the Magnificat" says Brown,[29] "are primarily spiritual, but we should not forget the physical realities faced by early Christians. The first followers of Jesus were Galileans; and Galilee, victimized by the absentee ownership of estates (cf Lk 20:9) was the spawning ground of first century revolts against a repressive occupation and the taxation it engendered (Acts 5:37). There was real poverty among the Jerusalem Christians who became the nucleus of the post-resurrection Church (Acts 2:44-5; 4:34-5; 5:1-2; Gal 2:10; 1 Cor 16:1-4; Rom 15:26-6). And when the gospel was proclaimed in the Diasopora among Jews and Gentiles, frequently it attracted the underprivileged social classes. The Epistle of James, with its eloquent denunciations of the rich (5:1-6), may represent Christianity in Diaspora Judaism. There were certainly slaves who were converts in the Pauline communities (1 Cor 12:13; Philemon; Eph 6:5). And Luke's peculiar and emphatic castigation of wealth (6:24-6; 12:19-20; 16:25; 21:1-4) points to the existence of many poor in the communities to be served by Luke's gospel. And so vss 51-3 of the Magnificat would resonate among such groups; for them the Christian good news meant that the ultimately blessed were not the mighty and the rich who tyrranized them. Reformers of all times have advocated revolutions that would level class distinctions by making the poor sufficiently rich and the powerless sufficiently powerful. But the Magnificat anticipates the Lucan Jesus in preaching that wealth and power are not real values since they have no standing in God's sight. This is not an easy message, even for those who profess credence in Jesus. By introducing it as a leitmotiv in the hymns of the infancy narrative, Luke has begun to introduce the offense of the cross into the good news proclaimed by Gabriel. If for Luke Mary is the first Christian disciple, it is fitting that he place on her lips sentiments that Jesus will make the hallmark of the disciple in the main gospel story (Lk 14:27). It is no accident, then that some of the offense of the cross rubbed off on Mary. In the early dialogue between Christians and Jews, one of the objections against

Christianity is that God would never have had His Messiah come into the world without fitting honor and glory, born of a woman who admitted that she was no more than a handmaid, a female slave."

Conclusion (v 54-6):

In conclusion we are reminded again that what is happening to Mary[30] is the result of God's mercy, the fulfilment of his promised support for his servant Israel (Is 41:8; 44:1; 45:4), the promise which he made to Abraham long ago—Abraham is mentioned 15 times in Luke and 7 times in Acts (1:55,73; Is 41:8ff; Ps 98:3; Mi 7:20). Luke closes the scene with another of Mary's journeys. She remained three months, i.e. until John's birth as she arrived in the sixth month of Elizabeth's pregnancy (1:26). But Luke, in typical fashion, removes Mary from the scene so that he can concentrate his reader's attention on his next scene, the birth of John.

D. The Birth, Circumcision and Naming of John the Baptist—Zechariah's Prophecy—1:57-80:

Here we begin Luke's second set of diptychs in which the birth, circumcision, naming of John the Baptist and Jesus are put before us with a song, also added in each case—the Benedictus and Nunc Dimittis. With regard to John the emphasis is on the two wonders which take place at his circumcision and naming. With Jesus the emphasis is on the wonders which take place at his birth.

The angel's message (1:13f) of the birth of a son, named John, to Elizabeth, the great joy which it would occasion and Zechariah's release from dumbness, is fulfilled. The presence of relatives and neighbors at the celebration and their involvement in the naming, would have been quite natural and what one would expect (Ruth 4:17). Circumcision, a symbol of the covenant relation between Yahweh and Israel,[31] took place on the eighth day (Lv 12:3). We are not fully clear about customs of naming a child, whether after his grandfather (the more common one), or father,[32] or even that it took place on the precise day of circumcision (as the Rabbis relate about Moses). One should remember the importance of names among the Jewish people. They were not mere labels but contained something essential of the bearer and his career, e.g. Elijah signifying that Yahweh, not Baal is my God, Peter the Rock. Often also a new career is signified by a new name in the Bible.

There is something unusual in Luke's text here which escapes the commentators—Luke does not explain the name John and it is difficult to imagine that his mainly Gentile audience would understand its meaning "Yahweh has favored" (in giving a child to barren parents). Does the imposition of a new name, not a family name, mean that John was to follow a different way from the priestly tradition of his father and perhaps make a new beginning for the Hebrew people? Luke emphasizes two wonders in the scene: the agreement of Zechariah with Elizabeth on the unusual name (he perhaps intends us to presuppose that they had not previously agreed on the name); the talking of Zechariah who evidently was both deaf and dumb. The same word "to bless" which expresses Zechariah's reaction, will be used of Simeon (2:28) and of the disciples in the temple after the ascension (24:53). Typically, Luke gives the crowds' reaction of fear before the supernatural intervention (1:12,30), of "storing up these things in their hearts" (2:19; 3:15; 15:22), their wondering about the child's career which Zechariah's hymn will answer.

The Benedictus—1:26-79: (The title comes from the first word in the Latin).

The Benedictus, like Mary's Magnificat, is inserted by Luke into his story to give a prophetic interpretation of God's gift to Zechariah of a son. It is not essential to the flow of Luke's text which would proceed quite well without it from v 66-v 80. As it gives a Christian interpretation of John in its present form (especially v 77) it probably is not a composition from Baptist circles. Also it says nothing about John's work as a baptizer, his death or the suffering Messiah and thus is little colored by the later events. Like the Magnificat, it is a hymn of praise and is a mosaic of Old Testament and other Jewish concepts and even phrases (e.g. Psalms; Is 9; Mal 4: QM xiv 4-5).[33]

The Benedictus, though called a prophecy (67,76,70) follows the usual threefold division of a hymn of praise—introduction, motives of praise and summarizing conclusion. The central section describes first the fulfilment of the Old Testament promises to David and Abraham, the two antecedents of Jesus most stressed in the early Christian preaching. Secondly (76-9) it addresses the child, the prophet who will prepare the way of the Lord.

Introduction v 68a:

Zechariah begins with a verse of praise which is found like a refrain at the end of four of the five books of psalms and also at a very significant point in 1 K 1:48 on David's lips "Blessed be Yahweh the God of Israel who has allowed my eyes to see one of my descendants (Solomon) sitting on my throne today." This refrain also introduces the Qumran victory hymn (1 QM xiv 4-5), which speaking also of mercy and salvation was intended to be sung after the eschatological battle for which they were waiting.

Strophe One—(68b-71b):

The reason for praise is Yahweh's visit to accomplish the redemption of his people had promised through the prophets (Ac 3:21). Visit is an Old Testament term which when used of Yahweh generally signifies a favorable deliverance.[34] It is used later (7:16) of the crowds reaction at Nain. Here the deliverance is explained as the raising up of a mighty Davidic (Zechariah and John were of the house of Aaron) Savior; the power of Yahweh, who raised up saviors in Israel's history.[35] Salvation is from the enemies who hate (Neh 9:27; Ps 106:9f). Perhaps for Luke these are the persecutors of the early Christians, whereas in the psalms, they are personal enemies or pagans. However, they are not defined here but in v 74 salvation means *freedom to serve,* in v 77 the forgiveness of sins is specified and in v 79 peace.

Strophe Two (72-5):

Here we go back behind David to the covenant sworn to Abraham (13:16; 16:24-30; Gn 22:16f; Jer 11:5; 31:31ff). Its fulfilment would mean that without fear (of their enemies) they would enjoy a positive freedom *to* (not only a negative *from*) serve God in holiness and justice, a beautiful description of the vocation to which Israel of old was called but often failed to realize (Ex 19:6; Amos).

Strophe Three (76-77):

Here John is directly addressed and his mission outlined, echoing Gabriel's words (1:16-17). He will be the last of the prophets (16:16; 17:16) who will make ready the ways of the Lord, i.e. Jesus (1:43; 3:24; 7:27), giving knowledge (see 3:10-14) of salvation. This will consist not in national independence but in the forgiveness of sins, a favorite theme in Luke (24:26). In 3:3 John will preach a baptism of repentance leading to the forgiveness of sins. In Jeremiah (Jer 31:34) the new covenant (Lk 22:20) will result in all knowing Yahweh and having their sins forgiven.[36]

Conclusion—(78a-79b):

The conclusion summarizes the main ideas of the psalm—God's visit (strophe 1), based on his heartfelt or really genuine covenant kindness (strophe 2) and the Jesus, the Davidic horn (strophe 1), whom the Baptist will prepare for (strophe 3). Malachi, after describing the messenger who will prepare the way (Mal 3:1), also (3:20) describes the sun of justice who will shine out with healing in its rays. Perhaps this is what Luke means by that difficult phrase *"anatole* from on high"—anatole was a name for the Davidic Messiah (Zech 3:8; 6:12; Jer 23:5) and literally means "rising" light.[37] This rising or dawning light, i.e. the sun or the morning star leads to a favorite Isaian theme[38] of those sitting in darkness and the shadow of death.[39] Later in Luke the Zacchaeus episode (18:35-42) is immediately preceded by a blind man episode. Together they show Luke's way of explaining the salvation of Jesus.

Luke uses the expression peace in his gospel more frequently than the other three evangelists combined—Isaiah had foretold a Prince of Peace and in Luke it will be proclaimed by the angels, by Simeon, by Jesus (8:48), by the seventy-two to an audience which may be hostile (10:5-6), according to some texts in the first words of the risen Jesus to his fearful disciples (24:36). In Acts, Peter will tell the

Roman Cornelius about the good news of peace brought by Jesus (Ac 10:36). Obviously, it is not political freedom which is referred to in Luke but a reinterpretation of the Old Testament concept in terms of a renewed relationship with God, the forgiveness of sins, the salvation from fear of one's enemies, the conquest of death—a peace that is offered to and sometimes rejected by all men in this world. Peace in the New Testament means especially a restored friendship with God. The offering of Jesus' peace brings division on earth (12:51)—Jerusalem did not know what was for her peace (19:42).

Luke finishes this Baptist episode by preparing us in his orderly way for John's next solemn appearance in the desert (3:2). He gives us one of his growth refrains (2:40,50) on the physical and spiritual development of John which reminds us of the development of Samson (Jdg 13:24-5) and Samuel (1 S 2:21). The desert was the historical training place for the Hebrew people (Exodus, Deuteronomy, Hosea) and for such individuals as Moses, the leader of the Exodus (Ex 3). The Qumran group, contemporaries with John, is familiar to us since the discovery of a library at Qumran on the Dead Sea in 1947. Certainly, there are smiliarities between John and Qumran but there is no clear cut evidence that he was closely associated with them. Quite likely there were other groups in the wilderness. There is quite a difference between the message of John as presented in the gospels and their highly selective and exclusive approach. John had a message to all Israel.

E. *The Birth, Circumcision and Naming of Jesus: Shepherds and Angels—(2:1-21):*

Here we come to what is one of the most familiar parts of the whole Bible told in simple direct, yet profound

Luke's Infancy Narratives

language.[40] Luke moves out from the Jewish world, from its center, Jerusalem and its periphery at Nazareth to the center of the whole world, Rome, to Augustus, the Emperor himself B.C. 44/42—A.D. 14. He gives us first the census which brought Mary and Joseph to David's city (five verses), next the birth itself in just two verses (6-7) with emphasis on the placing of the baby in the manger (mentioned 3 times v 7,12,16); finally Luke gives the biggest section (v 8-20) to the angels and to their interpretation of the event and the various reactions of the shepherds, of those who were told by the shepherds (v 18) and of Mary herself.

The Census—(1-5):

Luke begins his birth story of Jesus, unlike John (1:57) with a touch of solemnity (see 1:5; 1:39). Luke is the only New Testament writer to mention a Roman Emperor by name.[41] But apart from the obvious reason to explain Mary and Joseph coming to Bethlehem which is stressed as David's city,[42] several reasons can be sugested for Luke's mention of Augustus and his Roman census here. Luke, writing during the Roman Empire, is often at pains to show that the early Christians are law abiding people like Joseph and Mary here, unlike the Zealots of Judaism who advocated rebellion.

It is quite likely that Luke sees Augustus unknowingly (like King Cyrus before him, Is 45:1), helping to accomplish the plan of Yahweh, the Lord of history. Jesus' birth at Bethlehem fulfills the prophecy of Micah 4. Augustus was called savior, his word and proclamation called good news (gospel) and his great achievement, peace in the world. By Luke's time some emperors were even addressed as Lord and God. Luke seems to suggest here, especially for his Gentile seekers, that Jesus is the true savior, the bringer of true peace to the whole world (2:1) which he then knew. Later Luke is the only evangelist to record that Jesus came to make a different enrolment of citizens for heaven (10:17-20) whereas Augustus' census was for taxation purposes, which the Jews of course hated (not for military service from which the Jews were exempt).[43]

But Luke's historical note that this was "the first census under Quirinius as governor of Syria" has led to an unresolved historical problem as far as our information about the time goes. We know of no general Roman census which included Palestine, and would thus give a perfect solution to all the data we possess. Quirinius became governor of Syria in A.D. 6-7, some ten years after the death of Herod the Great (B.C. 4, Lk 1:5), according to Josephus, our sole authority (Antiquities 18:1.1). The census is referred to in Acts 5:37. But if Jesus was born in A.D. 6-7 it is difficult to explain how he was about thirty in the year 28-9 (?)-(Lk 3:23). Obviously, the discovery of new historical information is needed for an adequate solution to a difficult problem. Many scholars conclude that Luke seems to be inaccurate here. Some conclude from Luke's expression "the first census" that there were several censuses under Quirinius. There is some evidence that he was in Syria after B.C. 12 though not yet governor. It is quite possible that a puppet king like Herod would have co-operated in such a census to please his Roman masters. The reference to a census of the whole of humanity was theologically important for Luke as he stresses that Jesus of Nazareth was actually born in the Messianic city of David and at the same time shows that it has significance for all men.

The Birth, the Swaddling, the Manger—(6-7):

Luke seems especially interested in the swaddling and the manger as he repeats them (v 12,16). The "swaddling" is perhaps a reminder of the kingship of Jesus recalling David's son, Solomon's affirmation "I was nursed in swaddling clothes, with every care for no king has any other way to begin at birth" (Wis 7:4-5). The manger (phatne) which recurs in v 12,16 as a sign for the shepherds is perhaps a reference to the complaint in the first verses of Isaiah—

> The Ox knows its owner
> and the ass its master's crib (phatne)
> But Israel does not know,
> My people does not understand (Is 1:3).

Does it mean that in the shepherds Israel has at last begun to know its master? One wonders how many of Luke's predominantly Gentile audience would catch such allusions! One should be cautious about reading "heartlessness" or "acutely impoverished conditions" into (eisegesis), the phrase "no room" in the katalyma, a word which may mean a private home, a room (see 22:11) or an inn.[44] The word katalyma is associated in the LXX with the divine presence in Israel "not in the grandeur of the temple but in obscruity and humility."[45] There is a tradition going back at least to the second century that Jesus was actually born in a cave. Yet it is quite possible that the manger was in a house. Even to this day it is not uncommon to keep domestic animals in the lower part of a Palestinian house.

The reference to Jesus as first-born prepares us for the Presentation of Jesus as first-born and makes it clear that he has the rights and privileges of the throne of David (Ex 13:2; Num 3:12; 18:15-16).

The Announcement to the Shepherds—(2:8-14):

Some see this scene in the words of Jesus' response to John's disciples "the poor have the good news preached to them" (7:22; 18:17; 1:52). For Luke's audience it is quite likely that shepherds were a nomadic kind of people not in high regard. Many shepherds in Palestine also it seems were despised by the strictly orthodox as they were unable to keep the details of the Jewish ceremonial law. Some see these shepherds as the special shepherds who looked after the Temple lambs and thus are the first to recognize the true lamb of God. However, one should remember that in the Jewish background the great king David was once a simple boy shepherd (1 S 16; Ex 3:2; Ps 23).

Here then the symbolism seems to be (Is 1:3) that Israel is finally coming to know the manger of its true Lord. The reference to shepherds being in the open country by night leads many commentators to date the birth of Jesus between March and November, when such would be possible according to the Palestinian climate. December 25 was chosen in the fourth century to coincide with the "pagan" festival of the sun. There are traditions found in Clement of Alexandria (c A.D. 200) that Jesus was born on May 20 or April 20/1.

Here we find Luke's third announcement scene again following the typical pattern which we have already noted at 1:5-25. The glory, perhaps a metaphor from the glory of the sun shining, is frequently associated with a cloud and is a very old symbol for God's powerful presence and meeting with men.[46] Joy for Luke is the effect of the receiving of God's favor.[47] He is imitating the style of an imperial proclamation of good news for all the people. Luke, who stresses joy more than any other New Testament writer, here refers to "great joy" which the true gospel brings to men. He applies to Jesus three titles familiar to the early Christians—Savior, Christ (Messiah), Lord.[48] These are the early Church's confession as to who Jesus really was in the light of Easter.[49] The combination, Christ Lord (lit) occurs nowhere else in the New Testament and only by error for Christ *of* the Lord in the LXX translation of Lam 4:20 and Ps Sol 17:32.

The sign which the shepherds are given is the infant wrapped in swaddling clothes. Perhaps Luke is referring to Isaiah here and his famous sign (Is 7:14). Like Mary then respond in *haste* to the sign, the ideal response (1:39; 2:16).

Gloria in Excelsis:

The song of praise[50] of the angels (Dan 7:10) who live in God's presence is not without difficulties in translation. Basically it resembles the angels song at creation, described in the Book of Jubilees (2:2-3) and the song which Isaiah heard "Holy, Holy, Holy, the whole earth full of his glory" (Is 6:3). Glory, i.e. honor and praise to God in his transcendant dwelling (heaven). Peace (see 1:79) on earth be to men (not just Jews!) favored (by God). The problem is with the word favored or pleased. Does it mean a disposition of men, i.e. men who please God, men of good will as Latin versions translated it, or a disposition of God towards all men. Recently discovered parallels in the Dead Sea Scrolls indicate the meaning "men of God's good pleasure." Thus peace is not a politician's peace or a sentimental or even Pharisaical good will but is based on God's forgiveness.[51] Only God's good will (in Jesus!) can bring true peace to men. In the disciple's echo (19:38) peace is significantly in heaven as Jesus enters Jerusalem (19:42).

To Bethlehem—(15-20):

Luke brings the actors of both previous scenes together and gives us in a dramatic scene the various reactions around the manger. The shepherds, the first messengers, tell their story and as with John (1:63ff) all (he does not tell who) are astonished. But here only Mary is said to have treasured all these things and reflected on them like the ideal disciple (8:15,19ff; Ac 1:14). The same verb is found in Gn 37:11 of Jacob's remembering Joseph's dream of future greatness. Some think that Luke is suggesting that Mary was a source for the narrative which he is writing. She is the only bridge from Jesus' early life, to his ministry and the early church (8:15ff; Ac 1:14). The shepherds, who echo the angels, are the first of a long series in Luke who glorify and praise God for what they have heard and seen.[52]

The Circumcision and Naming (v 21):

One verse suffices here for what was the key scene in his treatment of John the Baptist. In dealing with John, Luke just gave a notice about his actual birth to concentrate on the naming scene. With Jesus the naming is passed over quickly and the emphasis is on the birth scene. It is clear that the duties of a pious Jewish family are fulfilled just as the angels command (1:31,60). But Luke, as with John, does not explain Jesus' name as Matthew does (1:21).[52a] The popular explanation, "Yahweh saves," must have been presupposed by him and it seems to be at least hinted at in 1:69; 2:11,30f; Ac 4:12.

F. *The Presentation of Jesus in the Temple—Simeon and Anna Prophecy—(2:22-40):*

Here, the Law, the prophets and the Temple provide a background as the future career and mission of Jesus is predicted. The Mosaic Law commended three ceremonies to follow the birth of a first-born male child: circumcision, redemption, purification (Lv 12:1ff; Ex 13:1ff; Num 18:15). Here Luke emphasizes some 5 times[53] the Law (Gal 4:4) and the fact that Jesus' parents like John's (1:6) were faithful people,[54] who carefully carried out all its commandments. Also, Luke shows us here Jesus coming (on his way home to Nazareth) to Jerusalem for the first time. Hitherto only Zechariah was portrayed in Jerusalem and he was unable to give a blessing, unlike here. We have no angel's revelation but Jesus is welcomed by the best of Judaism (not priests!). In a son and daughter of Israel who are waiting for its consolation, the spirit of prophecy comes alive as Joel had foretold (Joel 3:2; Ac 2:18) about the last days which have *now* (2:29) arrived. Two further clarifications about the mission of Jesus are also made here (compare 1:69ff and 2:30). The universal aspect of world wide mission to the Gentiles (from Jerusalem) is mentioned for the first time. Secondly, in contrast to the joy of the announcement and birth stories, a stark note of opposition, contradiction and suffering is struck as Jesus is recognized as the Suffering Servant of Isaiah. One should note the influence of the Samuel Old Testament story in Luke's reconstruction of this scene. Hannah and her husband brought their God-given child, Samuel, to the sanctuary at Shiloh and presented him for service to the Lord (1 S 1:24-8). The old priest, Eli, blessed them as Simeon did. There is also a conclusion similar to Luke's (1 S 2:21-6; Lk 2:40).

This section easily divides into four parts—the setting (22-4), Simeon's greeting and Nunc Dimittis (25-35), Anna's greeting (36-8), the conclusion with a growth refrain (39-40). Simeon's scene clearly gets the lion's share whereas the purification and presentation are not stressed by Luke in his simplified presentation of the Jewish customs.

The Setting—(2:22-4):

Leviticus commanded purification forty days after childbirth (*their* purification, i.e. Joseph and Mary). This was probably originally an ancient tatoo which was brought within the covenant. The offering of two birds is the offering of the poor people who cannot afford a lamb and a bird (Lv 12:6-8)—a subtle way of telling us about Jesus' poverty. Exodus 13:1ff commanded that every first-born male be consecrated to Yahweh in remembrance of his saving their first-born in Egypt (Ex 13:15). But as the descendants of Aaron and Levi had taken over the priesthood it was customary for all other families to buy back their own sons for five shekels (Num 8:15-16). Luke omits any reference to buying back, perhaps suggesting that like Samuel, Jesus was permanently in God's service.

Simeon's Greeting—(2:25-35):

The activity of the Spirit is mentioned three times with regard to Simeon, one of the two typical figures of Judaism and its expectations at its best, whom Luke now brings on in a key section of his narrative. Here Simeon takes the child in his arms (as Jesus does in Mk 9:36) and blessed God and the parents (v 36)—the same word is used of Zechariah after his cure (1:64) and of the disciples in the temple after the ascension (24:53). Simeon is described as an upright man,[55] devout (a Lucan word meaning careful about religious duties), (Ac 2:5; 8:2; 22:12), waiting for the "paraklesis" of Israel[56] as Anna wait for the "lutrosis" of Israel (1:38; see Is 52:9)[57]—all synonyms for the messianic deliverance. The consolation of Israel takes us back to the opening words of the prophecies of Second Isaiah (cf 40:1ff) just before the verse applied to the Baptist (the voice of one crying in the wilderness; Prepare the way of the Lord) where we read "Console, Console (parakalein), my people: speak priests to the heart of Jerusalem" (40:1; 66:12-13)—the rich have already got their paraklesis according to Luke 6:24. Simeon can be seen to symbolize the waiting Judaism and can now depart with his function completed.

Nunc Dimittis—(2:29-32): (first words of the Latin).

Simeon's prophecy is the address of a faithful, aged servant (12:42f) to his Master[58] now that the Holy Spirit has fulfilled his promise that before his death he would see the Christ of Yahweh, i.e. the long awaited salvation. The opening "now" is emphasized to signify that with Simeon we came to the end of an age that lived in hope. Mary too was called a servant (female) in the Magnificat (1:48). Servant, it should be remembered, was Paul's description for himself (Rom 1:1) and it was applied also in the Old Testament to Moses (Josh 1:2), Joshua (24:9), the prophets Amos (3:7) and Jeremiah (7:25).

The verb used ("you can let die" "apolueis"; Num 20:29; Tob 3:6, 13) is not an imperative or an entreaty but is an indicative and declarative—the function of the Old Testament if fulfilled. Simeon realizes that his death is near and now he can die in peace (complete happiness), like Abraham of old (Gn 15:15). This brief thanksgiving psalm is full of the phrases of Second Isaiah "seeing salvation"

(Is 52:9f), the sight of all the peoples (ibid.) "a light to the Gentiles" (Is 42:6; 49:6), the glory of Israel (Is 46:13; 45:25). Here is what has often been called "the scandal of particularity"—in a unique person, a unique place, a unique time, a unique people, God saves all men.

There is mention of a light, a revelation to the Gentiles, not a conquest of them as many contemporary revolutionaries would have expected.[59] To be a light so that "all mankind shall see the salvation of God" (3:6) will be the destiny of Jesus. He will guide people from the shadow of death into the way of God's forgiveness (1:79; 15:24). The wonder of the parents of Jesus at this new revelation which goes beyond the angel's words (1:32-3) is the typical and rather stereotyped reaction in Luke's two works to a manifestation of the divine.[60]

Simeon's Second Prophecy—(34c-35):

Simeon had just spoken of the messianic peace but as will also be explained later (12:52-3) it is a peace which divides as he now explains to Mary. Thus one can see Simeon's prophecies as a summary of the whole life of Jesus and the early church up to the end of Acts. Jesus is *set* (an image from building with stones) like the cornerstone on which people will stumble (Is 8:14) or like the cornerstone on which a house is built (Ps 118:22; Is 28:16). This "stone" explanation was used in the early church (Lk 20:17-18; Rom 9:30-32; 1 Pet 2:8). In the fall and rise of many in Israel, i.e. it will effect the whole people, we have an echo of Mary's Magnificat, e.g. 1:51 "confused the proud in their inmost thoughts." It is the story of Luke's gospel and Acts where only some Jews accepted Jesus and the gospel was accepted by many Gentiles. Jesus will be a sign that is contradicted[61] by a rebellious people (Nm 20:13; Dt 32:51).

Many interpretations have been offered of the "sword passing through Mary's soul," a phrase which is best understood as in parenthesis. Therefore the following phrase "the inmost thoughts of many will be revealed" is a continuation of "the sign that is contradicted" (so that the inmost thoughts . . .). The phrase inmost thoughts[62] is always used in a negative sense for hostile, vain or questioning thoughts. Men, by encountering Jesus will be compelled to reveal their true, inmost selves and take sides.[63] Perhaps the "sworn passing through" (Ezek 14:17) is best explained in Luke as a reference to the following scene where she will begin to realize that the claims of Jesus' heavenly Father and therefore his mission, will come before any human attachments to his mother and that therefore she must lose him.

Anna's Greeting—(2:36-8):

With Anna's presence Luke returns to his positive tone and reminds us that in case we look on the Jews too negatively there were "all those waiting for the redemption of Jerusalem" (2:38; 24:21). Anna had remained a widow, a decision which was highly regarded both in the Old estament and the New Testament. Widows were among the defenseless in society.[64] In Paul's churches which Luke must have known, widows had a special place.[65] Anna was a prophetess (Apoc 2:20) we are pointedly told though no word of hers is recorded. In the Old Testament seven women prophets are recognized—Sarah, Miriam, Deborah, Hanna (1 S2), Abigail, Hulda and Esther. Anna is the only woman in the New Testament to receive the title although the prophetic activity of women is mentioned several times.[66] She resembles the heroine, Judith, who also had remained a widow and spent her days observing the Law and fasting (Judith 15:5ff; 8:1-8). When she delivered Israel she gave thanks just like Anna (Jd 15:14ff). Her age, 105, is close to that of Anna if we take the 84 years to refer to Anna's period of widowhood. Anna belonged to one of the most insignificant of the lost tribes of Israel which lived north of Mt. Carmel and was closely assimilated to the Canaanites (Jdg 1:31-2; 1 K 4:16 Apoc 7:6). One wonders why Luke records such details as "the daughter of Phanuel" and "of the tribe of Asher," details which he does not seem to have or record about Simeon. Asher in Hebrew means "blessed" and Phanuel (peniel) is explained by Jacob in Gen 32:30 (LXX) after his night of wrestling as "I have seen God face to face and my soul has been saved." Thus some detect a symbolism in the names here—Anna has wrestled long with God in prayer and now sees his face in Jesus.

Conclusion—(2:39-40):

The conclusion again emphasizes that the Law was fulfilled by Jesus' parents and that they then returned to "their own town" Nazareth. Matthew does not mention that Mary and Joseph lived in Nazareth before Jesus was born. Yet all four gospels agree that Jesus' home was at Nazareth. The growth refrain about Jesus—grew, became strong, filled with wisdom, favored by God (Gn 21:8; Jdg 13:24; 1 S 2:21ff), in contrast to that about John (1:80) omits a reference to "spirit." Probably Luke's view was that Jesus who was conceived by the spirit did not have to grow in the spirit like John (Lk 4:1 *full* of the Holy Spirit; 4:14,18).

G. *The Boy Jesus in the Temple—(2:41-52):*

Here Luke gives us as the final episode in his infancy stories an illustration of Jesus' growing in wisdom and God's favor, a growth refrain which is repeated before and after the episode (2:40-53). It is also an illustration of Simeon's prophecy to Mary about the sword passing through her as Jesus recognizes his heavenly Father's claim and mission. For John, Luke is content to hint as his training in the desert (1:80). But for Jesus, alone of all the gospels, Luke gives us a childhood story—he will give us nothing more for the next 18 years (3:23). The next time in Luke's gospel that Jesus will visit Jerusalem apart from the temptation story (4:9) will be for his passion. But this bridge story between Jesus' infancy and public life is not told for purely biographical purposes as none of the evangelists show much interest in purely biographical details. The chief point of the story (called a paradigm or apophthegm), is not the unusual intelligence of the twelve year old boy but his statement about God as his Father (v 19). This episode is so often used in reconstruction of Jesus' psychological awareness and development that Brown's remarks should be carefully kept in mind—

> "The present setting and saying are no less and no more historical than are the divine voice and its setting at the baptism of Jesus. Jesus was baptized; Jesus had a boyhood—those are historical facts. But in Luke those historical reminiscences serve as the occasion for the articulation of a revelation apprehended by post-resurrection faith, namely, the divine sonship.
>
> And so, whether one is liberal or conservative, one must desist from using the present scene to establish a historical

development (or lack of development) in Jesus' self-awareness. It is not possible to argue from v 49 that Jesus as a boy knew he was the Son of God. It is equally impossible to argue from v 25 (which is a standard description of growth) that Jesus grew in knowledge. At most one can argue that Luke's appreciation of Jesus did not cause him to see any difficulty in stating that Jewus grew in wisdom and God's favor, and that Luke's christology did not cause him to see any difficulty in affirming that, already as a boy, Jesus was God's Son. Nor finally can we determine anything historical about Mary's understanding of Jesus from the statement in 50 that she and Joseph did not understand when Jesus spoke of his Father. As already indicated, this story or a form of it may well have first circulated in circles ignorant of the annunciation story and ignorant of the virginal conception. But the fact that Luke who is aware of such traditions, sees no difficulty in reporting Mary's lack of understanding means that *for him* v 50 is only an instance of the standard misunderstanding that greets a parabolic revelation or a prophetic statement. It is a stylized reaction in Gospel literature and tells us nothing historical of Mary's psychology."[67]

Setting—(2:41-5):

Luke's infancy stories end as they begin in the Temple in Jerusalem (1:5,46). Here we have a "going up," a journey from Nazareth in Galilee to Jerusalem for the Passover, an anticipation of the great final journey which began at 9:51ff. It was a distance of about eighty miles, a three day journey. The Law commanded every *male* Jew to go to Jerusalem for the three feasts of Passover, Pentecost and Tabernacles (Ex 23:14-19; 34:23; Dt 16:16). Women, it seems did not have to go but frequently did, like Samuel's parents (1 S 1:3-28). Probably it was the custom for those at a distance to go up once a year (1:41). We are not clear that boys of twelve, the age of discretion, were obliged to

Luke's Infancy Narratives

go at this time. For modern Jews the beginning of adulthood is celebrated by the "bar mitzvah" ceremony when a boy about age thirteen enters the synagogue and reads a lesson from the Law and the Prophets and then expounds on the text. Thus he becomes a "son of the Law" and is able to accept the responsibilities that his parents pledged for him at circumcision. The celebration normally lasted seven days; the boy Jesus remained behind and his absence was not noticed for a day—the three days include a day's journey out and back and a day searching. One should remember the vast crowds coming to Jerusalem and people's custom of travelling in large caravans as a protection against robbers. Some see in the episode a prophetic hint by Luke of the final visit of Jesus to Jerusalem when he again is teaching in the Temple and is lost for three days.

Jesus in the Temple—(2:45-50):

Jesus is found seated (Ac 22:3) in the midst of the teachers, an example of a pious, but brilliant, youth who is fascinated with learning the Law—hearing and asking questions is a Jewish phrase for a student learning. The amazement "of all who heard" should not be exaggerated (4:32; 20:26). One apocryphal gospel imagines Jesus instructing the rabbis in the Law and the Prophets in addition to such learning as astronomy and medicine. Mary's words of astonishment are the natural, spontaneous reaction of worry and even rebuke[68] which one might expect in such circumstances.

Now Jesus speaks for the first time in Luke—hitherto we have had words about Jesus by others such as angels and Simeon. The Greek of Jesus' answer or rather rhetorical questions is somewhat ambiguous. The Greek literally translates as ". . . I must be in the (the plural of the definite article but without a qualifying noun) . . . of my Father." "Must" is one of Luke's favorite terms and is frequently used when Jesus is speaking of the plan of the Father which he must fulfill, the mission which he must carry out.[69]

"House" (Luke 19:46; 6:4; Jn 2:16) or "affairs" i.e. discussing the Law are the two most frequent ways of supplying the missing word. The emphasis is on *my* Father as Jesus replies to his mother who spoke of "your father and I." Jesus' heavenly Father's mission will call him away from family obligations. There is a note of foreboding here and no wonder. Luke adds that Mary and Joseph did not understand (i.e. how his Father's mission would be worked out), as the disciples would fail later when his passion was predicted to them (Lk 9:45; 18:34). Whether one translates the missing word as "house" or "business" the meaning is clear. Jesus' presence among the teachers in the Temple shows where his future mission lies. He will have to leave his family to dedicate himself to his heavenly Father's mission. Thus this section forms an excellent climax to Jesus' early years and an introduction to his public mission.

Conclusion—(2:51-2):

Nevertheles, despite the clear reference to his obligations to his heavenly Father, Luke as he returns Jesus to Nazareth, the base from which his career will be launched (4:16), stresses his *obedience* to his parents—again an emphasis on the pious law-abiding family background of Jesus who honored his parents as the Decalogue commanded. This explains why the inhabitants of Nazareth suspected nothing only that he was Joseph's son despite the evident "grace" when he speaks to them (4:22). In case one got a wrong impression of Mary's rebuke and amazement and lack of understanding (v 48-50), Luke repeats what he said of her after the shepherd's report (2:19,51)

Luke's Infancy Narratives

and prepares the way for her full participation in the believing community in Acts 1:14. Luke adds a new word to his growth refrain about Jesus (compare 1:80; 2:40,52) i.e. maturity.[70] He is probably suggesting the general progress of Jesus both in age and stature. This new development of Jesus is clearly evident from the variety of progressing words which Luke uses to describe him—"baby" (2:16), "child" (2:17,27,40 where a diminutive is used), "the boy Jesus" (v 43,48) and finally simply Jesus (52).

4. PREPARATION FOR THE PUBLIC MINISTRY

(Lk 3:1-4:13)

Here Luke begins to make contact with the other three evangelists in his account of John the Baptist. In particular, he has in common with the other synoptics, Matthew and Mark, the well known trilogy, the preaching of John, John's Baptism, Jesus' Temptation.[1] It is interesting to compare Luke's account with that of the other synoptics in particular, as it frequently helps to see more clearly his special emphasis and insights and the points which he stresses for his own particular audience. Even a cursory comparison shows how he begins with a great effort at a synchronism (3:1-2) and inserts a genealogy between the Baptism of Jesus and his temptation (3:23-38). This section which describes the preparation for the public ministry of Jesus in Galilee falls easily into four parts——

  A. John the Baptist (3:1-20).

  B. The Baptism of Jesus (3:21-2).

  C. The Genealogy of Jesus (3:23-37).

  D. The Temptation in the Desert (4:1-13).

A. *John the Baptist—(3:1-20):*

Eighteen years have passed since the last scene and in all some thirty years have elapsed since Jesus' birth. Caesar

Preparation For The Public Ministry

Augustus (died A.D. 14) and Herod the Great (B.C. 37-34) have by now passed from the scene (1:5; 2:11). As Luke now prepares us for the public ministry of Jesus and introduces John's proclamation, he gives us a six fold synchronization which is so elaborate that some have suggested that this was the beginning of Luke's gospel in an earlier version and that the first two chapters are a preface which was added afterwards. On the contrary, it is interesting to note that the famous Greek historian, Thucydides, has a similar multiple dating for his key event (2:2-1), the attack on Plataea which began the Peloponnesian War about which he wrote. It is also important to note here that Luke who has already given a large place to John in the infancy stories continues his parallel treatment.[2]

Both are found in the desert (3:2; 4:1) and are written of by Isaiah (3:4-6; 4:17-19). Both issue warnings drawn from the Old Testament (3:7-9; 4:24-7). Both are questioned about their identity (3:15; 4:34). Both preach the good news (3:6,18; 4:18,43); John, about the future, Jesus about "today." Both are rejected (7:29ff; 3:18-20; 4:18-30). Yet there is a decisive difference between them as Jesus is the Son of God (3:22; in 3:2a the word comes to John). The Spirit of the Lord rests on Jesus (4:18) so that he will baptize in the Holy Spirit whereas the forerunner's baptism is in water.[3] Jesus is given an elaborate genealogy whereas with John, Luke is content to call him son of Zechariah and add no further information than he gave in the first chapters (3:2,23). Jesus alone will preach the kingdom, i.e. its presence[4] and will say that "the least born into the kingdom of God is greater than" John even though no man born of woman is greater than him who is more than a prophet (7:27).

A comparison between Luke's presentation and that of Mark and especially Matthew, brings out certain distinctive characteristics. Luke does not have Mt 3:2, "The

Kingdom of God is at hand," an expression which he leaves to Jesus; or the description of the person of John (Mt 3:6; Mc 1:6), which would give him Elijah's role, which Luke prefers to use in his description of Jesus himself;[5] or a description of his baptizing activity as in Mt 3:5-6; or give him the title The Baptizer, as in Mt 3:1. But Luke alone has the synchronization (3:1-2); a longer version of the quotation from Isaiah, so that John clearly anticipates the universal significance of Jesus (3:5-6); illustrations of John's preaching (3:10-15); the hesitation of the people as to whether John is the Messiah (3:15-16a); the summary v 18; the imprisonment of John before the baptism of Jesus (3:19-20). Two key texts illustrating Luke's attitude to John are 16:16—

> "The Law and the prophets were in force until John. From his time on, the good news of the kingdom of God has been proclaimed . . ."

and 7:27 "more than a prophet yet the least . . ."

Thus while for Luke, John is unique even among prophets yet he makes a decisive separation between them as between two periods in history the first of which reaches its climax in John. Some also see here a gentle polemic against the followers of John, a polemic which is more emphatic in John's gospel (Jn 1:8,20).

Luke's Synchronism—(3:1-2a):

Here Luke synchronizes the activity of John (and Jesus) not only on the world scene with the Roman political situation, but also on the local Palestinian scene with both the political and religious situation—a real world full of corruption and problems which John will challenge with lhis message. However careful and elaborate Luke's

Preparation For The Public Ministry

sixfold chronology is by ancient standards—in fact he gives us the only real date in the whole of the New Testament—nevertheless, it is difficult to analyze his dating by modern standards of accuracy as we lack the necessary data for an exact interpretation. If Augustus Caesar died 19th August A.D. 14, then does the fifteenth year of his successor Tiberius give us A.D. 28-9? However, it seems that for the Syrians and the Jews (also Luke), the new civil year began on the first day of October. Therefore, the first year of the new Emperor, Tiberius, would be from 19th August A.D. 14—30th September and the fifteenth year would be from 1st October A.D.27—30th September 28. This would perhaps lead us to putting the preaching of John and Jesus' baptism at the end of A.D. 27 and Jesus' death at the Pasch A.D. 30.

Pontius Pilate was "hegemon" (Lk 10:20; Ac 23:24; Mt 27:2) from A.D. 26-36. An inscription found at Caesarea, the Roman capital city, describes Pilate as "Praefectus." After Herod the Great's death B.C. 4 his kingdom was divided among three sons; Archelaus for Judea, Samaria and Idumaea, but because of Jewish complaints at his high handed ways he was exiled in A.D. 6 and Roman procurators were installed; Herod Antipas became tetrarch[6] of Galilee and Perea until A.D. 39. Much of Jesus' life was lived in his region and dominions (Lk 3:19; 8:3; 13:32). Herod Philip was tetrarch of the regions North and East of the sea of Galilee (Ituraea and Trachonitis) from A.D. 34. He built Caesarea Philippi and his brother, Antipas built Tiberias. We know little about Lysanias and the territory of Abilene which was centered on the city of Abila about twenty miles North West of Damascus. Josephus twice mentions that it came into Jewish hands and it seems from inscriptions that Lysanias was the hereditary name of the king there.

Next as Luke gives the religious setting he mentions the high priesthood of Annas and Caiaphas, a curious fact as the Jews had only one high-priest at a time and it was a lifelong appointment. However, Annas was actually high priest from A.D. 6-15 when he was deposed by the Roman authorities although it seems that he was still very influential among his successors who included five of his sons and also his son-in-law, Caiaphas, who was high priest from A.D. 18-36. Perhaps he was regarded by the Jews as still the legitimate high priest (Ac 4:6; Jn 18:13-24).

The Call of John—(3:2b-3):

The precise Greek phrase (the word of God came to), although resembling closely the opening phrases of several prophetic books (Hos, Mich, Hag, Joel), is found exactly only in Jeremiah 1:1 (LXX). While John is thus put within the prophetic tradition of the Old Testament there is also perhaps a suggestion to a resemblance between John and Jeremiah.[7] The word of Yahweh in the Old Testament was all powerful and possessed a sovereign efficacy.[8] It was at work in the history of Israel from the creation (Gn 1:3) to the rebuilding of Jerusalem (Is 44:28), from the call of Abraham to the present call of John.

John did not stay in one place but moved about the Jordan valley proclaiming a baptism of repentance which would lead to the forgiveness of sins. It is important to remember that in the Old Testament to obtain forgiveness of serious sin (Nm 15:30; 1 S 3:14), to achieve the restoration of community with Yahweh, there was nothing man could do. The ritual expiation found in Leviticus an Numbers was not directed to the ritual obtaining of forgiveness. Only Yahweh could forgive and forgiveness was his nature,[9] although he demanded conversion, ' 'a genuine interior change of attitude that issues in a revolution in personal conduct.''[10]

Preparation For The Public Ministry

John's use of the external symbol of baptism (Ac 2:38; 8:36) is quite interesting. It was the familiar rite of initiating converts into Judaism. It was also used in Qumran as a purification rite but they would never have used it for such a wide audience as John but for select initiates only. Thus in effect John was proclaiming:

> "You call yourselves Jews, you claim to be descendants of Abraham, you demand the privileges that belong to Israel. You have no right to the name, no right to the status; you have forfeited all by your wickedness. You have only one chance. You must begin where the unclean Gentile begins—at the bottom. You must re-discover, and re-learn your Judaism from the beginning. Only so can you hope to have any part in the good time that is coming."[11]

John's baptism was a preparation for the Messiah (Ac 19:4) and was an occasion of repentance (clarified in v 10-14), which would lead to God's forgiveness, i.e. salvation (1:77).

Luke's Quotation from Isaiah—(Lk 3:4-6):

All four gospels apply Isaiah 40:3 to John and claim for him the humble role of the voice (in Jn 1:23 John applies it to himself). This text was popular at Qumran to explain why they lived in the desert.[12] The phrase "as is written in" shows that the ministry of John is part of the divine plan as is also the life of Jesus.[13] In Isaiah, the text originally referred to the role of angels, who like a bulldozer, would level a highway through the desert hills and valleys so that the Hebrews might return from their Babylonian exile to the Promised Land. But John is to prepare a way so that all men can see the salvation of God (2:30; 1:77), the story of Acts (Ac 28:28). By preaching and baptizing, he would bring about a radical change in values, a redistribution of wealth (3:10), a levelling of the proud and an exalting of the lowly, a preparation of straight paths (1:77) for the Lord.

Luke's quotation is the most extensive of the four gospels. He adds Isaiah 40:4-5, which would suit his emphasis on the universality of the salvation which Jesus would bring (4:5,40). Note how "the paths of our God" (LXX, Mt) is changed to "his paths" (i.e., Jesus) and also the omission of the "glory" line[14] and further how Mark 1:2[15] is found in Lk 7:27.

Repent—(3:7-9):

Of the sixty three Greek words of John in these verses, sixty are identical between Matthew and Luke. Luke has "fruits" and "begin" in v 8, whereas Matthew has "fruit" and "presume." But Luke has John speaking to the "crowds" (see 7:29f; 13:17) whereas Matthew has Pharisees and Sadducees. Luke's version is obviously more suited to his audience, his own community and probably was used there for instruction. John describes his audience as like a brood of vipers (a Qumran phrase), fleeing from a desert fire. The answer to John's rhetorical question is "Nobody!" "Certainly I have not shown you how to escape."

The anger of Yahweh is an important theme in the Old Testament but is always ethically motivated and associated with his covenant love, his holiness, his justice—as opposed to the Mesopotamian conception of an unmotivated and irrational divine anger. Further, it is not the habitual attitude of Yahweh which is rather covenant love (Ps 30:6). It is his personal reaction to Israel's breaking of the covenant, to their "unbelief, distrust, rebellion, worship of false gods," their inhumanity and pride and refusal to obey his laws.[16] But though always controlled, it could reach a limit where intercession would be no longer effective (Jer 14:11-12; Ez 14:14). Going back at least to Amos (5:18-20; 3:2), a great day of judgment on Israel was expected. Isaiah (2:10-17) spoke of a universal judgment when Yahweh would act against all pride and arrogance, "all that is great to bring it down . . ." "all things of price" (Lk 1:51; Zeph 1). John insists upon fruits of repentance, actions like Zacchaeus which are evidence of repentance (Lk 19:1ff; Ac 26:20), a real listening to the prophets, unlike the rich man who is content to call on Father Abraham, the constant Jewish temptation to rely on the fact that they were chosen people.[17] God can create a new posterity for Abraham even out of stones. If John's words are translated back into Aramaic, there is a play on words between children (benayyâ) and stones (abnayyâ). That the crisis is already present is described in a vivid metaphor of the axe laid to the root of the tree, a metaphor which the Jordan jungle, Israel's largest forest land, provided.

What ought we to do?—(3:10-14):

The leaders rejected John's teaching (7:30) but the crowds asked the basic question which is a veritable theme in Luke, recurring at 10:25; 18:18; Jn 6:28. Peter would also be asked the same question at Pentecost (Ac 2:37) and the goaler would ask Paul and Silas (16:30; 22:10). The example which Luke selects for John emphasizes his concern with social justice for his audience. Repentance is not just an emotional experience but a transformation of the total person, leading to decisive action. Luke is very concerned about the material things of life and one of the great tests for him is the way a man uses his possessions and money, a frequent theme of his parables.[18] John for Luke is the forerunner also of Jesus' moral teaching. The same question is asked three times to show its importance. Basically, Luke's ideal is a sharing community which was the ideal throughout Jewish history (Lk 12:33f; Ac 2:44-5; Pr 13:7; Wis 7:14). He does not propose a revolution in the Roman Empire and its system of taxes. His attitude to such unpopular outcasts as tax-collectors and their soldiers must have shocked the Jewish society of John's day as they were local Jews who collaborated with the foreign power. He tells the tax-collectors to collect only the correct sum—the system was notoriously corrupt.[19] His advice to the soldiers is interesting as their profession was often considered incompatible with membership of the Jewish and later the Christian community. He is content to warn them against the special temptations of their profession—don't intimidate or bully, don't extort but be content with your pay. John is called Teacher (didaskalos) here, a title frequently used of Jesus in the rest of the gospel which was equivalent of Rabbi as the inscription on a first century tomb confirms (Jn 1:38).

The Messiah?—(3:15-8);

Finally, Luke shows that John distinguished himself from the coming Messiah who will execute the coming judgment which John proclaimed and will have a superior baptism. Like his baptism, John himself is inferior to the one to come. Here again Luke is quite close to Matthew's text. Messianic expectations were in the air. Late Judaism's expectations however were not as precise as many later Christians often presuppose. They had quite a variety of salvific figures who might appear from the anointed[20] king of the Davidic line to Elijah, the prophet-like Moses and perhaps also the Son of Man, the Suffering Servant, the Anointed Priest, not to forget the special activity of the Spirit which was awaited.[21]

A spiritual Messiah like Jesus can be said to have been far from the popular expectation which is also described in Jn 1:20-5. John emphasizes the urgency of the situation and uses the agricultural image of a farmer winnowing corn by casting it into the air with a wooden shovel so that the chaff can be blown apart and then burned with tremendous heat.[22] But the Messiah is so superior in power to John (Lk 11:20-22) that John is not worthy to be his slave. Luke (and Matthew) adds "fire" to his description of the superior baptism to come. In the Old Testament and Qumran texts, fire is often associated with the presence of God in judgment.[23] But it is quite likely that Luke is thinking of Pentecost when the spirit descended in the form of fire. Perhaps there is a double aspect here of both purification by fire and strengthening by the spirit.[24] This then says Luke is a typical summary of the good news with which John exhorted the people.

Conclusion: John in Prison—(3:19-20):

It is intersting to note how Luke describes the imprisonment of John by Herod Antipas[25] before he records the actual baptism of Jesus (3:21f). This is not just Luke's typical technique of closing a story before he goes on to the next one.[26] Rather he seems to be removing John from the stage of his gospel—he does not appear again apart from his disciples question in 7:18—before the public appearances of Jesus begin. Thus Luke puts John carefully into the preparatory stage of good news about Jesus to come and his future Messianic work so that he can turn his spotlight fully on to Jesus at his baptism.

It seems that Herod the Great had two sons named Philip, one, the son of Cleopatra, the tetrarch, the other the son of Marianne who is called Herod in Josephus and of whom we know almost nothing except that his wife

Herodias abandoned him to marry the tetrarch, Herod Antipas. Mark calls her "the wife of his brother Philip" (Mk 6:17), whereas Luke is content to call her "his brother's wife," to avoid confusion with Philip the tetrarch mentioned in 3:1. John censures Herod not just for his marital affairs but according to Luke "for all his crimes as well" (3:19). Luke does not tell of the death of John and is content with an illusion in 9:9 about his rising from the dead. Some suggest that as he does not tell of Peter's or Paul's deaths also it was due to his gentle character that he found such crude and barbarous descriptions too much to repeat. John was also a forerunner of Jesus in his own suffering (Mt 17:12). But Luke has made his point—with the baptism of Jesus the period of John is finished.

3. *The Baptism of Jesus—(3:21-2):*

Jesus who last appeared as a growing twelve year old at Nazareth is now baptized among the sinful people of Israel with whom he identifies himself. One should read the text carefully here and avoid reading into it any romantic notions about Jesus' religious experience and Messianic awakening. For the gospel writers, this scene's purpose would be to explain to their readers who Jesus really was and what his purpose would be. Each evangelist has his own particular emphasis in narrating the baptism of Jesus. John emphasizes that Jesus is the Anointed One and also the Lamb while the actual baptism is not mentioned. In Matthew, there is a discussion as to why the baptism of Jesus is "fitting." Luke, who passes quickly over the actual baptism has more than in Mark and Matthew. He has a distinction between the baptism and the theophany—this is where Luke's emphasis is placed. He alone stresses that Jesus was at prayer *after* the baptism of all including Jesus

Preparation For The Public Ministry

himself, thus carefully again separating Jesus' experience of the Spirit from John's activity. Luke, who loves to show Jesus as one who prayed constantly to God particularly at important moments in his life,[27] later will have Jesus tell us that the Father will give the Holy Spirit to those who ask him (11:13).

The Greek text of "the opening of the skies"[28] is close to the LXX version of Isaiah 63:19, where the prophet longs for God to open the heavens and come down and repeat his great redemption of the people in a new Exodus. One should compare Ez 1:1 also Stephen's vision of the opening in the sky (Ac 7:56) and Peter's vision of the sky opening (Ac 10:11), to see how the expression signifies a vision of heaven. Jesus here is the point of contact between heaven and earth, the Bethel of the New Testament, as John described it (Jn 1:51; Gn 28:17).

Luke's description of the Holy Spirit decending in visible form like a dove is difficult to understand. Is he implying that the spirit was visible to others besides Jesus? (Jn 1:32). Or does he mean that the Holy Spirit descended in a permanent form, unlike the often transient form which prophets experienced? Clearly Luke is using some kind of picture language to capture a unique experience, to stress for his audience that it was not just a subjective experience but that Jesus really possessed the Spirit. At Pentecost it would be "a noise *like* a strong driving wind" and "tongues *like* fire" which descended. However, on Jesus all four evangelists stress that it was "like a dove."

Different explanations of the dove symbolism are given—the dove was not a symbol of the Holy Spirit but rather of Israel. In Jewish tradition the hovering of the creative spirit over the waters in Genesis (1:2) suggested the hovering of a bird as in Dt 32:11. Some suggest that the dove is an allusion to the New Israel, the fruit of the Spirit.

Perhaps the most likely is in the traditional gentleness of the dove, the symbol of love of the beloved (SS 2:14; Ps 74:19). There is no need for "fire" in the case of Jesus as he was conceived by the Spirit (1:35). Jesus is the beloved and no objections typical of the prophets are recorded in his case. He will send the Spirit to others (24:49). His life is *the* life of the Spirit which will reach a climax in his ascension (Ac 2:23).

The "voice from heaven" is found in Rabbinical writings and in the Old Testament[29] to express a revelation from God. In Mark and Luke Jesus is addressed directly whereas in Matthew it is John and the people who are addressed. Here it expresses for Luke's audience the Father's approval and authentication of Jesus. To one who said "my Father" (2:49) there is a response from heaven saying "my son"—the phrase "son of" will characterize the next three sections of Luke, the genealogy, the temptation scene (4:3,9) and the Nazareth scene (4:22, Is not this the son of Joseph?). The first part of the quotation resembles Ps 2:7 and actually the Western Manuscript tradition which was widespread during the first three centuries, continues the quotation adding "Today I have become your father." This addition could easily be omitted due to possible "adoptionist" interpretations and an apparent conflict with Luke's infancy account (1:32,35; 2:49). It is quoted in Acts 13:33 by Paul. However, it is essential to remember in general that a quotation in the New Testament from the Old Testament should not be read by itself alone but in its context—as it would have been understood in first century Judaism and early Christianity.

Originally, in Old Testament times this Psalm (Ps 2:7) was probably applied to the king at his enthronement ceremony. It was a reminder for the king of God's gift of the nations to the ends of the earth for his heritage and domain—these he will break with an iron sceptre and shatter like a pot. However, some have argued that the word "son" comes from the Greek word "pais" which can be translated as either servant or son (e.g. Ac 3:13) and that therefore the whole quotation is based on Isaiah and his suffering servant theme. Certainly the second part of the quotation reflects Isaiah 42:11 and 44:2. Both together suggest that Jesus will exercise his mission (kingship 19:38) in the manner of God's favored servant who will bring justice to the nations (Is 42:1) but who will not violently crush opposition (Is 42:1) but will be gentle with the "crushed reed" and "the smoking flame" (Luke's outcasts), and will redeem man through his suffering love for others' sins (Is 53:5ff) and the indignities of rejection and death which he will endure, though innocent. Somewhat surprisingly, it is only Luke who gives a direct quotation from a Servant Song of Isaiah on the lips of Jesus (Lk 22:37; Is 53:12). "It is written in Scripture 'He was counted among the wicked' and this I tell you must be fulfilled in me."

C. *The Genealogy of Jesus—(3:23-37):*

The genalogy of Jesus is a typical example of putting pericopes side by side and leaving it to the observant reader to tease out the connections on either side and Luke's particular emphasis. Unlike Matthew and Mark, who have the temptation immediately following the baptism, Luke prefers to insert a genealogy. Luke refers to Jesus being "about thirty." This seems to have been the age among Jewish people when a man was considered fully mature and capable of public teaching. It was the age when David became king (2 S 5:4), that Joseph in Egypt received high office (Gen 41:46), that a man was fit to bear arms and serve as a priest (Nm 4:3,47; 8:23; Jn 8:57). Comparing the genealogy with the baptism scene and its proclamation that

Jesus is God's son, one can conclude that here Luke is interested in stressing the real humanity of Jesus before he comes to the temptation scene, to show his audience that Jesus was no (Hellenistic) divine phantom, but a real human, with a real family genealogy. Yet it should be remembered also that all three scenes—Baptism, Genealogy, Temptation, stress that Jesus is the son of God, e.g. here Luke emphasizes that Jesus was only "the supposed" son of Joseph through whom Jesus' genealogy is traced. In the ancient world adoptive parents were considered real parents (Gal 4:5) and could be used for tracing a genealogy.

While a modern reader finds a genealogy dull reading and tends to skip over it easily, it should be remembered that for the Jewish people they were of the utmost importance as the many genealogies in the Old Testament testify. Josephus tells us how carefully such records were kept in Jerusalem. Especially after the chaos of the Exile, genealogies were important in establishing membership of a particular tribe and clan and the privileges and rights for such as property and entry into the priesthood (Ezra 2:59-63; Neh 7:61-5). However, this should not blind us to the obvious artificial character of many genealogies as they loved to trace themselves back to the famous heroes of Israel. Clearly, Luke is primarily interested in showing how Jesus, in God's providential plan, is the climax of human history from Adam onwards, having his solidarity with all mankind (Ac 17:24-9). Paul also stresses that Jesus is the new Adam who came from God in a unique way like the old Adam. He is the prototype of a new humanity as God would like it to be.[30] He will restore paradise (23:43).

A comaparison between the genealogies in Luke and Matthew brings out some very interesting points. However, it should be emphasized that there are still many

Preparation For The Public Ministry

unsolved problems in them both and that no fully coherent explanations of their differences has been discovered. Neither genealogy should be seen to be completely factual but their theological aims should be seen as primary.[31]

(a) The position in both gospels is different. In Matthew it is a preface to his whole book and his infancy stories and thus precedes the story of Jesus like the genealogy of Noah is given in Genesis before the story of Noah (Gn 5:1ff). Luke tells of Jesus' birth, youth and inauguration of his ministry first, just as Exodus describes Moses' birth, youth and inaugural call before listing his ancestors (Ex 6:14-25).

(b) Each proceeds in the opposite direction to the other. Matthew begins with Abraham and stresses David and all the kings of Judah. He uses the words "A was the father of B." Luke begins with Joseph and goes back in history adding a pre-Abraham period back to God himself, thus having a longer list of names, seventy-seven to Mathew's forty-one. From Abraham to Joseph, Matthew has forty-one to Luke's fifty-six names. Luke uses the formula A *of* B of C to which translators usually supply "son," giving "A (son) of B."

(c) Matthew's list gives three periods of Jewish history — 3x2x7 = 42, whereas Luke has the artificial pattern of 11x17 — Adam to Abraham 3x7 generations; Isaac to David 2x7; Nathan to Salathiel (pre-exilic) 3x7; Zerubbabel to Jesus 3x7, thus making Jesus the seventy-seventh human descendant of Adam. However, the numbers in many manuscripts are different, varying from seventy-seven to sixty-three. Both use multiples of seven, the holy number. For ancient peoples, numbers were quite important and were seen as expressing profound truths.

(d) The lists of names differ with only fourteen names, the same in both. No harmonization seems possible as both trace the genealogy through Joseph. Such explanations as that Matthew uses a levirate marriage, that Joseph's mother married twice (Dt 25:5f) and gives the royal genealogy, whereas, Luke gives the historical genealogy, are unproven.

(e) As he goes through the key periods of Jewish history, Luke seems to stress every seventh, e.g. Enoch (7); Shelah (14); Abraham (21); Admin (28); David (35); Joseph (42); Joshua (Jesus) (49 i.e. 7x7); Shealtiel (56); Mattathias (63); Joseph (70). If one takes the total in Luke as 11x7 then Jesus is seen as beginning the twelfth, or perfect generation, eleven is an incomplete number (Ac 1:26). In 2 Baruch 53-74 and 4 Ezra 14:11 there is division of world history into twelve sections (see also 1 Ezra 5:5). One notices also the presence of several prophets, Eli (v 23), Amos, Nahum (v 25), Nathan? (v 31). Luke perhaps is choosing a messianic line through David's son, Nathan (2 S 5:14) rather than Solomon whose scandalous life was unsuitable.

(f) The aims of both are different, Matthew sets Jesus against the background of Jewish history as the last and final king in David's line. However, neither is content to show Jesus as merely a descendant of David. Matthew begins with Abraham, the father of the chosen people. Luke puts more emphasis on Jesus' Davidic ancestry in his first two chapters (1:27,32,69). But in his genealogy he goes back to Adam, thus removing the natural and racial boundaries, and to God himself who in 3:22 had attested the uniqueness of Jesus' sonship and thus stresses Jesus as the climax of all history. By linking Jesus with all men, Luke stresses one of his favorite themes that the gospel is for all men even though Jesus was a Jew.

D. *The Temptation in the Desert—(4:1-13):*

"My Son" says Ben Sira (2:1) "if you aspire to serve the Lord prepare yourself for temptation." Temptation is an important idea in Luke's gospel. In his version of the Our Father the disciples are to pray "subject us not to the *trial* (peirasmos 11:4) and the same word is used both of Jesus "You are the ones who have stood loyally by me in my trials" (22:28) and of the disciples in Jesus' advice to them "Pray that you may not be subjected to the trial" (22:40,46). The English word temptation, which suggests "enticement to moral evil," is not an accurate translation of the Greek word which suggests rather the humanity of the "son of God" as he struggles to follow his mission of suffering service, his true greatness (22:26; 23:39), which was hinted at by the heavenly voice during the Baptism scene. It is an introduction and interpretation of Jesus' ministry which will reach a climax in his passion especially, and is a model for Luke's community to follow. Jesus overcame temptation and therefore can be a compassionate High Priest, able to help us (Heb 2:17f; 4:15).

Traditional Interpretations:

It is interesting to note how the second and third century writers such as Justin, Irenaeus, Tertullian and Origen stress rather an Adam background than an Exodus background to the temptation scene, maybe because of the explicit reference to Adam in the genealogy (3:38). Unlike the first Adam, the new Adam conquers the devil and his temptation. They further see the temptation as an annunciation of his forthcoming trial (passion) and as prefiguring the temptations of the Church.[32] Later writers, Chrysostom, Ambrose, Augustine, Jerome, Gregory the

Great, give a moral and psychological interpretation as they see Jesus as the exemplar for Christians in time of Temptation and concretized the temptations into gluttony (stones into bread), ambition and greed (the kingdoms of this world), vain glory (leaping from the pinnacle of the Temple). Origen who wrote one of the first commentaries on the temptation scene concludes that it is a story in picture language because there was no mountain in Israel from which a man could see India and Persia.

Modern Interpretations:

These are quite varied as scholars dispute the historicity of the episode and its meaning in Luke, while in general stressing the Exodus background, investigating its connection with the rest of the gospel, its differences from Matthew's account and John's unusual presentation. It is often described as a typically Lucan picture story which describes in external form an inner experience of Jesus which he must have revealed to his disciples. As Hunter comments—

> ". . . to interpret the story in terms of an incarnate Devil engaging in some dialectical passage of arms with Jesus in some glimy picture-book wilderness is to betray a crude occidental literalism. The story describes inward experiences, not external events. It is the record of a searching spiritual experience—a real, not a sham flight—told in the figurative language of one who was steeped in the Old Testament."[33]

Here, before we comment on Luke's text, five interesting points are worth mentioning — (i) There is no need to posit an Adam or Exodus dilemma. The Genesis writer[34] describes man and woman as he knew them, the suffering or dominated woman desiring companionship, the suffering of man at work, guilty men, their lack of harmony, their fear of Yahweh, the attraction of the Canaanite fertility cults and their sysmbol of the snake (Gn 3:8-12). His faith in a good god told him that this was not what Yahweh had intended in creating a wonderful world with man (and woman) as its crown and his representative. He lays the blame squarely on man and produces his story, a profound psychological analysis of temptation which is always true whether of the Hebrews in the desert or modern man. In temptation there is (a) a command or law of a good God for man's good; (b) man begins by weighing up the attractiveness of the alternative and tends to distort the picture; (c) he convinces himself that the alternative will really be a good thing for him and lead to greater happiness; (d) he likes to have a partner in evil to spread it; (e) when wrong is done, shame and guilt follow; (f) man then tends to excuse himself and to blame others, even God; (g) man's situation is worse; (h) man must struggle with evil.[35]

(ii) As R.E. Brown points out, the three requests made of Jesus in John 6 and 7, closely resemble the temptations of Matthew and Luke:

Jn 6:15: The people want to make Jesus king—Satan offers Jesus the kingdoms of the world.
Jn 6:31: The people ask for miraculous bread—Satan incites Jesus to turn the stones into bread.
JN 7:3: The unbelieving brothers want Jesus to go to Jerusalem to show his power—Satan wants Jesus to jump from the pinnacle.

Brown concludes that—

> "It seems that Matthew and Luke are giving, in dramatic form the type of temptations that Jesus actually faced in a more prosaic way during his ministry."[36]

(iii) Modern writers, while often tending to confuse the differing presentations of the synoptics, see them as not only describing the kind of Messiahship which Jesus rejected, but as also decribing the kind of Church which he intended—living by God's word, not testing or challenging God, but adoring and serving him alone and rejecting political domination and power seeking. Luke's first temptation teaches that man lives by more than bread, i.e. there is more to life than just pleasure.[37] Man's real hunger needs to be satisfied. This is the "Waste Land" described by T.S. Eliot, the aridness void, alienation and meaninglessness created by greed and materialism in the most sophisticated of modern societies. The second temptation (Lk 4:5-8) is one to power or social status and prestige, to be well thought of, to influence people. For Jesus, real power comes from the worship and service of God and our neighbor—all else is illusion. The third temptation, the most subtle, is to avoid personal struggle and responsibility, to shortcut life and suffering, so as to achieve the spectacular, instantaneous and complete conversion of the people (Lk 16:31).

(iv) It should be remembered that Luke places the temptation scene side by side with the Nazareth scene, where using quotations from Isaiah, Jesus gives a more positive exposé of his proposed Messianic activity as God's servant and Anointed one as opposed to the negative temptation scene, where he rejects certain ideas which must have been popular in his time, whether an economic Messiah ministering to man's social and bodily needs or a political Messiah compelling belief by a theatrical display of supernatural power.

(v) Luke's particular presentation should be examined carefully and the key which is to be found in the last verse (4:13) and in the phrase "full of the Holy Spirit" (4:1),

Preparation For The Public Ministry 177

both of which Luke alone records as also the reference to the devil's claim to have authority over all the kingdoms of the world (4:5-6).

Luke, Matthew and Mark:

Luke, who closely resembles Matthew, does not have Matthew's reference to "forty nights" (Mt 4:2) or the "high mountain" (Mt 4:8), or the angels (Mt 4:11). Neither does he have Mark's mention of the "wild beasts" (Mk 1:15) or the ministering angels (Mk 1:13)—Jesus is alone.

Luke and Mark, unlike Matthew, agree that Jesus was tempted during the forty days—thus Luke's three temptations are the climax of the trial. In particular the order of the second and third temptations differs in Luke and Matthew. One cannot prove which order was original to their sources. However, Luke's climax in Jerusalem's temple which is typical of the emphasis on the Temple[38] makes it quite possible that he inverted the order. Matthew develops the resemblance to Moses on a high mountain[39] and builds up to a climax where Jesus rejects "the kingdom of the world." Later Matthew will put Jesus on another mountain in Galilee proclaiming the kingdom of heaven the true kingdom.

Setting—(4:1-2):

This is in Luke's style and is typical of his orderly presentation. The word "returned" is found in Luke's writings some 35 times and only 4 times in the rest of the New Testament. Only Luke among the synoptics emphasizes here in his typical phrase that Jesus was *continually* "full of the Holy Spirit" and therefore able to face temptation as the early church would be, e.g. the Seven, Stephen and Barnabas were also filled with the Holy Spirit (Ac 6:3-5; 7:55; 11:24), likewise at Pentecost, Peter and the first Christians; also Paul on receiving Baptism (Ac 2:4; 4:8,31; 6:3,5; 7:55; 9:17,24). It was in (not *by*) the Spirit that Jesus was led, i.e. he goes himself and is in control of the Spirit as it were, he is not driven as Mark puts it (Mk 1:12).

The importance of the desert imagery for the Hebrew people should be remembered. It was an inhospitable wild and dangerous land full of demons and wild animals (Is 13:20; 30:6). Here Israel first encountered Yahweh and its wandering there is a common image of man's encounter with God particularly in time of crisis (1 K 19:8). It was Yahweh who carried Israel through its desert period (Dt 8:14ff; Jer 2:6) and it was there that Israel was tested and failed (Ac 7:36ff; 13:18). Hosea had stressed that Yahweh would lead Israel back to the desert to speak to her and restore her love (Hos 2:16; Is 35.1). The reference to "in the desert for forty days" is an allusion to Israel's desert experience when, filled with manna, it rebelled and tempted God, whereas Jesus refused to tempt God.[40]

Moses also fasted forty days and nights on his journey to Horeb (Ex 34:28; 1 K 19:8). It is interesting to note that all Jesus' replies come from Moses' second sermon in Deuteronomy (ch 6-8), which probably was the original book of the law discovered long ago in King Josiah's time and made the basis of his reform. In particular, they come from that section which is an exposition of the Great Commandment to love God, which contains lessons from Israel's past experience and describes the temptations to which Israel succumbed in the desert as Yahweh tested them to know their inmost heart (Dt 8:2; 6:16,13). Here then we have the great eschatological battle between the man of the spirit and Satan (diabolos), the power of evil.[41] Only Luke has the three "power" texts (4:6,14; 10:19), which stress the great eschatological battle between Jesus and the power of evil.

First Temptation—(4:3-4):

The devil recognizes Jesus as Son of God[42] and suggests that he profit from this relationship and use his miraculous power to turn this stone (Mt stones) into bread. It is a more personal temptation for Jesus than Matthew's portrayal, which suggests a repetition of the manna miracle which many expected to happen in Messianic times (Is 25:6-8; Jn 6:30). It is a temptation to an impatient misuse of his power for himself alone. Jesus' answer recalls the lesson Moses drew from their desert experience. They had impatiently cried out for bread when their hunger was meant to teach them to trust God and his covenant, that his love would provide for them. For Jesus, once it is written it is final and to be obeyed—no argument. Each time Jesus puts God first, whereas the devil puts Jesus first and ignores God. Man must not live by bread alone (Matthew adds—"but by every word . . .").

Second Temptation—(4:5-8):

The second temptation provides an easy way for Jesus to obtain his kingdom (Ps 2:8), a kingdom which in Luke's thought, he has not already achieved.[43] All kingdoms are seen in a moment of time, i.e. in visionary internal view as the verb "took up" suggests. Luke's two expressions the "inhabited" (world)[44] and authority or power (exousia)[45] suggest political power and popular glory and domination over the world which Satan possesses.[46] It is a temptation to be the popularly expected political Messiah, to join perhaps with the Zealots in their war of liberation against the Romans. To Satan's condition that Jesus worship him, Jesus answers with the basic commandment (Dt 6:13) that Yahweh alone is to be feared (i.e. respected) and served in the way he wants—for Jesus by suffering and rejection and not by political domination. Note Luke's silence about many of the kings of Judah in his genealogy.

The Third Temptation—(4:9-12):

Luke alone mentions that "the devil led him to Jerusalem." The scene of the climax is one of the temple's pinnacles which we cannot identify precisely. Jesus has twice silenced Satan with a scripture text and now the devil leads off with two scripture quotations from Psalm 91:11-12, a psalm of trust which describes the wonderful protection enjoyed by the man who trusts in God and God's power to make him victorious over deadly perils. This psalm was occasionally quoted perhaps as far back as the first century with a Jewish midrash which expected that the Messiah would "stand on the roof of the temple." It is a temptation to be a spectacular bizzare kind of Messiah who would try to compel people into a superficial belief rather than by the way of the cross and resurrection, the true way in which the Messiah will be revealed. It was a temptation to pander to the Jewish love of signs. Jesus' reply (Dt 6:16) recalls the Jewish distrust of God's providence on their behalf at Massah (Ex 17:1-7; Num 20:2-13), their belief that he had abandoned them and their testing of him to find reassurance.[47] It is interesting to note that according to A. Schweitzer's unsuccessful theory, Jesus finally succumbed to this temptation—

" . . . The baptist appears and cries: 'Repent, for the Kingdom of Heaven is at hand.' Soon after that comes Jesus, and in the knowledge that He is the coming Son of Man lays hold of the wheel of the world to set it moving on that last revolution which is to bring all ordinary history to a close. It refuses to turn and He throws himself upon it. Then it does turn; and crushes Him. Instead of bringing in the eschatological conditions, He has destroyed them. The wheel rolls onwards and the mangled body of the one immesurably great Man, who was strong enough to think of Himself as the spiritual ruler of mankind and to bend history to His purpose, is hanging upon it still. That is His victory and His reign."[48]

Conclusion—(4:13):

In this final verse, we find Luke's main emphasis in telling the temptation scene, i.e. to relate it to the passion of Jesus. The devil leaves Jesus[48] to await another opportunity. The Passion for Luke is the devil's hour and the power of darkness (22:3,53; 23:39; Ac 26:18) and it is foreshadowed in the temptation. The early church believed that Jesus had conquered the evil one through his passion and resurrection (Ac 10:13,31; 16:11). Thus in Luke the temptations are to a great extent unique to Jesus, which he alone could conquer but in whose fruits all could share through the power of the Spirit.

5. MINISTRY IN GALILEE—(4:14-9:50)

"I take it you know what has been reported all over Judea about Jesus of Nazareth, beginning in Galilee with the Baptism John preached; of the way God anointed him with the Holy Spirit and power. He went about doing good works and healing all who were in the grip of the devil and God was with him."

(Ac 10:37-8; Lk 23:15).

"In my first account Theophilus, I dealt with all that Jesus *did and taught.*"

(Ac 1:1).

Thus in Acts Luke summarizes the activity of Jesus the Messiah, the one *anointed* with the Spirit and power, as teaching, doing good and healing those oppressed by the devil. In our present section, 4:14-9:50, Luke describes Jesus' manifestation and activity in his homeland of Galilee, to which he returned (a Lucan word as we saw in 4:1) in the power of the Spirit which he will later share with his apostles (24:49; Ac 1:8; 10:38; Rom 15:13). The last scene of the temptations reached its climax in Jerusalem, to which, in Luke, Jesus will not return until the end of the gospel.

However, John, in contrast to the synoptics, describes a Judean Ministry before Jesus' Galilean ministry and places here the cleansing of the Temple at Passover time

Ministry In Galilee

(Jn 2:13-22), the meeting with Nicodemus (Jn 3:1ff), a journey through Samaria and a meeting with the Samaritan woman (Jn 4:3ff); "he left Judaea and started back for Galilee *again*" and a reference that the Galileans welcomed him because they had seen "all that he had done in Jerusalem" (Jn 4:45). Matthew says that when Jesus heard that John was arrested he withdrew to Galilee, left Nazareth and went down to live in Capernaum (Mt 54:12-13).

Now Luke begins with a scene on a grand scale in Jesus' hometown of Nazareth where he gives his inaugural or programmatic sermon based on Isaiah (61:1f; 58:6). Luke will stress continually in this section, especially in his redactional summaries and special emphasis, how Jesus fulfills the prophecies of Isaiah[1] as he goes about preaching and healing. There are 24 episodes or Messianic acts in this section 4:31-9:50. Of 18 detailed descriptions of miracles in Luke, 14 are found here, thus putting the main emphasis of the whole section on miracles. Much of the material is shared with Matthew but in particular from 4:32 onwards, Luke parallels Mark's outline of the words and deeds of Jesus (Mk 1:14-9:41) with of course his own special emphasis. What he shares with Matthew he stamps in his own individual way to fit his own aims and audience.

However, Luke omits the material found in Mark 6:45-8:26. In Luke's "orderly treatment" he seems to avoid repetitions of similar episodes and thus gives one anointing of Jesus (7:36-50); one account of the barren fig tree (13:6-9); one return of Jesus to the disciples in Gethsemane (22:39-46); one trial scene before the Jewish leaders (22:66-71). As compared with Mark's outline, we find that Luke has his own material not only in his opening scene (4:14-30) but in his description of the call of the first disciples (5:1-11) and especially in the six episodes of the non-Markan section from 6:12-7:50. Most commentators are content to name the twenty-four individual sections in Luke here and do not discover any structured subdivisions or plan in this part of Luke, a procedure which they also follow in the journey narrative (9:51ff). However, it will be convenient for our purpose here to divide this Galilean section of Luke into four—

A. 4:16-30— The Inaugural Sermon at Nazareth and Jesus' rejection.
B. 4:31-6:11— Jesus' activity around Caphernaum, call of the disciples, healings and controversies.
C. 6:12-7:50— The choice of the twelve and a Manual of Instruction (the Sermon on the Level Place), Miracles.
D. 8:1-9:50— The Twelve with Jesus proclaim the Kingdom—Instructions to the disciples who begin to penetrate the mystery of Jesus, the multiplication of the loaves (9:10-17), the confession of Peter (9:18-22), the transfiguration (9:28-36).

A. *Jesus' Inaugural Sermon at Nazareth and his Rejection—(4:16-30):*

All the gospels begin their particular versions of Jesus' public ministry with a section which interprets its general character and meaning. Matthew and Mark give in condensed form the initial preaching of Jesus. Matthew stresses his appeal to conversion as the reign of God is approaching (Mt 4:17), while Mark further describes Jesus as proclaiming the good news and the time of fulfillment. In John the Wedding at Cana and the cleansing of the Temple (Jn 2:1ff) interpret the orientation of Jesus' ministry.

Ministry In Galilee 185

Luke, who well knows that Jesus did not really begin his ministry in his home town of Nazareth, as he makes it clear from his passing remark in 4:23 that previous work was done at Capernaum, opens rather with one of his vivid dramatic picture scenes. This enables him to give a manifesto which highlights his understanding both of Jesus and his church's mission and the source of his power (the Spirit). In particular, Luke seems to root Jesus' concern for the Gentiles and the subsquent Gentile mission in the opening scene of Jesus' own ministry. Luke speaks like Mark about the good news (4:18) and the fulfillment of Scripture, but for him the center of the message is not the reign of God. Rather as in John and Paul, it is the person of Jesus himself as the embodiment of that reign on whom Luke concentrates. For his theological purpose then, Luke somewhat artifically puts before the reader a scene which seems to combine at least two different visits of Jesus to his home town.[2] Only Luke gives the text of Isaiah explaining that Jesus was not a political conqueror. Also he alone gives the proverb about the doctor, the references to the Gentiles in the stories of Elijah and Elisha and the threat to kill Jesus. We notice several references in the gospels to Jesus' attendance (i.e. faithful Jew) at the synagogue services.[3] Only Luke emphasizes that this was Jesus' custom.[4]

The importance which Luke attaches to the words from Isaiah is evident from the fact that they are substantially repeated in Jesus' answer to John the Baptist's messenger (7:22). Obviously, Luke is modifying somewhat the traditional interpretation of the Spirit of power which John expected. Isaiah was perhaps the favorite prophet of those who expected God's salvation. People like John the Baptist and the Essene communities based their lives on his book. Luke will give concrete examples in the following sections of what he means by his *poetic* decription of

Jesus' ministry drawn from Isaiah; sight to the blind;[5] curing the lame;[6] lepers;[7] the deaf;[8] raising the dead (7:11-17; 8:40-56); preaching the good news to the poor (67:20ff). In general, in describing miracles it should be noted that Luke's emphasis is not so much on the actual details or even wonders of the miracles, but on the miracles as fulfillment of Scripture and especially on the power of the faith (compare Lk 7:1ff and Mt 8:5-13). Here we are referred to two of the most famous miracle workers of the Old Testament as examples of Jesus' future miracle working—Elijah and Elisha. One can also see in this scene a rejection of the false messianic temptations to be a political conqueror, to give a sign in proof of his claims, to give a spectacular messianic display to an unbelieving audience and to jump from a height.

Jesus' failure (Luke omits Mk 6:5) at Nazareth[9] and success at Capernaum in the next scene (4:31ff) can be seen as a commentary on Simeon's words to Mary that Jesus will be a sign that is contradicted "and one who will be the fall and rising of many in Israel" (2:34). This is the visitation which was prophesized in the early songs in Luke. This note of opposition to Jesus is a foretaste to what both he and the early Christians will encounter at the hands of the Jewish people. This rejection is actually placed by Mark near the end of Jesus' first year of ministry (Mk 6:1-6). Yet Luke insists in his program that man's evil cannot frustrate God's plan for Jesus (4:28-30) and of course he has in mind for his readers the triumphant spread of the gospel despite the many obstacles it would encounter.

Setting—(4:14-16):

Luke as usual begins with a careful setting of the scene. Here however, his opening two verses summarize Jesus' Galilee ministry rather than give a preparatory introduction. Luke refers to the "power of the Spirit" which will be evident in his miracles and teaching in *their* synagogues—"their" synagogues is a frequent expression in Matthew,[10] probably signifying that when he was writing the Christians had already broken away. In Acts this same Spirit will be available for all believers (Lk 12:12; Ac 19:1ff). This summary of the Galilean ministry stresses that *all* i.e. except those at Nazareth where he had been *brought up,* were loud in their praise[11] of Jesus.

Historically speaking this is the earliest description of a synagogue service that we possess and it is consistent with what we know from later Jewish sources. The service began with prayers[12] and then a reading from the Law.[13] Next a (prominent) member or visitor in the congregation (Ac 13:15), as they had no regular minister in our sense,[14] would be invited to stand and read from one of the prophets and then would conclude with the blessing from Numbers (6:24-26).

Jesus' Sermon from Isaiah—(Lk 4:17-21):

Modern researches into the text of the Old Testament at the time of Jesus show that there was considerable variety among different textual traditions in Palestine.[16] Luke, in common with the mainly Greek-speaking Christian Church, used the Greek Bible and thus usually quotes from it. However, some quotations in Acts 7:3,32; 13:22, seem to come from the Samaritan tradition. Quite likely, quotations from the Old Testament in general were somewhat loosely done and not as precisely as we might like. Here Luke's passage, which he carefully notes that Jesus "found," is from the Greek Septuagint of Isaiah 61:1-2, with three main changes which show an adaptation to Jesus' situation—

(a) He omits "to bind up the hearts that are broken."

(b) He adds in Luke 4:18 words from Isaiah 58:6 "to proclaim liberty to the captives" (see also Is 42:6).

(c) He stops the quotation just before the words Is 61:2b "a day of vengeance for our God," which would not have been a suitable description of Jesus' Galilean ministry.[17]

Originally, this was a prophecy describing the mission of the prophetic servant of Yahweh to bring the good news to the Babylonian exiles that they would be free to return to Jerusalem to celebrate the Lord's year of favor, i.e. the Jubilee year, when debts were cancelled, slaves freed and property reshared (Lv 25). Isaiah's dream had not been realized and was gradually applied to the future and became the hope of the oppressed and conquered Jewish people for the future. The text describes first how the bringer of good news is endowed with the spirit, like the Servant of Isaiah (Is 42:1; Lk 3:22; 4:18). He in turn will endow his servants (24:48-9). Secondly, the text describes the kind of work which Jesus and Luke's community will accomplish through the Spirit—the poor, the captives, the oppressed.[18] Here it is a manifesto which must be interpreted according to the examples which Luke gives subsequently and in the light of his insights into Jesus' mission. The Greek word which Luke uses here for liberty and freedom he has already used and explained as meaning the forgiveness of or freedom from the captivity of sin (1:77; 24:47). Luke will conclude and climax his gospel with a mission to preach repentance for the forgiveness of sins to all the nations.[19]

What would have been particularly astounding to Jesus' audience was his claim that *today* in his person and mission their hopes, which Isaiah had so eloquently expressed, were fulfilled. Today is an "obsessive" and

Ministry In Galilee 189

solemn word in Deuteronomy as the writer invites his audience to stand once again with Moses at Sinai and really listen and accept the covenant and choose life.[20] Salvation for Luke is a present option and reality (19:1ff), the kingdom which they had long waited for was here and now but different from their expectations as they soon realized. Jesus himself in person, whom they thought they knew so well is the fulfillment of the prophecy of the Old Testament and in himself and his ministry the year of God's favor is also fulfilled. Thus Luke's gospel is not unlike John's where the message is more about Jesus himself than the kingdom of God. At the end of Luke's gospel we find Jesus interpreting for his disciples "every passage of scripture which referred to him" as he points out their slowness "to believe all that the prophets had announced," that "it was written that the Messiah must suffer and rise from the dead on the third day" (24:25ff,46). Here (4:21) the scripture is fulfilled in your "*hearing*," as expression (Ac 28:27) which seems to indicate Luke's own audience and his understanding of the Jesus event as something challenging that they must *hear*[21] and accept.

Reactions—(4:22):

The first impression was quite favorable (Ac 6:15), although Luke seems to indicate that it was a rather superficial astonishment at the attractive way of speaking of one of their own rather than acceptance or real understanding of what he was actually saying. However, on deeper reflection their attitude changes. Many scholars think that Luke is inserting a subsequent visit here (Mk 6:1-6; Mt 13:54-8). Disbelief and rejection gradually take over leading to a murderous atmosphere.

Jesus' Reaction—(4:23-7):

Jesus bluntly puts into words their thinking and answers, their skepticism and temptation, again quoting scripture as in the temptation scene. The proverb (lit "parable" as also in 5:36; 6:39), "Physician heal yourself" could possibly suggest some personal sickness of Jesus but is best explained by the parallel saying which describes a demand for evidence, for miracles which they had *heard* he worked at Capernaum but which did not lead them to believe in him themselves, as Mark explains (in Mk 6:5, he actually performs some cures at the end of his visit). As his fellow townsmen, they seem to demand miracles as a right to satisfy their curiosity—thus, as one who claimed to be a prophet should prove himself (Dt 13:2f). This was the Devil's request (4:3) and would be repeated later even immediately after Jesus had cast out a devil (11:16) and especially during the crucifixion scene (22:64; 23:8,35ff). Jesus' signs would be for those with faith (9:9; 11:29-36). Here Jesus classifies himself (or his fate) among the prophets, a favorite title for Jesus in Luke. Some of his disciples would use this title of him even after the crucifixion.[23] Stephen would see Jesus also as in line with the Old Testament prophetic "forth speakers" who were all likewise persecuted.[24]

Jesus answers somewhat unexpectedly with one of the six Amen sayings which Luke gives.[25] Jesus' use of Amen is unique to himself and always introduces a solemn statement like a prophetic oracle. It substitutes quite likely for their phrase "thus says Yahweh." It is found in Matthew 31 times; Mark 13 times. Jesus here appeals to two of the best known miracle workers in the Old Testament as exemplars for his activity, Elijah and Elisha. Both carried out their activity by the power of the spirit as Jesus and his followers would.[26] Both also experienced some rejection at

Ministry In Galilee

home and worked miracles for non Jews, Elijah for the widow from Phoenician Sidon (1 K 17:8-16) and Elisha for the leprous Syrian Officer (2 K 5:1-14)—note how Luke again balances a story of a woman and a man. These two stories will be echoed again in the story of the widow at Nain. Jesus seems to be suggesting here that it is possible that God cares as much or rather more for the Sidonians and Syrians than for his own (unbelieving) Jewish people. He hints for the first time here an important theme of Luke's, namely, that the good news will be given to the Gentiles and received by them. Paul and Barnabas will put it quite bluntly to the jealous and violently abusive Jews at Antioch in Pisidia.

> "The word of God has to be declared to you first of all; but since you reject it . . . we now turn to the Gentiles. For thus were we instructed by the Lord . . . " (Ac 13:46-7).

Later Jesus will declare that in a Gentile centurion he found a faith unlike any in Israel.[27]

Conclusion—(4:28-30):

Their indignant and violent rejection (on the sabbath) is part of Luke's introduction to Jesus' ministry, foreseen by Simeon (2:35) and reaching a climax in the final fatal events of Jerusalem—to be repeated in the rejection of Stephen (Ac 7:58) and Paul (Ac 13:50). Luke's concluding words do not so much describe a miraculous escape (Jn 10:39) as insist that their murderous rejection could not stop Jesus or frustrate God's plan; that Jesus went on his way to his ultimate glorification—John would say his hour had not come.[28] Perhaps Jesus is seen as refusing the kind of miracle which the Nazarenes tried to force out of him (the third temptation).

B. *Jesus' Activity around Capernaum, Call of the Disciples, Miracles and Controversies—(4:31-6:11):*

This section begins by recording a typical day at Capernaum, an important trading town which Luke identifies for his Gentile and foreign readers as a town in Galilee, mentioning that Jesus had to *come down* from the mountain village (1,300') of Nazareth to Capernaum some 686' below sea level. It is a successful day in contrast to the day at Nazareth. Then Jesus (4:42) moves to open country and other towns. Now we hear of the call of the first disciples (5:1ff). Then there is the healing of a leper and a paralytic which is the beginning of a series illustrating the conflict between Jesus and a growing opposition to him. Jesus' itinerant preaching in this section has a double function. The kingdom and its demands are proclaimed to the Jews and Jesus' own disciples are formed into a group and taught by him. Only Luke uses the formula "to announce the kingdom of God" and it is frequently used from 4:43-9:60.

1. *A Sabbath in Capernaum and a Preaching Tour—(4:31-44):*

Again Luke puts before us a scene in a synagogue on a sabbath day where Jesus again makes a deep impression, not so much by the graciousness as the authority of his words. Three incidents illustrate how Jesus sets at liberty those who are oppressed; the healing by a mere word of a possessed man and (to balance) a sick woman, then the healing of a variety of sick people. This is the reign (kingdom) of God (4:43) in action, a reign of peace, justice and health and forgiveness which was long expected and is now present in Jesus (7:22; 17:21). Finally, Jesus leaves for a preaching tour.

Ministry In Galilee

Here Luke (4:31-44) parallels Mark's account Mk 1:21-34) quite closely. However, he omits Mark's blunt remark that Jesus' teaching was "not like the scribes" (Mk 1:22) and does not mention Simon and his companions as he will tell later of their call at a more logical place (but note 4:38).

Teaching with Authority—(4:31-2):

Originality was not common among Jewish teachers but rather the emphasis was on tradition and the quoting of famous predecessors. Jesus' teaching consisted both in words and powerful deeds which were closely connected (2 S 1:4). "What is this word?" they asked, "for he commands with authority and power . . . " (4:36).[29] For Luke, Jesus' word is clearly more than mere teaching but is unusual in that (like God's creative word) it produces action, conviction, obedience, like a command (4:32,36; 24:19). The message of the early church would be the preaching of the Word.[30] The Christian movement could be called "the word."[31] Jesus was no mere patient teacher of timeless truths but was a man who "went about doing good and healing all who were oppressed by the devil (Ac 10:38). Jesus had the power which Satan had offered (4:6,36; 9:1).

The Healing of the Man with an Unclean Spirit—(4:33-7):

This is the first of five *healings on the Sabbath* which Luke relates (4:38f; 6:6ff; 13:10ff; 14:1ff). It is noteworthy how little the Bible says about demon possession and exorcism. In the New Testament only the synoptic gospels and Acts specifically refer to it as prominent during Jesus' ministry. Luke describes the healing of the Capernaum demoniac here, the Gerasene madman (8:26-39), the epileptic boy (9:37-43), the bent woman (13:11). He refers to it in summary statements (7:21; Ac 10:38) and tells show it was entrusted to the disciples (9:1) and became part of the Christian mission (10:17).[32]

While it is difficult to make a precise difference between exorcisms and other healings, Luke seems to make such a distinction (4:40-1). It should be remembered that ancient opinion generally attributed such diseases involving loss of self-control like madness, epilepsy, convulsions, to the control of evil powers as a matter of fact which was not questioned. Jesus later points out that other Jews also drive out demons (11:19), but that he himself is the stronger one who overcomes Satan (13:16; Ac 10:38).

An unclean spirit is a description of an evil spirit (9:39ff; Mk 9:25). For Luke, the casting out of demons is a sign that the reign of God has come (11:20; 4:43). The demon shrieks out in a rhetorical question Jesus' mission to destroy evil.[33] He uses an unusual title for Jesus (a magical attempt to control by uttering a name?)—"The Holy One of God" which is found elsewhere only in Mk 1:24; Jn 6:69; see Lk 1:35. In the Old Testament it expresses consecration to God's service, e.g. Samson in Judges (LXX) 13:7; 16:17. Aaron (Ps 106:16; also 1 K 17:18; 2 K 4:9; Ac 3:14; 4:27,30). Jesus performs the exorcism simply with a blunt word "muzzle your mouth" with none of the incantations so frequent in his time. Jesus rebukes the demon as he rebukes the fever of Simon's mother-in-law (4:38-9). Luke uses the word twelve times (Mk 6 times, Mt 9 times) with the meaning of authoritative control over an evil power (Zech 3:2; Jubil 10:5-9). Comparing the words which Mark (sparassein) and Luke (riptein) use to describe the man's convulsions, some suggest that Luke uses a technical medical word and also notices his "high fever" at 4:38 (Mk 2:30), and "they consult" him, whereas Mark has they "tell him." Luke notes that

Ministry In Galilee

the demon came out without harming the man. He mentions, the reactions of the crowds and the spread of the news as Jesus quickly becomes a well-known figure.[34]

Simon's Mother-in-Law—(4:38-9):

Here Jesus is again pushing back the frontiers of suffering (here malaria?), as he heals Simon's mother-in-law. Note how he presupposes that his audience know who Simon is although this is his first appearance in the text. Luke's account is similar to Mark's. However, like Matthew, he omits the presence of Andrew, James and John whose calling he will tell later (5:1-10). The omission has the advantage of focusing attention on Jesus alone who leans over her in a kindly gesture as the Jerusalem Bible version translates. Luke notes how she immediately waits on the others when cured.

Many Healings—(4:40-1):

These take place after sunset as now the Sabbath is over and a new day has begun and people can carry burdens. The crowds thus were more cautious than Jesus, who seems deliberately to have broken the traditional Sabbath regulations which permitted healing only when life was actually in danger. Luke notes that Jesus also broke taboos in his very personal approach of laying hands[35] on *each* of the sick (4:40; 13:13); as later with lepers (5:13) and again by touching a bier carrying a dead body (7:14) and even a dead body itself (8:54), even though he could heal at a distance (7:1-10).

Some of the sick had demons, we are told, thus making a distinction perhaps between two kinds of illness. Jesus again rebukes and silences the demons who were calling him the "Son of God" "because they know that he was the Messiah" (i.e. the anointed one 4:18). The sudden testimony of a demon (without faith) was not what interested Jesus. He was interested in gradually leading his disciples to a full free acceptance and understanding of himself and his suffering mission. Jesus consistently refused to be publicly identified as Messiah because of the false implications which it signified (5:24; 8:28) and its inadequacy to express both the mystery of himself and his mission. Luke does not develop the title Son of God apart from what is found in his sources.[36]

A Preaching Tour—(4:42-4):

From now on Jesus is constantly on the move, and his horizon is expanding: Nazareth to Capernaum which he leaves next day despite the crowds who try to keep him from leaving (Mark mentions Simon 1:46). In Luke it is the crowds and not the disciples as in Mark who pursue Jesus. Curiously Luke is not precise about Jesus going out to the desert place to pray as Mark puts it (Mk 1:35; 9:9). Perhaps he thinks that this is the obvious interpretation as he portrays Jesus as constantly at prayer with God (e.g. 3:21; 6:12). Jesus' answer (4:43) portrays himself as an exemplar evangelist on the move like Paul in Acts, moving from synagogue to synagogue in Asia Minor. Here Luke introduces for the first time the Kingdom of God which is the principal concern of Jesus' preaching in the synoptics. Luke introduces the preaching of the kingdom in such places as this, where it is not found in Mark.[37] The preaching of the kingdom will be done by the disciples (9:2) but especially in Acts.[38] For Luke, the kingdom, or God's activity, is already present in the proclamation of Jesus' word and in his activity and not at hand as in Mark (1:15). Jesus is king (19:38) and the secrets of the kingdom are confided to the disciples (11:2,20; 1 Cor 15:25; Heb

Ministry In Galilee

2:8). For Luke Jesus is "announcing the good news of the Kingdom of God," a favorite theme of Paul but found once only outside Luke in the synoptics.[39] Luke actually uses the expression "The Kingdom of God" 31 times—Mark 14 times, Matthew 3 times, but Matthew uses the expression the Kingdom of the Heavens 30 times. Here we find one of Luke's favorite terms "I must" which expresses his total commitment to his Father's business (2:49) and his plan of history which will reach a climax in Jerusalem[40] and be continued in Acts in the lives of his witnesses.[41] "I was sent" is the passive voice implying God as the sender and that therefore Jesus is the Father's Apostle (9:48; 10:16), a favorite theme in John (Jn 4:34; 5:23). The area of Jesus' tour is described as "the synagogues of Judea" which probably in Luke is a general term for Palestine.[42] It refers especially to Galilee and not the Judean ministry which we find described in John.

2. *The Call of the Leading Disciples: Healings: Controversies (5:1-6:11):*

This section in Luke is arranged in quite a symmetrical fashion leading up to the naming of the Twelve which can be seen as beginning a new section in Luke (a b c b'a')—

a. The Call of the Three Leading Disciples—(5:1-11).
b. Two incidents, the healing of a leper and a paralytic which lead to controversy—(5:12-36).
c. The Call of Levi—A Feast—The Question about Fasting (5:27-39).
d. Two Sabbath incidents, plucking grain, healing a man's hand, leading to controversy—(6:1-11).
e. The Choosing of the Twelve—(6:12-16)—see section (c).

a. *The Call of the Three Leading Disciples—(5:1-11):*
—*Simon Peter, James and John.*

Jesus is still a lone figure after his escape at Nazareth and his acclamation at Capernaum. Now he is preaching the word of God[43] to the crowd, not in the synagogues as he was accustomed to, as he was perhaps no longer welcome there and he was avoiding the possibility of further riots (see Mk 1:45). In Luke this is Jesus' only public appearance at "the lake of Gennesaret" (his hearers applied the term "sea" to the Mediteranean) as Luke alone describes the sea of Galilee using the name of the plain North of the Lake which was some seven by thirteen miles long.

For Conzelmann, it is not a geographic lake but the setting for the manifestation of Jesus' power as here and later in the stilling of the storm (8:22-5). Against the background of an extraordinary catch of fish, Luke describes Jesus catching Peter (whose mother-in-law he had already cured) away from all his affairs.[44] Jesus takes the initiative right through the story and Peter becomes his first follower. Jesus says to Peter, not to the others as in Mark 1:17-18, "From *now* on *you* will be *taking men alive.*"[45] This commission to Peter comes when he has begun to recognize his own unworthiness and the true nature of the Lord. It prepares us for Peter's prominent role of leadership in Acts (1-15), where his missionary activity is singled out among the Twelve for emphasis and he takes the lead in accepting a Gentile as a Christian. The wonderful catch of fishes can also be seen as an anticipation of the spread of Christianity in Acts.

A comparison with Matthew and Mark's versions of the calling of Jesus' first disciples (Mt 4:18-22; Mk 1:16-20), shows that Luke is giving special prominence to Peter in his account. The simple account found in Mark as

Ministry In Galilee

the first act of Jesus' ministry has been extended quite plausibly in Luke with the addition of a miracle story and placed at the end of several days ministry and miracle working near Capernaum. It is full of symbolic detail, anticipating the world mission of Acts. "Put out into the deep"—the deep is symbolically the abyss from which the disciples save men (8:31), or perhaps it signifies the Gentile world to which Peter reluctantly puts out in Acts and needs to have his hestiation overcome by a specific command of Jesus, or could well be a summary of the mission in Acts. Perhaps too one can see Luke here as giving a message of risk to his own Church. They probably were tired and tended to slaken off their mission and to be expert, "know all's," like Peter, the fisherman, who had to learn the power of the word of Jesus which seemed to be the foolishness of men.

The other three gospels mention Andrew, Simon's brother, in their accounts of the call of the first disciples. Probably Luke is interested only in describing the call of the "inner three" of Jesus' disciples, who will be closely associated with Jesus—"When he came to the house he allowed no one in with him except Peter, and John and James"—(Lk 8:51—the raising of Jairus' daughter, also at the transfiguration 9:28). Peter and John are closely associated in Acts (3:1; 4:13; 8:14). Luke alone has Peter's confession of sinful unworthiness like that of Isaiah[46] (or simply human unworthiness before such a wonderful display of power?), stressing that the apostolic ministry is based on a gracious call or command of Jesus and not on the worthiness or talent of the person or human failure (22:54-62). Peter, through his obedience, learned that Jesus was more than Master (Epistata),[47] but "Lord" as he addresses Jesus in his amazement after the catch of fish. Jesus replies with "do not be afraid" as in a typical apparition scene or post-resurrection appearance. Here is Luke's only use of the double name, Simon Peter—a phrase found also in John (e.g. Jn 21:2,3,7,11), even though he has not yet mentioned that Jesus gave him the name Peter—from 6:14 where Luke describes the choice of the Twelve, Simon is simply called Peter.

The nearest parallel to this story is found in the post-resurrection epilogue of John's gospel (Jn 21:1-11), where the risen Jesus appears to his disciples in Galilee and commissioned Peter after a huge haul of one hundred and fifty three fish to carry out his mission while teaching the apostles the lesson of not relying on their own "fishing" resources. Scholars discuss whether two different events are involved or that both accounts go back to a single original event, which both evangelists have written up to bring out the symbolic meaning to suit their purpose and the place in which they insert the story in their gospel.

R.E. Brown[48] thus finds the following details shared by both—

1) The disciples have fished all night and have caught nothing.
2) Jesus tells them to put out the net(s) for a catch.
3) His directions are followed and an extraordinary large catch of fish is made.
4) The effect on the nets is mentioned.
5) Peter is one who reacts to the catch.
6) Jesus is called Lord.
7) The other fishermen take part in the catch but say nothing.
8) The theme of following Jesus occurs at the end (Jn 21:19,22).
9) The catch of fish symbolizes a successful Christian missionary endeavor in Luke, implicitly in John.
10. The same words are used for getting aboard, landing, net, etc., some of which may be coincidental. Their common use of the name "Simon Peter" when he responds to the

catch (Lk 5:18; Jn 21:7) is significant for this is the only instance of the double name in Luke.

Brown, while recognizing that there are many differences in vocabulary and detail, concludes that Luke and John have preserved variant forms of the same miracle story. He rejects the idea of the same event taking place twice as then one would have to explain how in John 21 Peter could go through the same situation and much of the same dialogue a second time without recognizing Jesus!

b. *Two Healings: (1) The Cure of a Leper—(5:12-16):*

Now after his insertion of 5:1-11, Luke returns to Mark's order for the next six episodes, the leper, the paralytic, Levi, the debate on fasting, the disciples and the Sabbath, the man with the withered hand (Mk 1:40-3:6; Lk 5:12-6:11). This provided Luke with good illustrations of Jesus' Nazareth program and so he makes few if any important changes. He omits the detail that *four* men carried the paralytic. However, we do not find in Luke such human sentiments of anger and sternness as in Mark 1:41-3, or the statement that it was no longer possible for Jesus to enter a town openly (Mk 1:45). A typical Lucan touch is 5:16, "He often retired to deserted places and prayed," a sentence which leads into Jesus' first conflict with the Jewish leaders.

Luke, unlike Mark (1:39), seems to place the leper in a town where it was rather unlikely that a leper would appear (Lv 13:46). This statement together with Luke's description of the Palestinian house in the cure of the paralytic, are often suggested as evidence that Luke was ignorant of Palestinian life and customs, or that he altered his descriptions to suit his audience. Perhaps the leper in his desperation or having heard the fame of Jesus, ignored the regulation or Luke means on the edge of the town. Here, Luke uses the unusual (medical?) yet Lucan phrase (4:1) "full of" leprosy and that the leper, confident of Jesus' power, asks to be made "clean" from his ritual uncleanness, which excluded him from the Jewish cult and society. Jesus deliberately stretches out his hand[49] and touches the unclean leper, something which was forbidden. Yet in respect for the Law, and especially the man's acceptance back into society, Jesus orders him to show himself to the priests, who were the public health examiners of the time, as Leviticus commanded (Lv 14:1-32; Mt 5:17). Luke, unlike Mark, does not say directly that the man ignored Jesus' request for silence but stresses that his fame as a healer spread and notes that Jesus was constantly retiring to the wilderness to pray. This note on prayer is particularly meaningful and Luke is perhaps teaching a vital lesson to his community not to mention his modern readers.

(2) *The Cure of a Paralytic—(5:17-26):*

Luke's introduction differs from Mark (Mk 2:1ff) and Matthew (Mt 9:1ff) in that he introduces at the beginning Jesus' opponents, the Pharisees and Scribes,[50] who provide the main opposition to Jesus during his public ministry. He explains for his audience that the Scribes are teachers of the Law. Probably Luke's presentation of the opposition to Jesus and especially his disciples during his lifetime was intended to reassure the faith of his audience who were suffering a similar kind of opposition. The Pharisees and Scribes typify what a number of modern studies have shown to be true, namely, that religious people tend to be more authoritarian and prejudicial and less compassionate than non-religious people.

It is interesting to note how Luke here presents the growing opposition to Jesus by describing as Mark does

Ministry In Galilee

(Mk 2:1-3:6) five conflicts between Jesus and his opponents, arranged in progressive order.[51] At the cure of the paralytic his opponents "question in their hearts" (5:22). During the dinner at Levi's house the attack on Jesus is directed at the disciples (5:30). Next in the question of fasting Jesus himself is questioned but concerning his disciples' omission (5:33). Then Jesus is questioned about their direct violation of the Sabbath as they walk through the grain fields. In the final episode they are watching Jesus "so that they could find a charge against him" (6:7) and so plot what can be done to him (6:11). Quite probably we have here a pre-existing collection of episodes from the catechesis of the early church which both Mark and Luke used. Originally these episodes did not all take place as described in the early period of Jesus' ministry but rather throughout his public ministry with the plot coming at the end.[52]

Here Jesus is described as almost compelled to heal by the "power of the Lord." It is interesting to note that Luke calls the man "paralelumenos," which is perhaps a more correct medical term than "paralutikos," which Mark uses. Mark describes the men as "unroofing the roof" and "digging it out," a description which would suit the flat, mud roofs of ordinary Palestinian houses. In Luke the bearers go through the tiles, a description which would suit his audiences' houses, although it is not unlikely that there were some tiled roofs in use in Palestine in Jesus' time. While Mark uses what was almost a soldier's slang word for a bed (krabbatos), Luke uses a refined diminutive of the normal word (klinidion)) the diminutive of kline (Mt 9:2).

For his opening controversy Luke selects an episode where Jesus deliberately seems to have challenged the Phraisees and Scribes who were expecting a cure, with his surprising words "'My friend, your sins are forgiven you." Here he is claiming to share Yahweh's power to forgive sins (i.e. salvation 1:77) and questions his incredulous audience (i.e. some in Luke's audience also) and incited them to see a proof for themselves. Thus for Luke "the forgiveness of sins" is more fundamental than a physical cure.[53] Jesus , who has shown his mastery over sickness, unclean spirits and even nature itself (the catch of fishes), now reveals himself as the master who can forgive sins. The Jews of course from the opening pages of their Bible believed that sin and sickness were interconnected. One of the Rabbis had the statement "A sick man does not recover from his sickness until all his sins have been forgiven him."[54] Here we find the first of Luke's 26 uses of Jesus' favorite self-description as "the Son of Man," a mysterious expression which is found only on Jesus' lips and in the gospels (except Ac 7:56). Actually the peculiar form with the definite article is not found before Jesus' time apart from one instance in the Qumran documents. The use of the definite article seems to be a direct allusion to Daniel 7 as a decription of the mission of Jesus. Evidently, Jesus, as far as we can see avoided the more traditional and especially political messianic titles and used a mysterious title which would combine the Suffering Servant theme of Isaiah and Daniel's eschatological figure and would also be open to expressing the mystery of his own personality and mission.[55] It is worth noting here the tendency of some recent scholars to explain the expression "Son of Man" on the lips of Jesus as not a title but as a circumlocation for "I."

Luke notes their reaction to Jesus with the frequent phrase "Who is this man who . . . "[56]. He mentions that it is "their faith" (5:20); how the man went off glorifying God,[57] also the "ecstatic" reaction of the people "We have seen incredible things today."

c. *The Call of Levi—A Feast—The Question of Fasting (5:27-39):*

The "forgiveness of sins" leads naturally to a further example where Jesus invites the public sinner, Levi, to follow him and then Jesus publicly dines with him. The episode which is well connected in Luke leads into the dispute about fasting. Here Luke shows us in action what the forgiveness of sins means—it leads to an intimate (i.e. *table*) fellowship with Jesus and a radical newness of life. For Luke's community this fellowship was experienced in particular at the eucharist. Jesus shows his forgiveness and full acceptance of Levi into the kingdom by eating with him and Levi responds by leaving everything behind and by his repentance.[58]

The Call of Levi—(5:27-8):

Luke and Matthew's versions both look like a simplified version of Mark, omitting any reference to the crowd by the sea and Jesus teaching them and that Levi was the son of Alphaeus. Both focus directly on the call itself and the response. In Matthew the tax-collector is called Matthew but in Mark and Luke he is called Levi. However, all three synoptics list Matthew among the twelve but not Levi. Matthew alone identifies him in the list as a tax-collector (Mt 10:3). Many Jews had two names, one Hebrew and one Greek, for business affairs. Both Matthew (the gift of God) and Levi are Hebrew names. It is suggested that Jesus gave Levi a new name as he also did to Peter (Mk 3:16; Lk 6:14).

The important fact about Levi is that he was one of the hated tax-collectors, a collaborator in the service of Herod Antipas, who was a Roman vassal king. For Jews, "murderers, robbers and tax-collectors" were classified together and a tax-collector was debarred from the synagogue (see 18:13) and could not be a witness in a law case as he was considered a public sinner (15:1f; 19:1-10). He is an example of Jesus' concern for the outcasts of society. It must have been surprising to find among Jesus' followers such extremes as a Zealot and a tax-collector. Jesus' call brings about a radical change in his life. Luke alone notes that he leaves everything to follow Jesus.[59]

Levi's Feat—(5:29-32):

In Mark the feast appears to be in Jesus' house but in Luke, for whom Jesus is too poor to have a house, Levi is the host to Jesus and a large crowd of his fellow tax-collectors and others ("sinners," in Mark and Matthew). Luke loves to portray Jesus at a banquet for his Greek audience for whom it was a well known background for discussions.[60] These banquets are the fulfillment of the Old Testament messianic prophecies which had expected the messiah to form his banquet community (symbolizing the restored communion between God and man and among men), especially from the poor and afflicted.[61] The final coming of the kingdom is pictured in terms of a great banquet scene (13:29; 14:16-24; 22:30). While the Pharisees and *their* Scribes [62] would not actually be partakers of the feast due to their strict segregation ideas, in typical oriental custom there was nothing to prevent them from being onlookers at the feast. Jesus' reply to their criticism is devastating in its ironical yet unanswerable logic. It shows the absurdity of their segregationist approach as if to hold that a doctor should only associate with the healthy lest he

Ministry In Galilee

catch a disease. Jesus' mission (4:18ff) was to bring healing to sinners and this could not be achieved by avoiding them but by associating with them, the very opposite to the approach of the Pharisees whom Jesus ironically calls "virtuous." Levi's behavior is a concrete example of the revolution in one's thinking and behavior which repentance for Luke brings about.[63] One can see Jesus' climactic statement in v 32 as an invitation to Luke's somewhat complacent community to remember their basic duty towards the sick in society who have most need of Jesus.

The Jewish scholar, Geza Vermes, has given an excellent description of the uniqueness of Jesus' approach—

> "It should be added that in one respect more than any other he differed from both his contemporaries and even his prophetic predecessors. The prophets spoke on behalf of the honest poor, and defended the widows and the fatherless, those exploited by the wicked, rich and powerful. Jesus went further. In addition to proclaiming these blessed, he actually took his stand among the pariahs of the world, those despised by the respectable. Sinners were his table companions and the ostracized tax-collectors and prostitutes his friends."[64]

On Fasting—The Radical Newness of the Gospel (5:33-9):

A banquet leads naturally to a criticism of the non-ascetic habits of his disciples as compared with those of John and the Pharisees, who fasted twice a week (18:12) even though the Law only prescribed fasting on the day of the Atonement (Lv 16:29ff; 23:17ff; Nm 29:7; also Zc 7:3ff; 8:19). Here we find the typical judgmental attitude which "elitism" tends to adopt as it is not content with the prescriptions of the Law. Luke here is explaining also why his community emphasized fasting when obviously Jesus had not (Ac 13:2ff; Mt 6:16ff). Jesus' answer is in his typical form of a rhetorical question (5:23,34). Can you not see that the marriage foretold by the prophets[65] is taking place so this is not a suitable time for the friends of the bridegroom (Hebrew "sons of") to fast? Jesus' answer is really a statement that he is the expected bridegroom, an image which the early Christians often used though found only here in Luke.[66] With the presence of Jesus, the kingdom or reign of God was present. But when he is taken away by force[67] there will be fasting as a sign of grief and of expectation of his second coming.

Similar to Mark (2:18-22), Luke (5:36-9) adds sayings which contrast the incompatibility of the new kind of behavior which results from the coming of Jesus, with the traditional Jewish behavior. He uses the term "parabole" which he applies equally (as the Old Testament Mashal is applied) to simple proverbs such as are found in his favorite books, Samuel and Kings (Lk 4:23; 5:36; 6:39) and also such moral stories as the Rich Fool (12:16), the Fig Tree (13:6) and the Unjust Judge (18:1).[68] His illustrations are homely, a patched coat and a suitable wineskin and he concludes with an unusual saying in v 39 about the old wine being better. Luke's version of the patched coat differs from Mark's. It is adapted to his second illustration. In Luke you do not tear a new coat to patch an old one, whereas in Mark and Matthew one does not sew a piece of unshrunk cloth on an old coat. In Luke the new one is ruined also in the process. Salvation for Luke is a gift (Ac 5:31), a decision, [69] a new reality of life.[70]

Levi leaves *all*. No compromise is possible—no patching up of the deficiencies of Judaism, its customs and traditions. One cannot select from the gospel and add it to Judaism. The Christian mission differs radically from the approach of Judaism. Jesus himself is the radical newness of the gospel, who must be followed. New wine cannot be contained in old wineskins—the result is disastrous to both new and old. The final proverb is difficult: "No one drink-

Ministry In Galilee

ing old wine wants new, for he says the old (Law) is good" (some Mss read "better"). Does it mean that the conservative misses the new approach of Jesus as is illustrated in the next episode? Is it a sad, yet understanding, reflection on those who reject the newness of Jesus, the new wine for the old ways of Judaism? The new wine will take time to establish itself! Or is it a warning of the abiding value of the old (see Mt 13:52)?

d. *Two Sabbath Incidents—Controversies—(6:1-11):*

Jesus' deliberate attitude to the Sabbath, the most public and distinctive sign of Judaism in a Gentile world, is an example of the newness which conflicts with traditional Judaism. All four gospels stress that one of the main disputes between Jesus and the Jewish leaders concerned the proper way of keeping the Sabbath. In the second of the two incidents here Jesus deliberately seems to challenge the Scribes and Pharisees who see themselves as the guardians of the Mosaic Law and even take the initiative in discussing his new approach. Relations between Jesus and his opponents then reach a climax.

Plucking Grain on the Sabbath—(6:1-5):

The Law allowed the poor to pull some ears of corn when passing a neighbor's cornfield (Dt 23:25). The objection here is the fact that it is done on the sabbath (Ex 34:21). It was one of the 39 works which the Scribes considered to be violations of the sabbath. However, at the sabbath exorcism (4:33-7) there was no objection. Luke's version of this episode is shorter than Mark's but his added description of the disciples "rubbing the grain heads with their hands" makes the scene rather vivid. With Matthew, he omits the difficult phrase of Mark "when Abiathar was high priest" (Mk 2:26) and also Mark's statement "The sabbath was made for man, not man for the sabbath" and half of the typical two-step Markan phrase "when (David) was in need and was hungry" (Mk 2:25).

Jesus answers the objection typically with a rhetorical question in return. He uses the rabbinical appeal to scripture (1 S 21:1ff) as the supreme authority. He cites the story of David who when he was running for his life from Saul asked food from the priest, Ahimelech.[71] Ahimelech gave him the bread of the presence (Lv 24:5-9) which only the priests could eat after it was left as an offering to God on a dish in the sanctuary for a week. Thus it should be obvious that human need was more important than ritual law (see also Mt 12:5). Thus, if David, the ideal king of Israel could break the law . . . ! There is perhaps a hint here that Jesus is at least equal to David in his authority (20:41). This implication is more evident in the second justification which Jesus gave "The Son of Man is Lord of the Sabbath." Mark further explains that the sabbath was made for God's people. Luke's community would understand the full implications of the explosive statement that the Son of Man (i.e. Jesus as it hardly means that "man" is Lord of the sabbath), who according to Daniel (ch 7) received authority over all the earth, was master of the sabbath.

The sabbath was a divine institution (Ex 20:8-11; Gen 2:2f) whose purpose was to remind people not only of their past redemption but the future rest, the Messianic age (Heb 3:7-4:10) to which God was leading them and which

Ministry In Galilee

was now present in Jesus. At Luke 6:5, the Western Text (Codex Bezae), inserts a third incident concerning Jesus and the Sabbath, perhaps under the influence of Romans (14:14,22f).

> "On the same day he saw a man working on the sabbath, and said to him, 'Man if you know what you are doing you are blessed; but if you do not know, you are accursed and a transgressor of the law'."

Healing on the Sabbath—6:6-11:

In comparison with Mark, Luke does not have the reference to Jesus' anger and grief at their hardness of heart. Luke tends to make Jesus rise above human emotions, unlike Mark's presentation. However, he notes that it was the man's right hand which was healed.[72] Again he notes that Jesus knew their thoughts. According to Jerome's commentary on Matthew 12:13, the gospel of the Nazarenes adds the man's words as follows:—

> "I was a mason and earned my livelihood with my hands; I beseech you, Jesus, to restore to me my health that I may not have to beg for my food in shame."

Jesus, taking the initiative, has the man stand evidently in a public place for all to see and boldly challenges the opposition who as the word implies, are closely scrutinizing him. The only alternatives for Jesus are to do good (Ac 10:38) or to do evil—the refusal to do good is to do evil.

He excludes the middle or neutral position between good and evil. The Rabbis only allowed healing of the Sabbath when there was danger to life. Jesus came to save even on the sabbath. For him the whole purpose of the Law was the doing of good. For Luke, Jesus himself was obedient to the Law (2:21-2) and respected its regulations (5:14) and could commend its observance as leading to eternal life (10:26). Here he is correcting their misinterpretations of the law to bring out its proper meaning, its fulfillment and "newness" in himself. It is interesting that we do not find in Luke such criticisms of the Mosaic Law as found in Matthew (5:21-8; 19:1-9), and Mark (10:1-12)—but see Acts 13:39-40; 15:10,21.

Luke concludes the episode by noting their "foolish anger" (2 Tim 3:9) over the defiant healing and their inability to get the better of Jesus in the controversy. But he does not have those strange (to his readers!) bed fellows, the Herodians (Mk 3:6) in what was, ironically, their Sabbath plot to destroy Jesus. The disciples who witnessed all this are being prepared to be leaders and to accept the newness of Jesus their leader.

C. *The Choice of the Twelve and a Manual of Instruction —the Sermon on the Level Place—Miracles— (6:12-7:50):*

Luke in his orderly presentation has dealt with the general character of Jesus' ministry and the rising opposition to him. Now he turns to Jesus' preparation of his new

Ministry In Galilee 213

Israel, his selection of special disciples who will be his apostles and their special instruction so that they can be witnesses and penetrate the "Who is?" of Jesus[73] and carry on his mission (e.g. the opposition they will encounter 6:22). This section begins with (i) the choice of the twelve apostles (6:12-16) which is followed appropriately by (ii) Jesus' great sermon of Instruction for them on the kingdom (6:17-49). Then (iii) the cure of the Centurion's Servant (7:1-10) and (iv) the Widow's Son (7:11-17) show Jesus as the Lord of Death and by now Luke has prepared the ground for an answer to (v) John's question about Jesus (7:18-35), where Jesus is shown to be more than a prophet yet neither he nor Jesus was accepted by the Pharisees and lawyers. Finally, the episode (vi) of the Penitent Woman (7:36-50) is an example of one who repented and listened to both John and Jesus. It also teaches the importance of love and forgiveness. Then the Twelve are ready in the next section to join with Jesus to begin proclaiming the kingdom. Apart from the opening section, Lk 6:12-8:3 has no parallel in Mark.

(i) *The Choice of the Twelve Apostles—(6:12-16):*

Luke, whose time indication (in those days v 12) is quite vague, gives the reverse order to Mark who describes the mass healings before the call of the twelve (Mk 3:10f; Lk 6:18f). Luke thus emphasizes the choice of the twelve, then the crowd and thirdly has Jesus give his sermon to the disciples in the presence of the crowds. Typically, Luke alone tells that before the choice of the twelve Jesus went out to the mountain and spent the night in prayerful communion with God, to stress the importance both of the event and of prayer in the decision making of his community. The mountain was important in Jewish tradition as the place where God spoke to men and gave them his law (e.g. Moses and Elijah). At daybreak we are told that Jesus took the initiative, called his disciples to himself and chose twelve whom he named Apostles—the same verb is used of God's choice of the patriarchs (Ac 13:17), of the church's choice of special men[74] as of Jesus' choice of the apostles (Ac 1:2; 9:15).

There are evidently three stages in Jesus' relationship with his twelve—a call (Lk 5:1-11), a *choice* of twelve from a larger group (Lk 6:13) and thirdly their mission.[75] One can imagine among Jesus' followers a series of concentric circles, the inner three who receive special attention (8:51; 9:28), the twelve who are selected from the disciples or learners, the wider group of seventy (10:1-20), the crowds who are distinct from the disciples (6:17) also the women who accompanied the twelve (8:2).

The deliberate choice of the twelve, which is in the earliest New Testament tradition (1 Cor 15:5), is highly symbolic in Jewish history, as Israel was composed of Twelve Tribes and Twelve patriarchs. Twelve was a common number in ancient leagues such as among the Arameans, the Ishmaelites and Edomites[76] with each tribe doing a month at the central shrine. Curiously also, it should be noted that the Old Testament has four different lists of the twelve tribes.[77] Here then we have a kind of acted

Ministry In Galilee

parable showing Jesus the Messiah, in opposition to its present leadership of Israel, rebuilding a new people of Israel (a phrase not found in the New Testament). The twelve are given the kingdom which the Father gave Jesus (22:29) and the promise that they will "sit on the thrones judging the twelve tribes of Israel." While Mark explains their function—to be companions to Jesus, to be sent to preach the good news and to have authority to expel demons (Mk 1:14), Luke states simply that Jesus named the twelve apostles, i.e. "someone sent" such as Jesus himself (4:43). Thus he probably reads back into Jesus' ministry, a term which was popular during the period of Acts.[78] The term, which means a witness to the resurrection, is properly used only after the resurrection, especially when they become *permanent* apostles.[79] Many associate the term with the Jewish "shaliach," a term which in Jesus' time meant a representative sent by another with full authority to act in his name and to be just like the person himself (Jn 13:16), e.g. "He who hears you hears me. ." (10:16; Ac 1:8). The group are usually referred to in the gospels as the twelve.[80]

In all, the New Testament has four different lists of the twelve.[81] Are these lists the result of varying traditions within the early Church or typical of its lack of precision in handing on the details of the Jesus tradition? In each list Peter comes first and Judas last. It seems that the traditions handed on the names in three series of four in which Peter, Philip and James are always put first in the respective sections but variety was normal in the placing of the others except Judas. Luke however, has in both lists (also John 14:22) Judas son of Jacob where Mark and Matthew have Thaddaeus,[82] perhaps another name for the same person, yet an obscure name not given elsewhere in the New Testament. The name Iscariot is obscure. It possibly means "a man of Kerioth," a town in Judea (Josh 15:25) or Moab (Jer 48:24) and if so it possibly makes Judas the only non-Galilean in the twelve.

The twelve, Jesus' new leaders, included quite a variety of men, fishermen, a tax-collector, a Zealot freedom fighter, mainly from Galilee—very different from such as the Sadducees and the Pharisees, the traditional religious leaders.

(ii) *The Sermon on the Level Place—(6:17-49):*

Having described the calling of the twelve, the foundation of Jesus' new community, Luke naturally places next a great Sermon of Jesus which is a charter or inaugural description of the life of the new community. This is the kingdom, blessed by God and especially subject to his reign here and now already.

There is an obvious similarity between Luke's sermon and Matthew's more famous Sermon on the Mount which is more than three times as long and takes three chapters—chapters 5-7, containing 107 verses compared to Luke's 30. Both insert their sermon at similar points. Matthew, after the call of the first four disciples (Mk 1:16-20) and Luke after the call of the twelve (Mk 3:13-19). Both have the same general sequence beginning with the

Beatitudes—Matthew has 9 to Luke's 4. Both have a central section dealing with love and end with the parable of the two houses. Except for a few verses, almost all of Luke's is found mainly in the same order in the longer Matthew.[83] Matthew in general stresses the fulfillment and perfection of the Jewish religion. Luke puts his emphasis on the love and forgiveness which the poor should have even towards their enemies.

It is difficult to argue which version in a particular verse is the original one. Some scholars, like Dupont, have argued for example that originally Q contained four beatitudes, those found in common in the two sermons. Luke adds his woes and other modifications to bring out the social concern of the gospel and the contrast between present suffering and future reward. Matthew, on the other hand by adding other beatitudes and making different modifications, has produced a program about Christian righteousness.

Luke omits what would not be of interest to his Gentile audience (e.g. Mt 5:17-6:18) and in general it is correct to say that the Jewish Christian conflict which is so prominent in Matthew is scarcely found in Luke. It is noteworthy that such "positive" beatitudes of the meek, the merciful and the peacemakers, which are not found in Luke would have made a better introduction to the main themes of his sermon than those which he actually included. An indication that the teaching here is somewhat artificially assembled is seen from the fact that the text switches from "you" plural in 6:20-8, to "you" singular in 6:29-30, to you plural in 6:31-8, to the third person in 6:39-40 and back to the second person in 6:41-2. Curiously, there is a similar fluctuation between the singular and the plural in Deuteronomy (compare 6:4ff and 6:14,16f).

Scholars generally agree that both are based originally on the same scene and probably the same collection of Jesus' teaching (i.e. Q), while neither is an exact tape recording of the original. Luke seems to have omitted parts of Q while Matthew may have added to it as he did with the collection of parables in Mt 13 and the Our Father. Each has a distinctive emphasis and variety in details. Both owe much to the early Church and especially the community problems which they were facing. Matthew, dealing with the problem of a church tempted to pharisaic self-righteousness, portrays Jesus as the Jewish Messiah who is Emmanuel, "God with us," proclaiming his "teaching in *their* synagogues," the gospel of a kingdom which is both a summary and a fulfillment of the Law and the Prophets. Luke is more concerned with his Gentile community, their treatment in their society (6:22) and especially such dangers as that of riches in their lives. Luke, too, is concerned to teach the characteristics, e.g. reversal of values, love, obedience, which those who accept God's reign or kingdom should exhibit here and now and also its promises for the future. The phrase "kingdom" has only appeared once in Luke so far (4:43) but becomes almost a theme in this section.[84]

Other characteristics are stressed in the following episodes—the essential requirement of faith[85] in receiving the kingdom, its power over sickness, sin and death

Ministry In Galilee

(6:21ff; 7:10ff), the extraordinary statement that the new so much surpasses the old, that the least in the kingdom is greater than John (7:28). The kingdom of God *and his sons* (6:35) is a kingdom of *mercy* especially towards the oppressed poor but even towards one's enemies and thus very different from the power kingdoms of the world (4:5f). It is a new way of life for the disciples with a radical change of values *now*. The kingdom demands love even of one's enemies, forgiveness, self-criticism, not condemning others, obedience to the person of Jesus and his words. The poor, the outcasts of society, are open to accepting, but the rich, the satisfied, alas are closed. They rejected both John and Jesus—the cold neutral observations of the Pharisee are bluntly contrasted with the faith, great love, and peace of the prostitute (7:33ff).

Outline: Luke's version after his setting of the scene may conveniently be divided as follows into five sections:

Setting: (Lk 6:17-19): (Mk 3:7-12; Mt 4:25; 5:1-2).

A. *Four Beatitudes and Four Woes* (6:20-23); Matthew has nine beatitudes (including 5:11) and a chapter of woes (23).
B. *Love of Enemies* (6:27-36); (Mt 5:39-42,44-8).
C. *Self Criticism—not Judging Others* (6:37-42); (Mt 7:1-5).
D. *Fruit, the Test of True Discipleship* (6:43-5); (Mt 7:16-21; 12:33-5).
E. *Be Hearers and Doers*—the parable of the Builders (6:46-9); Mt (7:24-7).

Setting: Somewhat different to Matthew's, Luke's sermon is not delivered on the mountain, the place of prayer and special communication with God. Rather, like Moses descending to meet the people (Ex 32:15; 34:29), so Jesus *and his twelve* (6:17; Ex 19:24) descend to a level stretch (still on the mountain? an unusual word for plain is used). There they meet a large crowd of people from Judea,[86] Jerusalem and from the Gentile country to the north of Galilee, i.e. Tyre (Ac 21:3-7) and Sidon (Lk 10:13f), an audience symbolic of the universality of Jesus' salvation. They came to hear and to be healed—Luke particularly stresses those troubled with unclean spirits and that the whole crowd tried to touch him (cf 8:46), as a healing power (5:17), went out from him to cure *all*.[87] For Luke a miracle is an example of the saving *power* of God.

In Luke the Sermon is clearly directed to the disciples in the hearing of the crowds (6:20; 7:1) i.e, the poor are poor disciples, not all the poor as such. They are poor because they are like the Son of Man. They suffer like the prophets of old.

A. *Four Beatitudes and Four Woes—(6:20-23):*

Solemnity is indicated by Jesus' gesture of "raising his eyes to his disciples."[88] "How happy are the poor . . . ". Beatitudes were a frequent literary form used by Jesus[89] and provide a very thought-provoking opening to the Sermon on the Mount both in Luke and Matthew, whose version differs in number and style and sequence.[90] A beatitude is basically a paradox, a union of opposites (happy and poor), which at first sight does not seem quite true yet provokes and leaves an uneasy feeling that it might be true. It reverses the accepted values of a society which considers being born a Jew, being rich, powerful—prosperity, comfort ("full") and popularity ("laughing now") as the basic signs of true happiness. It contrasts the values of the world and the values of God and his reign.

Basically, the beatitudes are a description of Jesus himself and what a true disciple can be if he responds to the good news which Jesus brings to the poor (4:18). A beatitude is a highly emotional and congratulatory statement of fact, a consolation and an assurance but also a challenge and a summons to join the disciples of Jesus. It recognizes the real situation of the disciple, poor,[91] hungry, weeping, hated but surprisingly it emphasizes a present happiness—"the reign of God *is* yours," "who hunger *now*," "your consolation is *now*." Such are the people who are regarded fortunate by God as they take him seriously and thus enjoy his favor. The beatitudes are a proclamation that God's saving activity has drawn near in Jesus now. The poor (there is no blessing of poverty as such) have a long Old Testament background. They are the pious of Israel who like Simeon are awaiting the coming of the Lord and the consolation of Israel. The poor, those who lack the world's resources (Dt 15:4,11) are therefore the oppressed in society (Amos 2:6; 8:4) and having no wordly influence or power, turn to God for salvation.[92] Those who hunger now *will be filled* and the weeping (Mt "mourners") *will laugh* (Mt "will be comforted")—these are the real have-nots of Luke's world and are different from Matthew's version whose terms are more spiritually messianic.[93]

Luke's final beatitude is particularly stressed and probably refers to the situation of persecution in which many of his audience (12:32) existed. It decribes the four stages "hate, ostracize, insult, proscribe" whereby a Jew was excommunicated from the synagogue.[94] The response of rejoicing is typical of Acts (e.g. 4:23-31; also Lk 1:41). Here Jesus places his disciples in the line of prophets persecuted by the Hebrew people.[95] Evidently while salvation is already present and enjoyed in part here and now, nevertheless, it remains to be completed and fulfilled. Thus it must not be forgotten that there is a future dimension to a beatitude, a prophetic promise, a hope for the future, a reversal of the present world situation such as we find described in the story of Dives and Lazarus (16:19-31; also 12:13-34; 14:7-11).

The reversal of the situation and the contrast between the beatitudes and the woes fit in well with Luke's double edged theology which he expressed in the Magnificat (1:51-5; see also Is 5 and 65; Dt 11:26; 28:1ff).[96]

Luke's four parallel woes which are not found in Matthew's sermon, teach the same basic lesson by antithesis and contrast. The first three can be described as "apostrophes to the rich" who are not actually present (they are rather expressions of regret, a statement of fact "alas" rather than curses), while at the same time they are words of encouragement and warning to the disciples and to Luke's community for whom wealth was obviously a danger. They reflect the typical prophetic condemnation of oppressors (Is 65:11-16; Amos 5:7ff). The rich are paid in full (a metaphor from a receipt for a bill), unlike Simeon who actually saw the messianic times, the consolation of Israel (2:25-6). It is interesting to note that at Qumran a similar collection of Blessings and Woes formed part of the rite of admission to the community and perhaps had a similar function in Luke's day. The fourth woe is a warning to the disciples about excessive popularity, the sign of a false prophet (Jer 5:31; 1 Tim 3:7).

B. *Love of Enemies—(6:27-36):*

Luke brings forward and emphasizes as a basic principle, the saying "Love your enemies" which in Matthew derives from Jesus' interpretation of the familiar "Love your neighbor." It is introduced by the authoritative proclamation "I say to you who hear me" and is followed in

Ministry In Galilee

Luke by a series of examples also found in Matthew. The unit is rounded in v 35a with the repetition (i.e. an "inclusion") of the sentence "Love your enemies and do good." The explanation of this unusual and distinctive *command* is also found in v 35, where the statement is made "Then your reward will be great and you will rightly be called (by God) sons of the Most High" since he too is good to the ungrateful and the wicked. The motive is to imitate, to be like God in his unconditional and universal love of all men. Here the Old Testament commandment to "Be holy like God and love your neighbor as yourself" (Lv 19:18; Lk 10:27f; Mt 5:45), receives a radical, new and distinctive interpretation (fulfillment). A man's neighbor is every person, even his enemy. The opposite is found particularly in the Qumran command "to hate all the sons of darkness, each according to the measure of his guilt which God will ultimately require," and also in the attitude of some of the Old Testament Psalms (58:7-12; 137:7-9). However, it should be remembered that the principle of exact retaliation formulated in Mosaic law ("an eye for an eye") was actually a kind of early legal reform. It placed precise limitations upon the extent of permissible revenge. There is also a well known quotation from Lenin "Hatred is the basis for Communism."

Here we find Luke's first use of the special Greek New Testament word "agape" for Christian love (found some 120 times in the New Testament, its verb 130 times). Other available words which give different meanings of love were *eros*, the love of passion; *storge* or family affection; *philia*, friendship. The New Testament noun is scarcely found outside the Bible, although the verb agapan is—it was a new container for new wine.[97] This approach to persecutors is not found in Jewish tradition before this time (Rom 12:14; Jas 3:9; Mk 11:21; Mt 25:41). Lest there be a misinterpretation of the meaning of love it is illustrated concretely with a touch of Jesus' frequent use of hyperbole. It is *doing good* to those who hate, blessing those who curse, praying for those who ill-treat one. It is offering the other cheek not revenge to those who punch one on the other, giving one's shirt as well to one who takes a man's coat (Matthew has the other first), giving to all who beg, not demanding back what others have taken. Jesus is of course *the* example of doing good.[98] The Golden Rule in its positive form as a command *to do* not just to avoid as it was traditionally formulated[99] sums up the attitude of love (in Matthew it is found later at 7:12). In v 32-4, three illustrations by question and answer show how different Christian love is from the natural reciprocity of mutual friends.[100] Luke alone has (6:35) the phrase "lend without expecting to be repaid," which although here applied significantly to the poor, blends in with his emphasis on the responsible stewardship of wealth (14:13f; 16:9; 19:3). If such statements were taken literally they would be an invitation to "nudism." Yet there is a real demand in them which a Christian cannot evade by over-rationalization.

God's compassion is the model (Lk 1:50,54; Ex 34:6; 2 S 7:15; Hos 2:16-22). The word *hesed*, grace or covenant love which describes the incredible generosity by which Yahweh manifests a kindness and forgiveness which goes beyond any law, is an essential part of the Old Testament definition of Yahweh.

C. *Self-Criticism—not Judging Others—(6:37-42):*

God's compassion leads Luke to reflect on the problem of judging the motives of others especially by the leaders within the community of brothers (v 41). Here Luke has a longer commentary on Jesus' command to judge not which is not found in Matthew (Mt 7:1ff; Lk 6:37ff). The command is illustrated negatively "condemn not," probably referring to Pharisaical attitudes towards others (e.g. 18:11ff; 5:33; 9:54) and positively ("forgive").[101] While Matthew tends to stress the Last Judgment, Luke emphasizes the justice, the measure, the proportion of our giving and forgiving compared to what we get back in life, not forgetting God's generous compassion. This is illustrated with an image of a very generous grain merchant—"good measure, pressed down, shaken together, running over, will they (God) pour into the fold of your garment." This fold which was formed above the girdle was often used as a kind of pocket.

"He also told them a parable" (v 39), in fact some five brief parables or expanded metaphors follow this statement showing the relationship between Jesus and his disciples. Thus, he is no blind guide but a teacher who sees and knows the way for them to follow, the way of forgiveness, not judging, unlike the Pharisees to whom the saying about the blind guides may have originally been applied (Mt 15:14). A guide can only guide if he sees the way and a teacher can only teach what he has been taught.[102] Luke (6:41-2), which is almost word for word identical with Matthew (7:3-5), is a humerous satire on the hypocritical teacher, blind to his faults (e.g. the Pharisee) who tries to reform his *brother*—the imagery of the plank and the speck is drawn from Jesus' carpenter's experience. The lesson is self-criticism, not to judge others. On hypocrisy see commentary on 12:1.

D. *Fruit, the Test of True Discipleship—(6:43-5):*

How then can one distinguish a true disciple of Jesus from the hypocrite? A man's fruit, his deeds, show what he is really like in his heart, i.e., whether it is loving, forgiving or censorious. This argument was also used by John the Baptist (3:8). The heart is the source of his doing and thinking which Jesus will expose (2:35). In Matthew

(7:15ff) the two trees and their fruit are used as a warning against false prophets but in Luke the message is addressed to the disciples.

E. *Be Hearers and Doers—the Parable of the Builders—(6:46-9):*

Faith, unless living and obedient, i.e., leading to action, is disastrous, e.g., the rich young man who refused to sell all (18:18ff). The question "Why do you call me Lord, Lord . . .?" is addressed to the disciples, to the contradictory life style of some members of Luke's community (Rom 2:13; Jam 1:21ff; Lk 8:21). Originally perhaps it was addressed to the Pharisees. The New Life is summed up in obedience to a person, Jesus, not mere intellectual approval or an internal assent. Thus the concluding climax of the sermon is an incredible and total claim by Jesus that the lives of the disciples should be based on his teaching or *disaster* would result. Luke seems to imagine a man building a house, working hard to dig deep and finding a rock (rock foundation), near one of the European rivers which often overflowed its banks. Matthew thinks of a sudden flood coming down a dry *wadi* in Palestine. Ultimately, it is the *foundation* which counts in time of testing, is Luke's message to his community (17:26ff; 1 Cor 3:11ff). Man falls unless his life is a *doing* of Jesus' teaching.

(iii) *The Cure of the Centurion's Servant—(7:1-10):*

Like Matthew, Luke follows his sermon with an account of how Jesus went to Capernaum, a border town with a tax office and a garrison. There Jesus healed an unnamed centurion's servant and praised the Gentile centurion's humble faith: "I have never found so much faith among the Israelites." But in Matthew, the cure of a leper comes between the sermon and the cure of the centurion's servant. A similar story is also found in John who seems to give an independent version of the same incident now closer to Matthew and again closer to Luke in other details while also having details of his own.[103] There is almost an identity of language in the dialogue of both Matthew and Luke but the presentation of the episode is different as Matthew typically seems to have abbreviated the narrative. In Matthew, it is the centurion's "pais" which could mean son or "boy" (servant) and he is "paralysed, suffering dreadfully." In Luke he is clearly a servant, very dear to the centurion and was at the point of death. In Matthew, the centurion comes personally to Jesus, whereas in Luke, who never has Jesus preaching to Gentiles directly, the centurion sends two delegates, one of Jewish elders (a phrase only found here in the gospels) and a second of friends. Thus Luke effectively keeps the Gentile offstage as the time for the Gentiles would come later (Lk 21:24; Acts). Perhaps this is also a reason why Luke also omits Mk 7:24-8:26, which can be called Jesus' Gentile mission. Nevertheless, it gives Luke the opportunity to record Jesus' finest praise as given to a Gentile and anticipates as it were the Gentile mission which is thus begun indirectly by Jesus himself and could serve as an example for the early Christians. In fact, it should be noted that the first Gentile convert described in Acts 10 was a Gentile centurion also "who gave generously to the (Jewish) people" (Ac 10:2) and who had faith in Jesus of whom he heard without meeting him.

Matthew's emphasis on the exclusion of the Jews is found in a sentence which Luke uses elsewhere (Lk 13:28-30). "I tell you many will come from east to west and sit at table with Abraham, Isaac and Jacob in the kingdom of heaven while the sons of the kingdom . . . " (Mt 8:11-12).

In the first episode which Luke describes after his sermon, the interest is not in the healing which is scarcely described and the servant to be "rescued" is only mentioned at the beginning and the end. Luke is interested in describing the behavior of a Gentile of such faith (see also 7:50; 8:25,48,50), in contrast with Jewish faith, that he is an ideal member of the New Israel which he has just described (no mention of circumcision see Gal 6:3). He is a man who showed his love in good deeds by building a synagogue. Clearly too he is a man who understands Jesus' authority and the importance of obedience (7:7-8), a point highlighted in the sermon (6:46). He describes Jesus' power in terms of his own soldier's profession. The centurion here is quite likely a Roman seconded to Herod Antipas' administration. In Luke's writings the centurions who are described are all men of character and integrity[104]—note the contrast between the Jewish elders' estimate of the centurion as worthy, and his own opinion that like Peter he is unworthy (5:8; 7:4,6). This perhaps is typical of Luke's treatment of Roman authorities in both gospel and Acts. Here he pictures, somewhat ideally, good relations between Romans and Jews who intercede for them and emphasizes a Roman's actual admiration of Jesus himself—a representative of the mighty empire asking a favor of Jesus who heals at a distance by his powerful word alone.

Luke, in telling this story about a servant who almost died and his next story about a widow's son who actually had died, is preparing the way for Jesus' reply to John the Baptist's question, which will include a reference both to healing and raising from the dead to life (7:22). Jesus is the author of life (Ac 3:15).

(iv) *The Widow's Son at Nain—(7:11-17):*

The raising of the widow's son to (earthly) life, which is the climax of Luke's healing stories before the question of the Baptist, presents a very interesting comparison with the previous episode, the cure of the centurion's servant. It gives other complementary aspects of Jesus' approach and in particular shows him taking the initiative although there is no appeal for help. The first cure concerns a Gentile *man's* servant, the second, a Jewish *woman's* only son. The first cure shows Jesus' power at a distance; in the second Jesus comes into close contact. In the first the boy is at the point of death, in the second he is dead. The first stresses faith, whereas, the second stresses Jesus' compassion for the nameless widow and there is no mention of faith.

The episode is found only in Luke although a similar miracle, Jairus' daughter (Lk 8:40; Mk 5:21; Mt 9:18) is also told in the three synoptics, while John tells of the raising of Lazarus (Jn 11). It is inserted into a series of "Q" material (Lk 7:1-35) and begins a series of stories about women, which only Luke tells (e.g. 13:10ff; 14:1ff). It follows the simple structure common to miracle stories, a description of the evil, Jesus' intervention with a word, the result or healing, the religious reaction of the crowd.

Many commentators, noting the tendency in the New Testament to tell stories in Old Testament language, point out the resemblances between this story, which is very Hebraic in its language, and 1 K 17, where Elijah has an encounter also at the gate of the city and raises the only son of a widow from the dead and 2 K 4, where Elisha restores to life the only son of a Shunamite woman—influence of course does not negate the historicity of a story. For Luke, the prophet Elijah is a kind of "type," one of the great prophets who prefigures Jesus.[105] Nain (Heb Na'im), probably the present day Nein, some six miles South East of Nazareth, is not mentioned elsewhere in the Bible but was rather close to Shunem where Elisha performed his miracle (2 K 4:18-37). The phrase "give him back to his mother" (7:15; also 9L42) is found exactly in 1 K 17:23. The crowd evidently recognized that God was at work again through a great prophet with their cry "A great prophet has arisen among us."[106] With the Old Testament exclamation (Ruth 1:6; 1 S 2:21), (v 16), "God has visited his people" which indicates the fulfillment of Zechariah's prophecy (1:68,78b), we find one of Luke's three important christological statements on the lips of people about Jesus which are in the center of his gospel (see Peter's confession 9:20; the centurion's statement 23:47; also that of the Eleven after the resurrection 24:34).

Yet a close comparison between the Elijah stories and Jesus' shows that the resemblance is quite superficial and that Jesus' method and power are quite different. Jesus touches the bier on which the body lay (typically oblivious of Jewish taboos Num 19:11) and cures him with an all powerful word. Elijah has to have recourse to prayer and effort.[107]

Luke's artistic hand paints a simple yet dramatic picture as is his custom. One can easily visualize the meeting of the two crowds at the city gate. Jesus, his disciples and the large crowd with him meet the considerable crowd of sympathizing townspeople on their way out to bury the widow's only son, i.e., the end of her line as the pathetic description emphasizes (8:42; 9:38). Jesus touches the bier in the sight of all and commands the young man to get up. He sits up (this unusual word is possibly the technical medical word for a patient sitting up in bed), and begins to talk. The crowds' exclamation that God was visiting his people in this prophet is a reference to 1:67ff "the Daystar shall visit us in his mercy to shine on those who sit in darkness and in the *shadow of death*" (9:8,19). Luke also notes the fear which seized them (1:12,65; 8:25,37), their glorifying of God as the centurion and others also reacted,[108] and the spread of the story throughout Judaea (i.e. Palestine). This latter prepares the way for John's hearing of the news in 7:18).

In this event we find that Luke alone of the synoptics begins to call Jesus "the Lord," a title commonly found in Acts (1:21; 4:33 etc.), but found also some 16 times in his gospel.[109] Jesus is for Luke the compassionate Lord of life who delivers man from the captivity, not of the Romans but of death. This is only the beginning, although the young man would still have to face death—Jesus would finally face and conquer death in his own suffering and resurrection.

Luke in particular stresses the compassion of Jesus. The weeping woman would weep no longer as the sermon at 6:17 puts it. The word used for "moved to compassion" has an interesting etymology which makes it the strongest word in the Greek language describing an emotion which moves a man to the very depths of his being.[110] It is only found in the synoptics in the New Testament and apart from three uses in parables, is always used of Jesus. Three uses of it in Luke describe compassion in the presence of death—the half dead man in the parable of the Good Samaritan and the Prodigal Son who was dead and came back to life. Curiously, Luke has none of the four occurrences found in Mark (Mk 1:41; 6:34; 8:2; 9:22) and does not use the word in Acts. All of the gospels speak of the compassion of Jesus but no single reference is found in all the synoptics.

(v) *John's Question about Jesus—(7:18-35):*

Having carefully set the stage, Luke now introduces the messianic question of John, a question that will be frequently asked from this until Peter's answer (7:49; 8:25; 9:9,18ff). It is a challenge, not just to John and the actual actors of the gospel, but especially to Luke's audience, who were perhaps waning in their enthusiasm, to rethink their understanding of the compassionate Jesus and his Father who sent him. Luke's interest is not so much to give a complete historical account of the great martyr, John, as to help his audience answer the question "Who is Jesus?"

Luke's version of the episode is close to Matthew's shorter version but is in a different context. In Matthew, it comes after the Missionary Sermon, almost a digression. Luke fits it much better into his work just after two very exceptional miracles. In Matthew, unlike Luke, who has already mentioned it (3:20), we are told that John is in prison, sends his *disciples,* but Luke, who usually likes *two* witnesses, notes that two disciples were sent and also repeats their question twice for emphasis (7:19,20). In Matthew Jesus simply answers "Go tell John what you hear and see . . . " (Mt 11:1ff), whereas, in Luke, with his interest in eyewitnesses and evidence, Jesus' answer is preceded by an account of miracles worked in the presence of the two witnesses who actually see them. Luke also has (7:29-30) the contrast between popular belief in John and the unbelief of the Pharisees and the lawyers.

This episode can be conveniently divided into three—

    A. John's question is answered (7:18-23).
    B. Jesus praises John (7:24-30).
    C. Jesus describes his own generation (7:31-5).

A. *John's Question is Answer—(7:18-23):*

It should be remembered that in Luke (like Mark but unlike Matthew 3:14 and John 1:29) it is not stated that John, Jesus' cousin, recognized Jesus as the Messiah at his baptism. For Luke, John is unique in that he begins the time of fulfillment but his ministry is quite separate from that of Jesus and they never appear on the stage together. Luke, who describes Jesus in terms of Elijah, does not clearly identify John as Elijah yet he does not have the polemical attitude towards John and his disciples who survived his death such as we find in John's Gospel.[111] The question must have been asked why Jesus did not save or raise John!

Three approaches can be taken to John's question with a combination of the second and third as the most likely[112]—

(a) Because he was becoming discouraged in prison and was losing faith in Jesus,[113] yet Jesus describes him as no wavering reed (7:24).
(b) His disciples needed to be strengthened. Jesus states that he is blessed who is not scandalized in him.
(c) John, who still kept his disciples somewhat aloof from the Jesus movement, is genuinely puzzled at Jesus' ministry which he had heard was one of teaching and healing yet was far from the figure of wrath and fire and judgment which he had expected.

In his answer to John[114] Jesus alludes to three passages from Isaiah (35:5f; 29:18f; 61:1) which are quite similar to his prophetic program statement which he had also taken from Isaiah (Lk 4:17ff). Each of the three stresses both blessing and a threat of Judgment,[115] but Jesus stresses the blessing as characterizing his ministry, the year of God's favor and ignores the judgment as not yet (see his Woes). Jesus' answer is typically not direct but rather indirect and almost a riddle. He invites John to a second reflection on the works of his ministry which had originally caused his question: the blind (Is 35:5); the cripples (Is 35:6); lepers and deaf (Is 35:8); the dead (61:1) and especially the poor (i.e. Luke's community—the list also resembles the great banquet (14:15-24) have the good news preached to them. These come from Isaiah's description of the messianic times although Isaiah does not mention precisely the cure of lepers and the raising of the dead. Jesus' beatitude (7:23) shows his appreciation of the problem people had in interpreting his ministry which did not quite confrom to their expectations. It is like a trap into which people can fall (the metaphor comes from bird catching).

B. *Jesus Praises John—(7:24-30):*

When John's disciples left, Jesus challenges his audience with three questions (24,25,26f) about the character and role of John. A man easily swayed like a reed in the wind? A man of luxury? (Luke alone has the phrase "and live in luxury"). A prophet? Jesus answers himself—John was more than a prophet and identifies him with the eschatological messenger of Mal 3:1, while at the same time pointing out the finality and superiority of his mission. The text quoted is actually a combination of Exodus 23:20 (Moses) and Malachy (Elijah), a text which Mark has in 1:2 joined with Isaiah (see also Ac 13:24). Moses and Elijah will again appear at the transfiguration (9:30) as fulfilled in Jesus.

> "The apparent sting in the tail of Jesus' praise of John—"the least in the kingdom of heaven is greater than he'—has baffled many an interpreter" writes Vermes. "Some have seen in it a contrast between the future glory of the elect and John's generation on earth. Others

Ministry In Galilee

identify "the kingdom" as the realm of the spirit resulting from the ministry of Jesus and belonging to a higher sphere than the world of the Baptist. Others still understand the phrase 'the least in the kingdom' as a description of Jesus as the servant of God. The first two interpretations are too theological for serious consideration by a historian, but the third is plausible at least as far as its acceptance as a reference to Jesus is concerned. The Servant concept itself becomes less relevant when it is recalled that in Aramaic and Hebrew the phrase 'the least one', 'the smallest one', can be used in the chronological sense to designate the youngest or last person in a series. In the belief of the evangelists, Jesus was God's ultimate envoy, and although it is by no means sure that the words are his own, their significance is: John was very great, but I am greater."[116]

Certainly it does not teach that John is outside the kingdom (e.g. 13:28). Rather it teaches that the important thing for Jesus' hearers is to be a member of the kingdom, more important than admiration of John, more important even than being the greatest of the prophets.

Luke, who does not have here Matthew 11:12f (see Lk 16:16) or Matthew 11:14 (Lk 1:17), has the explanatory parenthesis of v 29,30 (Mt 21:32) in the middle of Jesus' words on John. It gives a twofold response to Jesus as a preparation for what is next, especially v 35 and vss 36-50 (the repentant woman and the Pharisee). The entire people, even the tax collectors, "justified God" i.e. accepted his judgment on their sinfulness and received baptism, whereas the Pharisees and the lawyers saw no need for repentance and thus rejected God's plan (Ac 28:25-8) by which John should bring them to repentance.

C. *Jesus Describes his own Generation—(7:31-5):*

Jesus concludes with a parable rebuking the Pharisees and the lawyers—"the men of this generation," who are disobedient hearers (6:46-9) of both John and himself. They are like peevish children who will neither play a game of weddings nor funerals. They neither accepted the ascetic call of John to repentance nor the social message of good news of Jesus, but criticized one as mad and the other as debauched and a friend of sinners as Luke will describe in the next story. But God's plan is wise (Is 55:8) and is shown to be just (v 29f and v 30) by the results, her wise children who accept the preaching both of John and Jesus.[117]

(vi) *The Penitent Woman—(7:36-50):*

All four gospels describe how a woman anointed Jesus at a dinner.[118] However, there are differences of scene,[119] characters,[120] details.[121] It seems quite likely that originally there were two distinct episodes and that, in the telling, details passed from one to the other.

There is no proof that the woman was Mary Magdalene, a woman who is described in the next scene in Lk 8:2. In Luke it is an example of the cold judgmental Pharisee (6:31ff) and the loving sinners in their differing responses to Jesus, the friend of sinners (7:30) and the emphasis is on love of the sinner and her proportionate forgiveness. It shows his favorite contrast between a man and a woman and also his reversal themes are evident as God's wisdom is shown (1:51f; 18:9-14). In the other gospels there is a hidden preparation for Jesus' death and a discussion about selling the oil and giving the money to the poor instead of her extravagant waste on Jesus.

In Luke, who delights in showing Jesus to his Greek audience as teaching at banquets, this is one of three occasions which he alone describes where Jesus dines with the Pharisees (also 11:37f; 14:1; 7:30f). Jesus "lay on a couch" which was the Roman custom of reclining and which the Jews adopted on formal occasions. Jesus' host

Ministry In Galilee

here is a suspicious Pharisee who probably invited the popular teacher, as he addresses him (v 40 not Lord), to test whether he was a genuine prophet or not. The fact that he ignored the usual courtesies to Jesus is significant of his attitude to him.[122]

"And behold" as Luke tells us in his Septuagintal style (v 37) a woman known in the town to be a sinner (a prostitute?) without saying anything (e.g. a confession of faith), lets herself go and gives an extraordinary demonstration of her love for Jesus—her tears fell on Jesus' feet and to remedy this she uses her hair, her kisses and her perfume.

Simon's Pharisaical idea of a prophet is one who can see through others (not himself), one who would have nothing to do with a sinner. Jesus ironically fulfills this criterion by seeing through Simon himself and by reading his judgmental thoughts about the woman (1 S 16:7). Jesus then formally interrogates Simon himself beginning with a parable which should have trapped Simon into seeing himself in a mirror.

Simon gives a grudging "I suppose" to Jesus' parable of the two debtors who are let off by an extraordinary creditor (God), unaware that he himself is one of the debtors. Debt was a Jewish description of sin and Luke uses the same word in the Our Father (11:4). Simon misses the point that the woman had experienced such a wonderful forgiveness that she is responding with loving gratitude. She is typical of Luke's argument that despite the gravity of their evident sins, those furthest from the kingdom are giving the best response to Jesus. Jesus' gentle approach to the woman is in contrast with the blunt way he attacks the blind Simon who resembles the brother of the Prodigal Son or the Pharisee at prayer in the Temple. There is a striking contrast between the woman's "total" response and Simon's minimal hospitality—as Simeon prophesized, Jesus is the rise and fall of many in Israel.

Simon sees the possibility that Jesus is a prophet. But Jesus goes on to proclaim the forgiveness of sins which was the main element in his (spiritual) salvation as Zechariah had prophesized (1:77, forgiveness of sins *leading to peace* as here, 7:50; 1 S 1:17) and as the early preaching would emphasize.[123] Thus Luke emphasizes again the continuity between his own time and the ministry of Jesus.

The climax of the episode is the question of the guests—"Who is Jesus?" (7:49), a question which will dominate the next chapters in Luke leading up to Jesus' own question at 9:20.[124]

Commentators have experienced difficulties in interpreting several of Jesus' statements at the end of this episode. Thus the Jerusalem Bible translates 7:47 ". . . her many sins *must* have been forgiven her, or she would not have shown such great love" i.e. love and gratitude coming from forgiveness and not vice versa. The statement "your faith has saved you" is normally used in healing stories (8:48f; 17:19; 18:42), meaning that faith makes possible a person's healing, but here there is no physical healing—it seems to be loosely attached to the narrative and the word faith is probably used in a vague sense but certainly not as *causing* salvation. This "faith" brought her into the Pharisee's house and issued in a loving deed to Jesus.

D. *Jesus with the Twelve proclaims the Kingdom as he moves from Capernaum to a wider Tour—Instructions to the disciples who begin to penetrate the mystery of Jesus—(8:1-9:50):*

Now Jesus leaves the area of Capernaum and a new stage begins as he journeys around from town to town until 9:51, when he sets his face to go to Jerusalem. Here

Ministry In Galilee

Luke parallels Mark again (Mk 4:1-9:41) with the famous omission of Mark 6:45-8:26. He also omits the parable of the seed growing quietly (Mk 4:26-9), the visit of Jesus to Nazareth (Mk 6:1-6) which he had included in his inaugural episode at Nazareth (4:16ff). He does not describe the execution of John just as in Acts he does not tell of the deaths of Peter and Paul. The Twelve are frequently mentioned by Luke in this section[125] showing the important interest for Luke here as he prepares the way for their role in Acts. An important theme also for Luke is the reflection on the question just stated at the end of the previous episode—Who is Jesus? (7:49). Peter will speak out at 9:20 and Jesus will perform miracles, give teaching about his person (e.g. the Transfiguration, the Passion predictions) and his mission of suffering and what their approach as disciples and apostles should be in their mission. The varied material in this section can be outlined as follows in seventeen sections:—

(1) Jesus' tour with the Twelve and some Women—(8:1-3).

(2) The Parable of the Sower—(8:4-15).

(3) The Parable of the Lamp—(8:16-18)

(4) The True Kindred of Jesus—(8:19-21).

(5) The Calming of the Storm—(8:22-5).

(6) The Healing of the Gerasene Demoniac—(8:26-39).

(7) Jairus' Daughter and the Woman who touched Jesus' garment (8:40-56).

(8) The Mission of the Twelve—(9:1-6).

(9) Herold's Anxiety—(9:7-9).

(10) The Return of the Twelve—the Feeding of the Five Thousand (9:10-17).

(11) Peter's Profession of Faith—(9:18-21).

(12) Jesus' first Prediction of his Passion and Resurrection—(9:22).

(13) The Conditions for Discipleship—(9:23-7).
Discipleship—(9:23-7).

(14) The Transfiguration—(9:28-36).
(15) The Cure of a Boy with an Unclean Spirit — (9:37-43a).
(16) Jesus' Second Passion Prediction—(9:43b-45).
Prediction—(9:43b-45).
(17) The Dispute about Greatness—(9:46-50).

(1) *Jesus on Tour with the Twelve and Some Women—(8:1-3):*

Now Jesus goes on a more extended tour through towns and villages proclaiming and preaching the good news of the kingdom. The absence of mention of synagogues perhaps means that they were closed to him but the crowds follow him nevertheless.[126] It is interesting to note that Luke uses the word "Kathexes" to describe Jesus' journey, the same word that he used of his own aim to write "in order."[127] Luke here agrees with the other synoptics (Mk 1:14f; Mt 4:17) in stating that Jesus' preaching was especially concerned with the kingdom of God. He later calls it "the word of God" (8:11ff; 21) and in his life it resembles the powerful creative word of God (e.g. Gen 1:1ff), as Jesus speaks to the sick, demons, the wind, the dead and a new creation takes place. Faith is *the* response (8:13,25,48,50) and only those who obey, who hear and keep it are his true family, the true sons of the kingdom (6:47; 8:15,21). The Twelve who are given its secrets[128] and later the Apostles, continue Jesus' proclamation.[129]

Here Luke typically parallels the twelve men with many women (8:3) who, as he alone tells, help to provide for Jesus and the Twelve from their resources, like Simon's mother-in-law (4:39). Women are very important for Luke in contrast to the Rabbis, and they will be witnesses of the resurrection when the men have run away.[130] Mark does not mention the women who accompanied Jesus until the resurrection. Luke mentions in particular that some had been cured by Jesus—Mary Magdalene's "seven devils" probably means not a dissolute life but some serious mental disease (11:26); Joanna (also in 24:10) and Susanna are named only in Luke's gospel. The mention of Joanna's husband, Chuza, a steward of Herod Antipas, the tetrarch of Galilee, is an indication that Luke had special information about Herod's court (9:7-9; 23:6-8).

(2) *The Parable of the Sower—(8:4-15).*

The parable of the sower which is one of only three extended parables common to the synoptics (also the Mustard Seed and the Wicked Vinedressers) is very suitably placed here to explain the differing responses to Jesus' message, e.g. the questions of those like John, the hostility of the Pharisees, the impatience of some in Luke's community. The use of extended parables is a new aspect here of Jesus' teaching. Mark, it should be noted, collects his parables into a day of parables and Matthew in his turn has symbolically seven parables formed into one of his main sermons (Mk 4; Mt 13). Jesus' parables which no previous teacher of Israel used so well or so frequently,[131] are developed comparisons based on the daily commonplace experiences of the people of Palestine. Thus they reveal God's workings which are not at first sight obvious to man. They do not give a precise logical answer but they arouse the listener's curiosity and trap the listener into an application to his own situation, to question his assumptions and open the way to new conclusions if one is sincere. At this point Jesus is challenging the somewhat superficial adherence of the crowds and disciples (8:4,9,13) to a deeper penetration of God's working through himself.

Luke's version is substantially the same as Mark's but with some interesting variations in detail such as his vague opening as compared with Mark's seaside picture.

To understand the parable it should be remembered that in Palestine ploughing was done after the seed was scattered as we read in Jubilees 11:11—"Mastema (the devil) sent ravens and birds (Lk 8:5,12) to devour the seed which was sown in the land . . . *Before they could plough in the seed* the ravens picked it up from the surface of the ground." The four different soils are described—perhaps an adaptation to Luke's audience: the footpath (at the side?), rock which had *no moisture,* whereas, in Mark and Matthew it is rocky ground which had no depth of soil, soil with thorns growing in it, good soil. Despite three disastrous soils the harvest from the fourth is "a hundred fold" (i.e. abundant harvest Gn 26:12). Luke does not have Mark's thirty and sixtyfold which perhaps suggests some limitation in God's harvest.[132] Jesus then challenges his audience to really hear what he was saying (6:4ff).

All the synoptic gospels follow this parable with a reflection on Jesus' purpose for speaking in parables. In comparison with Mark's explanation, Luke applies his reflection only to the present parable and does not say that the explanation was given only to the twelve, but they ask for it publicly. He describes those who do not understand as the "others" (Mk "for those outside everything is . . . "). In particular, Luke does not have Mark's final line that Jesus speaks in parables "lest perhaps they repent and be forgiven" (Mk 4:12). Finally, Luke does not have Jesus' criticism of the disciples (Mk 4:13).

In Luke as in Mark, it is emphasized that fuller understanding of the secrets of God's rule which a parable communicates, is a gift from God which is given primarily to the disciples. Many hear the word of God from Jesus (and see the miracles) but only some adequately receive the word—for "the others" it remains "in parables" *with the result that* ("that" in text) they see and hear yet do not perceive or understand (or want to, like the people of

Ministry In Galilee 243

Nazareth or the two disciples at Emmaus 24:25). Even though a parable was intended to be an illustration leading to a deeper perception, in Luke's view the responsibility is clearly not on God's or Jesus' part. The Greek word for "mysteries" (plural in Mt, Lk, singular in Mk) is not found elsewhere in the gospels. It is frequently found in the Dead Sea Scrolls and in the epistles and the Apocalypse (Rom 11:25; 16:25; Eph 1:9; 3:9; Apoc 1:20; 10:7; 17:5,7) to describe the secret purpose of God which has now been made known. It incorporates the Jewish idea of God's secret plan (Dn 2:18f,27ff; 4:6; Wis 2:22). The quotation from Isaiah (6:9) occurs 5 other times in the New Testament.[133] Luke repeats it at the end of Acts as the conclusion to his two volumes when he describes how the majority of the Jews, though given the first opportunity to hear the good news, stubbornly refused to receive it.

The Explanation of the Parable—(8:11-15):

The complete rejection by many scholars since A. Jülicher (1898-9) of the allegorical explanations of the details and characters in the parables[134] as the inventions of the early Christians is seen by several recent scholars to be an oversimplification. While recognizing that the parables have been adapted to the new situations of the various evangelists, nevertheless, this does not deny that there could and actually was an allegorical explanation originally given by Jesus himself as all three synoptics agree.

Originally, the parable could have had a "nil desperandum" message to Jesus' perplexed followers. The seed is sown and will ultimately triumph and will yield a harvest beyond expectations despite its small beginnings and many poor responses—hardness, superficiality, weakness in persecution, preoccupation with cares and riches. Luke interprets the seed as "the Word of God," a phrase which was a technical term for the gospel in the early church.[135] Rather than the final harvest, he stresses the hearer's (his own audience) individual responsibility in receiving the word (8:21; 11:27). It is a picture of four different responses to the gospel. Satan takes the word from the first group according to Luke as it leads to faith and thus (spiritual) salvation (8:12). Luke mentions temptation (peirasmos), the daily battle with Satan[136] and more bluntly, the "riches and pleasures of life" where Mark has "the *desire* for wealth." Luke's anxieties are illustrated in 10:32-42; riches in 12:16ff; pleasures 15:13. Three conditions are required for the proper harvest—a spirit of openness (literally "a good and noble heart" e.g. the centurion's faith); secondly, to retain the word despite temptations and thirdly to bear fruit by perseverance (21:16-19; 6:43f; 12:51-3).

(3) *The Parable of the Lamp—(8:16-18):*

Luke follows the explanation of the parable of the Sower with a brief parable about a lamp, a collection of sayings found in other contexts in Matthew (5:15; 10:26; 13:12) and Mark (4:21-5), some of which are later in Luke himself (11:33; 12:2; 19:26). In Luke the parable of the light fits in with his context. To the disciples the mysteries are revealed but it should be remembered that they have a responsibility to the others not to keep God's word hidden to themselves. They are a lamp of faith to the others (8:10) that they might see and enter the kingdom. While Matthew seems to imagine the one roomed Jewish house with its weak lamp, Luke seems to picture a Roman villa with different lamps and one in particular which is outside to light the way for guests to enter. Thus in the light whatever is hidden will be brought to light (i.e. the hidden character of Jesus' person and mission or perhaps that of men; see

Ministry In Galilee

2:32,35). The section concludes with the advice to listen carefully as in the parable of the pounds. Talents which are used such as knowledge increase, but lack of use can cause a man to lose even what "he thinks he has" (Mk "what he has").

(4) *The True Kindred of Jesus—(8:19-21):*

This incident is found in Matthew and Mark after the mention of the sin against the Holy Spirit but before the parable of the sower (Mk 3:21-5; Mt 12:46-50). Luke removes it out of this embarrassing context and puts it after the parable of the Lamp to illustrate the parables as an example of true faith and the true kindred of Jesus. Like Matthew, Luke omits the first part of Mark where his mother and brothers come to take charge of Jesus because his ministry was so frenzied that it was impossible for him and his disciples to get food and he seemed "out of his mind" (Mk 3:20ff). He also abbreviates the second part and omits Mk 3:34 and the reference to the "will of God" in v 35 for "hear the word of God" which is a theme in his gospel and in Acts (e.g. Lk 8:11).

In Luke Jesus does not down his family as R.E. Brown puts it—this scene is

> "not to be read as if the hearers of the word of God replace Jesus' mother and his brothers as his real family (so Mark), but as a statement that his mother and his brothers are among his disciples. The physical family of Jesus is truly his family because they hear the word of God. Luke preserves Jesus' insistence that hearing the word of God and doing it is what is constitutive of his family, but Luke thinks that Jesus' mother and brothers meet that criticism."[137]

Luke does not name the brothers of Jesus although he mentions them twice (here and in Ac 1:14).[138] In early Christian debate it was disputed whether they were step-brothers of Jesus from an earlier marriage of Joseph (the second century (?) Gospel of James; the fourth century Epiphanius) or cousins (Jerome) or full brothers (fourth century Helvivius). Catholic scholars and the sixteenth century reformers held that Mary had only one child, Jesus,[139] a view which is not necessarily contrary to the text of the gospels, as according to Semitic custom, a brother can stand for a close relation.[140]

(5) *The Calming of the Storm—(8:22-5):*

Again, with a vague historical context ("one day" where Mark has "the evening"), Luke tells a further story which illustrates his faith and perseverance theme—the teacher calmly asleep before and during the storm, is sharply contrasted with the little faith of the disciples. But it should be noted that typically Luke's reproach to the disciples is not as strong as Mark's whose version he summarizes omitting the disciples "do not care if we perish?" and toning down "Why are you afraid? Have you *no* faith" to "Where is your faith?" In Matthew, whose word for storm is characteristic of the apocalyptic scenes of the end of time (Apoc 6:12; 8:5), the order is different and the rebuke to the disciples comes before the miracle.

Many commentators describe this miracle under the category of "nature miracles" with such miracles as the walking on the water, the feeding of the crowd, the large catch of fish, the coin in the fish's mouth and the fig tree, a rather small group compared with the majority of Jesus' miracles which deal with mental and physical disease. However, this triumph over the forces of nature is described by Luke as a rebuking just as Jesus rebuked men possessed by devils (4:35; 9:42).

In Jewish thinking, nature was alive and often under the control of a spirit (see Apoc 4:6; 21:1, where the sea is no more). Yahweh, from the creation story onwards was pictured as subduing the forces of the deep, the symbol of the hostile powers which were yet to be brought fully under his rule.[141] The lake, as Luke calls it, is again the setting for a manifestation of Jesus' power (5:1). This then the first of four miracles which demonstrate Jesus' power over nature, demons, disease and even death naturally leads to a reaction of "fear and admiration" (5:9f) and the key question "Who is this?" who can do what God himself can do?

(6) *The Gerasene Demoniac—(8:26-39):*

Here the power of Jesus' word over demons even in Gentile country[142] is illustrated for Luke's Gentile audience—the only time in Luke where Jesus goes outside Jewish territory. The textual tradition gives several variant readings for the name of the place. "Gerasene" has probably the best attestation in Luke. Gadarene seems to be an assimilation to Matthew (8:28) and Gergesene an attempt at correction by Origen. Of the different locations proposed, the modern Kursi on the eastern shore seems best as the town Gadara is six miles from the lake and Gerasa some forty miles to the southeast in Perea. The man is what a modern doctor would probably decribe as a violent schizophrenic who did not live in a house, notes the highly domesticated Luke. It is interesting to note that Luke takes 284 words to tell the story, whereas Mark with 382 has nearly three times as many as Matthew with 136, who had two demoniacs and an immediate cure (Mk 5:8; Lk 8:39), an indication perhaps that Matthew is summarizing Mark. Luke's summary has more verses than Matthew's. The episode is unusual in that there is a further part after the normal exorcism dealing with a herd of swine and finally the cure and the man receives a mission from Jesus. The demon (Legion, i.e. many demons with the power of an occupying Roman legion) with whom Jesus has an unusual conversation as he tries to apply counter magic to Jesus by using his name, recognizes Jesus as "the Son of God Most High," a common Gentile title for God according to Josephus.[143]

Jesus' command to "come out of the man" is surprisingly not immediately fulfilled (compare v 29 with Mk 5:8). But Jesus saves the man (8:36), i.e. sets him free from his bonds as he had proclaimed in his program (4:18; 8:29). Luke re-emphasizes the man's bondage (v 29f) and he alone tells of the demon's unusual request—not to be sent into the abyss (Mk "out of the country"). The abyss was the prison for demons at the end of time (Apoc 20:1-3; Rom 10:7) but in the Septuagint it is often used for the sea. Swine were unclean animals for the Jews and forbidden as food (Lv 11:7-8; Lk 15:15). Jesus is kind even to the evil spirit but the result of their presence even for swine is disastrous. All three synoptics stress that Jesus is asked to leave the place yet the response of the people is not the unbelief of the Pharisees but one of terror before the unusual power. The man's request to go with Jesus (although a Gentile) is denied yet he is sent to be a missionary at home (see 5:14; 8:56) and the man *obeyed* as Luke notes, an example of his theme of *hearing* Jesus and doing.

Nevertheless, when one has explained this story one is left with the suspicion that it is a story which has developed in the early tradition. Such unusual elements as the 2,000 pigs diving into the lake and the rather tame reaction of the villagers could possibly have been added to an original exorcism story as it was popularly retold in early Christian circles.

Ministry In Galilee 249

(7) Jairus' Daughter and the Woman who
Touched Jesus' Garment (8:40-56):

Jesus returns to find a welcoming crowd. Luke often stresses his popularity with the people in Galilee. They are in fact waiting for Jesus with a request for a healing for Jairus' daughter. Jairus was possibly the organizing official of the synagogue where Jesus had already worked a miracle (4:33-7). The miracle forms a "sandwich" with another miracle for a woman, worked on the way—the sandwich technique is more frequent in Mark.[144] The two stories showing Jesus calm, unhurried but confident with power over sickness and death (as in Jn 11:6 with Lazarus) form an interesting contrast. Both emphasize that faith leads to salvation (8:48,50). Jairus was obviously a public and respected leader in the Jewish community while the woman, due to her affliction, was a social outcast and ceremonially unclean (Lv 15:25ff). Yet Jesus interrupts his more important petitioner who was begging him urgently to concentrate on the less important. Curiously, there is a series of twelves which follow one another here in Luke—the only daughter was about twelve (8:42); the twelve year old hemorrhage (8:43); the Twelve (9:1); twelve baskets (9:17).

While Matthew (135 words) omits six main points found in Mark (316) Luke's (288) account differs only in details, e.g. the only daughter was dying (7:12; 9:38). Luke omits Mark's diminutive "my little daughter" (Mk 5:23). The MSS tradition of v 43 is uncertain but some of the best omit Mark's derogatory remarks that she had suffered much under many doctors and had spent all her money on them (Mk 5:26), simply saying that "she could not be healed by anyone," more in keeping with Dr. Luke (Col 4:14). Luke omits Mk 5:28 but adds to Mark's account Jesus' statement (v 46) "Someone has touched me for I perceive that power has gone out from me." Only a touch[145] was needed to make Jesus unclean (Lv 15:25ff; Num 19:11; Lk 8:54; 5:13). Luke omits Jesus' turning to the crowd and tones down the disciples' reply, making Peter the spokesman.[146] For the woman "proclaiming before all the people," one of Luke's favorite words for apostolic preaching, is used. She is called daughter as the sinner in 7:50; 23:28 and is sent away in peace, no longer isolated from the community due to her uncleanness, as her faith has *saved* her.[147] The same Greek word means both healing and salvation.

Meanwhile, as Jesus delays, word comes not to trouble the Teacher for it seems there is nothing he can do as the child is dead. Jesus again reflects that faith (the opposite of fear) leads to salvation. Jesus has publicized the first miracle but singles out Peter, John and James[148] and the parents who are amazed at what happens. The mourners laugh at Jesus and have not the proper disposition (6:25). Luke translates Mark's Aramaic phrase and he alone notes that "her spirit returned" ("pneuma" is used here but "psyche" in 9:24). To sleep is the New Testament expression for to die (e.g. Ac 7:60). Jesus commanded that she be given something to eat and that they tell no one (Mk "no one should know")—the first occurrence of the so-called Messianic secret in Luke (see 9:21; 8:39; 5:17ff; 7:16).

(8) *The Mission of the Twelve—(9:1-6):*

Jesus has been training his twelve and now they are sent out on a mission of their own. Probably his difficulties with the authorities taught him that the time was short and that it was urgent to spread the good news of the

Ministry In Galilee

kingdom as widely as possible as his instructions indicate (9:3ff). This "trial" run confined to Palestine (24:46ff; Ac 1:8) would prepare the twelve for their future career and would explain to Luke's audience that the many journeys and activities in Acts were continuous with the activity of Jesus himself and his preparation for his disciples (5:10). Luke is unique in that the central part of his gospel, which includes the Feeding of the Crowd, Peter's Profession of Faith, the Transfiguration and Prayer and Passion education for the disciples, is framed by two missions of the disciples (9:1ff; 10:1ff). John does not have Mark's account of Jesus' rejection at Nazareth here as he has already used it (Mk 6:1-6; Lk 4:16-30), but parallels Mark's account of the mission rather closely. He omits Mark's "two by two" here (see 10:1) and agrees with Matthew, unlike Mark, on the prohibition of a staff (Mt 10:10; Mk 6:8; Lk 9:3). In Luke the apostles are given "power" over evil, like Jesus himself (4:36; 8:46) and are sent to preach the presence of "the kingdom of God"[149] and "to heal," thus showing that Acts is clearly a continuation of what Jesus had begun.[150] Nothing is told of the actual course of the mission. The emphasis lies on Jesus' instructions, the empowering of the disciples, their preaching of the good news of the kingdom, and the minimum of possessions which they carry with them.

Jesus' instructions demand a radical dependence on God, not on possessions and the preparation which a normal traveller would do. The differences between the various synoptic accounts are not important. Note Luke has John's advice about the two coats here (3:11). The instructions are for this one urgent journey through the villages "everywhere." They will be changed later (22:36,49; Ex 12). Like the Levites of old they were entitled to live off the people's generosity (Nm 18:31; 1 Cor 9:7-18) and should be content, not moving from house to house nor overpressing their message of good news (Mk "repentance"), but shaking off the dust and moving elsewhere if not received—for Jews even foreign dust was unclean and to be shaken off when coming on pilgrimage (10:11; Mt 18:17; Ac 13:51).

(9) *Herod's Anxiety—(9:7-9):*

As in Mark, the mission and return of the twelve form a "sandwich" around Herod's anxiety as to the identity of Jesus, due probably to the widespread activity just reported. Luke however greatly abbreviates Mark's version and omitting Mark 6:17-29, only directly tells of the death of John who was alive in 7:18. Luke alone adds that Herod (Antipas) whom he correctly describes as tetrarch (3:19; 9:7; Mark:king) was "perplexed" and "sought to *see*" Jesus: "That fox" (13:31f) would actually see Jesus at his trial (23:6-12). In Mark, Herod himself thinks that John is risen but in Luke Herod is much more cold blooded. While the people think Jesus is either a resurrected John or Elijah or one of the ancient prophets,[151] Herod bluntly explains that Jesus cannot be John whom he beheaded. Herod's curiosity to see Jesus is not the faith needed to really see Jesus and enter the kingdom (9:27; 11:29f; 13:35,31; 19:4).

(10) *The Return of the Twelve—The Feeding of the Five Thousand (9:10-17):*

The Apostles, as Luke calls them here (6:13; 22:14), report back to Jesus. However, without giving the actual report apart from his mention of the unrest caused even in Herod's court, Luke tells us Jesus withdrew with them to a desert place (9:12)s near Bethsaida, which is one of the few places named by Luke (Mk 6:45). Perhaps he thinks that his audience will know that Bethsaida was outside Herod's territory and that Jesus is avoiding Herod's intentions to see him (9:9; 13:33). Matthew alone connects Jesus' departure with John's execution (Mt 14:13, John says that Passover was near Jn 6:4). Bethsaida (Julia after Augustus' daughter), actually in the territory of Philip (3:1) who had rebuilt it, was northeast of Lake Galilee and the birthplace of Peter and Andrew (Jn 1:44). The crowd follow and Luke alone notes Jesus' welcome and his twofold activity of preaching the kingdom and healing as he had instructed the twelve (9:2).

Next we find the Feeding of the Five Thousand which is the only miracle story which all four evangelists recite. However, none of th six versions in the four gospels say that Jesus multiplied the loaves. One should note for example that in Luke, who only slightly abbreviates Mark, the typical description of the people's amazement is not found. The episode which forms the climax of Jesus' Galilean ministry (henceforth Jesus will concentrate on the disciples though not exclusively), has a deep theological significance. Jesus had clearly turned down the mere production of bread in the temptation scene (4:1-11). There is a rich background in the feeding of Israel, likewise in the *desert* with manna (Ex 16:12-15)—possibly the numbers have significance, the five thousand, the perfection of Israel (Ac 4:4), the twelve baskets, the abundance of Jesus' feeding which would be adequate for the future feeding of Israel from the sea (Num 11:22,32).

The feeding of the crowd also recalls Elisha's provision for a hundred men (2 K 4:42-4), see v 42. The Jews had expected a great messianic banquet with the banishing of hunger[152] and here we have a symbolic banquet, an enacted parable of the arrival of the Messianic age as Peter would confess. The dialogue emphasizes the inability of the disciples to deal with the people's situation due to their limited faith and resources without Jesus as in the scene after the Transfiguration. The account is closely linked in the gospels with Jesus' passion prediction and especially with the Eucharistic scenes.[153] The Greek word for the fragments which filled twelve baskets (Klasmata) was used in the early church as a kind of technical word for the broken parts of the Eucharist.

(11) Peter's Profession of Faith—(9:18-21):

In Mark this episode is the watershed of his gospel, the climax of his first part and the introduction to the second. Luke's gospel is not so simply divided into two, the scene is presented immediately after his one great feeding, thus offering an unusual parallel to John's gospel (Jn 6:67-71, note how he skips from Mark 6:44 to 8:27). Nevertheless, it serves Luke well as a climax to Jesus' Galilean ministry and the various responses[154] which it evoked while also a preparation for both Jesus' passion and resurrection prediction and the transfiguration scene. It is the only time in the synoptics where Jesus shows an interest in what people think of him.

Luke does not indicate the Gentile setting of the scene (Caesarea Philippi), but notes, as on significant occasions that Jesus was praying alone when he began the dialogue to elicit a personal response from his disciples. The three answers, all *old* dead characters (Luke has *old* prophets), are basically the same as the reports which Herod received (9:18). There is no mention that Jesus was recognized publicly as a Messiah, obviously more than a prophet. Peter is the first of Jesus' followers to identify him as God's Messiah, an Old Testament expression (1 S 24:7,11;

26:9) and a title connected with Isaiah's prophecy,[155] whose coming was a basic element of popular Jewish belief at the time. Though both a political and spiritual savior (not necessarily a transcendent figure however), his purpose would be to bring to Israel and the world the definitive kingdom or ideal rule of Yahweh himself.

An interesting, almost contemporary (c B.C. 50-30 from its political allusions) description of Jewish Messianic hopes is found in the seventeenth Psalm of Solomon, a Pharisaical production. Its emphasis is primarily political as they considered it an insult to God himself that his land was under Roman domination. Yet it also speaks of religious activity—the expulsion of sinners, the rebuking of the proud, the restoration of Israel's glory—

> "Behold, O Lord and raise up for them their king, the Son of David,
> ready for the time which thou, O God, choosest for him
> to begin his reign over Israel thy servant,
> And gird him with strength to shatter unrighteous rulers,
> And to purge Jerusalem from Gentiles that trample her down to destruction."

In Luke the title Messiah is found in the infancy narrative (2:11,26), in the mouth of demons (4:41) and of Jesus himself (23:2) also in the Jewish leaders' jeers (23:36).[156] The word of Peter's confession differ slightly in all three synoptics but all three agree that Peter called him the Messiah. As in Mark and unlike Matthew, Jesus does not praise Peter or refuse the title but strictly commands silence (8:56) and goes on to use a different title "the Son of Man" and to talk of suffering—thus it seems that Peter's insight was incomplete and probably over political. In the next scene, the transfiguration, the full revelation of Jesus as God's son and Chosen One will be made to Peter by God himself.

(12) *Jesus' First Passion and Resurrection Prediction—(9:22):*

Luke, in respect to the apostles, omits the rebuke to Peter as well as Peter's attempt to dissuade Jesus from his suffering service (Mk 8:27-33). Jesus, for the first time, explains how the Messiah's kingdom will come. The word "must" recalls that Yahweh's plan and purpose included suffering as told in the Old Testament.[157] From now on the shadow of Jerusalem hangs over Jesus' ministry but only after his hour (22:53) of death and resurrection would the disciples really understand what he was saying[158] and therefore be able to publicly proclaim it (Ac 2:14-36). In Daniel 7:13ff, the Son of Man who personifies both Israel and the saints of the Most High, must suffer at the hands of others but God's reign triumphs. Hitherto in Luke the Son of Man is associated only with power and glory. He will suffer death at the hands of the Sanhedrin, whose three categories are mentioned (20:1) but be raised on the third day, i.e. shortly afterwards, as the expression means in Hos 6:2; Gn 40:13; Jdg 19:4. Mark has "after three days."

(13) *The Conditions of Discipleship—(9:23-7):*

With the absence of the rebuke to Peter found in both Matthew and Mark the sayings about the conditions for true discipleship addressed in Luke to *all*, lose some of their harshness. All disciples must follow the way of Jesus in his suffering: If you wish (freedom) . . . deny your very self (the same word is used of Peter's denial of Jesus), i.e. to die to self-centeredness . . . *take up* your cross each day—Luke adds this, stressing the daily struggle of the Christian.[159]

Ministry In Galilee

But the way is not just a negative way of self-denial. It is noteworthy that this is the only place in the New Testament where the idea of self-denial actually occurs. Paul, of course, speaks of dying to self and sin but here it has the positive purpose of taking up the suffering of the world and following Jesus and his way.[160] The image, a familiar one to Galileans,[161] was of a condemned person carrying his own cross to the place of crucifixion. Although such descriptions of the cross in the synoptics must have been influenced by the actual events of Jesus' passion, there is no difficulty in saying that Jesus could have actually used this image. It was considered by Romans, Greeks and Jews as the most debased and cruel form of execution. Its metaphorical use was mainly Christian although we do find some other examples, e.g. Gen R 56, which describes Isaac carrying the wood (Gn 22:6) like one carrying his cross on his shoulders. Plato, in his Republic (366A) speaks of the crucifixion of the just. The following paradoxes in Luke expand the symbol of the cross for the Christian life. To lose one's life (soul) for Jesus' sake is really to save it (i.e. not to escape the Roman persecution in Luke's time). This important antithetical statement is found 6 times and in all four gospels.[162] It has been described by A.E. Housman (not a believer) as "the most important truth which has ever been uttered and the greatest discovery ever made in the moral world." However, there is a similarity with Buddha's famous parable of fire where everything is burning with desire and whose point is that it does no good to try and satisfy desire as it simply adds fuel to the fire. What real profit does a man gain if he destroys (Luke adds this word) or ruins himself.

In v 26 we have a typically indirect statement of Jesus that a man's personal loyalty and acceptance of Jesus *and his words* (on suffering) will determine his relation with the Son of Man when he comes *in his own glory* (6:22f;

13:25f). Luke emphasizes *his own* glory as distinct from that of the Father and omits Mark's reference to "this adulterous and sinful generation." The next verse, 27, has been much disputed among commentators as to what future coming of Jesus' kingdom it refers. (Jn 3:3; Wis 10:10). It is already of course present with power in Jesus. Luke omits Mark's final words "come in power." Does it mean that the suffering of some will not begin until after the resurrection? Pentecost? Probably it refers to the vision of "some' ' in the next episode, the Transfiguration, or possibly the destruction of Jerusalem? or the second coming? As it stands in the text, it is to be understood as an exhortation to constancy in discipleship.

(14) *The Transfiguration—(9:28-36):*

In all three synoptics the transfiguration is a climax to the week of the confession episode and, unusually for them, there is a chronological connection. Mark and Matthew have "after six days" (Ex 24:15f). Luke perhaps precisely, or using the term for a Roman week or possibly indicating the first day of the week, the day of the resurrection, has "about eight days after saying this." All three agree on the basic elements: Jesus going up the mountain with the inner three; his luminous transformation; the appearance of Moses (first in Luke) and Elijah; the words of the confused Peter; the theophany in the cloud; the words addressed to the disciples to listen to Jesus, "Jesus only"; the silence imposed on the disciples. Here we find a profound revelation from God himself as to who Jesus is, a question which was partially answered by the great feeding scene and by Peter. It both looks back to the baptismal voice and anticipates his future passion and paschal glory just referred to (9:26).

Ministry In Galilee 259

Such a profound experience could only be described in Luke's typical picture language or myth, as it also can be called to express, not a story which is untrue, but one which endeavors to capture the inexpressible in a material portrait. None of the more rationalistic interpretations of this scene, e.g. a displaced post-resurrection "mystical" ' scene, a parable of spiritual realities, a hazy sunrise and half sleepy disciples, adequately explain this unique scene which is quite different from any other in the gospels and was considered historical in the early church (2 Pet 1:16-18). It taught clearly the unity between true glory and suffering in the Christian, showing that in Jesus' life (Ac 7:56) suffering is the necessary path in God's decree to true glory (24:26; Ac 7:56). Also it is both preceded and followed by references to Jesus' suffering in Jerusalem.

Its importance for Luke is seen in the many details which he alone tells and the fact that untypically, his account is somewhat longer than Mark's even though he has omitted the question about Elijah (Mk 9:9-13). In Luke, as one would expect, it takes place while Jesus was actually praying, a similar scene to the Mount of Olives, where there was also a heavenly apparition and the disciples were asleep. The (high) mountain here (Hermon hear Caesarea Philippi? or possibly Tabor near the following episodes), is a traditional place for revelation. Here, John comes before James, a Johannine tradition. Luke does not speak of transfiguration (lit metamorphose) as the other synoptics do, as it possibly is too reminiscent of Hellenistic deities and literature and also avoids Mark's garments "white as no fuller on the earth could bleach them." He speaks of his face changing in appearance and his clothes dazzling white[163] and his glory. This description would recall Moses on Mt. Sinai—he also heard a voice from the cloud. But he reflected God's glory whereas Jesus' glory, a divine symbol, was his own.[164] Similar luminous transformations are recorded of various saints.

Moses and Elijah (the Law and the Prophets) appear in glory (Lk) talking with Jesus (24:4; Ac 1:10), and the subject of their conversation, though not in words, is given in Luke alone. Both had met God on the mountain, suffered greatly (Ac 7:17-44; 1 K 19:10) and tradition had spoken of them, especially Elijah, being taken up to heaven. Both were closely associated with the hope of Israel (Ac 3:22; Mal 3:1; 4:5; Deut 18:5). In Rabbinic tradition they arrived together at the end of time.

They discussed Jesus "exodus" (Greek) which he would "fulfill" (a favorite word in Luke) in Jerusalem. Note how in Ac 13:24 Jesus' "eisodos" or coming into the world is described. Thus the Old Testament Exodus is a type, an anticipation of the New Exodus which Jesus will lead (Ac 3:15; 5:31; Heb 11:22) to deliver God's people, according to God's plan—forty days before his ascension. The word "exodus" is also a euphemism for death (2 Pet 1:15; Wis 3:2; 7:6). Jesus is the fulfillment of the Law and the Prophets, the hope of Israel. Peter and those with him are in a deep sleep (like Adam) and on awakening, see Jesus' glory (2:9; Jn 1:14). Peter addresses Jesus (Epistata, Master) as they are leaving and in confusion and fear, probably of losing Jesus, stammers (in all three versions), how good it is to be there and that they should make three tents for the three glorious figures—an attempt to prolong the wonderful moment, just as the desert tent contained the glory of God or perhaps an allusion to Zech 14:16-19; Lv 23:42; Jn 7:2ff, where the feast of tents, a reminder to the Jews of the Exodus, is seen as symbolic of the future when

Ministry In Galilee

all the Gentiles will come to Jerusalem. For Peter, the messianic time has arrived (Apoc 21:3). But it is the cloud, the Exodus symbol of God's presence, which was expected again in the last days (not Peter's tents), which overshadowed the three.[165] The reaction of the disciples is natural fear in the presence of the divine. The voice (at the baptism 3:22) describes Jesus as God's Son (in the best MSS as his Chosen One[166])—"Listen to him"—there is no further need for tents.[167]

This is the climax of the episode. Jesus is the New Moses, the prophet like Moses, the fulfillment of their hopes, of all that Moses and Elijah stood for, the one to be listened to (Dt 18:15). Finally, there is Jesus alone (Phil 2:6). Luke does not have the conversation in Mark 9:1-13 about John and Elijah nor the command to silence. He simply states that they told no one in those days—their real understanding will be emphasized in 9:45.

(15) *The Cure of the Boy with the Unclean Spirit—(9:37-43a):*

Moses came down from the mountain to find the crowd confused and unbelieving.[168] Similarly, Jesus, in the first of four incidents which describe in turn the lack of faith, of understanding, the pride and intolerance of the disciples. Thus Luke concludes his Galilean ministry. Mark, in the story of the epileptic boy (9:14-29) gives a detailed description of the boy's condition and Jesus' conquest of the demon, and draws the conclusion about the necessity of prayer. In Matthew it is a lesson about the disciples' need for faith (Mt 17:14-21). Luke considerably abbreviates Mark's version, omitting much of Mark's detail about the disease and surprisingly, the reference to the need for prayer (Mk 9:28-9), probably out of a reverence for the disciples' reputation. Luke's purpose is to emphasize v 41—Jesus' urgent "how long," which echoes God's impatience with Israel (Dt 32:5,20) as he omits Mark's address to the Father "All things are possible to him who believes . . . " (Mk 9:23f; Lk 9:45).

Luke adds such human Lucan touches as "the only son" (l7:12; 8:42), "he gave him back to his father" (7:15; 1 K 17:23), and gives a different ending, describing how the onlookers "marvelled at the greatness of God" (11:14), the power which Jesus had but not yet his disciples. Luke's phrase (v 38) where the father asks the teacher (didaskale) "to look upon" his son is probably a technical phrase for a doctor's examination of a patient and in general his description of the epileptic symptoms can be described as more professional than Mark's. Jesus' "rebuking and healing" is seen by the great crowd in Luke, unlike Mark, as a manifestation of the greatness of God. In Luke this reaction of the crowd is different quite often from that of their leaders.

(16) *Jesus' Second Passion Prediction—(9:43b-45):*

Unlike Mark, Luke closely connects this second Passion prediction with the foregoing—it took place in the midst of the amazement of all but is addressed to the disciples (v 43b) to bring them down to hard reality lest they get carried away by the superficial wonder of the crowds. Luke does not have Mark's remark that Jesus returned to Galilee as he had never pointed out clearly that Jesus had left it. The announcement of Jesus is made with a very Semitic introduction (lit) "Place you into your ears these words" (Ex 17:14), i.e. pay close attention. There is no mention of the resurrection as in Mark and in Luke

Ministry In Galilee 263

9:22, but here he concentrates on Jesus being handed over (Is 53:12), the aspect of suffering. Mark says they did not understand and were afraid to ask—a very human reaction to the mystery of human suffering heightened by Peter's previous rebuke. For Luke, suffering is mysterious although he accepts it as part of the Father's plan. Luke excuses the disciples and suggests a reason "it was concealed from them so that they should not perceive it." Understanding only comes with the resurrection (18:34; 22:14ff; 24:6ff). To understand is a gift (8:10).

(17) *The Dispute about Greatness—Tolerance—(9:46-50):*

In Luke, the disciples' subsequent behavior (to the special treatment of the inner three) shows their lack of understanding of Jesus (rare in Luke), as they quarrel about prestige and precedence in the coming kingdom. He omits Mark's reference to Capernaum (only Jerusalem will be mentioned from now on) and also Jesus' question about the dispute on the way as he knew their thoughts. In Matthew, it forms part of his ecclesiastical discourse (Mt 18:1-35). Luke probably is also dealing with some misconceptions in his community teaching them that true Christian greatness lies not in seeking praise or power but in caring for the insignificant, the helpless, the unimportant, like a child without rights in society (1 Cor 1:27). Jesus, as in the Magnificat and the Beatitudes, reverses again the values of society. There are two ideas here, the great (not the greatest) is the lowly and to receive the lowly is to receive not only Jesus, but "the Father" who sent him. Another example of the disciples' pride and self importance is their attitude towards the exorcist who is using Jesus' name (remember their own recent failure 9:40), yet does not belong to the official group (probably a problem in the Lucan Church).[169] The lesson for Luke, who again abbreviates Mark here, is that allegiance to Jesus is the all important thing and that such people are to be seen as friends, not enemies. The final line makes a paradox with 11:23, a contrary statement which, however, is applied to a different situation. Here the lesson is tolerance for those who are not against *you* (v 49). Thus there is no contradiction with 11:23 where Luke has "with me." Allegiance to Jesus is all important and typically Jesus excludes the neutral position, yet encourages tolerance (6:43f) as the following episode will show.

Thus concludes the Galilean Mission of Jesus as he shows forth the mystery of himself and the messiahship. Despite the disciples' lack of faith and perception, their self-centered ambition and even intolerance, they begin to have their eyes opened and to see more than either the crowds who stand in amazement, or the hostile leaders. More teaching is needed before Jesus finishes his work in Jerusalem with his passion and resurrection.

6. A TEACHING JOURNEY TO JERUSALEM (9:51-19:44)

Here we come to what has been described as one of the great riddles of gospel study. It contains almost half Jesus' public ministry with a tremendous variety of juxtaposed sayings, controversies, parables, miracles, discourses, incidents against the obviously artificial background of a journey to Jerusalem. The emphasis is on the teaching of Jesus yet there is no clear structure upon which scholars are agreed.[1] Something similar of course was the case with the variety of material which Luke included in his Galilean ministry. Perhaps the search for too structured and organized a plan is for something which was never part of Luke's orderly account. Mark, in decribing this decisive journey to Jerusalem (his "Perean ministry"), is content with one chapter and Matthew with two, but Luke takes about ten for what becomes in fact a series of journeys. In Luke certain short editorial remarks give the whole the appearance of a journey and enable us to divide it into three sections—

9:51 ". . . he firmly resolved to proceed toward Jerusalem."
13:22: "He went through cities and towns teaching and making his way towards Jerusalem."
17:11: "On his journey to Jerusalem he passed along the borders of Samaria and Galilee."
19:29: "Having spoken thus he went ahead with his ascent to Jerusalem."

This section ends best at 19:44 as the journeys after that fall within Jesus' Jerusalem ministry (19:46,8) and the previous ones are the resumption of the great journey to Jerusalem (19:11,18,41). This conveniently divides the ten chapters into three—

Stage A: — (9:51-13:21) — Samaritan refusal — the Seventy Two — Sayings — Controversies — Parables — a Miracle (13:10-17).

Stage B: — (13:22-17:10) — Sayings — Controversies — Parables — A Miracle (14:1-6).

Stage C: — (17:11-19:44) — Two Miracles — Discourses — Parables — Sayings — Zaccheus — Entry.

Here Luke abandons Mark who has probably been his chief source since chapter three and does not resume following Mark until 18:15 (Jesus and the children, Mk 10:13). Only three sections are in common with Mark: the lawyers' question, the Beelzebul controversy and the Mustard Seed Parable. Therefore, this section can be described as a combination of Q which Luke shares with Matthew and especially "L," Luke's special tradition, which is characterized by a number of familiar and striking parables and some short sayings. The content is didactic and Jesus is presented as the teacher of his disciples, the new community, with some twenty parables, with many sayings and stories about discipleship[2] and as a debater with his critics' controversies (11:14ff; 13:10ff; 14:1ff) and polemics against his opponents are found here.[3] After the high point of his revelation at the Transfiguration, Jesus is now clearly the Messiah and his salvation is present but a decision and commitment are required to recognize the signs of the times (12:54ff), to enter by the narrow door (13:22,30), to answer the invitation to the Messiah's Banquet (14:15-25). Thus the journey, "the Way" has ecclesial, ethical and parenetic characteristics as Jesus educates his disciples into the cost and way of discipleship and forms them into his community which is characterized by perseverance, ceaseless prayer, a sense of love and sharing.

Here we see Luke, the creative writer giving his own peculiar stamp, his theology of the way of the Lord, on the material available to him. Many of Luke's distinct emphases are here, the universalism of the gospel (the Samaritans), men and women, outcasts, the joy of the kingdom, the final coming ("speedily but not immediately"). Thus, while the sense of real progress in the journey (Galilee, Samaria, Bethany, Jericho; 10:38; 17:11) is rather vague, attention on Jerusalem as the goal is emphasized.[4] Since the Transfiguration it has been specified as the place of Jesus' suffering, and now the final journey begins. It should be remembered that the homeless Jesus (9:58) has been journeying constantly since 4:42. Now it is Jerusalem which makes the difference. The previous section closed with Jesus' interpretation of his mission and that of his disciples as suffering service and now Jesus goes to Jerusalem to perform his great example of suffering service. There are few time indications and they are quite general.[5]

In general, it is a rambling journey around central Palestine and at 17:11 Jesus is no nearer Jerusalem than at the beginning. Yet all other topographical references are omitted (9:56; 10:1,38; 11:1). The way to Jerusalem has both symbolic and theological meaning for Luke. It is the center of his gospel, the place of Jesus' suffering, resurrection (no appearances outside Jerusalem are recorded by

Luke) and ascension, his theological goal since "no prophet" can be allowed to die anywhere except in Jerusalem 13:33, and on the way Jesus explains what is required of his disciples as they follow him. Jesus is preparing his disciples to carry on his mission after his death (9:60; 10:3,16; 17:22ff).

A useful thematic analysis is given by John Drury of Luke's creation here which he describes as—

"a single tract of teaching relieved by frequent and various narrative settings and enlivened by stories peculiar to Luke . . . which add so much vivacity, movement and body to the whole" . . . "First things are put first by beginning with calls to discipleship. Last things are put last by a conclusion which teaches the coming of the kingdom and judgment. Hopes are thus raised that the intervening material is also in an historical order, and the hopes are fulfilled. The call of the disciples is followed by their successful mission, the basic things of the disciples' life are illustrated by the Good Samaritan loving his neighbor and Mark's love of God developing into teaching about prayer. Then with its historical and spiritual basis established, the Beelzebub controversy brings the kingdom up against its enemies; a confrontation which is seen as an opposition of sound perception against the perverted and superficial vision of the Jewish leaders who are castigated in the woes which follow and prophecy the doom of the Jewish nation, rooted in its failure to see or react positively to the crisis. Luke shows the disciples' role in this world of dispute: trust, readiness, faithfulness and a clear head. From this fundamental contrast emerges the major theme of the historical problem of the Jewish nation, which comes into the open again at Luke 13:5ff and gets covert dramatic treatment in the healings of the bent woman and the dropsical man, both polemically set on the Sabbath day, and the parable of the Supper. The moral stories of the Prodigal Son and the Unjust Steward exemplify by contrast the positive reaction to crisis which the nation lacks. Judgment concludes the whole. The

A Teaching Journey To Jerusalem

history of the beginning of Christianity thus underpins and shapes the whole section. The Church is called, sent, established, flung into controversy with the opposition, contrasted with the ancient people of God, and the whole story pointed towards judgment. Central to it all is Luke's grand theme of the passing of religious initiative and authority from Israel to the Christian Church."[6]

STAGE A — 9:51-13:21

(1)	A Samaritan Village refuses to Receive Jesus	9:51-6.
(2)	Would-be-Followers of Jesus	9:57-62.
(3)	The Mission of the Seventy Two	10:1-24.
(4)	The Good Samaritan	10:25-37.
(5)	Visiting Martha and Mary	10:38-42.
(6)	Teaching about Prayer	11:1-13.
(7)	Opposition and Temptation for Jesus	11:14-36.
(8)	The Hypocrisy of the Pharisees and Lawyers	11:37-52.
(9)	Courage under Persecution	12:1-12.
(10)	The Rich Fool	12:13-21.
(11)	Trust in Providence	12:22-34.
(12)	Vigilance for the Master's Return	12:35-48.
(13)	The Mission of Jesus	12:49-53.
(14)	Discerning the Signs of the Times	12:54-9.
(15)	A Call to Repentance—The Fig Tree	13:1-9.
(16)	The Bent Woman on the Sabbath	13:10-17.
(17)	Ultimate Success — Parables of the Mustard Seed and the Leaven	13:18-21.

(1) *A Samaritan Village Refuses to receive Jesus—(9:51-6):*

As Jesus began his Galilean ministry with a reference to Elijah and with rejection (4:16-30) so also Luke alone and somewhat ominously, describes Jesus' very solemn determined beginning of his journey to Jerusalem with an allusion to Elijah, who called down fire from heaven to consume Ahaziah's soldiers (2 K 1:9-15; Si 48:1-14) and a rejection scene. Jesus' single-minded determination to do the Father's will contrasts with the "would-be-disciples" of 9:57-62. The failures even of Jesus himself are openly acknowledged as a warning and a consolation to Luke's community who must have been concerned with the rejection of Jesus by many Jews. Twice we are told (9:51,53) in Septuagint style (Jer 21:10; Is 50:7)[7] that Jesus "set his face," that he was heading with determination towards Jerusalem. Now the time of his "assumption" was at hand. This is the only use of the noun in the Bible but the verb was used by Luke for the ascension (Ac 1:2,11,22) and was already used in the Old Testament times for the assumption of Elijah,[8] of the Suffering Servant (Is 42:1), Enoch (Sir 49:14) and even of the mysterious death of Moses himself (i.e. the first century A.D. work, The Assumption of Moses; see Joel 9). It recalls the "exodus" of the transfiguration story and is equivalent to the "glorified" or "raised up" of John's gospel (Jn 3:14ff; 8:28; 12:33-4). It signifies the complex of events especially from Jesus' passion to his ascension, his journey to the Father.

Like Moses, Jesus sends messengers before his face (Ex 23:20). But, unlike Elijah, Jesus refuses to call down fire at the request of the Sons of Thunder (Mk 3:17) on the Samaritan Village which refuses to receive him (2 K 1:10; Sir 48:1-4). Only Luke tells of this hostile encounter with Samaritans although John has a favorable episode at the well of Sychar (Jn 4:44ff). The hostility between the Jews and the half pagan Samaritans, who worshipped on Mount Gerizem (Dt 12), was proverbial.[9] The Samaritans were especially hostile to anyone going to worship in Jerusalem as Josephus, the Jewish historian from Galilee, tells us. The point of the story is that the disciples misunderstood the nature of Jesus' suffering and rejected but nonviolent service, and see Jesus as an Elijah type of Messiah as John the Baptist had expected (Lk 7:19; 12:49f).

Jesus rebuked his revengeful disciples as he had dealt with the devils (4:35; 8:24; 9:42) and did not reject the Samaritans in return but rather gave an example of discipleship, of loving his enemies (6:27; 23:24) and moving to another village (9:5; 10:10). The expanded text here v 56[10] found in many ancient manuscripts (like the scribal addition "As Elijah did" to 9:54; also "You do not know of what spirit you are" to 9:55) makes good sense in the text and in fact it is more difficult to explain its omission than its inclusion. Soon, however, Luke will tell of model Samaritans (10:30-7; 17:11-19) and warn the Jewish cities of their own coming disaster. Samaria will be emphasized in Acts 1:8 and will be a fruitful mission in Acts 8:4ff.

(2) *Would-be-Followers of Jesus—(9:57-62):*

These three scenes about "following" Jesus on his Exodus journey continue the reflection on Christian discipleship. Of the three proverbial sayings given Matthew also has the first two earlier in the Galilean ministry (Mt 8:18-22) but only Luke has the third. The emphasis in all three is not so much on the disciple, about whom little is told (the first and the third are volunteers, the second is called by Jesus) as on the teaching, the sayings of Jesus which are recorded. All emphasize the urgency, the immediacy and the absolute, "all or nothingness" of discipleship which the would-be-disciple, in imitation of Jesus, must bluntly face even though it conflicts with many of his important loyalties.

The first, an emotional enthusiast (a Scribe Mt 8:19), is reminded honestly and bluntly that Jesus (and a disciple) has nowhere to call his own, no home, no security (9:23f "must deny himself . . . "). The second, who is called by Jesus, wants to bury his father first, like Abraham at Haran. Whether the father is actually dead or not is not made clear. Jesus is not denying the importance of family ties (18:20; Mt 15:3-6; Tb 4:3; 6:15) but indicating the priority of preaching the Kingdom (Luke). All other loyalties can be left to those who are (spiritually) dead to Jesus' call (14:25f; 15:32)—a proverb which seems at first sight ridiculous. The third, a volunteer, requests (not unreasonably as 5:29) permission from "the Lord" to take leave of his family just as Elisha, who was ploughing, received from Elijah (1 K 19:19-21). He is refused. Ploughs in Palestine had only one handle and required total concentration to go straight in the hard earth. Sacrifice and total dedication are essential to discipleship. All three stress the same message basically of the sacrifice, particularly of home—leaving without saying goodbye, the undivided loyalty required (14:26-33; 2 Tim 2:4). It should be noticed that in the call scenes in the gospels there is no mention of rewards but only of the cost of discipleship (Mk 1:16-20; 2:13-14; Mt 8:18-22).

(3) *The Mission of the Seventy Two—(10:1-24):*

Thirty six teams of two, urgently going ahead of Jesus to every town and place he intended going to visit, reads like a modern presidential campaign. Though it is a blitz mission on a much grander scale than is usually associated with Jesus, yet it provides perhaps a more reasonable background for his cleansing of the Temple and his crucifixion than is usually imagined. The possibility that the episode is a symbolic Lucan creation is a continuing debate among critics, as only Luke describes this new mission of the fur-

A Teaching Journey To Jerusalem

ther seventy two (9:1,51). After a description of the initial mission which emphasizes its instructions (10:1-12) he gives a series of woes on such towns as Chorozin, Bethsaida and Capernaum with their unbelief (v 13-16). Finally there is a joyful reflection on the return of the seventy two, the conquest of evil and the privilege of Christian knowledge (v 17-24).

The number is given as seventy two in such MSS as P 75, P 45, B? D, but an almost equal number of MSS have seventy. However, this does not affect the symbolism which many commentators find here since the Jewish tradition, about 70/72 also oscillates between the two.[11] The symbolism, if here, that is normally stressed is that the selection of the seventy two symbolizes the future Gentile mission by the number of the Gentile nations (Ac 1:8), as the number twelve symbolized the mission of Israel and the creation of a new Israel. As in Acts, the missionaries go two by two, e.g. Peter and John in Acts 8:14; Paul and Barnabas in Acts 13; Paul and Silas in Acts 15:40. However, Luke's main interest is clearly in the defeat of the powers of evil (10:18-20), in the fall of Satan, the prince of demons (Is 14:12), like lightening from a height (heaven) and the fact that the disciples should rejoice that their names are written in heaven (v 17-20). The phrase "from heaven" is best taken with "lightning" signifying the sudden and swift fall of Satan but not actually from heaven.

Almost every detail of the instructions given by the Lord himself describing (7:13) this urgent mission, are found in his previous instructions to the twelve (9:1-5) or in Matthew's missionary discourse in 10:7-16. In Matthew also, the message is a proclamation of the kingdom but Luke does not have his "Go nowhere among the Gentiles and enter no Samaritan town . . " (10:5; also 7:5 is missing in Luke). A note of urgency, not found in 9:1-6, is given by the insruction not to waste time on the elaborate salutations, typical of the East (2 K 4:29), as also not to waste time on those who do not welcome them, or to move from house to house. They are not to worry whether food is clean or unclean (10:7; 1 Cor 10:27; Ac 10:25), or about receiving meals free as they deserve their wages,[12] unlike the Rabbis who taught gratuitously. No (spare) sandals, no beggar's bag—they would be poor dependent missionaries (10:4). This entirely negative list seems to deny even the basic equipment for a journey (22:35ff). They are to cure the sick and their message is peace (10:5; 1:79; 2:14ff), the reign of God is near. Luke's only use of this phrase does not mean that a future reality is chronologically near but that Jesus is near and he is the kingdom and is present (17:21). God's harvest is ready and so urgent that they should pray that the Lord will send more workers.[13] No force is to be used but they are to be like helpless lambs among dangerous wolves (Ac 20:29; Is 11:6; 53:7). The result will be Peace or eventual disaster.

Here Luke has a reflection on the refusal, the unbelief of the cities on Lake Galilee, using the historical example of the destruction of the wicked city of Sodom (Gn 19) as a warning of the future punishment—on "that day" i.e. judgment (21:34; Mt 7:22; 2 Thes 1:10). Curiously, no ministry of Jesus at Chorazin is mentioned in the gospels but it was close to Bethsaida and Capernaum on the northeastern shore of Lake Galilee. All three are uninhabited today. Sodom did not have their opportunities for repentance. Likewise, the Gentile commercial cities of Tyre and Sidon (4:26; 6:17) would have repented long ago if they had seen his miracles (Am 1:9ff; Is 23; Ezek 26-28). The important statement for Luke's church is that he who hears or rejects you, hears and rejects not just "me but him who sent me" (v 16). Capernaum, where Jesus was so popular, in contrast with Nazareth (4:21ff), receives the strongest condemnation in language which recalls the condemnation of arrogant cities of the past (e.g. Is 14:13f; Ezek 26:20; 28:6f)—to Hades or Sheol, the realm of the dead (v 15). "Capernaum did you think that because I visited you, you would be raised up to heaven?" is perhaps the implication of the question (10:15).

But the present mission is a highly successful one. Despite failures, the seed is producing the hundredfold. Not only Satan but all his forces which enslave man[14] are given into their power, "in your name," and as the Magnificat predicted (1:52) deposed from the heights. But the disciples are reminded that the important thing for them is not the working of wonders but the fact that *they themselves* already share in God's kingdom, that they have the knowledge of the Father revealed to them (not the powerful, learned or clever, but mere children) for which the great men of faith of the past have longed.[15]

The conquest of evil leads Jesus to rejoice in the Holy Spirit (a unique phrase) and to praise the Father. The Rabbis actually had a phrase which said: "Where the Spirit is, there is the kingdom."[16] Jesus' joy is the Father's will, his love for the little ones. Here we have one of Luke's most important christological statements (v 21-4, see also v 16, 19) which has the rhythm of Hebrew poetry and because of its similarity to the statements on Jesus' unique sonship so common in John's gospel (Jn 3:35; 6:46; 14:9; 17:10), has been described as "a meteorite from the Johannine heaven."

The section in Luke consists of a prayer of praise (v 21-22) concluding in a private beatitude to the fortunate disciples (v 23-4). Jesus is the Son as we heard in the Transfiguration (9:35) and it is through him alone that knowledge of the Father is given, knowledge of how he is fulfilling the Old Testament, the hope of Israel in Jesus' teaching and works. Jesus is here claiming to uniquely announce God's will because of his exclusive relationship as Son—the absolute use of the Son here is typical of John's gospel (Jn 10:15; 17:2; Mk 13:32) and knowledge is also used with the Johannine meaning of an interpersonal commitment and relationship.

Claude Montefiore, a well known Jewish commentator, has remarked that he would like to prove these words of Jesus spurious, because if it could be proved that Jesus really spoke them, then orthodox Christianity would receive notable encouragement.[17] Curiously, the hymn to the Son of Pharoah Akhenaten has a similar line "No one knows thee except thy Son Akhenaten." Some suggest that here is a "declaration of war" on Qumran and such teachers like the Teacher of Righteousness, who claimed to reveal God.[18] Matthew has this final beatitude in a different context connected with the parable teaching of Jesus (Mt 13:16-17).

(4) *The Good Samaritan—(10:25-37):*

Jesus has claimed a unique revelation which the learned in the Law did not have and now he is tested[19] by an expert in the law which enshrined the Jewish revelation—a Lawyer was Luke's name for a Scribe (11:45,53). The highlight of the scene is Luke's unique parable, known as The Good Samaritan. In particular, the brilliant character-drawing of the three actors from whom we are to deduce a model for our behavior, makes it one of the most unforgettable of all stories. The theme of men journeying is quite relevant both to Luke's context here and to his general love of journeys. We find the same question put to Jesus in 18:18 by one of the rulers (Mk 10:17)[20] and a similar answer to a somewhat different question by a Scribe in

A Teaching Journey To Jerusalem

Mark 12:28 (about the greatest commandment) and by a Lawyer who is a Pharisee in Matthew 22:24 (see also 22:34ff). However, in Luke it is the Lawyer and not Jesus himself, as in Mark, who summarizes the 248 commandments and 265 prohibitions of the Old Testament into the two of love of God (Dt 6:5) and love of one's neighbor (Lv 19:18).[21] This shows that Jesus was probably not the first to combine the two commandments thus, as contemporary Jewish literature also confirms.[22] His originality and uniqueness was in his person and in particular his life and death. Mark's Scribe receives a sympathetic reception but in Matthew and Luke he tries to test Jesus. In Luke when Jesus turns the tables on him by responding with a question to which he knows the answer, he seeks to justify himself by another question. Either all versions go back to the same event or more likely, details of different events were intermingled during the oral transmission. Luke alone has the second question followed by the parable. The structure of both sections is parallel, a question (10:25,29), a counterquestion (10:26,30-36), the Lawyer's answer (10:27,37a) concluding with a command to do this continually.[23]

The phrase "inherit eternal life" is a Johannine concept and will be explained in 18:18ff as entering the kingdom, being saved. Here it is not a question of the much maligned salvation by "works" but as in the Old Testament, the keeping of the law was considered essential to eternal life and the law-abiding Jesus, as Luke insists, affirms the lawyer's interpretation.[24]

The Old Testament describes the loving of God with three faculties, i.e. the whole person being in love with God, but in Luke and Mark "the mind" (in Hebrew it was part of the heart) is added, probably as a clarification for Luke's audience with its Greek psychology. The emphasis in the episode is on love of neighbor by which love of God was expressed. Love your neighbor "as if he were yourself" is probably the best translation of Lv 19:18, remembering that Leviticus commanded the alien to be treated as if he were a Jew (Lv 19:34). There is then agreement between Jesus and the Lawyer on general principles. In practice the Lawyer's second question showed that he had some limitations in application. Jesus through his parable compels him to rethink his application and his understanding of how man should love God in the concrete. A proper understanding of man's love would depend on the heart of the lover. It would not entail any limitation based on the worthiness of its object. Quite a variety of interpretations for neighbor were possible—a fellow Jew or even a proselyte, a fellow Pharisee perhaps for a Pharisee, at Qumran they were taught to hate outsiders. Judaism was no monolithic society and it should be remembered that the ordinary people hated the Sadducees and that the Pharisees in their turn had little time for the ordinary people. A boundless love of man qua man was not held by any, not to mention their Roman and Samaritan enemies.

Jesus' parable, a typical answer in Luke,[25] tells how two pillars of Judaism did not fulfill their plain duty and help their fellow Jew in his need.[26] The 17 mile "Bloody Way" from Jerusalem to Jericho, a noted residence of priestly families, drops about 3,300 feet and passes through barren, desolate and dangerous country, notorious for its robbers until modern times. The priest and the Levite or temple assistant cautiously pass by on the other side lest perhaps they incur defilement by touching a body to see if the man were alive (Lv 21:1ff; Num 19:11). Thirdly (popular stories have *three* characters) one might expect, in proper anti-clerical style, a layman or even a Pharisee or Scribe to please the audience. Instead there is a surprise—a hated Samaritan, a "half breed heretic with a half bible and mixed blood" (Jn 4:9). Nevertheless, the Samaritan's interpretation of the Torah was better than that of his Jewish enemies. The compassion of the Samaritan (the point of the story repeated at v 37)[27] is spelled out in loving detail.[28] He is an example of a man who did not hesitate to get involved and who did far more than the minimum. The story is not complete, no names, no conclusion about the beaten man or further cost, and Luke's expansive detail clearly shows where his emphasis lies.

It is therefore wrong to ask of such stories questions which the author never intended, e.g., if the ass of the Good Samaritan had arrived more quickly what would he have done to the robbers? To Jesus' different question "Who was neighbor," the Lawyer answers rightly but does not pronounce the name Samaritan but uses "the one who . . . " Jesus put the emphasis on the subject, the Lawyer himself and his attitude and removed any limitation from the object—"ask what you can do for . . . ." Jesus' conclusion is a command to imitate the Samaritan (a life of self-criticism, seeing, empathy, courage, active involvement), an invitation to a revolution in the Jewish life style and their understanding of the claim of love. But basically Jesus' parable was not merely an invitation to love one's neighbor, to social activity as it were. It was an attack on one of the bitterest religious and racial conflicts in the ancient world (Gal 3:28). The Jews considered the Samaritans as stupid, heretical, uncouth and lazy and Jesus could have demanded no greater act from them than to regard one such as an example, as a brother.

(5) *Visiting Martha and Mary—(10:38-42):*

To balance the Samaritan parable, Luke introduces artifically here a story about a *woman* listening to Jesus—a disciple's "doing" is motivated and guided by listening to Jesus. T.S. Eliot made the point well in his poem Ash Wednesday

> "Teach us to care and not to care
> Teach us to sit still."

The Good Samaritan activity of Mary is not enough, as Luke stresses from the first temptation to live on bread alone.[29] Even women must be disciples (Ac 22:3), contrary to Jewish custom which restricted women to a domestic role and they must listen to Jesus the Word of God, to the gospel before performing loving service. (He is the motivating force and example.)

The sharing of a meal is a typical situation for Jesus in Luke.[30] He does not mention the place as Bethany (Jn 11:1) was only two miles from Jerusalem and would destroy Luke's artificial journey, which had barely begun,if mentioned. Only Luke gives us this information about Martha and Mary, a link with John, where they are sisters of Lazarus and have similar temperaments (Jn 12:2; 11:20). Mary sits at the Lord's feet like a disciple (Ac 22:3) but the focus is on the busy Martha who was "anxious and concerned about many things"[31]—an example of domestic strain! Jesus' defense of Mary is a gentle rebuke as the repetition of the name Martha, Martha signifies (22:31; Jn 1:51). Only one thing is important, i.e. discipleship or more precisely as the next episode shows "prayer." The confusion in the textual tradition here seems to have come from understanding "one" as referring merely to the

A Teaching Journey To Jerusalem

number of dishes for the meal—some read "few things are needful or only one." Mary has chosen the good portion, i.e. to listen to the Lord.[32]

(6) Teaching about Prayer—(11:1-13):

Teaching about prayer naturally follows, thus giving us the three fundamentals of the Christian life, active love, listening to God's word and prayer. Possibly the Our Father is an example of the "one thing" required by the disciple. The teaching can be divided into three sections, the disciples' prayer (v 1-4), the parable of the Disobliging Neighbor (5-8) and sayings about God's answer to petitions (9:13). Jesus, for Luke, is the model for the disciples' prayer. Typically in Luke he is found at prayer on such an important occasion when he teaches his disciples in response to their question. "As John taught his disciples" again suggests a parallelism between John and Jesus. Such sects in Judaism like the Pharisees had distinctive prayers expressed their particular beliefs (5:33; "Lex orandi Lex credendi"). Matthew, who had seven petitions to Luke's five[33] gives a different setting in his collection of teaching on prayer in the Sermon on the Mount (6:9-13—Luke has 38 words in Greek to Matthew's 57). In Matthew, Jesus' prayer is contrasted with the lengthy and ostentatious prayers of some Jews and Gentiles while he emphasizes forgiveness. Thus Matthew is dealing with people who were familiar with prayer and was correcting their bad habits. Luke is rather dealing with how to pray and teaching the importance of simple, brief, confident prayer—keep asking but remember the kind Father to whom you are praying. As it is doubtful if Luke and his community would have omitted petitions which Jesus taught historically, the theory that the longer version found in Matthew's Syrian community is composed also of additional sayings of Jesus which are paralleled elsewhere in the gospels and contemporary Jewish prayers, can be accepted as plausible. Matthew's extra petitions, his third and seventh, in fact are parallel to his second and sixth and add nothing new to them (Mt 26:39,42). There is also a close identity of language between the two, but careful study of the Aramaic background suggests that Matthew's wording is more original, whereas Luke gives the more probable context.

No gospel shows that Jesus taught the prayer twice or indicates that the disciples forgot it after the first time. The differing formulations preserved by the early church show that they did not regard it as a fixed formula but rather a guide for prayer, as Matthew seems to point out (6:9).

It is noteworthy how neither the language nor the form of the prayer is original but could have been used by the Jews themselves and is as Bligh puts it—

> "A brief formula which will remind them of the lessons which Israel should have learned in the desert—to think of God as a loving Father, but also to fear him and hold his Name in veneration, to recognize that all good gifts come from him and to desire to pass out of the period of temptation into the peace of the kingdom."[33]

There is no reference to the cross and resurrection or the spirit. Its originality lies not in the materials used but in its brevity, its arrangement of the petitions putting first things first and its universality as a prayer for all men (e.g. the Good Samaritan). In addition, the meaning of such words as "Father," "Kingdom," "Temptation" received a distinctively Christian meaning from the person, life and teaching of Jesus. Recent writers stress the eschatological emphasis of the prayer—eschatological refers to the final

A Teaching Journey To Jerusalem

establishment of God's kingdom, the Messianic banquet, the return of Christ, the deliverance from the final time of trial, the destruction of the forces of evil. But Luke's version in particular combines both the everyday concerns of the Christian and the eschatological meaning—the kingdom has come but is still yet to come.

The structure of the prayer is simple—an address to God as Father, two petitions with regard to God's name and kingdom, now and in the future, and three for "us" believers, our needs, bread, forgiveness, help in temptation. All the prayers of Jesus, the unique Son (10:21f) in the gospels (except Mk 15:34; Mt 27:46) begin with Father (Abba, the word of a child for its father). Here the disciples are invited to share in Jesus' sonship and his intimate but non-Jewish way of addressing God.[34] The whole prayer it should be noted is in the plural—a Christian can never omit his brother from his prayers.

The phrase Father in heaven is a semitic way of saying heavenly (i.e. transcendent or majestic) Father. It is a typical Matthaean phrase which he uses 20 times (Luke never; Mk once in 11:25). It is not clear whether God's name (his personality, fame, reputation, nature, status, purpose, e.g. Ps 124:8; 22:22) is to be hallowed or glorified by himself as in Ezek 36:23 or by the action of men, by the holiness of their lives (Lv 11:45)—probably both. This is the first concern of a disciple.

The second and third (Mt) petitions are explanatory paraphrases (Zech 14:9). In Hebrew and Aramaic the expression Kingdom is an active noun for the kingly power of God. It is incipient in the life of Jesus but is yet to come to fullness (22:29f) and was frequently prayed for in Judaism. Some MSS of Luke read instead "Your Holy Spirit come upon us and cleanse us," a sentence which would fit in well with Luke's theology. Luke does not have the prayer "your will be done" here, unlike Matthew,[35] or the phrase "as in heaven also on earth." Possibly Matthew gives a liturgical expansion of the original prayer. "Keep on giving us" (not "me") each day[36] out "epiousion" bread (4:3; 7:33). The meaning of the Greek adjective here which we normally translate daily is uncertain as it occurs nowhere else. Unfortunately, an ancient papyrus MSS which contained it has been lost and its etymology is disputed. Two suggestions are made most frequently: (a) the word means a soldier's or a workman's ration for tomorrow—the Aramaic underlying word could be "delimhar," "the bread of the poor"—thus we are completely dependent of God for our daily bread, necessities (Mt 6:34); (b) the bread which the Jews expected in the last times. In John bread had a double sense—the teaching (Word) of Jesus and the Eucharist[37]—interestingly, in three late MSS of 2 Maccabees 1:8, the word refers to the Jewish showbread (Ex 25:30; 1 S 21:5-7; 1 K 7:48).

The petition, forgive us our sins (against God) is followed in Luke by the statement which in Aramaic probably means "for we ourselves forgive our debtors," thus making a distinction, unlike Matthew, between sins against God and debts to our fellow men.[38] This is the only action of the Christian in the whole prayer. No one can accept God's forgiveness if he has not a forgiving heart for others. Luke's version concludes with a plea that despite our weakness, God will keep us faithful from succumbing to the trial—the same basic verb in Mark 14:36 means "remove" (22:28,40,46). Luke possibly is referring to the great final trial, the danger of falling away completely from God, described in Rev 3:10; 1 Thess 1:6ff; 3:2ff; 5:6 but also to the daily trial of the Christian. God, of course, may test man[39] but does not incite him to commit evil.[40] Marcion, the early heretic, read here "Do not allow us to be led into temptation." Matthew adds a final word "save us from the evil one," making it personal.

Next we have in Luke, alone, a humorous parable in question form: Which of You? This kind of rhetorical question (can anyone of you imagine that . . . ?) is frequent in Q and L and seems to be characteristic of Jesus alone in Judaism (e.g. Lk 11:11; 12:25; 14:5,28; 17:7; Mt 6:27; 7:9). The Disobliging Neighbor at Midnight (11:5-8) teaches that we should not be half hearted but urgent and persistent in our prayer (for daily bread?) but also that our prayer should be directed to a Father always ready to give (18:1-8). A neighbor grudging to give is not a likeness but a contrasting shadow of God's generosity. This parable is more easily understood when one realizes that in a one roomed Palestinian village house, where the family sleep on mats on a raised section and the domestic animals on the other, the bolting and opening of the door with its iron bars and locks, was quite an inconvenience to all. Persistence (shamelessness) wins where neighborliness does not.

Next (v 9-13) we find a group of sayings almost identical with Matthew's version but in a different context. Like Matthew's Our Father they are in his Sermon on the Mount (Mt 7:7-11) after a statement on profaining the holy which Luke does not have (Mt 7:6). A disciple should *continually* (present imperative) ask, seek and knock and God will always answer ("it shall be" is a divine passive)—he is the perfect father who knows and wants what is good for us. The point is made by contrasting the lesser with the greatest, "if a human father . . . " so *much more* generous is God. This is a rabbinical form of reasoning known as "light and heavy" as it argues from the less to the more important. Matthew has a stone and a serpent but Luke exaggerates further and has a serpent and a scorpion (Dt 8:15). If even a sinful, human father can give good things (here is the mixture of good and bad) how much more the heavenly Father . . . But the Father's gift is not just "good things" as in Matthew (Lk 1:53) but the Holy Spirit to those who ask. See the prayer in Acts 1:14 also 8:15; Rom 8; Gal 5:22. Luke will give us the contrast of the Holy Spirit, i.e. Beelzeboul in his next episode.

(7) *Opposition and Temptation for Jesus—(11:14-36):*

Jesus and Evil Spirits (11:14-26):

Consideration of the gift of the Holy Spirit (God's kingdom in action) leads Luke to consider the opposing spirits and the temptation of Jesus to perform a sign. In the temptation paradigm scene Luke has shown us how Jesus, full of the Holy Spirit, resisted the temptations of the devil (4:1ff).

The scene opens with Jesus casting out a devil (continuous tense, i.e. not an instantaneous cure?) from a dumb man (in Matthew he is also blind). Luke, as often before gives us the crowd's reaction of amazement but here also he notes two kinds of opposition to Jesus. They accept the reality of his miracle but attribute his power to Beelzeboul, the prince of devils, making it a kind of black magic. Here, of course, we have the popular demonology of the times, e.g. the kingdom of Beelzeboul and the wandering demons seeking rest in a human person.[41] The form Beelzeboul ("b" in some MSS) is not found outside the Bible but "Baalzebul" occurs in the Ras Shamra (Ugarit) tablets as the name of a Canaanite god (Lord of the divine abode, or Baal the prince). Baalzebul was the high god of the Philistine city of Ekron (2 K 1:2ff). Quite likely the Hebrews had taken the name of the Philistine god and understood it in terms of similar Hebrew words meaning "lord of the flies" and "lord of the dung." Others were seeking a (different) sign from heaven. First we have the reply (to their thinking, v 17 as in 5:22; 6:8) to the Beelzeboul accusation and the second is answered in v

29ff. Luke's opposition is a confused crowd but in Mark 3:22 they are "scribes who came down from Jerusalem" and in Matthew 12:24, they are Pharisees. In general (see v 20) Luke's version is quite close to Matthew (Q) but he omits the difficult verses found in Matthew 12:31-32 (Mk 3:28-9).

Jesus answers the Beelzeboul accusation with a triple argument building up to a climax which neatly reverses the attack and puts the dilemma (the power of Satan or God!) back on his accusers. This is one of the few places where we are given Jesus' own explanation of his miraculous activity and it is therefore important. Firstly, it is evident that Satan (= Beelzeboul) is not engaged in civil war and foolish enough to destroy his own kingdom (of sickness) by dissension—he is the one who binds not looses. Secondly, what about their own Jewish exorcists (Ac 19:13f) their own sons (= pupils)? They, and Jesus obviously accepts their works, are worthy of the same charge. Ask them whose power is used. Possibly the pupils refer to Jesus' own disciples as it is difficult to see the activity of Jewish exorcists as a sign of the arrival of the kingdom. The argument from the similarity of miracles would at a later date be used by Clement of Alexandria to advance Christian claims.[42] Thirdly, if God and his power are at work in Jesus then they must draw the obvious conclusion that God's rule or the kingdom of God's Spirit (4:18; Ac 1:2,5ff) is here in the power which conquers the kingdom, which makes men victims (10:18; 13:16; Ac 2:22; 26:18). The expression "by the finger of God" (= the Spirit, see Ezek 8:1ff; Mt 12:28) which signifies God's concrete and direct intervention, is a rare expression,[43] found only in Ex 8:19; 31:18; Dt 9:10 (the giving of the covenant) and in Psalm 8:3 (creation). In the Exodus scene (Ex 8:19) the foreign magicians who are unable to reproduce Moses' third plague, confess to Pharoah that "this is the finger of

God" while Pharoah's heart remains stubborn. Thus Jesus' opposition is more blind than the pagan magicians. They are invited to see Jesus as the stronger one (the same Greek word as in John's speech at 3:16)—unless possibly the strong man is the man with the false sense of security who is overcome v 26.

Jesus overcomes the strong man, Satan, described in Luke like a prince in his castle (Beelzeboul meant "Lord of the House") and divides the spoils (a reference to the Suffering Servant Is 53:12; 2 S 2:21). They are warned that there is no neutrality in this war—either Jesus or Satan (v 23—see 9:50). They are either gathering the scattered flock of Israel together or scattering it. Matthew here puts a parable about a tree and the sign of Jonah but in Luke the parable of the tidied house follows with its message that exorcism once or conversion once does not make one immune from further and worse (seven) demonic attacks. It is not sufficient to get rid of evil and create a vacuum of self righteousness as it were. Unless one replaces it with good, the last state can be worse than the first. The Jews, unless they accept God's power in Jesus can end up much worse than they were originally before they became clean through Moses. The next section will emphasize that they must be open to hearing and keeping the word of God.

True Happiness—(11:27-8):

In this brief episode which is peculiar to Luke but similar to his message about Jesus' true kindred (8:19-21), a woman's spontaneous praise of Mary and indirect praise of Jesus himself in typical Eastern rhetoric, becomes the occasion for one of Luke's most important stresses. Jesus' true family, who are truly happy and holy are those who really listen to his word (here equated with "the word of God" Ac 4:29ff) and live according to it (1:38; 8:21). This

A Teaching Journey To Jerusalem

relationship is available to all men. This is what the Assyrian did when Jonah preached.

Tempting Jesus—The Sign of Jonah—(11:29-32):

The sign of Jonah is almost identical with Matthew's version. In Luke it is addressed to the crowds gathering thickly, who are bluntly addressed by Jesus as an evil generation (11:45). In Matthew, the audience is composed of some scribes and Pharisees who are described as an evil and *adulterous* generation—it comes before the description of the return of the unclean spirit (Mt 12:38-42). Luke does not have Mt v 40, describing Jonah as "three days and three nights . . . " but as "a sign to the men of Nineveh so will the Son of man be to this generation." Possibly "adulterous" with its Biblical background of the marriage love between Yahweh and Israel would be unclear to Luke's audience. The sin of this evil generation (an allusion to Moses' song Dt 32:5) was that they wanted to prescribe a conclusive, compelling sign to Yahweh and were not satisfied with Jesus' deeds and his way of saving man. Their heart was wrong and no sign therefore could satisfy it. Jesus turns their request for a different sign or conclusive, visible proof back upon themselves and especially on the condition of their own inner thinking and openness to God's way.

The theme, like that of the previous section and also so many of Luke's parables, is repentant hearing now of Jesus. But scholars dispute as to what is the sign to this generation according to Luke. In Matthew it is a clear (post resurrection?) reference to the resurrection (Ac 17:30)—just as Jonah had appeared to the Ninevites after being apparently dead for three days. It is similar in Luke if one sees him as emphasizing the future tense—"will be a sign" (16:30f; Ac 1:3; 17:31). However, the Ninevites in the story were not witnesses to the prophet Jonah's escapade. It seems more logical to take his sign as signifying the person of Jesus and his preaching of repentance and thus no sign at all (see Mk 8:12). This kind of sign permitted a genuine free response. In fact, both the Ninevites (Jonah 3) and the Queen of the South (i.e. modern Yemen 1 K 10:1ff) acted upon the evidence which God gave them. Both episodes involved journeys so dear to Luke's heart and successful preachers to the Gentiles. Jesus had rejected the spectacular sign approach at the temptation.[44] Significantly, Luke has two Gentile examples of open-mindedness here. They are superior to the Jewish response to God and will condemn the present generation on the day of judgment (i.e. unless they repent—it is a warning). Here we find a claim of Jesus which must have astonished his audience—greater than the wisdom of Solomon, greater than the prophet of repentance, Jonah.

The Parable of the Lamp—(11:33-36):

These sayings scattered in Matthew but linked together in Luke by the "catchword" lamp (v 33,34,36) go to the heart of the problem of the opposition and negative reception of Jesus. He is like the lamp (the sign) at the door of a Greek house, shining on all who wish to enter (also used in 8:16). The light of Jesus' preaching (and that of Luke's mission) is clear for all to see. But the problem with this evil generation is that its eye is not sound, its ability to see and to be fully illumined is faulty and turns the whole body into darkness. The eye in its turn was understood as a kind of lamp for the inside of the person;[45] somewhat similarly in John's gospel light, seeing, darkness, unbelief, are used of the (spiritual) reception of Jesus' message.[46] In the Old Testament times both God himself (Is 60:19; Ps 27:1) and the Law (Is 51:4; Ps 119:105) were described in terms of light.

A Teaching Journey To Jerusalem 291

(8) *The Hypocrisy of the Pharisees and Lawyers—(11:37-53):*

The theme of opposition to Jesus is continued in Luke's fourth "table talk" scene (see 5:17ff; 7:36; 11:37) with Jesus' devastatingly blunt criticism of the Pharisees, his hosts and the Lawyers (see also 19:47; 20:19f; 22:2). Luke's construction of the scene seems rather artificial and staged to give a narrative background to a long stretch of teaching. The setting seems to recede as the chapter builds up to an attack once again on "this generation" (11:32,51). Thus, in Luke, Jesus makes a very abrupt and blunt polemic against a Pharisee who invited him to a meal and who merely was genuinely (?) surprised at the unusual fact that a famous teacher did not carry out the customary *ritual* ablutions (i.e. not because of dirt) for which both the quantity of water and method of washing were prescribed in detail by Pharasaic tradition, e.g. one and a half egg shells of water poured from the finger-tip to the wrist. Matthew's somewhat longer version of this criticism is found in a different setting at the end of the Jerusalem ministry. He has all of Luke's criticisms in a different order with seven woes.[47] Luke's structure begins with his reflection on the "inside and outside" (v 37-42) and leads into six woes divided into two threes (two fours in 6:20ff), three directed to the Pharisees (v 42,43,44) and three (v 46,47,52) in answer to a Lawyer's complaint that his group were being insulted also (v 45 "hubrizein," a strong word is used as in 18:32 also Ac 14:5; 1 Thess 2:2; Mt 22:6). A woe should not be seen as a vindictive curse but rather as a sorrowful statement of fact, an anticipation of judgment, yet not without a hope of remedy, being more open than the Old Testament curses as it were. Nevertheless, the blunt insulting picture of Jesus presented by Luke here should be noted as far from the romantic "gentle Jesus, meek and mild" portrayal for which Luke is often taken for granted. Unlike Matthew, Luke distinguishes between the Pharisees, the pious living, aloof, yet admired, and progressive sect among the Jews and Lawyers (= Scribes in v 53 and the other gospels), the theoreticians who were mainly Pharisees and who taught the theories according to which the Pharisees lived. Here also Luke has an opening for his "rich and poor" almsgiving and reversal theme (e.g. 11:41; 12:13ff).

Verses 39-41, the opening criticism of the foolish Pharisees ("fools" as below 12:20) are somewhat obscure. Matthew's text at 23:25 makes a clear comparison between the outside and the inside, accusing them of cleansing the outside and leaving the inside filled with extortion and selfishness. Verse 39 in Luke says they cleanse the outside but leave the inside full of rapaciousness and evil. Verse 40, not in Matthew, gives the basic principle that God created both the outside and the inside (the heart). Verse 41 is particularly obscure, literally "But the things which are inside give for alms and behold everything is clean for you." Quite likely it is an invitation to purify the heart and the full sense is that almsgiving based on and expressing a pure heart (the kingdom inside 17:21; the whole person 11:36) is the true cleansing about which they should be concerned.[48]

The first woe (v 42) criticizes a religion which is obsessed with meticulous detail going even far beyond the tithing which the law prescribed,[49] while neglecting and escaping from what really is important, justice and love of God.[50] Secondly, (v 43), their preoccupation with the external was evident in their vanity, their desire for the front seats facing the congregation in the synagogue and for popular recognition and respect. Thirdly and most devastatingly, they are like unmarked graves which defile a man even though he walks on them unawares (Num 19:16).

A Teaching Journey To Jerusalem

Ironically, their superficial holiness (holiness was for Luke almsgiving, justice and the love of God) was an evil influence on the people of Israel and led them to reject Jesus. In Matthew 23:27 they are like tombs whitewashed on the outside but full of corruption within.

The lawyers are accused firstly (v 46) of making religion into a burden, of turning the Mosaic law into a complicated web of rules which were impossible for the people to bear while they do not "life a finger to lighten them" (Ac 15:10; Mk 2:23-8; 7:1-13).[51] Secondly, (v 47-51) and ironically they are accused of building tombs for the prophets whom people like themselves (their fathers) had killed (Ac 7:51-3). Their fathers did the killing while they, with their spirit, do the entombing of the prophets' teaching by their complicated, legalistic system. They canonize the prophets when they are dead and can no longer disturb their conscience. Here we can see the perpetual conflict between two kinds of religion, the prophetic and the legalistic, both of which are of course necessary but neither is adequate of itself.

Sayings such as 4:24; 13:33 show that Jesus saw himself among the prophet martyrs of Israel (Ac 3:22-6). The phrase "the wisdom of God has said" seems to be not so much a quotation from the lost Jewish book entitled The Wisdom of God (see also 2 Chron 24:19), as a kind of reverential way of saying God has said in his wisdom (7:35; 21:15). In Matthew 23:34 Jesus says "Therefore I send you prophets and wise men and Scribes . . ." Luke's anachronistic version which summarizes God's plan of salvation, has prophets and apostles or groups familiar to his own Christian audience. Luke is saying that Jesus knows and teaches God's wisdom, his plan for history while the scribes are rejecting God's wisdom and plan. This generation (11:29) is the climax of God's missions to Israel and will have to account for the blood which has been shed throughout Jewish history from the foundation of the world, i.e. from Abel, the first martyr (prophet? Gn 4:8) to Zechariah[52]—"All the prophets" is a frequent stereotype in Luke from here on.[53] Here many see in Luke a hint that the climax of old Israel's history is the destruction of Jerusalem (21:32).

The final woe is another paradoxical view of the obscurantist lawyers whose badge of office was a key, symbolizing their duty to unlock the law for the people (Is 22:22). This final woe is a devastating climax like the third woe to the Pharisees (v 42,52). They not only have not gained access themselves but have prevented others (from accepting Jesus) by taking away the key of knowledge (perhaps a Greek idea where Matthew has "shut the kingdom of heaven").

The final two verses which are proper to Luke, describe the menacing hostility of the lawyers and the Pharisees to Jesus as he is leaving. The text is complex but describes them pressing upon Jesus vehemently and trying to trap him into indiscreet sayings—the word trap is a metaphor from hunting wild beasts.

(9) *Courage under Persecution—(12:1-12):*

The hostile note which Luke has just emphasized leads naturally to a message of courage to Luke's own fellow Christians who were being persecuted for openly confessing Jesus. These sayings are found in different places in the other gospels, some addressed to crowds, some to disciples (see Mk 4:21-5; 8:13-21 and Matthew's missionary discourse 10:17ff). In Luke, Jesus is typically surrounded by crowds (lit "many thousands" e.g. 14:25; 18:36) "trampling on one another" but he addresses his disciples first (12:54). Three sections can be distinguished in Luke: (a) v 1-3, a warning against hypocrisy. Acceptance of Jesus must penetrate to the depth of their being. (b) The Son of Man will acknowledge those who profess him before men. God and the Holy Spirit will teach them when being judged by man.

The opening saying of Jesus sums up his opinion of the Pharisees—he attacks their hypocrisy, their leaven, their insidious corruptive influence (11:44; 1 Cor 5:6). This saying, leaven (yeast), is found in the other two synoptics—Mark (8:15) does not explain it (evil influence such as political collaboration or refusal?). In Matthew 16:5-12, it means teaching and in Luke hypocrisy. References to hypocrisy are found in 6:42; 12:1,56; 13:15. Mark has one (Mk 7:6) while Matthew has 13 references. In the New Testament it is found only in the synoptics and there always in the sayings of Jesus himself (Gal 2:13ff). The Greek word means an actor, one who plays a part. Theatres in the Greek and Roman settlements in Palestine must have made the word familiar even to the Jews. The concept hypocrisy is not found in the Old Testament but in the Septuagint the word is used twice to translate "hanep" "godless."

Wilkinson has an interesting reflection on the frequent misunderstandings of hypocrisy which are made:[54]

> "First a hypocrite is not somebody who fails to live up to his ideals. If a man lives up to his ideals, they are too low and it is time he found some better ones! Again, it is sometimes thought that a hyprocrite is somebody who 'acts a part' like a play actor, because the Greek word 'upocrites' has as its classical Greek background the Greek drama. But the way to find the meaning of New Testament words is not to trace them back through classical Greek, but through Aramaic, and beyond that, through the Greek of the Septuagint to the Hebrew of the Old Testament.

To find the meaning of 'hypocrite', we must look carefully at the ways in which Jesus used it, because it is Jesus who has brought it into prominence. In Jesus' use of it the essence of hypocrisy is found in three things. (1) In being more concerned about what other people think than about the truth itself: trying to project a good image, and preserve one's respectability at all costs. The hypocrite is concerned about 'appearances'. He wants his goodness to be seen by men. Examples of this are in Matthew 6:2; 6:5 and 6:16. The Pharisee wants it to be *seen* that he is making a generous gift to charity, that he says his prayers, that he is keeping the fast. (2) In being outwardly religious, but inwardly profane and ungodly. As Isaiah said (29:13) 'This people draw near with their mouth and honor me with their lips, while their hearts are far from me'. The example of this is Matthew 23:27. Jesus says that the Pharisees are like whitewashed graves which look nice from the outside but within are filled with corruption. (3) In being self-satisfied and self-admiring, sure of one's goodness. The example of this is in Luke 18:9-12 where the Pharisee parades his goodness before God in prayers and gives thanks that he is not like the tax collector. Hypocrites are not as plentiful in the Church as they were two generations ago, for it is now neither fashionable nor profitable to be a churchgoer."

The observation of the seventeenth century French moralist, Rochefoucauld, is also to the point here. "Hypocrisy is the homage that vice pays to virtue."

In the coming judgment the secret sins (true character) of Pharisaism will be disclosed to all[55]—this prophecy becomes a command in Matthew 10:26.

Here we have the only synoptic description of the disciples as Jesus' friends (also Jn 15:15). This means that they receive special encouragement and advice about the danger of apostasy in the face of persecution (Mt 10:16-33). Jesus asks of all of his disciples the denial of self

A Teaching Journey To Jerusalem

(9:23ff), to be without fear of anything even of those who kill the body (1:50,74; 5:26). "Proper" fear or reverence for God in the Old Testament is the recognition of God's sovereignty and his ultimate power and is considered as a necessary foundation of wisdom, of right living.[56] Here Luke is dealing with the natural human fear of being killed and uses the principle of the greater fear driving out the lesser. If you fear having your body killed, should you not the more fear him who can both kill and then cast into Gehenna—the Jerusalem rubbish dump with its continually smouldering fires which was used as a symbol for punishment of evil after death.[57] But a disciple should fear nothing (12:7). He should be encouraged and reassured by remembering that they were worth much more to God than many sparrows (the cheapest of the bird sold for food), which, though of little value, were still not neglected by an all seeing and caring God who is informed about the tiniest details of a disciple's life (2:18; Ac 27:34).

Reflection on secret sins and fear lead to the climax of the argument, a warning which looks forward to the future coming of the Son of Man (12:8,40), a warning to a persecuted community tempted to apostasy.

It is a reminder of the importance of public loyalty to and confession of Jesus (in 9:26 the saying is used to demand the full acceptance of Jesus' words). Obviously, Jesus took the future day of Judgment and the possibility of hell seriously. To acknowledge Jesus before men will mean that one will be acknowledged before God when the Son of Man comes—"before the angels of God" is the equivalent of Mark's "the Father with the holy angels" (Mk 8:38).[58] Verse 10 which is joined by the catchword Son of Man deals with the difficult distinction between the euphemism of "speaking a word against the Son of Man" and the blaspheming of the Holy Spirit which will never be forgiven. Matthew 12:31f and Mark 3:22-7, in the context of the Beelzeboul incident, develop more fully this sin against the Holy Spirit. Luke seems to be particularly concerned with the danger of apostasy in his own community and the encouragement of fearless confession and perseverance (Ac 14:22). Luke seems to distinguish between two periods of Jesus' activity on earth as Son of Man and later of activity through the Holy Spirit and also a time before and after a man has received the gift of the Holy Spirit (e.g. Ac 28:26f). Thus Peter spoke against Jesus before receiving the Holy Spirit (22:34,57). Therefore a man who refuses the influence of the Spirit (Ac 1:8; 28:25ff) or also after he has received the Spirit, deliberately and knowingly apostasises, cannot be forgiven until he repents (Heb 6:4-6; 1 Jn 5:16b).

In the final saying joined by the catchword Holy Spirit, the Holy Spirit appears in his positive function as the disciples' teacher (similar to John 14:26ff), their defender before synagogues, rulers and authorities (Mt 10:19-20; Mk 13:11). In Acts we find frequent remarks about their boldness of speech, e.g. Peter before the Jewish authorities is filled with the Holy Spirit.[59] The same word "merimnan" (do not worry) was used of Martha (10:41; 12:11).

(10) *The Rich Fool—(12:13-21):*

Jesus had claimed to be greater than Solomon, the wise man of Jewish history (11:31; Ac 10:42; 1 K 3:25) and now is invited like Solomon to settle a dispute, an incident found only in Luke. A rabbi who was expert in the Law of Moses was expected to be able to pronounce on all the aspects of life with which it dealt whether religious or secular, criminal or civil affairs. The questioner hoping for a favorable decision against his (older?) brother on the

A Teaching Journey To Jerusalem

problem of their inheritance (Dt 21:15ff; Num 27:1-11) receives at first a blunt rhetorical refusal which echoes the rejection of Moses in Exodus (2:14; Ac 7:27). Then Jesus goes on to give a lecture and far more than the questioner bargained for. Jesus penetrates to the attitude of greed behind the request. Here we find one of Luke's parables which stresses the right attitude and use of material possessions.[60] Jesus warns *the crowd* to take heed and guard against all kinds of "pleonexia," a word mainly used by Paul in the New Testament for greed, for more and more material possessions which tend to become one's God (Col 3:5; Eph 5:5). A man may be rich but possessions do not guarantee meaningful life. The structure here is a typical one with a saying of Jesus followed by a parable on a related theme.[61]

The parable of the Rich Fool is a brilliant character drawing and vividly told, e.g. the dialogue with himself, God's dramatic intervention. It is an "example" parable giving an illustration of what not to do in life. It is a parable of catastrophe for the foolish rich in Luke's community who think that they are secure (Am 6:1ff). It is a perfect description of a self-centered rich man (a narcissistic monologue with himself of I,I,I, My, My, My), but it should be noted that like the rich man (16:19ff) there is not a suggestion that he did not pay his wages, etc. He is a farmer who has an abundant crop and planned to build bigger barns to store it. He says to himself (soul Ps 41:6ff; 42:5) "You have plenty for the years to come, Relax, eat heartily, drink well. Enjoy yourself" (Si11:14f). He thinks only of indulgence not of others in need. In God's eyes he is a fool. He is not reproved for being rich. His possessions are of no use as he failed to take death into account that very night (his soul or life or animatory principle is required). One is reminded of Luke's Sermon with its threat of reversal in store for the rich (6:20ff; 1:52ff). A fool

(11:40) in the Biblical tradition is not the opposite of the intelligent man but the opposite of the wise man (Ps 14:1; 53:1; 73:22; Proverbs; 2 Cor 11:23). He is the practical atheist who ignores God in his practical life and lacks any life—influencing belief in God. He is condemned implicitly for his lack of concern for the poor (11:41; 12:23). "They require" is a circumlocution known as a "divine passive," a Jewish periphrasis for "God requires." While Jesus had no difficulty in using the word "God," in general he spoke of God by means of circumlocutions according to the custom of the pre-Christian period. It is used about a hundred times in his sayings in the gospels. Only in Luke's special material (6:38; 12:20,48c; 16:9; 23:31), do we find the third person plural used, the common periphrasis among Rabbinical literature.[62] The point of the parable is that the important thing is a proper relationship to God and our neighbor, to be rich where God is concerned (Mt 19:21; "treasure in heaven"; Lk 12:23), by almsgiving towards the poor (12:33; Ac 9:36; 10:2ff) and a proper appreciation of the relative value of the things of this world and a trust in providence as Luke next explains.[63] D omits the final verse probably accidentally, unlike the overwhelming number of the other manuscripts which include it.

(11) *Trust in Providence—(12:22-34):*

The disciples are to learn a lesson from the rich fool (v 22) not to be anxious about food and clothing, the basic needs of life. The treatment on anxiety which Luke gives here is found in a different setting in Matthew in the Sermon on the Mount and is quite similar apart from v 26 and v 32 (Mt 6:25-34; 19:21). The verb and noun for this kind of anxiety, caring, are used in Luke about the cares which choke the good seed (8:14), Martha's approach to life (10:41), the disciples' worry about answering charges (12:11), the attitude which the returning Christ should not find (21:34)—(see also 1 P 5:7; 1 Cor 12:25; Phil 2:20).

A man's life (or body, a parallel expression for the self) is much more than food or clothing. Five reasons are given for lack of anxiety. (One should note here how Jesus stresses the wonder of the ordinary things so taken for granted in the natural world.) Firstly, man is much more important than the unclean crows (Ps 147:9; Jb 38:41; Lv 11:15; "sparrows" 12:7) which God feeds even though they neither sow nor have barns like the rich fool. Secondly, since the smallest things such as adding to one's span of life ("stature" is another possible meaning) are beyond man's power, why be anxious about the rest and why not trust God in whose power they are. Thirdly, since God clothes the temporary grass (the lilies are perhaps the tiny scarlet anemones that fill the fields Ct 5:13) in a greater splendor than Solomon's, how much more will he provide for you "O ye of little faith." This favorite expression of Matthew is not found in Mark and only here in Luke (Mt 6:30; 8:26; 14:31; 16:8; 17:20).

Faith here is the opposite to worry and fear which lead unbelievers to run after what they are to eat and drink (12:16ff). With much hesitation the Committee of the Greek New Testament rejected the D reading in 12:27 ("they neither spin nor weave") as a stylistic refinement introduced due to the following mention of Solomon's clothing. The context helps us to understand the strong verb used in 12:29 ("meteorizo") which occurs only here in the New Testament. Two possibilities in meaning are—Do not be arrogant or fly high (Luther) and do not be anxious, unsettled, insecure, "swinging between heaven and earth" "hovering between fear and hope"—the second fits in better (see Phil 4:4-7; Rom 12:16; 1 Tim 6:17ff). Fourthly, the emphasis that your Father knows your needs. Except in the "Our Father," Jesus has hitherto spoken of God as Father only once in Luke 11:13, when he spoke of the Father giving the Holy Spirit, who next in v 32 is described as giving the kingdom (= the Holy Spirit who casts out fear as in Acts). Fifthly, Jesus turns from negatives to a positive climax (v 31) and commands his disciples to *seek* the Father's kingdom[64] and the rest will be added to them as well, i.e. make God's kingdom the object of all your energy and endeavor. This is one of the many imperatives of Jesus which we find in the New Testament (e.g. 13:24). Thus Jesus commands a main aim or priority for his disciples into which they can channel their normal human greed and self-seeking. The things of this world are not ignored but set in perspective against God's providence and kingdom and their relative importance in man's life.

The teaching is not an invitation to irresponsibility. The disciples are called by Jesus (the good shepherd Jn 10:1ff; 21:16ff), a little flock, a phrase only found here in the New Testament.[65] Here it describes the disciples, few in number and weak in power, in contrast to the crowds (12:1,22,32), but more so to the threatening world of Luke. They are like the faithful remnant which Isaiah encouraged with similar words (Is 41:8ff; 43:1ff). Jesus encourages them by recalling the Father's pleasure in giving them the kingdom—verse 32 is in Luke alone and echoes the shepherd scene (2:8-14). Man may seek the kingdom in Luke but on the other hand it is something which, like the Spirit (1:13), the Father gives (12:32; 6:20-23) and which is inherited but not built by men (10:25; 23:51; Mt 25:34; 1 Cor 6:9-10). But to seek the kingdom, to be open to receiving it as a gift one must sell 'what you have and give alms,'' unlike the rich fool. This must not be taken literally and totally as a command to sell *everything* down to the smallest possession and produce a class of destitutes (see

Zacchaeus in 19:1ff, also the ruler in 18:18ff). The early Jerusalem Christians did just that and had to be supported by the rest of the Christian world.[66] Luke sees the heart of the person as the key to the question. The twin foci of his morality are the total response of the heart, i.e. his thoughts, affections and actions and the Fatherhood of God to which it responds in love (10:27). The important thing is to decide on one's treasures because there one's heart will be. Here is the answer to the problem of 12:31 of how to amass a never failing treasure with the Lord (Mt 6:19-21; 1 Tim 6:17-19; Jam 2:5). Note how Matthew puts this reflection before his teaching on trust in God while Luke puts it after.

(12) *Vigilance for the Master's Return—(12:35-48):*

The Father's gift of the kingdom leads into a series of sayings (12:33-13:9), dealing with the urgency of preparedness and vigilance for the Master's return and the second coming in judgment. This is the first of Luke's three long eschatological sermons.[67] Four parables are included here, the Waiting Servants (12:35-8), the Sleeping Householder and the Thief at Night (v 39-40), the Faithful or Unfaithful Steward (42-6), the Responsible or Irresponsible Servants (47-8). Three stages can perhaps be distinguished in the development of such parables which deal with the delay of the Second Coming[68]—the original stage when Jesus used them to warn his audience, not about his future coming but of the crisis of the times; the second stage when the early Christians applied them to Jesus' future coming; the third stage, or Luke's use of them for his audience some of whom have lost interest evidently in the future coming of Jesus.

Instead of concern for earthly things, the disciple, who is a servant (1 Cor 4:1-2), should be constantly faithful, vigilant and prepared for his master's coming.

Luke is not so much interested in predicting the future as in teaching the proper attitude for the present. The fullness of the kingdom is clearly in the future and so the disciple should be watchful and ready like a man ready for action with his long Palestinian robe gathered into his belt (Ex 12:11; 1P 1:13), or a servant waiting to open up for his master's return from a wedding with his lamp burning, an echo of Matthew's parable of the wise and foolish virgins (Mt 25:1-3). The custom referred to was that of a man going to fetch his bride home and the enthusiastic preparation and watchfulness of the servants left behind to open the doors. There is a peculiar unlifelike twist to Luke's version here, a kind of allegorical interpretation pointing clearly to Jesus and the Messianic banquet. Unexpectedly, it is the master who girds himself, seats the servants at table and waits on them in a scene reminiscent of the washing of the feet in John 13:3ff; Lk 22:27; Mk 10:45. In v 38—"And if he comes in the second or third watch . . . blessed are they.," we find one of the problems of Luke's Church tackled as it faced the indefinite delay of Jesus' coming and the Church's existence—the length of the delay should not disturb them. Here Luke seems to have preserved the ancient Jewish division of the night into watches (Jdg 7:19) while Mark, with his cultural adaptaion to a Roman audience, uses the fourfold division of the Roman army Mk (13:35).

The parable of the surprising and obviously unannounced coming of the thief who digs through the mud wall of a Palestinian house v 39-40, leads to the command to be ready for the similar coming of the Son of Man)Dn 7:1; 1 Thess 5:2; Apoc 3:3; 2 Pet 3:8).

Peter, whose characteristic question is somewhat obscure, is typically answered indirectly with another question (10:26; 18:19). In Matthew 24:45-51, which is almost identical, the question which is in the style of Luke is missing. However, as in John 21:21, Peter receives the same kind of answer to his question. Here in the answer there is

A Teaching Journey To Jerusalem

a change from the servant of the parable to the steward or servant in authority, thus giving a direct message to the church leaders of Luke's time as represented by Peter about their greatest responsibility and need for watchfulness (8:45; Mk 5:21). His question implies a distinction between the privileges of the inner group of disciples (12:13,22) and the crowds. Is the banquet for all or only for the twelve Mk (10:3-40). Church leaders should not act in the manner of domineering stewards lording it over the others (22:24-7; Ac 20:30; 1 P 5:2f). If the steward acts faithfully and wisely as he is put to the test of time and sees that the other servants are properly fed (Jn 21:15ff), his reward will be greater responsibility, "in charge of all his property". But if, like the rich fool (12:19), he abuses his responsibility during the Master's long delay (v 45) and ill treats the others he will be cut off from the community and have "his lot with the unbelievers", i.e. on the day of judgment[69]. In the final verses 47 and 48, which Luke alone adds, he distinguishes between culpability and culpability, between the leader who knew but did not fulfil his master's wishes (a severe beating) and the one who did not know fully but still deserved to be flogged (a lighter beating).

Peter, in Acts 3:17 and Paul, Acts 17:30 and Jesus himself (23:34) speak of those acting in ignorance (Jas 4:17; Rom 1:20; 2:14f; Dt 17:12; Num 15:30; Ps 19:13). As in Amos 3:2 they (i.e. God) demand (v 48) a higher responsibility and also a corresponding higher punishment because of the special privileges of Israel, Israel "to whom much has been given" (19:11-27; Hos 4:4-11; Jer 2:19).

(13) *The Mission of Jesus—(12:49-53):*

The remarks about the future division and judgment of the leaders of the disciples lead to the small, rather rare section where Jesus, speaking of himself in the first person, defines his mission, speaks of his future suffering and the divisions which his mission will cause among men. Verses 49 and 50b are proper to Luke while 50a is parallel to Mark 10:38b and v 51-3 are parallel to Matthew 10:34-6. Here we see Jesus as an example of what a Christian should really be anxious about, "thy kingdom come." The word ("synechomai" 4:38; 8:37; Ac 18:5) denotes actual distress as Jesus looks forward with anxious impatience to the goal of his journey (9:31; 13:32; 22:15; Jn 12:27). Jesus pronounces that he has come to light a fire on earth. It is important to note in explaining this mysterious phrase that verses 49 and 50 form a Semitic parallelism—the purifying elements of fire and baptism. Dunn fills out the thought of each verse by adding what is extra in the other as follows:

"Jesus came to cast fire on earth,
and how he wishes it was already kindled *on himself;*
How he longs for the baptism *which he came to administer, to be accomplished on himself.*"

"Here then" he comments, "we come across a most striking and startling development of the Baptist's metaphor. Not only does Jesus accept the Baptist's expectation as an aspect of his ministry. But he sees also tht purgative judgment which the Baptist predicted must first be experienced by himself."[70]

Fire was an eschatological symbol frequent in the Jewish prophets for the final judgment where the elect were purified[71] and the impious destroyed.[72] Jesus then is pointing out his role as inaugurating the eschatological time by passing through the fire of trouble and testing (Is 43:2; Ps 66:12; 69:2-3). However, it is quite probable that Luke here is referring to the fire of Pentecost (Ac 2:3,19) and the gift of the spirit by the risen Jesus and his church (24:49; Ac 2:33), which inaugurates the last days (Ac 2:17; 2 Cor 1:22; Rom 8:23).

A Teaching Journey To Jerusalem

Baptism, which is not an Old Testament word, refers to Jesus' passion and death (17:25 and 24).[73] But as Jesus must go through testing so must the world. Jesus has come to bring the Messianic peace between man and God, man and man, promised by the prophets,[74] but it is not the superficial, apathetic peace of the false prophets, a distinction that was familiar in the Old Testament prophets.[75] It is the peace where God's will is done. Jesus, who demands a personal decision for or against himself and his way of suffering (9:23f; 14:27) and provokes division even in families (21:16), is set for the rise and fall of many, a sign that will be contradicted (see 2:34; Mt 10:34). Jesus himself, the new element in Israel's history, is the crisis, the division (the same root word as in v 46; Mt 10:34 has "a sword") between believers and those who refuse to believe[76] and will disrupt even family relationships, a common element of the Jewish view of the last days (Mi 7:6; Sanhedrin 97a; Dt 13:6-11). Jesus divides, because the good news which he brings to one group is superficially at least, bad news for another, e.g. oppressors, the rich. But Jesus' division leads to a deeper unity through repentance to unity in brotherhood, sharing justice and true peace. Jesus produces "from now on" (22:69; the period of Acts onwards) a new family (8:21; Ac 2:44-7; 4:32)—the five members in v 52 are given in detail in v 53, where the mother and mother-in-law are the same person.

(14) *Discerning the Signs of the Times—(12:54-9):*

Jesus now turns to the crowds to appeal to them to discern the signs of the present times and see the critical situation in which they are (12:54-6) so that they will be converted before the coming judgment (12:57-13:9). Jesus' contemporaries demanded a sign from heaven yet failed to discern the signs of the times which were in fact in front of their very eyes. The tragedy of the people was that they were blind to what was really happening before their eyes in Jesus, the sign (2:34). They failed to use in religion their intelligence which they displayed in ordinary affairs. The signs of the times which would lead to the destruction of Jerusalem were no more difficult to read than signs of the coming weather. Matthew's weather interpretation depends on the redness of the sky in the evening or in the morning (Mt 16:2-3), whereas, Luke's depends on the wind from the West (1 K 18:44), the sea bringing the rain or the desert bringing parching heat from the South. But they did not live with a watchful attitude towards the things which really were important and urgent and demanding repentance and reconciliation. They are hypocrites who deal in superficialities and do not face the real issues (Mt 15:7) and Luke's readers are intended to take a message of watchfulness for their time. The word for time here ("kairos' ' and not "chronos," the word for measured time in the New Testament), means the time of Messianic fulfilment, the key moment which is disastrous to neglect (2 Cor 6:2). To strengthen his appeal, to get them to judge Jesus' teaching for themselves (v 57; 2 P 1:13) and to repent, Jesus uses two parables and two statements (12:58-13:9).

The parable here (12:58f) which Matthew in the Sermon on the Mount has used as an example story about the general need for reconciliation with one's brother, is a sound piece of practical worldly common sense. But read against its first background before the destruction of Jerusalem and also its background in Luke of the delay in the second coming of Jesus, it has a very different meaning. We quote some of Hunter's remarks about its first background:

A Teaching Journey To Jerusalem

"Jesus was far more interested in politics—the politics of his own nation in relation to God's eternal purpose—than many pious Christians have supposed. One of the many gospel evidences in proof of this is the parable of the Way to Court, or, as it is often called, the Defendant. It concludes a passage (Luke 12:35-9) heavy with Jesus' foreboding about the crisis which overhung Israel. Read it again, and you will see that the parable is the last of five (the others are the Waiting Servants, the Sleeping Householder, the Man in Charge, and the Weather Signs) in which Jesus foresees the coming crisis and calls on his country-men to read the signs of the times and act accordingly. 'How weatherwise you can all be' he says to them, 'O, if only you could be as spiritually wide-awake to what is happening in this nation now!' Then he speaks the parable of the Way to Court . . . There are four parties in the parable—the insolent debtor, the creditor, the judge and the constable. How do we interpret it? The insolent debtor on the way to court in Israel. The way to court is Jesus' way of describing the impending crisis in his nation's history, a crisis which, he says, will bring testing for his followers, God's judgment on the nation, and a blood baptism for himself. Israel stands at the cross-roads, and she must decide which way she will go. She must choose whether to align herself with God's purpose embodied in himself and his ministry, or, refusing and pursuing the path of nationalism, enter on a collision course with Rome which must end in her ruin. What makes the decision so urgent is the shortness of the time. If his countrymen were in similar straits financially, if they were insolent debtors on the way to court, they would settle with their creditor long before they reached it. But, alas, in the far more momentous crisis of their nation, 'eyes have they but they see not'. Could they but realize their peril, they would see that the only right thing to do was to turn, before it was too late, and come penitently to the living God whose great purpose in history goes forward whether men will or not!

Consider the historical situation as Jesus saw it in the light of God's purpose for the world. God has chosen Israel to be his servant—to be the bearer to the world of a 'light to lighten the Gentiles' that they too might come to a knowledge of his saving truth. But Israel, by rejecting God's kingdom and Messiah, was repudiating her part in God's great plan.''"

In Luke it is part of an exhortation (12:54-13:9) to his community to repentance "on the way" (v 58) and is a very powerful argument especially if written after the disaster of A.D. 70. Note that whereas Matthew has only two, Luke has three officials, the magistrate, the judge, and the jailer, in keeping with the "law" of three characters in popular story telling. Luke also has the good Greek word "lepton" (used also of the widow's mite in 21:2), whereas, Matthew has a colloquial Latinism (Greek Kodrantes, Latin quadrans).

(15) *A Call to Repentance—The Fig Tree—(13:1-9):*

Two tragic episodes from recent history and the parable of the barren fig tree, reinforce the urgent need for the sinner (lit debtor 13:2; 12:59; 11:4) Israel to repent. The two recent disasters on which Jesus comments are not mentioned elsewhere in any other source but the first which describes the cruelty of Pilate fits in well with what such writers as Josephus and Philo tell us of Pilate's dislike of the Jews (see Ac 3:13; 4:27; Lk 23:13-31). In fact, after the killing of some Samaritans in A.D. 36, Pilate was recalled to Rome for punishment. Jesus, himself a Galilean, is invited to comment (sympathetically) on Pilate's mingling of the blood of some fellow Galileans with that of their sacrifices, a particularly revolting death. Galilee was a hotbed of revolt against Romans. Possibly, here we have a reference to Pilate's violent slaughter of the Jews who protested when he used the Temple money to finance a new water aqueduct for Jerusalem. Jesus rejects the common fatalistic idea that such disasters must be a judgment of God on their sin.[78] As in the case of those killed by the collapse of the tower in Siloam, he concludes that they were not worse sinners than those who did not die and twice repeats the warning (13:3-5) that such disasters are just a first taste of what will happen to everybody (i.e. all sinners) if Israel does not reform herself. The warnings so often applied to Jesus' opponents are now applied to all. Thus while the kingdom is a gift it is also a decision to which every man is challenged and which he must strive to enter.[79] Unless they changed their minds and attitudes to Jesus they would end in destruction. Like the Old Testament prophets (e.g. Amos, 4:6ff), Jesus sees such events as God's warnings to repent and not an invitation to judge the victims. The risen Jesus would command that repentance should be preached in his name to all nations.[80]

Jesus therefore gives no abstract solution to the problem of human suffering. Possibly the disaster of the collapse of the tower at Siloam was seen as a judgment of God on those who collaborated and worked in the building of the Roman aqueduct.

The parable of the fig tree deals also with the coming judgment and in particular with the problem of delayed judgment and divine mercy and the urgency of repentance. It must be interpreted in the context of Jesus' repeated pronouncement that without repentance all will perish. Only Luke tells this parable. However, some scholars suggest that it has become an "acted out" miracle story in the style of the Old Testament prophets in Matthew and Mark (Mk 11:12-14,20f). Others see the reverse, that Luke has created the parable, thus removing the rather harsh cursing and rather arbitrary behavior of the other synoptics while adding the point of another year's grace (13:8).

The barren fig tree was an Old Testament symbol for an Israel in urgent need of repentance before it was too late.[81] Isaiah had similarly pictured God looking for fruit in his vineyard of Israel (Is 5:1-7). Fig trees were often planted in spare corners of vineyards and after three years fruit was expected. One can possibly read the mention of "three years I have kept coming" as the length of Jesus' public minsitry since John's preaching (see Lv 19:23—this makes the tree six years old v 7). John has preached a baptism of repentance and had seen the axe laid to the root of the trees and every tree not bringing forth good fruit being cut down (3:3,9). The manuring of the tree which is not mentioned in the Old Testament, symbolizes God's exceptional effort to save Israel by the life of Jesus (Amos 3:2). Probably, the parable should best be given the title, the parable of the interceding vinedresser (v 8f). He asks for one more final chance, one more year before it is too late and the door is closed.[82] The point is that punishment does not always follow immediately, but a merciful God normally gives a time for repentance (Ex 34:6). This is the present time, the now for Luke's audience.

(16) *The Bent Woman on the Sabbath—(13:10-17):*

This episode is peculiar to Luke but is a typical example of a Sabbath healing which leads into a controversy such as the man with the withered hand as Luke has already described (6:6-11). Its main teaching about the true meaning of the Law as opposed to Pharisaism, of the primacy of helping one's neighbor over the customary detailed Sabbath observance, is found in all of the gospels. However, one should note that it is one of the few miracle stories which are found in Luke's journey narrative of which about ninety per cent is teaching material.[83] Clearly this exorcism story (v 11,16) is also included here by Luke for its teaching value. Certainly its emphasis on Jesus' concern for a suffering person and a woman at that would have appealed to Luke, whose stories have so often such a special tenderness about them. It fits in with the teaching of the preceding section on the need to repent and accept Jesus as an example of the gift of salvation to which in particular the Jewish leaders were closed in their enthusiasm for the details of the Law. The person involved and her suffering may seem trivial but as the next two parables show, the beginnings of the kingdom can seem deceptively small—they are connected in v 18 with the word "therefore."

This episode would seem to belong in the earlier parts of Jesus' ministry when he frequently spoke in synagogues. It is the first and last time since Jesus set out for Jerusalem that we find him in a synagogue from which he probably was already banned. Curiously too the two parables (13:18) are the only recorded instance of the use of parables by Jesus in a synagogue. Luke typically gives a vivid word-picture of each of the three characters, the bent woman, the president of the synagogue and Jesus in action, in word and deed. Unasked as in 6:8 and 7:14; 14:4, Jesus takes the initiative, calls the woman and tells her that she is free from her infirmity and, fearless of taboos, lays his hands on her.[84] In this section we find a play on the words "freeing" and "binding." Jesus is the stronger one who binds the strong man, Satan (Mk 3:27; Lk 11:17-23) and sets the captives free (4:18f; 11:20; 10:18; Ac 26:18). There is no mention of faith here but a detailed diagnosis of the sickness and the immediate cure which typically leads the woman to thank God.[85] However, the synagogue official does not see an occasion for joy in the release of the woman from her eighteen year captivity. Alluding to Deut 5:14, he indignantly rebukes the congregation for coming to be healed on the Sabbath and thus indirectly, Jesus himself.

He is an example of the religious leaders who are missing the presence of the kingdom (11:20) and thus in need of repentance. He sees the healing as a mere "work" and not as a sign of the kingdom conquering evil, a sign of the times. The controversy here and not the miracle itself, has the real emphasis in Luke's story (6:9-11; 14:1-6). In a blunt answer Jesus calls his opponents hypocrites (12:56) as they concentrate on a detail and miss the true meaning of the law. In an "ad hominen" argument he answers them from their own actions—that they would not hesitate to release animals on the Sabbath (Luke: an ass or an ox in 14:5; Mt 12:11 has a sheep). Thus with devastating logic (argumentum a fortiori), he invites them to advance from a familiar truth to a further conviction (*how much more* should a daughter of Abraham . . .). They had a kinder interpretation of the law for animals than for men. Further, he adds a new point in his remark, that the Sabbath is best honored by doing God's work of salvation in releasing the woman (the "divine must" is used here as in 9:22; 2:49 and 24:44). Jesus does not attribute her disease to a specific sin but to Satan's bondage (13:2). As with Zacchaeus, Jesus stresses that the woman is a daughter of Abraham (a contrast to the Mosaic law which they would quote 19:9). Possibly, the bent woman symbolizes the Jewish nation in servitude to the law for Luke. The joyful reaction of everyone at the glorious deeds of Jesus is contrasted with the confusion of his opponents. Despite opposition there is a large harvest.

(17) *Ultimate Success—Parables of the Mustard Seed and the Leaven(13:18-21).*

The two parables inserted here of the *man* with the mustard and the *woman* with the yeast contrast the insignificant beginning (e.g. the healing of the bent woman) with the ultimate success of the kingdom (of the parable of the Sower and the story of Acts). These parables of contrast can also be seen as a message of encouragement for Luke's community, stressing the hiddenness of the present workings of the kingdom and pointing forward to its final glorious manifestation. In Matthew (13:31-33) both are found together, whereas Mark (4:30-32) has only the mustard seed. The introductory formula does not mean that the kingdom of God is like mustard seed or yeast, but rather should be taken as a rabbinical introduction. As in the case with the mustard seed so is it with the kingdom. Luke, unlike Matthew, and Mark, does not even mention the smallness of the mustard seed or that it was a *great* tree as some copyists have also added in Matthew 13:19). What happens to the seed is the significant thing and the kingdom is rather like the tree. The growth of the kingdom must not be interpreted to mean evolution or human achievement. The achievement is God's and the contrast is between humble beginnings and the future, while in Mark it is stressed the farmer sleeps (Mk 4:26-9).

It was difficult for people to see in the activity of Jesus the itinerant preacher, the dawning of God's universal and almighty kingdom. However, hindsight would help Luke's community to see that he was setting in motion an irreversible chain-reaction of events. "Birds of the air" was a rabbinical name for the Gentiles. In the Old Testament the tree which sheltered the birds was a symbol for the worldwide empire which embraced the nations of the world.[86]

The kingdom is also like what happens when yeast or leaven is put into flour and secretly and mysteriously transforms the whole from within—three measures was the amount used by Sarah (Gn 18:6), yet, it seems to have been a very large quantity. Leaven is used positively here for the good influence of Jesus (Rom 11:16) and not in its normal meaning of an evil influence (12:1; 1 Cor 5:6-8; Gal 5:7-10).

STAGE B

(1) The Narrow Door	13:22-30.
(2) Lament over Jerusalem	13:31-35.
(3) Four Parables at Dinner with Pharisees	14:1-24 .
(4) The Cost of Discipleship	14:25-35.
(5) Three Parables on God's Mercy	15:1-32.
(6) Parables on the Right Use of Money	16:1-31.
(7) Teaching on Service	17:1-10.

(1) *The Narrow Door—(13:22-30):*

The author reminds us here that Jesus is on the way towards Jerusalem, teaching as he goes through cities and towns. Then he gives us various sayings of Jesus associated with such words as door and exclusion. These are scattered in different contexts in Matthew, occasionally with changes in the wording.[87] They clarify thoughts implicit in the previous section about the inclusion of the Gentiles and the exclusion of the Jews from the kingdom. In fact, the reversal motif "The last shall be first" runs through the whole of Stage B from 13:22-17:10.

Luke's version begins with someone questioning Jesus: "Are only a few to be saved?" (Am 5:3; Is 120:19-22). The question seems to react to the "whole mass" which is leavened by Jesus in the previous section (v 21). The question is a relevant one at all times but it seems that it was discussed among the Rabbis of Jesus' day with varying conclusions.[88] It was commonly held that all Israelites would be saved except for a few notorious sinners. In Matthew 7:13-14 it is a narrow gate, whereas in Luke it is the narrow door of a home and in Luke the problem is not to find the door but to enter. In Matthew there is a statement that few find it, but in Luke many will seek to enter but will not be able. Jesus, typically, does not directly answer the questioner's curiosity about how many (yet see v 24 "many will try . . . !), but faces the questioner himself with the difficulty of being saved and his personal need for repentance. As so often, Jesus answers with a parable (10:29ff; 12:13ff; 14:15ff). Jesus insists that his Jewish listener must strive to enter by the narrow door (in Jn 10:7-8, Jesus is the door). The Greek word "strive" comes from the Greek noun *agon*, which means a contest, whence we get the English word agony. It means that one must do one's utmost and put everything into being open to receive the gift of the kingdom.[89] The many who do not enter do not strive until it is too late.

The narrow door in v 25 is locked and it is the entrance to the messianic banquet, to the kingdom (see Mt 25:10 where Jesus is the master). Secondly, Jesus points out the absurdity of the plea of those locked out. Mere social acquaintance which such as the Pharisees had with Jesus in synagogues and at meals is not enough (Ex 24:11). Thirdly, as with the virgins in Matthew 25, there is a finality to the opportunity to enter. There will be a time when the door is shut and the one more chance is over (13:8; 9:26). Jewish birth then is clearly not enough but only the truly faithful (Rom 4:16ff; Gal 3:6-9) will enter to dine "with Abraham, Isaac, Jacob and all the prophets,"[90] and the faithful Gentiles ("from the east . . .").[91] Matthew has Luke's lines 28-9 as the conclusion of his story about the centurion, unlike Luke 7:9f.

Luke is telling his audience that the decisive element at the judgment is one's active response to Jesus here and now and not one's familiarity with him. The latecomers are told "I do not know where you come from" and are rejected in the words of the Psalm 6:8 (also in Mt 7:23). Here is Luke's only use of the common phrase in Matthew about "the wailing and grinding of teeth." Luke's exclusion of some Jewish people is not as harsh as Matthew's (Mt 8:12). "Some who are last will be first . . . " is an example of the reversal of popular belief brought about by Jesus not just in the next life but also in this. This proverbial saying which appears several times in the synoptics, is applied here as a warning to Luke's community, a warning not to be too late for the kingdom (Mt 19:30; 20:16; Mk 10:31). The final verses (v 28f) are not just a prophecy of the last judgment but also of the spread of the gospel among the Gentiles recorded in Acts.

(2) *Lament over Jerusalem—(13:31-5):*

A warning of some Pharisees that Jesus should leave Herod Antipas' territory leads to Jesus' lamentation over the Jewish refusal to accept him and his prophecy about the resulting fate of Jerusalem. The incident probably takes place in Peraea, where Herod had already killed John. The attitude of the Pharisees involved whether they were giving a friendly warning or whether as friends of the Herodians (Mk 3:6) they were trying to get rid of Jesus (and his messianic hopes) from his area, is somewhat unclear. The reply of Jesus suggests that they brought a direct communication from Herod who, according to 9:9 was curious to see Jesus (23:8; Ac 4:27). Luke is the only synoptic who does not continually present the Pharisees as opponents to Jesus.[92] Jesus, in one of his sharpest rebukes, and a rare political remark at that, shows that the hen (v 34) is not intimidated by the fox (or perhaps Jackal), a symbol of crafty unscrupulous cunning for many people.

A Teaching Journey To Jerusalem

In Rabbinical literature, the fox was a worthless and insignificant man. In Ezekiel, the false prophets who had not gathered together the flocks of Israel, are called foxes (Ezek 13:4; Neh 3:35; Lk 9:58), whereas Jesus is a true prophet (v 33). Jesus' blunt reply which alludes to Ex 19:10 and its reference to God coming on the third day in the sight of the people, divides his ministry into a period of exorcisms and healings (4:39; 13:11-17; Ac 10:38) and his accomplishment or perfection on the third day (12:50). The phrase "today and tomorrow and on the third day" is an Aramaic idiom which refers to a short period followed by an important and certain event (Hos 6:2; Jonah 1:17; Lk 4:25; 1 Cor 15:4). "Today and Tomorrow" mean "day by day." Perhaps there is a reference to Daniel's "three and a half," the time of persecution followed by God's triumph (Dn 7:25; 8:14; 12:12). Jerusalem, the goal of his great journey, is to be the scene of Jesus' "perfection," whether Herod likes it or not. The Greek word "teleioumai' " (lit "I will be finished, I will complete, fulfill or accomplish) is used in Jesus' final cry from the cross in John (Jn 19:30; 5:36; 17:4) and in Hebrews (2:10; 5:9), where it echoes Exodus 29 and Leviticus 8 on the consecration of priests.

In the second part of Jesus' response, he ignores Herod completely and goes on to speak of the "divine must" of his journey and announces in somewhat ironical fashion his coming death like that of all the prophets. He has left Galilee, it is stressed, to journey to Jerusalem, not to escape Herold or fulfill his plan, but to conform to God's plan and his ordained sequence of events. Jesus' whole ministry lies under a divine constraint (2:49; 4:43; 13:14; 19:5) but especially *the days*, his "analempsis" (assumption 9:51), the entire paschal mystery which is described by its last event in which Jesus returns to the Father to send the Spirit.[93] His death in Jerusalem is not an accident but his goal. The reference to three days is repeated to emphasize the shortness of his time left (Jonah 1:17). In Luke, Jesus has been shown as a prophet, the bearer of God's word (4:18,23; 7:16; Ac 10:38). Now he must die like a prophet to give testimony with his life[94]—a second passion prediction (12:50). Thus to the Pharisees warning of danger in Galilee, Jesus replies that he is going knowingly to face his death in Jerusalem.

Mention of Jerusalem leads Luke to put here Jesus' apostrophe or lament over Jerusalem, symbolizing the Jewish people. An identical version is better placed in Matthew 23:37-9 after Jesus' confrontation with the city at the end of a long sermon against Pharisaism in particular, just before his crucifixion. This apostrophe is full of allusions to the scattered Jewish people (Is 31:5; 60:4; Zech 10:8-10). To be gathered safely under the wings of God was a constant Old Testament image.[95] Now God is abandoning his temple again (Ez 8-11) and destruction is coming (Jer 12:7; Mic 3:12). It is the tragic abandoning of a lover (Ps 87:2) because "you refused me' ' (v 34) and the rejection and responsibility is not God's but theirs. They had made a habit of killing God's messengers and prophets.[96] Jewish legend by this time had turned five of the great prophets into martyrs at the hands of the people. From the expression "how often" many conclude that this is not Jesus' first visit to Jerusalem but that here we have a reference to the Jerusalem ministry mentioned in the early chapters of John. However, Jerusalem can and must be taken in Luke as the symbol of the Jewish people and in particular their leaders (20:9-16).

The fate of Jesus and the fate of Jerusalem are closely intertwined for Luke. "Your house (temple?) will be abandoned," echoes the words of Jeremiah over the king's

A Teaching Journey To Jerusalem 321

house in Jerusalem.[97] This will be the case "until the times of the Gentiles are fulfilled" (21:24; Rom 11:25-32). Jesus concludes that the city will see him no more until it greets him in his triumphant entry with the words of Ps 118:26 (19:38). These words in Matthew 23:37-9 are found after the events of Palm Sunday and they refer rather to the second coming of Jesus.

(3) *Four Parables at Dinner with Pharisees—(14:1-24):*

This symposium at a dinner with one of the rulers who was a Pharisee (Jesus' third such, i.e. 7:36; 11:37) can conveniently be divided into three parts. In the first part (v 1-6) we have Jesus' interpretation of the Sabbath law as he heals a man with dropsy (a medical expression) on the Sabbath. Dropsy was a dreadful disease and was popularly thought to be a curse from God (Num 5:21-3). Only Luke tells this story but it is quite similar in its teaching to the healing of the man in Luke 6:6-11 and the woman in 13:10-17 (note 6:32-6). Secondly, in v 7-11 we have some table talk with Jesus as he gives two precepts (7-11,12-14) and teaches how people should live with one another in view of God's invitation to the future messianic banquet. Thirdly, (15-24) we are given the parable of the Great Banquet or "The Contemptuous Guests" as it can also be described. Only the poor and the Gentiles actually attend. Right through Luke continues the theme of repentance with the foolishness of the self-centered Pharisees, particularly in view. Here we find Luke's sixth dinner scene.[98] He has just mentioned the heavenly banquet in the preceding chapter at 13:29.

The frequency of dinner settings with intellectual discussions in Luke's presentation of the gospel is striking. He had plenty of antecedents in Jewish literature, such as

Esther, Ecclesiasticus (32), the Epistle of Aristeas, not to mention the famous symposium of the Greek philosopher, Plato. They are a fulfilment of the messianic prophecies,[99] which expected the Messiah to gather the poor and the scattered into his banquet community, thus restoring communion between God and man and between men themselves. Thus in Jesus, God is not only visiting men and entering into communion with them as a guest in their houses, but there is also a reverse or deeper level to the banquet scenes. Really it is Jesus who is the host, inviting to repentance, to the forgiveness of sins, to communion with God now.

This is Luke's fourth discussion of a healing on the Sabbath. The scene is dramatic as "they watch him lurkingly" (6:7; Mk 3:2). Jesus forces the issue with two questions to their silence (6:6f). Jesus, the radical goes back to the true meaning of the Sabbath (Gn 2:3). He again uses his devastating argument that they had more care and compassion for animals than for their suffering fellow man (13:15; Jn 5:17). It is noteworthy that in the stricter Qumran rules, whereas an animal could not be pulled out at all on the Sabbath, a man could provided no implements were used. The best and oldest manuscript reading here is "son or ox," a combination found in Deuteronomic legislation about working on the Sabbath (Dt 5:14). In the Aramaic there is a pun involved—son (bera), ox (beira), well (bera). This implies that their compassion only exists where self-interest is involved. The man is "set free" by Jesus (v 4; 4:18f).

Next Jesus tells a parable as Luke reminds us (v 7) and gives a precept on humility. It is not a rule of dinner etiquette or advice as in Prov 25:6, on which the parable is based, but is a parable about the messianic banquet and the revesal it will involve. Note that the invitation is to a marriage which was a messianic symbol (Is 62:4; 54:5; Hos

2:7; Jer 2:2). It recommends that humility in life which the Magnificat (1:46-55) had taught would be reversed. The parable of the Pharisee and the Tax Collector (18:9-14) will teach the same lesson with the same concluding verse (18:14; 14:11; Mt 23:12; 18:4; 1 P 5:5; Jam 4:6; Phil 2:5ff), which is the key to the interpretation. The Pharisees, with their exalted self-importance, tended to put themselves in the first places before God and men (11:43). All must recognize their need of salvation. The passive "shall be exalted" is an indirect reference to God's reversal of popular human values.

The second precept is based on Jesus' distinctive principle that one should do good without the common expectation of reciprocity (6:33). Pharisees always tend to exclusivism, to cut themselves off from others especially the common people, to invite their own people and kind, to measure the reponse, to expect the same in return. Four categories of those normally invited are named friends, brothers (close relatives), relatives, wealthy neighbors. Jesus' somewhat hyperbolic advice is different: do not so much invite these but the poor with selfless generosity. This was Jesus' own mission as he explained at Nazareth (4:18-19; 7:29). At the resurrection repayment will be based on how we have treatd the poor (e.g. Dives in 16:19ff; Mt 25:31ff). Here the expression "the resurrection of the just" does not mean that only the just will rise.[100] The rich, as the next two incidents insist, actually refuse the invitation to the kingdom because the cost of discipleship is too much for them, while the poor accept (7:22; 14:12,21).

The dissimularities between Luke's version of the parable of the great banquet and Matthew's are such that a common source is unlikely (Lk 14:15-24; Mt 22:1-14). Both make the point that the Jews reject the invitation which is then extended to the Gentiles. As with the closed door (13:24-30), clearly many are excluded. Luke's version takes its beginning from a pious, confident and almost self-congratulatory platitude which one in the party exclaims at Jesus' mention of the resurrection. Like the woman's beatitude (11:27ff), so also the man's beatitude here is corrected by the shocking story of the great eschatological banquet at which none of the many invited turn up. Jesus answers the statement from the bystander as so often with a parable in Luke (12:13ff; 10:29ff; 13:23ff), which is possibly a kind of midrash on Is 49:6. Matthew's king with many servants is in Luke unexpectedly, a man with one servant (i.e. Jesus, Is 42:6; 49:6). Matthew's brief statement "one went off to his farm, another to his business" is expanded in Luke and the excuse about the wife is added (14:20; 18:29). There are unexpected details in Matthew's incredible allegory of an invitation to a wedding feast, e.g. those invited kill the servants, the dinner preparations are interrupted while a military expedition destroys their city, servants are sent into the streets of the destroyed city to invite the bad and the good, one guest who came off the streets had no wedding garment.

The second invitation may seem unusual but it was customary in the East as a courteous reminder to those who had accepted the first that the meal was ready (Esth 5:8; 6:14; Lam 4:2). The Jews had accepted God's invitation (a key word repeated four times, v 13,16,17,24) but refused Jesus. The excuses which are close to those required by Deuteronomy for exemption from military service (e.g. Dt 20:7; 24:5) are what the parable of the sower calls being "stifled by the cares and riches and pleasures of life" even at dinner time (8:14). The angry master sends the servant next on a double mission both inside and outside (only Luke) the city, i.e. the Gentiles. The poor (the

A Teaching Journey To Jerusalem

streets and alleys) who cannot repay the invitation are the new community which Jesus forms from the old Israel (4:18; 7:29). Note that v 21 is a repeat of v 13. The blind and the lame were not only excluded from the Qumran community, but also from the Jewish temple itself (Lv 21:17-23). Those in the highways and hedges, the major roads outside the city, are the Gentiles who make the house *full*. Thus *some*Jews are excluded while some sit down at the feast with the Gentiles (13:28f; Rom 11:17-25; Eph 1:11-13). Originally, the parable was intended for Jesus' opponents but in Luke it is an explanation of the current situation.

The phrase "force them to come in" has often been disastrously interpreted since the time of Augustine, as a justification for the use of violence and persecution on non-Christians.[101] A better translation would be "urge," "persuade," or the compulsion of love (see the same word in Mt 14:22; Mk 6:45). Oriental courtesy demanded a moderate reluctance which the host should overcome. Note there is only one servant involved in Luke.

(4) *The Cost of True Discipleship—(14:25-35):*

But lest his audience become smug and secure, that they, unlike some Jews, have accepted Jesus' invitation, Luke now mentions in his most blunt and forcible presentation, three of the demands of discipleship—the hatred of one's family and even life itself, the taking up of the cross and following Jesus and thirdly the complete renunciation of all one's possessions. Note how Luke abandons the dinner setting in v 25. Typically in Luke Jesus is presented as the model for discipleship. The bluntness reminds one of

Garibaldi's famous offer to his followers of "hunger, thirst, forced marches, battles and death," or Churchill's "I have nothing to offer but blood, toil and sweat'. The message of complete dedication already given to the disciples (e.g. 9:18-27,57-62), is now for 'the great crowds' (e.g. Ac 2:41; 4:4), whereas in Matthew 10;37, the first is addressed to the disciples. The third is in Luke alone. Jesus turns to address them[102]—the image is like that in Mark where Jesus is striding ahead of the disciples and the following crowd (Mk 10:32).

The fact that Luke has already recorded the ten commandments and also the command to love even enemies (6:27; Mk 7:9ff) warns one that the harsh expression "hating" one's family (1:15ff) is a hyperbolic and dramatic semitism for preference to emphasize the absoluteness of the personal loyalty demanded. The Semitic language likes to use extremes, e.g. light and darkness, truth and falsehood, love and hate. Luke's version seems more semitic than Matthew 10:37, who has "Whoever loves father . . . more than . . .". Luke adds "wife, brothers, sisters, even his own life." To further stress the point the solemn refrain "He cannot be my disciple" is repeated three times (v 26,27,33). Thus in such texts as Gen 29:31ff; Dt 21:15; Rom 9:13, hating means loving less and not dislike, as some translations put it. The saying about the cross is already given at 9:23.[103]

Two short parables about a rash builder (1 Cor 3:10-15) and a reckless king going to war (12:54ff; Eph 6:6-11) are placed between the second and the third demands. The use of two short parables is frequent in Luke. They are found only in Luke and are intended to provoke the audience to self-examination and a deeper commitment (9:59ff). They warn the disciple against a hasty commitment and a foolish underestimation of the total renunciation involved. The third demand of the disciple which is again hyperbolic but nevertheless very real, extends the renunciation to all of one's possessions (e.g. Heb 10:34). A fully sacrificing disciple is like salt and is useful for society to preserve and purify and add flavor to it. But a half-committed one is like tasteless salt which is useless for any purpose and is thrown out like rubbish (Mk 9:49f; Mt 5:13).

(5) *Three Parables on God's Joyful Mercy—(15:1-32):*

Mention of the invitation of the poor to the heavenly banquet leads Luke in chapter 15 to give three parables describing God's joyous mercy to the lost sinner, as a defense of Jesus' mission to the lost, against the murmuring of the aloof Pharisees and scribes (Ps 1:1; 267:4-5; 51:13). These parables, which show little or no influence of adaptation by the early Church, are carefully combined into one unit with the repeated refrain "lost," "found," and "joy," which is found in v 6,9f,23f, and the final v 32 gives the stress or punch line of the parable. The first two particularly form a typical Lucan pair of parables about a man and a woman, to illustrate the same point.[104] The parables of the rich shepherd and the poor woman have a similar structure, loss, an anxious search, the joyful celebration of discovery. They make the same basic point that Jesus is as justified in searching for the lost as people are in searching for their lost goods. The joy of the finders is a reflection of the joy of God himself when he recovers the lost. In the third we turn from a lost object to two lost sons with a further unexpected twist at the end. The theme of repentance continues to be prominent, especially in the third parable about the son as opposed to the sheep and the coin, where it is artifically brought in.[105] The joy of God over a sinner's repentance is depicted as that of a joyful shepherd, a joyful housewife and especially a joyful father to whom a son is restored in fellowship. Only Matthew has any similar parables to this chapter with his version of the Lost Sheep (Mt 18:12-24) and his parable about two sons (Mt 21:28-32). It should be noted that recent linguistic investigation has shown that apart from the opening three verses, the language of this chapter is not Lucan. Therefore, the chapter should not be seen as a purely Lucan construction but as drawn from his special source.

The Lost Sheep—(15:1-7):

In Matthew the parable is used in his fourth major sermon which is addressed to the disciples on discipline within the community and is part of an exhortation to seek out any of the little ones in the Church who have strayed. He emphasizes seeking. In Luke, it is addressed to the third criticism of Jesus' association with sinners (5:30ff; 7:34) with its teaching that it is God's way which Jesus embodies in seeking the lost and accepting them into the intimacy of table fellowship. In Luke the emphasis is on the joy of finding and repentance. Thus Luke gives a life situation in the life of Jesus while Matthew gives that of the early post-resurrection church. For Luke, such meals indicate that Jesus is the doctor, saving the lost, bringing forgiveness of sins and newness of life (5:30-32; 19:9f). Luke is no doubt exaggerating when he mentions "all the tax collectors . . . ". There is a note of horrified contempt in their description of Jesus as "this man" (v 2) as also in the elder brother's description of his brother as "this son of yours" (v 30). The same basic word used here in 15:2 and 19:7 is also used in John 6:61 of the skepticism of the disciples

A Teaching Journey To Jerusalem

and in John 6:41,43, of the rejection of Jesus by the Jews—the elder son will similarly complain in v 28-30. Jer 31:10-20 and Ezek 34:11-16 (Jn 10:1ff; Lk 12:32) are examples of the Old Testament background to the parable of the lost sheep. Sheep is not a very complimentary biblical description of man. The carrying of the exhausted sheep on the shepherd's shoulders reveals his tenderness and care (Is 40:11; 49:22; Mt 9:36; Rom 5:6). Only Luke has the invitation to the neighbors for the celebration (v 6). The final line seems to end in irony, emphasizing God's "more" joy ("in heaven" is a reverential circumlocution) and higher regard for outcasts than that of the Pharisees and scribes—there are no ninety nine who have no need to repent (5:32; Rom 2:23; 1 Jn 1:8).

A Jewish saying which would perfectly express the feeling of Jesus' critics said that "There is joy before God when those who provoke him perish from the world." Scholars have noted how confidently in such parables (rhetorical questions both) Jesus speaks of what gives God joy and how what happens in heaven is perfectly reflected in his ministry as he acts with God's authority and in his place. Here it is pointed out that the shepherd leaves the ninety nine to search out the single lost sheep. The Jewish scholar, C. Montefiore, has noted a revolutionary and distinctive aspect of God taking the initiative and searching for the lost until it is found.

> "Here is a new figure which has never ceased to play its great part in the moral and religious development of the world."[106]

The Rabbis believed that God would welcome a sinner if he first repented and of course adopted his interpretation of the law (Is 55:7; Jer 3:12; Eph 2:4f). For them God could not love sinners and search them out.

The Lost Coin—(15:8-10):

A woman, as an example of God's searching love, is a very revolutionary idea among the Jews who considered that a woman was not even capable of learning the Law. Like the shepherd, she leaves everything aside and searches thoroughly until she finds. The drachma which she lost and which is only mentioned here in the New Testament, represented a day's wages for a working man. Possibly the ten were on a head-dress and represented a poor woman's dowry or wedding ring. In the dark windowless Palestinian house with its low door, she has to light a lamp and sweep the dark earthen floor to aid her search. The same application is made with the resultant joy before God's court of angels—Luke mentions the angels 23 times, Matthew 19 and Mark 5 times.

The Prodigal Son's Unloving Brother—(15:11-32):

Commentators tend to use superlatives when describing the artistry and appeal of this parable about repentance, so beloved of artists and writers, yet strangely omitted by the other gospels. Some even describe it as a mini-compendium of theology, a kind of Pilgrim's Progress, the story of Everyman, beginning with a man as God intended him to be, then describing the actual human condition and finally redeemed man as he can be. One thinks of W. Somerset Maugham's famous comparison of his life to a party which was "very nice to start with, but has become rather noisy as time has gone on. And I am not at all sorry to go home." However, as with writings which are popular over a long period like Dean Swift's Gulliver's Travels, which was written as a criticism of his society, one can miss the real point of the story. It is a defense of Jesus' good

A Teaching Journey To Jerusalem

news to the poor and a trap-like invitation to his opponents to repent. Thus the popular title "The Prodigal Son" distorts the point of the story as his prodigality is only a detail and as the opening line makes clear, it is about two sons and their loving father. Many better titles are suggested, e.g. The Loving Father, The Father's Love, The Waiting Father, The Two Sons, The Two Brothers.

The story has many Lucan characteristics. It is an almost purely secular story with little or no religious details. It involves journeys, a reversal, rich people with servants and an Old Testament background such as the preference for the younger brother, Semitic terminology.[107&108] It reflects actual conditions in Palestine, where a man could easily think that by escaping the rather stultifying Judaism of the half a million Jews who stayed at home, he would do far better by going to the diaspora of the approximately four million Jews scattered throughout the Roman Empire, some quite near to Palestine. However, the humorous story told by A.M. Hunter about the modern prodigal who was advised by the minister to return home, is a warning that the story is larger than much of real life. Months afterwards the minister who advised him "to go back home and his father would kill the fatted calf," met the prodigal "Well, and did he kill the fatted calf for you?" "No" was the rueful reply, "but he nearly killed the prodigal son."[109]

The first part of the story describes a foolish father who, disregarding the advice of the wise,[110] gives his younger "permissive age" son his share (one third) of his inheritance. This younger son is obviously anxious to be free and independent (Gn 3:5) of parental control and to have his own money and experience of life. He turned his share into cash as the text probably means and set off for a distant land where he squandered his money in a carefree and spendthrift fashion (Eph 5:18; Tobit 1:6; 1 P 4:4). The nature of his spendthrift life is not specified (see 15:30). He ended up in disaster as a result of a famine and its corresponding inflation. He had to hire himself out to a Gentile pig-keeper, an occupation which signified the bottom of the pit for a Jew, in whose religion pigs were considered impure and even the source of a curse (Lv 11:17). He was so reduced in poverty that he longed to eat swine fodder, the fruit of the carob tree, but no one gave him anything (1 K 8:47ff). There was a Jewish saying that "When the Jews are reduced to eating carob seeds they repent." But his repentance is based on the lowest motive possible, his misery. However, in a typical Lucan soliloquy, e.g. 12:16-21,45; 15:17-19; 16:3f; 18:4,14, he rehearses a speech of true repentance. He came to himself and saw that the situation with his father could never be the same again. He is content to return as a hired servant whose status was the lowest, lower even than the regular slaves. Sin as always for the Jews, is primarily against God (Ex 10:16)—heaven is a reverent periphrasis. They also had the idea of a forgiving father (Is 63:16-19). But what was his sin? The wasting of his possessions would fit in well with Luke's next teaching on the right use of money (16:1-31). Also he was certainly not honoring his parents by not being able to look after them in their old age as the commandment intended. But the Father sees him from a distance and has compassion (a key word also in 7:13; 10:33). The father, thinking only of his joy, cuts short his Son's confession and immediately welcomes him home, not as a servant, but as an honored son.

He runs to meet him—rather undignified behavior for an elderly oriental. He falls on his neck and kisses him as a sign of forgiveness and reunion.[111] The ring signifies rank and authority (Gn 41:42; Esth 8:2) and shoes signify a freeman while the fatted calf is an allusion to Abraham's

A Teaching Journey To Jerusalem

entertainment of the heavenly visitors (Gn 18:7; 1 S 28:24). The description of one who is spiritually lost, as a dead man capable of being restored to life, reminds one of the famous scene in Ezek 37:1-14 (see also Gn 46:29-30; Ps 103:10f; Lk 9:60). An interesting comparison can be made with the Buddhist story which begins like the Prodigal Son but when the boy returns home to his father he then begins to work off his guilt and the penalty for his behavior by years of servitude of his father. This is the principle of *Karma,* which is quite different from the principle of grace or free forgiveness and the full restoration of one who is clearly guilty.[112] The teaching is Paul's doctrine of justification in tender human terms (see also 18:9-14; Gal 4:5; Eph 1:7; Col 1:14).

But the real interest and the main challenge and emphasis lies in the second half of the parable with its unusual climax (v 25-32). It describes the unloving criticism and complaining of the elder brother which represents the complaining of the Pharisees and scribes at Jesus' conduct, which is not found in the first two parables. Both sons, it becomes quickly evident, were lost to their father. The concluding words more or less repeat the conclusion of the first part (v 24,32).

The father, again forgetting his dignity, goes out to plead with the second son who is at work in the fields (Gn 25:29), like the searching of v 4,8. A servant has fed his curiosity with the facts that his brother was received back safe and sound and that the fatted calf was killed. He had "refused to go in." He replies to his father that his life was one of slavery, unrewarded, and in still superior language, like the Pharisee in the Temple (18:11-12) that he was a model in his obedience and proceeds in a jealous rage to turn on his father and accuse him of not being similarly generous to himself (Mt 20:12). He does not call him father, in contrast to his brother. He accuses probably without evidence, his brother (i.e. "this son of yours") of consorting with loose women (Prov 29:3)—a Freudian projection of jealousy. The father is not deflected from his love of both and refuses to be drawn into taking sides and calls him "my son," an affectionate word meaning "my child" and quietly insists instead that the prodigal is "this brother of yours." The story has no moral attached but is an unanswered question and incomplete as we are not told whether the elder son, who was more lost than his brother, accepted the invitation to compassionate love and joy or not. He represents the complaining opponent to whom the parable was addressed by Jesus. He is a Jonah-like character without heart, the harsh, unforgiving righteous man, not just of Luke's community but of every age, who needs to learn to judge not and to find the true meaning of Christian joy and compassion. The first two parables stress that God loves wandering sinners and welcomes them back with joy. The third invites all to share in that joy.

(6) *Parables on the Right Use of Money—(16:1-31):*

This chapter which mainly contains teaching on the right use of wealth, consists of two parables, The Dishonest Steward and Dives and Lazarus, with a vivid collection of sayings in between.

The Astuteness of the Dishonest Stewart—(16:1-13):

Luke, who almost delights in using immoral characters such as the disobliging neighbor (11:5ff) and the unjust judge (18:2ff) as examples of the proper response in a crisis, excels himself here with a unique parable in which every character is a scoundrel (see Mt 21:31; Mk 7:24-30). Not only that, but Jesus seems to praise a crook for his as-

A Teaching Journey To Jerusalem

tuteness, not however for his dishonesty and to invite his disciples to imitate him—an example which has horrified many an earnest Christian who forgot that the Bible is full of such characters from Jacob to Judith, to Rahab, to David. The setting is typically Lucan, the rich household, the soliloquy which gives us the scoundrel's thinking, the big quantities.

Yet it is an ironical parable which is true to the economic situation of the times and is possibly even based on an actual recent occurence—an Egyptian papyrus has illustrated a similar corrupt embezzler engaged in bribery there in the second century. Palestine and Galilee in particular, had many large estates owned by rich absentee landlords who entrusted them to stewards with full powers and responsibilities to run the estate (e.g. 12:43ff). Here Luke changes his audience and addresses the parable to the disciples and of course his own community. Note how for variety he switches back and forth from the Pharisees 15:3 to the disciples 16:1 and back to the Pharisees 16:15 and again to the disciples 17:1, the Pharisees in 17:20 and the disciples in 17:22. The story tells how a steward was discovered selfishly (v 9) squandering (the same word is used of the prodigal son in 15:13 and connects the two parables) the estate and so faces dismissal. Some recent writers have suggested that his subsequent action was well within his powers and his normal profit making for himself which was permitted that he was only remitting his normal commission to ingratiate himself with his master's debtors by destroying the original records. Large debts are involved—the hundred "baths" of oil or about eight hundred gallons is the yield of one hundred and forty six olive trees, and the hundred "kors" of wheat or about one thousand bushels, the yield of one hundred acres, each is about ten years salary for a working man.

Possibly the use of oil and wheat was a Jewish subterfuge for getting round the law forbidding Jews to charge interest from their fellow Jews (Ex 22:25; Lv 25:36; Dt 23:19) and he was making the bills interest free. However, what is stressed here is how the Lord (an ambiguous word) praised or gave credit to the steward for acting wisely, for his realistic and enterprising action in the critical situation which he recognizes and faces up to ahead of time. Only here and 12:42 does Luke use the word "wisely." The ambiguity of the word Lord is that it can refer to the servant's master or to Jesus. It is unlikely that a master, unless grudgingly or sarcastically, would admire a servant who had squandered his property. Yet this possibly was its original meaning. But it seems more likely that as it normally does in Luke, the expression in the text refers to Jesus (see also 18:6). In 2:9 and 14:23 it refers to God. The Revised Standard Version of 1881 put in "his" to make sure that the commendation was not that of Jesus. The original purpose of the parable was an invitation to Jesus' still unconverted audience to decisive action before the crisis of the kingdom, to boldly stake all before it is too late (13:9,24ff). Like the steward, they faced an immediate crisis. They should use their minds and show as much intelligent realizm and face up to the facts of their critical situation just as the wordly use foresight in their own interests. The children of the light (an expression also found in Qumran, also Jn 12:36; 1 Th 5:5; Eph 5:8) often fail in the virtue which the children of the world often use to assure their future welfare and friends. Jesus is asking for inventiveness and resolute courage for a better cause. One is reminded of the saying attributed to Karl Barth that while the human sin is pride the sin of the Christian is laziness. Many Christians are not as dedicated to the spread of the good news as some communities are to their propaganda even though they have no hope of a future life. In Luke it is adapted to teach the proper use of wealth by the association of some three further and different lessons on the use of money (v 9-13). These additional remarks, which have been called the moralizing notes of an early Christian preacher, are linked together and with the parable by such catchwords as the repetition of "dishonest" or "unrighteous," which in differing forms occur from v 8-11, "mammon" which occurs in v 9,11,13 and servant or steward in v 13,1.

Verse 9 on the right use of money would be an excellent introduction to the story of Dives and Lazarus (16:19-31). It also clearly but ironically refers back to the dishonest steward who used mammon to win friends for himself who would help him in his coming crisis. The word "mammon" is found in Jewish literature to mean "money" or "profit." It is the opposite of true riches (v 11). Responsible stewardship of one's money which does not last for ever, but not its complete rejection, is what is commanded here (19:3; 14:13f; 6:30ff; 1 Jn 2:17). Money is merely a means whereby friends last even into the future life. "They" is a reverential way of saying God, thus giving the meaning of the verse as a command to use wealth so as to make God one's friend so that he will welcome one into heaven. One who is unfaithful in goods, will not be entrusted with greater things in the life to come. This contradicts the teaching of Karl Marx, who believed that Christians were so concerned with the future that they were not interested in the present (19:11-27). A man's use of money is, especially in Luke, a good test of his commitment to Christ. These applications also, it should be noted, correct possible misunderstandings of the parable by those who would see it as an invitation to financial misuse. Money is only given to man on trust (1 Chron 29:14; 1 Tim 6:7) and can prevent people like the Pharisees from an appreciation of true riches (v 14; 2:32f; Mt 25:34).

The final application on the impossibility of serving or giving complete dedication to two masters is found in identical words but in a different context in Matthew's Sermon on the Mount (Mt 6:24). Again, it corrects a possible misiunderstanding of the parable and teaches that the disciples' prudence and astuteness has to do with true riches. It is not God and money but either God or money (Col 3:5; 1 Tim 6:8-10). The word "mammon" found here is the common Aramaic word for wealth found in the Jewish literature of the times including the Dead Sea Scrolls. It literally meant "that in which one puts one's trust." The steward saw that money cannot be clung to and that it only benefits when given away (12:33). Here Luke recalls us to the teaching of John (3:10ff).

The Law and the Kingdom of God—(16:14-18):

These sayings which are grouped by the catchword "law" and which fit very loosely into the context, are a criticism of the Pharisees, their attitude towards money, the law, and in particular divorce. Verses 14 and 15 are found only in Luke while the other verses are found scattered in Mark and Matthew—v 16 and Mt 11:12-13; v 17 and Mt 5:118; v 18, Mk 10:11-12 and Mt 5:32.

The Pharisees, not unlike practitioners of the modern Protestant work ethic, who could quote such Old Testament texts as Dt 27:1ff, on wealth as a divine reward for keeping the Law and who practised almsgiving, must have considered Jesus' teaching as impractical naivety and so they "turned up their noses" at Jesus (Job 4:7-8; 8:6-7; Lk 132:1-5). They are hypocrites, content to justify themselves before men, but God, unlike men, can see through to their hearts (11:41; 1 S 16:7). God reverses the fortunes of men as Mary's song put it (1:51) and as the following parable illustrates.

A Teaching Journey To Jerusalem

Luke 16:16 (Mt 11:12-13) on the law and the prophets, John and the good news of God's kingdom, was the pivot argument for Conzelmann's tripartite division of history. However, many scholars today hold that Conzelmann tended to read too much into the text and to produce too rigid divisions. For Luke there is a dynamic continuity in the story of salvation, John's position, like that of the Ascension between the time of Jesus and the church, is rather ambivalent—like a bridge belonging to both eras, the last of the prophets and yet inaugurating the time of salvation. These verses clearly speak of the continuing and abiding value of the law in addition to the grace of the kingdom. The new has not so much destroyed the old or brought it to an end, as brought it to fulfilment and showed its proper and true depth of meaning down to its smallest details. The new element[113] is the universal aspect that now everyone, people of all kinds and not just the select few, are "forcing their way into" the kingdom (14:25). Matthew has this saying in a different context and in a reverse and expanded form (Mt 11:12; Gal 3:24). The Greek verb used here is a strong word and suggests the storming of a city by desperate people striving, as in a contest, as they were told to do in 13:24, and like the unjust steward above. Other interpretations here suggest the killing of John, the violence of the Zealot movement and also the oppression of the kingdom (present in Jesus) by his opponents such as the Pharisees. Verse 17 insists that the true spirit and meaning of the law down to its dots or smallest distinguishing marks or flourishes between letters, is to be found in Jesus and is more lasting than the universe (Ac 15:21; 21:20).

The statement on divorce shows that it is more demanding than some of the actual rules found in the Old Testament (Mt 5:18; Mk 10:11-12). The new freedom in Jesus does not get rid of the law as some obviously held, but is even more demanding. This is Luke's only reference to teaching on divorce and shows Jesus rejecting the looseness of the law as found in Dt 24:1-4. The liberal interpretation school of Hillel, to which many of the Pharisees belonged, allowed divorce for the most trivial reasons (e.g. a poor dinner), unlike the stricter school of Shammai which interpreted Deuteronomy as meaning only unfaithfulness. Here, Jesus is even stricter than Shammai and curiously for Luke, only the man's side is mentioned (see Mk 10:11-12; Mt 5:32; 19:19). Possibly there is an allusion to Herod who dismissed his wife to marry Herodias who was already married to his half-brother. Possibly Antipas had five brothers when the parable of Dives and Lazarus was composed (16:27).

The Rich Man and Lazarus—(16:19-31):

This parable illustrates the danger of riches, that they are no guarantee of God's blessings. It reminds us of the necessity of repentance before the coming reversal of fortune and the point which Luke has already stressed that there will come a time when it is too late (13:9,24ff). In a few haunting lines, Jesus has drawn a picture which has challenged mankind ever since, a blind mankind which is so used to Lazarus at the gate that it thanks God it is not like him. It is a parable which is revolutionary in its social and ethical challenge, for man's eternal destiny is decided by his relationship to Lazarus. The sin of the rich man is simply indifference and insensitivity, not positive cruelty—he lacks the compassion of the Good Samaritan.

When the young Albert Schweitzer (1875-1965), already a famous European theologian and musician and with a very successful career ahead of him, turned his back on his career to become a missionary doctor in Gabon, he had concluded that he was the rich man and Africa the poor man.

"Just as Dives sinned against Lazarus" he wrote in the opening page of his book, *On the Edge of the Primeval Forest,* "because for want of heart, he never put himself in his place and let his conscience tell him what to do, so we sin against the poor at our own gate." "Whatever benefits we confer upon the peoples of our colonies is not beneficience but atonement for the terrible sufferings which we white people have been bringing upon them ever since the day on which the first of our ships found its way to their shores."

Jesus seems to have taken a popular story about the selfish rich and their disregard for the misfortunes of the poor. A parallel is found in the Egyptian story about the reversal of fortune after death. Although here it is addressed to Pharisees, many think that it originally concerned the luxury living Sadducees who did not believe in the resurrection. As they disappeared with the fall of Jerusalem it may have been convenient to change the audience.

Lazarus is the only character in a parable of Jesus to be given a proper name. It is the rather common Jewish name, Eliezer (Gn 15:2) which must have been carefully chosen here for its significance, as it means "God helps," thus putting him among the poor who receive the kingdom (6:20). It recalls the Lazarus of Bethany whose resurrection failed to convince the Jewish people (Jn 11:1ff). Some have suggested that John's version is a dramatization of Luke's epilogue to the parable but it is a possibility that Luke's edition is based on John.[114] Abraham, a favorite character in Luke (1:55,73; 13:16; 19:9) is mentioned some 7 times in the story and in particular the rich man calls on him repeatedly, contrary to the warning which John had earlier expressed (3:8).

The story which has again three characters and two scenes and an epilogue, is painted in strongly contrasting colors. Like the prodigal son, Lazarus longed to eat the scraps. In the reversal of the situation after death (1:46-55; 6:2; Mt 5:4), Lazarus is at the banquet table in the place of honor, reclining in Abraham's bosom (5:34; Mt 8:11; Jn 13:23) and the rich man is outside in suffering. Popular ideas about the situation immediately after death are used. Hades is normally the abode of all the departed but in the New Testament it is especially the place of punishment, Gehenna (12:5; Ps 6:4-5). In Enoch (ch 22) Sheol is described as having two separate compartments where the good and evil can see each other as they wait for the final judgment. The emphasis on the "great chasm" in between signifies that after death nothing can be done to save the rich. It should be noted that the rich man is addressed by the same tender expression "my son," as the elder brother of the prodigal son. The emphasis of the parable is on the point made in the dialogue v 27ff. Lazarus is silent all through the parable. The rich man requests that Lazarus be sent as a warning to his brothers about conditions after death. It is implied that the rich man had not repented (v 28,30). The parable therefore properly understood, teaches not just a message of charity and a reflection that wordly success is not important in God's sight (16:15). The main point is that the teaching of the Bible which they knew so well in theory, the Word which was available to Luke's community,[115] was so clear and convincing that it should lead to repentant behavior. No other sign, however spectacular, would convince those who love their riches. "If a man with the revelation of God's will before him in the scriptures and Lazarus lying in misery at his door step, cannot be humane, nothing—neither a visitant from another world nor a revelation of the terrors of hell, will teach him otherwise."[116] The final line is an allusion to the refusal of some of Luke's contemporaries to be convinced by the resurrection of Jesus and their demand for signs (11:16).

A Teaching Journey To Jerusalem

(7) *Four Sayings about the Disciples' Duties—(17:1-10):*

The first three of these instructions to the disciples appear elsewhere in different settings and order in the other synoptics (Mk 9:42; 11:22ff; Mt 17:20; 18:6f,15; 21:21), while the third, a parable on service, is found only in Luke. The disciples are warned to be on their guard (v 30; 12:1; 21:34; Ac 5:35; 20:28) against scandal, lack of forgiveness, weakness of faith, self-satisfaction. Despite the inevitability of evil in the world, they are warned about their responsibility to the little ones. They must take care lest they be a scandal to such poor as Lazarus (Mt 25:45; Gn 19:11; 1 S 5:9). The metaphor is that of a snare in which one is trapped or an obstacle over which one stumbles—these were seen as sent by God to test his people or an individual (Is 8:14; Jer 6:21; Ezek 3:20). Possibly the reference as in Mt 18:6 is to the destruction of the weaker faith of some simpler members of the community. Drowning was a popular way of getting rid of demons and the millstone was the huge stone used for grinding corn. Secondly, when a brother does wrong there is the duty of rebuking him (4:39; 9:55; 19:39f; 23:40; Mk 10:13,248), and *if he repents,* the duty of endless forgiveness seven times *a day* (Mt 18:21f; has seventy times seven; seven is the perfect number Gn 4:24; 1 Cor 13:4f). Thirdly, v 5f, to the Apostles' request (see 6:13) to the Lord "increase our faith" which is probably a reaction to the second duty of endless forgiveness, Jesus replies with an hyperbolic "if" statement about the power of faith and its quality thus rejecting the idea of quantity. A sycamine tree was known for its deep roots, which according to some rabbis would remain in the ground for 600 years, and it seems an impossibility to plant something in the sea. Possibly Luke had joined two sayings together. It is noteworthy that

Paul, like Matthew and Mark, describes faith as moving mountains (1 Cor 13:2; Mt 21:21f; Mk 11:21ff).

Fourthly, Luke gives us again a difficult parable which describes the harsh reality of the slavery in his world to make a valid point, somewhat like the Unjust Steward. It is in the form of a question which expects an emphatic negative as an answer (11:5). However, its harshness evaporates when we recall 12:37, also 22:27, where Jesus is the servant, something which would have been almost incredible in antiquity. This parable about a slave, tired after a day's work, strikes at vain human pride, desire for perfection and self-righteousness, which is always a temptation (Rom 3:27; 1 Cor 9:19; 2 Tim 4:7f). It reminds the apostles that they are servants of God and unworthy (not useless or lazy, see Mt 25:3ff) servants at that. It is a reminder that man is not God. When the Jews had carried out all the "orders" (v 9) found in the Law of Moses what credit did they deserve? (1 Cor 9:16). God is entitled to man's total and unending service. Luke frequently uses the word slave or servant to describe a disciple.[117] Any recompense comes from grace, the generosity of the master (see 9:57-62; 19:7). Here we have an allusion to Paul's teaching about the insufficiency of human works and achievement and man's justification through God's mercy.

STAGE C — 17:11 — 19:44

(1) The Ten Lepers—Faith and Salvation—17:11-19.
(2) The Coming of the Kingdom—17:20-37.
(3) Two Parables on Prayer—18:1-4.
(4) Jesus and the Children—18:15-17.
(5) The Rich Ruler—18:18-30.
(6) Third Passion (and Resurrection) Prediction—18:31-4.

A Teaching Journey To Jerusalem

   (7) The Blind Beggar near Jericho—18:35-42.
   (8) Salvation for Zacchaeus the Tax Collector—19:1-10.
   (9) The Parable of the Sums of Money—19:11-27.
   (10) The Messiah of Peace enters Jerusalem—19:28-44.

(1) *The Ten Lepers—Faith and Salvation—(17:11-19):*

The lack of thanks of the servant's master (17:9) leads Luke to begin the final stage of his travel narrative with the story about the healing of the ten lepers and its emphasis on the importance of thanksgiving for God's mercy—the Pharisee will show the wrong kind of thanksgiving (18:11). This whole section stresses three of the basics in a proper prayerful attitude to God, thanksgiving, endurance and sorrowful repentance. In this story Luke begins with a reminder about the great journey to Jerusalem. Actually there is little sense of journeying and much of the description is about meals. In a phrase which is difficult to translate, he suggests that Jesus is on the borders of Samaria and Galilee, thus suggesting a cross country journey through Bethshan across the Jordan and down its eastern side until Jesus recrosses the Jordan near Jericho to go up to Jerusalem. Actually Luke's version is mainly a literary device as Jesus seems further from Jerusalem than in 13:22 and his mention of Samaria and Galilee prepares us for a story about Samaritans and Jews joined together in their common misery.

The story has so many puzzling details, e.g. the complaint of Jesus that the nine did not return to give thanks after he had sent them on a long journey to Jerusalem, also the unusual ending for a miracle in Luke with no statement of the people's admiration, that several scholars have suggested that it is a parable constructed by Luke from Mark 1:40-45 and the story of 2 Kings 5:1ff. One should remember Luke's characteristics of using Old Testament details to describe his stories. However, Luke has already given Mark's healing in 5:12-26 with a different point and further we must confess that we have not sufficient information to prove that it is a parable. Certainly Luke's emphasis here; his fourth description of a healing during the great teaching journey (11:14; 1:10ff; 14:4; 18:35) is as in the others, not on the healing act which was performed off stage, but on the teaching lesson to be gained from the episode, e.g. the repeated praise of God and Jesus (v 15,16), the repeated "this foreigner" (v 16, 18), faith (v 19). All ask for mercy like the tax collector (17:13; 18:13) but the point is the contrast between gratitude and ingratitude, between the lack of perseverance in faith of the Jews and the faith of the Samaritan, a contrast which was still evident in Luke's world. Outsiders like Samaritans would see the real significance of Jesus before his own people, the Jews, who receive God's gifts without a proper faith response (Ac 8:1ff). The details of the story fully accord with Jewish legislation about lepers (Lv 13:45-6; 14:1ff) and with such texts as Luke 16:17. Jesus is shown to send the ten to obey the Laws' requirements and present themselves to the priests who were like health inspectors (Lv 14:2ff) and could restore them to the community (5:14; Mk 1:44).

Like the case of Naaman, the Syrian (2 K 5:10-15), the cure is not immediate but a journey is demanded as a test of faith (5:15). Like Naaman (2 K 5:15) the foreigner turns back to glorify God (13:13; 2:20) and give thanks (an allusion to the Eucharist 22:17ff; 18:11). His priest was at Mt. Gerizim and not so far away but it is not clear if he even went that far. Note that it is only at v 15 that Luke dramatically describes his hero as a Samaritan. His hero, it should be noted, is not just like the Samaritan who was praised above the Jewish priestly aristocracy, but even

A Teaching Journey To Jerusalem 347

worse, one cursed by God as popular opinion had it, by a terrible disease. With a series of questions Jesus brings out the difference between a healing and the faith experience of salvation. he proposes the foreigners as an example to Israel (4:27). The final line on faith and salvation is found also in 7:50; 87:48; 18:42; Mk 5:34; 10:52; Mt 18:42. To those with a thankful faith it was no unexplained healing but a sign that the kingdom had broken in upon the kingdom of evil. The salvation of the leper, already given as an illustration of the presence of the kingdom to John (7:22; 10:9), leads Luke to a presentation of the two stages of the kingdom as already among them (17:22-37). This leads to an invitation to continual, but confident, prayer during the seeming delay (18:1-8)—One is reminded here of the Christian's prayer "Thy Kingdom come."

(2) *The Coming of the Kingdom—(17:20-37):*

Matthew and Mark have each only one discourse of Jesus on the last days (Mt 24:1ff; Mk 13:1ff), whereas Luke has three (12:35-59; 17:20-18:8; 21:5-36). While Matthew and Mark intertwine the return of the Son of Man with the destruction of Jerusalem, Luke seems to separate them more clearly as if the destruction of Jerusalem had already taken place. While Luke's third discourse is addressed to the people in the Temple, his second here, like the first, is directed to the disciples (v 22), although it is an artificial unity as the first two verses are addressed to the Pharisees. One should notice that here, however artificially, Luke has united in a combination, unique in the synoptics, the parousia or return of the Son of Man (v 24,30) and also the suffering of the Son of Man (v 25). Luke, like the other synoptics, confines the title Son of Man to Jesus' own lips (except Ac 7:56) as a description of the different aspects of his historical mission on earth,[118] his passion according to God's plan[119] and his eschatological role, especially as judge.[120] But where Luke is more free to compose himself for his own audience as in his infancy narratives and introductions, he prefers such titles as Lord, Christ, Son of God, Son of David. This discourse on the day(s) of the Son of Man has many parallels in Matthew 24, while the order of v 23, 26f, 37-39, 40f, 28, while Luke alone has v 20f, 25, 28f, 32, 37a. Just as Paul and Peter do in their letters,[121] Luke is quite likely correcting misunderstandings and speculations and perhaps even disappointments current in his community as he teaches that the Son of Man will return suddenly even if there seems to be a delay.

Luke begins with a question from the Pharisees about "when" and proceeds first with a negative reply (v 20f) and then with a positive statement (v 21f). Firstly, the kingdom will not come with dramatic signs which can be observed[122] such as the rising of a star which can be spotted by careful observations. Nor will there be need for a reporting that it is here or there as if it needed careful observations or guidance to check its authenticity. Rather the kingdom is "entos hymon," an unsual Greek phrase which in the context (i.e. the Pharisees) cannot have its more common meaning of an inner, individualistic experience "within you," as Origen, Jerome and the Gospel of Thomas have held, stressing the indwelling of the Holy Spirit (Rom 14:17). It stresses the fact that the kingdom has come (11:20) and is a present reality right now, i.e. "among you" or in your midst (Ac 2:22; Jn 1:10), in the person and activity of Jesus (10:9; 11:20; 16:16)—the view of Ephraem and Cyril of Alexandria, while Tertullian and Cyprian explain it as "within your grasp," i.e. by faith. Thus it can be described as a "riddle" answer which conceals its meaning from those who do not want to see.

A Teaching Journey To Jerusalem

In v 22f, Luke continues to expand the same theme with the disciples as the audience. He begins with a Semitic phrase which is the introductory phrase of an oracle of woe "the days will come."[123] In their trials they will impatiently long to see (2:29) "one of the day*s*" of the Son of Man, i.e. one of the unique days of Jesus' life—note a switch from day to days of Noah (v 26f), Lot and Sodom (v 28f). The expression recalls the days of Jesus' assumption (9:51), also the Rabbinic expression for the time preceding the Messianic age, "the days of the Messiah," or in particular "one" may be a Semitic expression for "the first." Luke excludes a "very soon" judgment (v 22f; 19:11; 21:8) and describes, not so much the final judgment (21:25b) as he gives an exhortation to immediate repentance to readiness (12:35ff; 21:34ff). They should not be misled into excited running about by those who say that he is to be found in this place or that (Ac 5:26). His coming will have a brightness and a shining like lightning visible to all. But first there is a divine "must" of suffering and rejection before the glory.[124] Then two sudden catastrophes from the Old Testament due to failure to repent, and be vigilant, are mentioned (see 2 Pet 2:5-6). The first describes the world before the flood, preoccupied with the cares of life (8:14), is also in Matthew (Gn 6:5ff). The second found only in Luke describes the inhabitants of Sodom (Gn 18:16ff). He has already described the rich fool who similarly thought himself secure (12:16-20). Both Noah and Lot, who were no saints themselves, read the signs of the times, took precautions and were saved.

Verses 31-33 seem to be a rather loose insertion by Luke here. In Matthew and Mark they make good sense in advising flight from the invading armies of A.D. 70. In Luke (typically) the two examples describe what men might do in a crisis—a man on a roof or in a field might think of saving his belongings in his house. But in Luke, wholehearted dedication to the coming of Jesus involves detachment from one's belongings. There must be no turning back in indecision like Lot's wife who was so attached to her belongings that she became a pillar of salt (Gn 19:26; Lk 9:61f). As for the nine lepers, salvation can quickly be lost even after a good beginning. Whoever is willing to lose his life will keep it alive—the same verse is found at 9:24 with the word save for "possess" and for "keep it alive."

Two further dramatic examples are given to illustrate the effect of the crisis of the coming kingdom: Two men in bed or two women at the mill. They may look outwardly the same but one expects and is taken (with Jesus) while the other is not (12:51-3; 1 Thess 4:17). Verse 36 should be omitted with the best manuscripts as an assimilation to Matthew 24:40. To their question of where? Jesus replies with a proverb, that as the farsighted and speedy vultures gather wherever there is a carcass, so will judgment find men everywhere, wherever they are—possibly a reference to the Roman standards of which eagles were the symbol,[125] circling around Jerusalem (Hab 1:8). Perhaps the text means that as clearly as the presence of vultures shows the location of a carcass, so will the judgment be evident to all.

(3) *Two Parables of Prayer—(18:1-14):*

Luke continues his eschatological theme with a parable, with an introduction "on praying always and not losing heart," as the disciples wait for the second coming. Both of these are frequent themes in Paul's letters on "constant prayer"[126] and "not losing heart."[127] Jewish tradition seemed to limit prayers to thrice a day (Dt 6:10) "lest God is wearied." Continued asking (not continuous)

A Teaching Journey To Jerusalem 351

for the kingdom would be a good definition of prayer for Luke. Again an aspect of an immoral character's behavior is used to make a point in a parable, this time by contrasting the behavior of God himself with that of an unjust or corrupt judge—the use of an adjective such as unjust to describe a character (v 6) is very rare in a parable. The key word of the parable in v 3,5,7,8 is "avenge," the vindication of a just cause against an opponent. The argument is the frequent *argumentum a fortiori* or "how much more . . . " will God, who is the just judge and who does care (2 Tim 4:8) vindicate his chosen, who continually call upon him. A judge in the Old Testament background was in particular the protector of the poor, the defenseless and oppressed, here symbolized by the dogged widow.[128] The image of the judge recalls Josephus' description of King Jehoiakim as "neither religious towards God nor kind toward men." Probably the judge was capricious and needed a bribe where the poor woman only had her persistence.[129] In his soliloquy he describes her as exhausting him (see 5:5) and is afraid lest (lit) "she give him a black eye" (1 Cor 9:27) and wear him out completely by her persistence. Jesus points to the judges' words and in a series of rhetorical questions argues how much more God will listen to the continual cries (Apoc 6:10) of his elect,[130] thus putting the stress rather on not losing heart or confidence in prayer than on mere persistence. The parable is similar to the story about the friend at midnight (11:5-8) and its aim is to strengthen the hope of Luke's community and give it confidence in God and in his ultimate vindication in a situation which was conducive to despair. The second part of v 7 is uncertain—(lit) "he is long suffering over them," which can be taken as a question or a statement, suggesting that God delays to help in his patience, "until the times of the Gentiles are fulfilled" (21:24). It seems obvious in the context that deliverance is not soon or immediate (21:9ff) yet is will be swift and sudden as at the Flood and at Sodom. The concluding question which is unique at the end of a parable, gives an eschatological note. This hanging question turns the reader's preoccupation with his trials and suffering to his faith (17:27f).

The Pharisee and the Tax Collector—(18:9-14):

> "Two men went up to pray. O rather say,
> One went to brag—the other went to pray."

Richard Crashaw's poem, *Steps to the Temple,* catches the point. Both parables on prayer begin with an introduction by Luke and end on an eschatological note. Having stressed the importance of thankful, yet confident, perservering prayer, Luke now teaches by contrasting the self-abasing tax collector and the self-righteous Pharisee—a right and a wrong attitude to God in prayer. The theme of the Pharisee's incapacity to see his need for repentance is still very much in evidence in Luke. Salvation is not a human achievement but a gift of God's compassion and mercy (17:9f). The parable is addressed to the self-righteous who hold everyone else in contempt. The contrast again is a striking and even a shocking one between the Pharisee, loaded with virtues, representative of Jewish religion at its best and the corrupt tax collector who worked for the Romans and was outside the law by common opinion and whose name was the equivalent of a sinner. The Pharisee's prayer as he typically stands apart, is a perfect reflection of his belief—his god is made in his own image (Lex Orandi, Lex Credendi).

Emphasizing "I," the selfish pronoun (the tax collector says "me" v 13), he thanks God that he is not like the

A Teaching Journey To Jerusalem

rest of men, particularly this tax collector. Prayer was aloud and by calling himself *the* sinner (v 13), the tax collector, in his humility, accepted the Pharisee's verdict. The Pharisee's religion is composed of negative virtues, a list of what he is not, of what he is against in addition to "works of supererogation," extra deeds which the law did not require. He fasted twice a week whereas the law only required one fast a year on the Day of Atonement (5:33ff; Lv 16:29ff; Num 29:7). The law required tithes of the main crops but he tithed everything (11:42; Num 18:21; Dt 14:22). Conspicuously, there is no emphasis on love, justice or mercy.

The tax collector is repentant and appraises himself honestly and receives mercy (O God be propitiated!) because he sees his need and asks for it, unlike the other. He stands "far off," beats his breast (13:48), does not dare to raise his eyes, accepts his neighbor's condemnation, but does not judge him in return. He has a broken and contrite heart (Ps 51:17; Is 64:5) and makes no claim to merit or excuse. It should be emphasized that the tax collector is not proposed as an ideal but rather an aspect of his life is praised. V14a concludes that God has justified or forgiven the sinful tax collector and not the other. Here we find one of Paul's important words "justified" used in a more Semitic way (Rom 4:5). Luke concludes with an eschatological statement already found in 14:11 (Mt 18:4; 23:13) which takes us back to the theme of the Magnificat—God in his great reversal will exalt the lowly and humble the proud.

(4) *Jesus and the Children—(18:15-17):*

From here up to his passion account Luke again begins to parallel the narrative order of Mark and Matthew after his long teaching section since 9:51. Now he gives, with little change, four episodes which Mark relates, the Children (18:15-17; Mk 10:13-16; Mt 19:13-15); The Rich Ruler (18:18-30; Mk 10:17-31; Mt 19:16-30); the Passion Prediction (18:31-4; Mk 10:32-4; Mt 20:17-19); the Healing of the Blind Man (18:35-42; Mk 10:46-52; Mt 20:29-34). Between the passion prediction and the healing of the blind man Luke omits the story of the ambition of the sons of Zebedee (Mk 10:35-45) as perhaps he did not find it to his kindly touch and he would tell a like story at the Last Supper (22:24-7). He also does not have Mark 10:2-12 on divorce as perhaps he had already included it at 16:18. Similarly, we find omitted the fig tree cursing (Mk 11:12ff, but see Lk 13:6-9) and the anointing at Bethany (Mk 14:3-9, but see Lk 7:36ff).

This story is called variously, a pronouncement story, a paradigm or an apophthegm. It is a story, short, vague, reduced to the minimum, whose main purpose is to give a particular saying of Jesus. Thus there is no description of where the event took place, who brought the children or why the disciples rebuked them (Mk 10:13-15; Mt 19:13-15).

The theme of the kingdom is continued and this story and the next about the rich ruler have the common theme of entering the kingdom (v 16,17,24,29; 17:20). The children who are mere infants, according to Luke and therefore completely helpless, dependent and insignificant with no earnings or accomplishments of their own, are a symbol of the little ones (17:2), the trusting, poor of whom is the kingdom (6:20) and the humble like the tax collector (18:9ff). Their welcome forms a contrast to the rejected, proud Pharisee with his accomplishments and the story of the rich ruler unable to surrender everything completely.

Luke notes the call of Jesus and his positive and negative statements that the kingdom belongs to such and

A Teaching Journey To Jerusalem

the "amen" statement (4:24) that those who do not have the acceptance of children will not enter (13:24ff). Some writers see in Jesus' command not to hinder children an implicit authorization for infant baptism in the early church (Mt 3:14; Ac 8:36; 10:47; 11:17). Luke does not have Mark's anger of Jesus at the disciple's action or his statement (Mk 10:16)—that Jesus took the children in his arms and blessed them and placed his hands on them. Like Matthew, Luke is hesitant to show Jesus in the grip of human emotions.

(5) *The Rich Ruler—(18:18-30):*

In Mark he is "a rich man," in Matthew he is also "young" and Luke uses a favorite word of his to describe him as a ruler of some kind, whether of the synagogue or of the sanhedrin is not clear (12:58; 14:1; 23:13,35). Luke omits some of Mark's vivid detail such as the man running and kneeling to Jesus, Jesus' expression of love and the repetition of some of the disciples' words on renunciation. The teaching is that one cannot serve God and Mammon, that it is very difficult for a rich man to get into the kingdom. The following of Jesus, which the rich man neither asked for nor wanted, involved for him even more than the law required, namely, the surrender of his possessions.

The young man begins by flattering Jesus. He hopes to be told the secret of eternal life and asks the same question which introduced the parable of the Good Samaritan.[131] However, Jesus leads the rich man in a different way to the lawyer. "Eternal life" probably is to be understood here as the final stage of the kingdom. Matthew (Mt 19:17) changes Jesus' question-response as he is perhaps worried that Jesus hesitates to be called good.

Luke has no such difficulty and sees Jesus' response as a criticism of an unusual and perhaps casual greeting. No example of such a greeting as "Good Teacher" has been found in Jewish literature—the term "good" was especially used of God. Quite likely, the rich man considered himself good and thus Jesus, with typical penetration to the heart of the matter, is laying down a principle for his subsequent criticism of the young man's goodness, to help him to see his own imperfect condition. This time it is Jesus who quotes the commandments (10:25-8; 16:29f), quoting five which deal with duties towards one's neighbors. It is interesting to note the fluidity in the order of the commandments at the time of Jesus as all three synoptics give a differing order. Mark has "Do not defraud" as one of the major manuscripts of the Septuagint reads (Dt 24:14). Luke seems to have the same order as the Codex Vaticanus and the Nash Papyrus (note Rom 13:9; Jas 2:11). To the rich man's confident reply about his goodness since youth and his implicit "What else?" Jesus makes a devastating response by zeroing in on his heart and the one further requirement which he lacks (10:47; Rom 3:21ff; Phil 3:7). It is an invitation to a revolutionary lifestyle, sell all (Luke), give to the poor and with treasure in heaven, follow me! (6:23ff; 12:13ff). This was the practice of the early Jerusalem Church and the disciples, as Peter is quick to point out.[132] However, a very different reply of Jesus is found in a version of the Gospel of the Hebrews, quoted by Origen (on Mt 15:14):

> "How can you say I have fulfilled the law and the prophets, when it is written in the law: You shall love your neighbor as yourself; and so many of your brothers, sons of Abraham, are clothed in filth, dying of hunger, and your house is full of many good things, none of which goes to them?".

A Teaching Journey To Jerusalem

Jesus' phrase, "There is still one thing you lack" possibly means that he has not fully kept the commandments as he thought.

In Luke the man does not go away or refuse but grows very sad for he is very rich and is present for Jesus' further remark on how hard it is for a rich man to enter the kingdom.[133] Jesus illustrates this difficulty with an amusing hyperbole of a camel hump and all going through the eye of a needle—Luke's word for needle suggests a surgeon's needle! The misunderstanding of the joke here has led to the creation of a small night gate at Jerusalem when the other gates were shut but there is no evidence of its existence. Others explain the hyperbole from the similarity between the Greek *kamelos* and the word for a cable or ship's hawser which evidently could not pass through a needle's eye.

Here again Jesus is bluntly reversing the popular notion that riches are necessarily a sign of God's favor. The twelve found Jesus' hyperbole difficult and conclude that scarcely anybody can be saved. In an enigmatic phrase (v 27), Jesus points out that things are possible with God which are impossible with men and that the salvation of all rich and poor alike depends on God.

Peter, as often spokesman, speaks up for the disciples who have, unlike the rich man, left their homes to follow him.[134] St. Jerome comments that all he left was a mere boat and a few nets! Luke in his version of Jesus' reply has "on account of the kingdom of God" (18:29; Mk 10:29; Mt 19:29) and also adds "wife" to the list of what they gave up (14:26; 1 Cor 9:5). All three synoptics stress that Jesus' reply is to everyone (not just the original twelve). It describes a two stage return as in the Beatitudes—a plentiful return now, in the age to come eternal life (compare Job 42:12f).

(6) *The Third Passion and Resurrection Prediction— (18:31-4):*

Jesus brings his disciples down to reality from the world of rewards with a prediction of future events at Jerusalem, his third major passion prediction, but actually the seventh which Luke has recorded.[135] This prediction which is made to the Twelve in confidence specifies Jerusalem, the goal of his long journey, as the place of accomplishment for the destiny of the Son of Man, as already written by the prophets (e.g. 21:27; Is 50; 53:8; Hos 6:2). Luke does not have Mark's introduction, describing the wonderment and fear of Jesus' followers nor his reference to Jewish responsibility, to the condemnation of Jesus by the chief priests and scribes (Mk 10:32f). Luke in particular among the synoptics emphasizes the fulfilment of Scripture,[136] using his favorite theme and phrase "the prophets" to show Jesus' death as part of God's plan.[137] But actually, he gives little detailed reference to the Old Testament to describe what he means.[138] He adds the expression "shamefully treated' " (Mt 22:6; Ac 14:5; 27:10, 21) or insulted in v 32 but does not clearly specify crucifixion and emphasizes "rising on the third day."

For the first time (see 9:44) the Gentiles or Romans are introduced as playing a part in the passion. Even though Jesus' suffering[139] was written in the prophets (e.g. Is 53) yet paradoxically its meaning was "hidden from them" by God, v 34, a typically kind interpretation found only in Luke at this point. As in his second major prediction (9:43ff; 24:16), Luke emphasizes their complete failure to understand what was about to happen, a point which he repeats in three different ways (v 34), thus preparing the way for the desertion of the Twelve (24:6ff). Only actually when they meet the Risen Lord would they begin to comprehend (Ac 3:17). The blindness of the disciples is a central theme in Mark.[140]

(7) *The Blind Beggar near Jericho—(18:35-43):*

The blindness of the apostles leads to a story, rich in symbol, of a blind man who wanted desperately to see (Jesus!) and whose eyes were opened by the Davidic Messiah so that he follows him as a disciple (Mk 10:52). Similarly, the eyes of the disciples must be opened. The scene is Jericho already mentioned in the Good Samaritan and the place where the Jews of old entered the promised land. There are interesting discrepancies among the synoptic accounts of the story.

Mark alone names his one man Bartimaeus and situates the episode as Jesus leaves Jericho (Mk 10:46-52). Matthew typically has two but no name and it takes place as they leave Jericho. Luke has one man, no name and it happens as they enter Jericho. Luke does not have Mark's story of the ambitious and contrasting request of the sons of Zebedee (Mk 10:35-40), nor the beggar's Aramaic address to Jesus (Rabboni). Typically he concludes the scene with the people praising God. The people are often contrasted with the leaders in Luke (see 19:47f; 20:19; 22:2; 23:13b).

Luke who alone tells the following story about Zacchaeus has constructed a convenient and interesting literary triptych with the episode of the blind man at the entry to Jericho, the story of Zacchaeus inside the town and then the parable of the sums of money as Jesus departs for Jerusalem (19:11). He omits the detailed exchange between the blind man and the crowd found in Mark. The center of the episode is the persistent prayer of the beggar. In v 39 an intense word for "cried out" is used of the beggar when he hears that Jesus of Nazareth is passing—probably the normal way of referring to Jesus. But he alone in Luke's gospel (20:41; 23:2,38) proclaims Jesus openly as the Son of David.[141] Jesus accepts the title and deliberately stops and dallies with the man despite the urgency of his journey. Jesus shows the kind of Messiah, i.e. of the poor, that he is by his deliberate concern and his opening of the man's eyes.[142] Hitherto, Jesus had only indirectly spoken to his Messiahship and refused to let people call him Messiah.[143] He again, here stresses that the man's faith has led to his salvation (7:50; 8:48f; 17:19).

(8) *Salvation for Zacchaeus, the Tax Collector—(19:1-10):*

Again we have an episode which illustrates the kind of Messiah which Jesus was in view of the contemporary, popular, nationalistic expectations and the kind of despised people with whom he concerned himself. Many of Luke's familiar themes are clustered here in this narrative in which he alone describes a tax collector; riches (18:24f); reversal and repentance; the joy of salvation; Jesus the divine visitor; seeking out the sinner (7:16; 1:78; 15:1ff); the invitation to and sharing of a meal with outcasts; Abraham.

Zacchaeus, the Greek form of the Jewish name Zakkai which meant the "pure" or "innocent one,"[144] was "chief" tax collector, a title found nowhere else in Greek literature, at the fertile oasis of Jericho on an important trading route in the Jordan Valley. Verse 2, which describes the rich Zacchaeus has a very Semitic touch about its construction. It is Luke's sixth reference to a tax collector.[145] Being of small stature (the phrase could

A Teaching Journey To Jerusalem

possibly apply to Jesus and not Zacchaeus) he sought to see Jesus, a phrase that recalls Herod and the blind man (9:9; 18:41). In his resourcefulness (16:1ff) he ignored his dignity and climbed into the lower boughs of a sycamore tree, a kind of fig tree or mulberry tree. Jesus who seems to know his name and all about him, stops and speaks as he did to the blind man even though he is only passing through Jericho. He invites himself to Zacchaeus' house with a "divine" must statement, signifying that his visit is prompted by his divine mission (22:37; 24:44; Ac 2:23). Here also we have two of the "today" statements,[146] signifying that some momentous fulfilment of God's dealings with Israel is taking place. The immediate and joyous repentance of Zacchaeus is contrasted with the hostile, murmuring of disapproval of all when they saw Jesus gone to be a guest at an outcast's house (5:30; 15:2).

Zacchaeus is a new man and shows his salvation to be a present reality by beginning a new way of life. He loses his dedication to riches (18:22; 3:13; 1:78f) as he stands up and publicly declares so to his new found Lord (v 8). He gives half his belongings to the poor (12:33; 16:9) and his restitution to those he had defrauded is not the one and one fifth, normally required by the law (Lv 6:1ff; Num 5:7), but a generous fourfold restitution which both Roman and Jewish law required in extreme cases of flagrant stealing.[147] Commentators note here that he does not leave all and is not required to give all away as Levi did (5:27f; 18:22). The salvation of his household looks forward to similar scenes in Acts.[148] The conclusion is an "ad hominem" statement to the murmurers. It implies that such outsiders as Zacchaeus are as much if not more genuine sons of Abraham than the respectable Jewish members of society.[149] Only Luke has the final statement based on Ezekiel (Ezek 34:16). "The Son of Man came to search out and save what was lost." This is a statement which would make a good summary of his whole theology and understanding of the mission of Jesus.[150] It recalls his program which he proclaimed at Nazareth.

(9) *The Parable of the Sums of Money—(19:11-27):*

This parable should be read not in isolation but in its context in Luke. Typical of so many of his periscopes, it both looks back and forward. Jesus had just been proclaimed Son of David by the blind man and had explained to the murmurers his mission of searching out and saving the lost such as Zacchaeus. Now to the same audience (v 11), Jesus tells a parable, to which Luke provides not only one of his introductory interpretations, "because he was near Jerusalem and they thought that the kingdom of God was about to appear," but also a conclusion "and having spoken thus he went ahead with his ascent to Jerusalem" (v 28).

Jesus, the king (v 22,35) is just about to make his deliberate Messianic entry to Jerusalem to offer a peace which will be refused, a refusal which will result in the destruction of Jerusalem. Thus Luke gives a historical context in the light of which he intends the parable to be understood. The times (Ac 1:6) were full of political hopes and frustrations and Luke in his writings is anxious to show Jesus' mission and that of his followers as clearly innocent of any accusations of political revolution that were frequently made. Luke has consistently concentrated on the present and insisted that the kingdom was already a reality while at the same time moderating excited hopes for its second stage or final fulfilment (9:27; 22:69).

The parable with its evident allegorical details has obviously close similarities with the parable of the talents or

A Teaching Journey To Jerusalem

personal gifts which Matthew has associated with his great parable of the Last Judgment and its separation of the sheep from the goats (Mt 25:14ff). However, comparison shows that Luke has a major extra section or even another whole parable which is added to make Matthew's merchant into a nobleman who goes to a far away country to acquire a kingdom which his fellow citizens, who despise him, try to prevent. Luke thus gives a reason for the departure. Two parables can then be seen combined in Luke, one about sums of money like Matthew (vv 12-13, 15b-26) and the other about a kingdom and the punishment of the nobleman's enemies (v 12, 14-15a,27). The combination is especially noticeable in v24, where a rather small sum of money is given to a man just made governor of ten towns. Possibly Matthew's version is closer to the original which Luke developed to express his theology, although abridgement by Matthew is also of course a possibility. Nevertheless, it is rather Luke who is interested in the kingship of Jesus[151] and in the family history of the Herods to which his account seems to refer. In Luke the parable is addressed not just to the audience of Jesus' day and their expectation of the kingdom at any moment as Jesus enters Jerusalem, but also to the audience of his gospel as they await the Parousia and especially to the leaders of his church. For them it is both a lesson in patience and especially responsible conduct and administration of the Church. It encourages the admission of new believers, unlike the approach of the Jewish people. Quite likely in fact it was originally a criticism of the Jewish use of the Word of God as they had been entrusted with its spread. But clearly there are allegorical aspects to the whole parable in Luke's version as he separates and combats the mistaken identification of Jesus' departure from the world and his return or parousia. A noble man (Jesus), departs to receive kingly power against the wishes of his fellow-citizens (the Jews). There is an unspecified period of trading by his servants (the disciples). There is the return of the king and his judgment of his servants and punishment of his enemies who "do not want him" (13:34). In the actual entry the crowds in Luke welcome a king about to ascend his throne (19:38). Luke stresses, not so much the lengthy absence of the nobleman as the responsible conduct expected from the servants, the leaders of his church.[152] He addresses it however to those who like the disciples misunderstood the suffering role of Jesus and expect the immediate end of the present age.[153] The verb "appearing" in v 11 refers to the parousia (2 Thess 2:8; 2 Tim 4:1). Now as the journey of Jesus reaches its climax we find Jerusalem is mentioned quite frequently (v 11,28,37,41).

The story of the man going abroad to receive a kingship seems to refer to the journey in 4 B.C. of Herod the Great's Son, Archelaus, to Rome to receive a kingship from the Roman Emperor as was the custom of the time. His father had left him Judea with the title of king but it needed to be confirmed in Rome. The Jews also sent a delegation to oppose him (see Josephus Antiq 17,9,3f; 17,11,1). The Emperor Augustus actually confirmed him as tetrarch but denied him the title king until he proved himself. He was a bad ruler and, according to Josephus, massacred about three thousand Jews at the first Passover after his return and was finally replaced by Augustus with a Roman governor in A.D. 6. Archelaus actually had a large white marble palace at Jericho and the sight of it may have suggested the parable.

A Teaching Journey To Jerusalem

The parable suggests a long delay as it was "a faraway country" and the verb "went" recalls its frequent use in Luke to suggest Jesus' journey to his destiny (e.g. 22:22). In Luke the sums (mina) are quite small. Matthew's talent is actually sixty times greater and the master there divides his wealth among his three servants. The little things suggest the insignificant daily tasks of the community. In Luke each of the ten receive the same amount but only three of the ten give a report which shows a parallel with Matthew's three. It is frequently remarked that Matthew's version shows the inequality of men's talents in life whereas Luke stresses equal opportunities for all before the gospel. In the version given in the Gospel according to the Hebrews, the first servant is rewarded, the second who hid his talent is rebuked and the third who had "wasted his master's money with harlots and flute-girls" is put in prison. Here again Luke uses the word slave for the disciples[154] and the generous rewards of the Master should not cause one to forget the parable of the slaves in 17:10. The reward here is further responsibility. The third slave, on whom the typical end stress of the parable lies, is treated according to his own distorted image of God. In Matthew the third servant buried the money thus acting safely and prudently and according to Rabbinical law was therefore released from liability, whereas the man in Luke who hid it in a scarf used for protection from the sun, was liable if it were stolen. He did not even put the money "on the table" of the moneylenders to make interest. Fear, the opposite of faith, the fear that paralyses and prevents courageous action and risk, was his problem. In Matthew it is idleness (Mt 25:26). He is a tragic figure as he knows what he should do and what is required of him. It is the fear of the cautious Pharisee with his "hard" idea of God, the fear of the conservative and orthodox Christian to launch out from his ghetto into the deep, into the wide world and bring new believers into the Church.

The protest in v25, whether it comes from Jesus' audience or the man's fellow slaves, is omitted in such manuscripts as D and W but fits in naturally in the background. It leads to two conclusions: (i) one which is also found in 8:18 (Mk 4:25; Mt 13:12), teaches that those who are responsible like the first two servants will be rewarded, while the converse is also true of the third servant; (ii) the enemies who refuse Jesus as king will be punished, unlike the repentant Zacchaeus who was saved in the previous episode (see Mt 27:30). This v 27 is an introduction to the following passage and the passion and is also possibly an allusion to the terrible events of A.D. 70.

(10) *The Messiah of Peace Enters the Temple in Jerusalem —(19:28-44):*

This is the climax of Luke's great journey narrative as the "non-political" king, "to be rejected" (19:12,14f,27) makes the ascent to Jerusalem to cleanse and take possession of its temple which will be the only place of his teaching activity (19:47; 20:21; 21:37f). All four gospels record Jesus' deliberate messianic entry which took the form of an acted parable like those of the prophets of old (Jer 27:1-11) but each has stressed his own insights. From now on it is not infrequent to find all four gospels parallel. Like Mark, whom he seems to follow, Luke mentions Bethpage and Bethany and the hill "called" as he puts it, Olivet. But unlike Mark, whose procession culminates with Jesus silently but ominously looking around the temple before withdrawing to Bethany, Luke includes the lament over Jerusalem and the cleansing of the Temple as part of the entry itself. The entry is carefully planned and obviously courageous, in view of the hostility of the Jewish leaders and Jesus' foreknowledge. Luke, like Mark, does not clearly point to a prophecy here but as Matthew actually points out (Mt 21:5) Jesus seems to be deliberately leading a royal procession and acting out the messianic words of Zechariah "Behold your king comes to you . . . humble and riding on an ass (Zech 9:9)."[155]

The selection of an ass in preference to the horse which signified war is not a gesture of false humility. It contrasts with the current, popular image of the Messiah as a military and nationalistic champion and shows that Jesus' approach here as throughout his ministry, is not that of military force but of peace. It takes one back to the prophets' picture of Jerusalem filled with the presence of Yahweh who comes to save the outcasts and to make Jerusalem a place of peace and refuge for all nations (Zeph 3:16ff; Zech 9:9). Zechariah, a prophecy of hope, describes a shepherd king who brings peace but suffers and is cut down among his followers.[156]

Animals which were never used before, were used especially for holy functions.[157] The instructions to the two disciples are similar to Mark's version and probably intended to indicate, not previous organization, but a miraculous confirmation of Jesus' prophetic prediction and extraordinary clairvoyance.[158] In John it is Jesus himself who finds the ass after the procession had begun. The phrase "The Lord has need of it" can possibly be interpreted as a password, as it is repeated twice or rather as only Luke notes the "owners" inquiry (v 33), it is intended to inculcate an attitude towards possessions (Ac 4:34ff). Here Jesus refers to himself as Lord (19:31,34), a title which normally in the gospel before the resurrection is used by the evangelist alone and not by others (except Lk43,76). In Luke, the disciples set Jesus on the ass and spread their garments, a gesture used for acclaiming a king

(2 K 9:13). The palm branches are omitted. Only Luke writes about the descent from the Mount of Olives thus laying bare the famous wide panorama of the city and its Temple which opened to the pilgrim. Typically, Luke notes the rejoicing and praising of God (the same word was used of the angels 2:13 and shepherds 2:20), but it is from the crowd of disciples. But like John's account (Jn 11:45) he stresses that it was the mighty works (10:13; 19:37) which were the cause of this enthusiasm. Psalm 118 is on their lips. It is a special psalm of national thanksgiving to Yahweh for his repeated deliverance of Israel over the ages and was sung during the ascent of the pilgrims for a festival. The actual verse (26) is the priestly blessing upon the procession. Luke, like John, inserts the word "king," thus proclaiming Jesus king and connecting the cry with Zechariah's prophecy (Zech 9:9; Mt 21:4f) and the preceding episode of the parable of the rejected king. Mark emphasizes the future, the kingdom to come (Mk 11:10). In Luke Jesus is proclaimed as King Messiah or the divinely anointed King now, and Jesus openly accepts the proclamation.

Luke omits the Jewish cry "Hosanna" and replaces it with glory (see Mt 21:9). He adds words which clearly recall the angel's song at Jesus' birth (2:14) but now the place of peace and glory is heaven and not on earth as the following verses (e.g. 42) will show (15:7; Apoc 12:10). The disciples recognize now what the angels knew from the beginning that Jesus is the king from heaven offering true peace. The Pharisees' reaction is a rebuke. They do not accept Jesus as king but "teacher" (v 39) and quite likely they fear a disturbance which will provoke the Romans (19:14,21). Mark does not mention this rebuke but Matthew has a similar complaint at the cleansing of the temple (Mt 21:14ff). Jesus answers them in a proverbial form, that

A Teaching Journey To Jerusalem

nature would cry out if the disciples were insensitive to what was happening. This must have seemed prophetic when Jerusalem was reduced to silent yet eloquent stones (v 44). The Babylonian Talmud has a similar comment on Heb 2:11 about the witness of stones against a man. The secret of Jesus is clearly revealed before his death (4:35,41; 9:21,36).

Next Luke inserts into the Markan narrative a prophetic oracle of Jesus just as they reach the top of the Mount of Olives, whence a panoramic view of Jerusalem spread before them. In strong contrast to the rejoicing disciples and the complaining and rejecting Pharisees, Luke alone who (see 13:34f; Mt 23:37ff) only exceptionally describes the emotions of Jesus, presents a weeping Jesus as the climax of his great journey narrative. The word used signifies a deep anguished emotion.[159] Josephus tells us that Jerusalem was so beautiful that Titus wept when he gave orders for its destruction in A.D. 70. In proper etymology the name Jerusalem signified "vision of peace" (Heb 7:1f) and Jesus like the prophets of old gives an oracle of destruction describing how Jerusalem is missing real peace by her refusal to accept him (v 38).

Whether Luke's description here was written after and in the light of the Roman destruction of A.D. 70 is a difficult question to answer definitely. Certainly the bank with which the enemies will encircle Jerusalem resembles the Roman siege technique of *circumvallatio*. However, this was the standard military procedure of the times and all the details can be found in the Septuagint, especially Jeremiah (Jer 6:1,6 13f,17,21; 52:1) who is quoted directly in v 46. See also Is 29:3; 37:33; Ez 4:2; Hos 14:1; Nah 3:10; Hag 2:15; Ps 137:9 and Josephus in his Jewish Wars 5;262. The path of peace with God and man was hidden (the passive probably refers to God as the agent)—see 9:9;

22:29f; Jn 9:39; 12:37ff; Is 48:18. They have not the faith of the blind man to understand their eyes must be opened to see Jesus as the leader to true peace (18:35ff). "Days will come" is an Old Testament phrase which Luke uses three times in these chapters (19:43; 21:6; 23:29). The repetition of "you" ten times in two verses (43,44) makes the passage very direct and very personal. The reason is that Jerusalem did not see the signs of the times and did not recognize the time of God's saving visit as the people of Nain had (7:16; 1:78). All would be destroyed and not a stone of the city would be left upon a stone (Hag 2:6ff; Ps 137:9).

7. JERUSALEM—19:29-24:53

In the final section of his gospel Luke has the same general plan as Mark and Matthew and his presentation, like theirs, easily falls into three parts. However, especially the second and third sections contain much that is unique to Luke.

    A. Jesus in the Temple—19:45-2:38.
    B. The Passion of Jesus—22:1-23:56.
    C. After the Resurrection—in Jerusalem—24:1-53.

A. *Jesus in the Temple—(19:45-21:35):*

The temple is the real goal of Jesus' triumphal entry and long journey (9:51ff; 13:22,33; 17:11; 18:31; 19:28).[1] Unlike Mark, where some of Jesus' activity takes place outside the temple (e.g. Mk 11:11-26; 13:1-37), Luke, who emphasizes the temple, situates this entire part in the temple. He begins and concludes by pointing out that Jesus was in the temple and that he taught there daily (19:45ff; 21:37). It opens with Jesus' authority being questioned and rejected by the authorities and closes with Jesus proclaiming the coming destruction of the temple (21:5-38). Jesus cleanses the temple and takes it over for his public (not private, see 21:37f) teaching of the people[2] and his disciples (20:45). He restores the temple as a place of prayer for Israel. In Luke, unlike Mark (compare Lk 20:1 and Mk 11:27) Jesus is at home in the temple. The early Christians will come daily to the temple for prayer and teaching.[3]

Here in the temple Jesus' conflicts take place as he is questioned and challenged, no longer by the Pharisees, who appeared for the last time in 19:39, but by the Scribes and the temple authorities (20:1-44). Luke emphasizes that Jesus' acceptance there by the people[4] is so great that these authorities cannot carry out their determination to get rid of him. The people come early in the morning to hear Jesus (21:38), listen to him attentively (19:48; 20:1) and are shocked at his death (23:48), in contrast with the plotting of the leaders (19:47). Jesus is clearly not a nationalistic Messiah, but a king visiting his people to restore its proper worship and cult of God and to proclaim God's word.

Here Luke gives us almost all the same episodes as Mark and Matthew but does not have their emphasis on the parousia. Thus Mark has some seven conflict scenes (Mk 11:27-12:44) of question and answer between Jesus and the Jerusalem leaders dealing with such fundamental contemporary issues as authority, God's messengers, the problem of the Roman Caesar, resurrection, the greatest commandment, the Messiah. Matthew has some additional parables but Luke parallels Mark closely except for the greatest commandment which he had earlier discussed in 10:25-28.

An examination of Mark chapter 11-16 gives a seven day format within which Mark, possibly telescoping somewhat, has decribed the concluding events of Jesus' life. This traditional interpretation has Jesus entering Jerusalem on Sunday, cleansing the temple on Monday, teaching and engaged in controversies on Tuesday, anointed at Bethany on Wednesday, coming in secretly and holding his Last Supper on Thursday before his arrest, trial and finally crucifixion on Friday.[5] Luke however, has no clear separation of days up to Thursday (e.g. 20:1 "one day"). He omits the cursing of the fig tree and for him the cleansing of the temple is the beginning of a teaching period without miracles in the temple which lasted an indefinite number of days (19:47).

(1) The Cleansing of the Temple—19:45-48.
(2) The Authority of Jesus is questioned—20:1-8.
(3) The Parable of the Vineyard and its Wicked Tenants—
    20:9-19.
(4) Paying Taxes to Caesar—20:20-26.
(5) The Sadducees and the Resurrection of the Dead—
    20:27-40.

- (6) Jesus, David's Son and Lord—20:41-44.
- (7) The Scribes are denounced—20:45-7.
- (8) The Widow's Mite—21:1-4.
- (9) The Destruction of the Temple is Foretold—21:5-7.
- (10) False Signs and Cosmic Disasters—21:8-11.
- (11) Persecution of Christians—21:12-19.
- (12) The Siege and Destruction of Jerusalem Foretold—21:20-24.
- (13) The Coming of the Son of Man—21:25-8.
- (14) The Lesson of the Fig Tree—21:29-33.
- (15) Exhortation to Watch—21:34-6.
- (16) The Last Days of Jesus—21:37-8.

(1) *The Cleansing of the Temple—(19:45-7):*

All four gospels describe a cleansing of the Temple, which is essentially the same in each—John at the beginning of his gospel as perhaps symbolic of the whole ministry of Jesus to cleanse Judaism, the synoptics at the end of the ministry, on Monday in Mark but on Sunday in Matthew and Luke. Luke's version, which follows Mark's, is the briefest of all. He has already described in prophecy its total destruction. He omits the cursing of the fig tree[6] and some of Mark's references to Jesus' coming and going to Bethany (Mk 11:11,19,27). In Luke Jesus is returning, not so much to Jerusalem as to the Temple to take possession of his Father's house where we last saw him as a boy in 2:46. In Mark, the triumphal entry ends with Jesus looking around the temple but in Luke it ends with the cleansing of the temple, an illustration of his description of the unreadiness of Jerusalem for the divine visitation (the previous verse 44). Malachy (Mal 3:1ff) had spoken of the Lord coming to purify his temple and Zechariah had spoken of an ideal temple without any kind of commerce (Zech 14:20ff; Tob 14:7ff).

Jewish tradition had also spoken of the Messiah coming from the Mount of Olives and revealing himself in the temple. The magnificent temple was the symbol of God's presence among his people, the center of their cult and pilgrimage and the lifetime goal of every Jew. However, as is evident particularly from the prophetic books, it was in constant need of reform like the Jews themselves (e.g. Jer 7:2ff; Is 1:12; Am 5:21; Hos 6:6; Mic 6:6f). There the Law which enshrined the true will of Yahweh, was intended to be taught. Here Jesus will now give his teaching, his authentic interpretation.

But it should be remembered that the Temple was the main source of employment in Jerusalem in keeping an estimated 18,000 priests and levites at work together with thousands of others in subordinate occupations and trades. It became a vast slaughter-house at Passover time. Every Jew had to pay the temple tax either in shekels of the temple or in Galilean shekels, the only coins which did not have the image of a king on them. It amounted to about half a shekel or about two days' wages. Money changers set up counters for changing money in the big courtyard of the Gentiles and charged rates for changing money. Also it was the most convenient place to buy animals for the sacrifice as the highly unpopular Sadducees who controlled the markets and the temple tended to pass animals (Lv 1:3) only bought at their stalls. It was then a place of exploitation. This is the only incident in the New Testament where Jesus is moved to violence at the thievery and the fact that the bustling market was the place of prayer for the Gentiles. John had prophesied that the Messiah would purge his floor (3:17). Luke passes over it quickly mentioning no whip, etc., but only that Jesus quoted scripture as he expelled those who sold, saying that instead of being a house of prayer as Isaiah had described it (Is 56:7; also a Lucan emphasis) it had become a hideout for robbers. This is a reference to Jeremiah's famous condemnation of the Temple and his prediction of its destruction (7:11). It is surprising that Luke, unlike the other synoptics, does not have the phrase "for the Gentiles" in the Isaian quotation as it would be very suitable to his Gentile theology (Mk 11:17). Possibly the temple was destroyed when he wrote. However, the omission is best explained when one takes into account his treatment of the temple in Acts, e.g. Ac 7:48. "Yet the Most High does not dwell in buildings made by human hands . . ." As in John (Jn 4:21) he quite likely thought the Gentiles did not have to worship in the temple which never actually fulfilled its full function. Jesus, not the temple, was a light to the Gentiles (2:32).

The result of Jesus' triumphal entry and his public provocative cleansing in the temple was that the leaders of Judaism could no longer ignore him but looked for a way to do away with him (6:11). Luke presents a sharp contrast between the hostile leaders and the people who hang on to Jesus' words. He describes three groups among the leaders, the chief priests, the scribes and with a new expression "the principal men of the people." He is probably referring to the three divisions of the Sanhedrin, the highest court of authority among the Jews. The people are not described as the crowd or the multitude as in Mark (e.g. Mk 11:12) but the "laos," a word which is the equivalent of Israel in the Septuagint and used for the Christian community, e.g. Acts 15:14; 18:10.

The references to teaching and to the authorities in v 47 prepare the way for the conflicts between Jesus and the Jewish authorities in the following chapter.

(2) *The Authority of Jesus is Questioned—(20:1-8):*

Jesus' assumption of authority to cleanse the temple and proclaim the good news as he taught there naturally led to a counterattack from the official teaching body and a conflict about his credentials and his authority. He was an unordained, country Rabbi, teaching in the temple. The same verb is used of Martha's sudden "attack" on Jesus in 10:40. Luke's version is close to Mark's but he adds that Jesus is preaching the good news and thus is preparing the way for similar conflicts over authority in Acts. Also Luke does not stress that it is the one important question as Mark does in 11:29. In Mark "these things" refers to the cursing of the fig tree and the cleansing of the temple, but in Luke, it seems to refer more especially to Jesus' authoritative teaching. Like John he had received no approval from them. Possibly they sought to trap Jesus between a public confession of Messiahship which would put him into the hands of the Romans or into some kind of refusal which would lower him in the eyes of the people.

Jesus characteristically answers their question by a concrete counter-question about the Baptist's authority which they had also refused to recognize, thus impaling them on the horns of a dilemma before the people. Obviously they would have liked to answer "from men" but because of John's popularity they were afraid of the people to give their true opinion (7:30; 9:19). But Jesus' question which exposed their embarrassed cowardice was no trick evasive question (Ac 23:6ff), because if they could answer it they could also obviously answer their own question about Jesus' own authority (see Jn 9:1-34). Jesus, who had recognized John's authority (7:26) is claiming that his own also is from God, as John himself had recognized (7:18-30).

(3) *The Parable of the Vineyard and its Wicked Tenants— (20:9-19);*

Having impaled the authorities in an embarrassing dilemma but still speaking directly to them as they realized (v 19), Jesus turns to the people and in typical fashion answers their question about himself and his authority with a parable which teaches his own unique transcendence as a Messiah. The parable clearly warns that their rejection of both John and himself will lead to their destruction (20:16,18f) and can be seen as a last appeal to the leaders of Israel in the face of the disaster to which they are inevitably leading Jerusalem.

The parable is clearly drawn from the real life situation of Palestine in Jesus' day. It was occupied land with many absentee landowners to whom the local tenants had to pay rent in the form of a percentage of the crop. Obviously it was a smouldering situation and frequently the tenants must have refused the often exorbitant rents and hoped that they could escape the wrath of the absentee owners. To kill the son, the heir, would have been a great temptation in a world where title deeds were often uncertain and Jewish Law presumed that whoever occupied and used land for three years was the owner unless there was a claim to the contrary. The people, in killing the heirs would, in Jewish eyes, be only taking back from oppressors the land which Yahweh had given for all to share. But there was more to Jesus' parable than just a story taken from real contemporary life. The image of the vineyard was very familiar, representing Yahweh's dealing with Israel in Scripture.[7] The story here is a brief history of Yahweh's patient and generous dealing with Israel despite the fact that they continually refused (Ac 28:32ff) to recognize the authority of his servants, the prophets, like John, and give him, the rightful owner, the fruit to which he was entitled.[8] It is the most allegorical of all the parables. The landowner is God, the tenants are the Jewish leaders, the servants are the prophets, the son Jesus, the others the Gentiles. Accepting that Jesus saw himself as God's unique son and in a long line of God's prophetic messengers and that his course was leading to death, the parable fits in well in the historical background. Quite likely, this parable actually helped to sign Jesus' death warrant. Possibly the original version ended with the death of the son as in the Gospel according to Thomas. Thus having no mention of the resurrection, the further additions in the gospels would then have been made by the early Christians in the light of the subsequent events.

Luke's differences from the versions of Mark and Matthew are small but interesting to note. He does not have their Isaian details such as the digging of the winepress and the building of the watch tower. Perhaps they would be uninteresting for his Gentile audience. The owner goes to another country *for a long time* (9:12). Luke's version is more climactic as the third servant is not killed, a fate left for the beloved son (a reference to the baptism scene—Lk 3:22; 9:35). Here is a Lucan touch as like the unjust steward and the rich fool, God soliloquises "What shall I do?" In Luke and Matthew but unlike Mark's version, the son is dragged outside the vineyard so as not to defile it, and is killed there. Symbolically, this means that Jerusalem rejects Jesus but that also his salvific death is meant not just for Jerusalem alone but also for the Gentiles (Rom 9:11; Is 42:6; 49:6). In Matthew 21:40f, Jesus' question about what the owner will do is answered by the audience and Jesus replies by quoting Psalm 118:22f. But in Luke Jesus answers his own question and the audience interjects "God forbid" before Jesus quotes the Psalm. The phrase "he looked on them' ' (v 17) will later be used in 22:61 as Jesus looks on Peter.

All three synoptics somewhat awkwardly and perhaps artificially conclude the parable with a prophetic quotation from Psalm 118, a Psalm already quoted at the triumphant entry (19:38). The Psalm was a very popular one in early Christian circles as it is found also applied to Jesus' resurrection in Acts 4:11; Rom 9:32f; 1 P 2:4ff; Eph 2:19ff. It comes from a section of the processional psalms celebrating God's repeated deliverance and perhaps originally sung at the restoration of the walls of Jerusalem about B.C. 444. At times in Israel's history she had seemed God forsaken and as useless as a stone rejected by a builder. But disciplined by Yahweh and refined through suffering, she had experienced a wonderful reversal of fortunes by God's hand, became worthy to be a foundation stone, and even a corner store for a new Israel (Is 28:16; 1 Cor 3:9). Similarly, the rejected Jesus would become the keystone for the new Israel, the new people of God. This again is an example of the reversal theme in Luke (1:52). Luke alone adds a second reflection on Jesus the keystone, this time quite artificially through the catchword stone (as he joined 11:33-6). It is quite difficult to imagine one falling on a cornerstone and being smashed to pieces or on the other hand a cornerstone falling on a person. Two Old Testament references immediately come to mind as fulfilled in Jesus, Is8:14 where Yahweh becomes for Israel "a stone of offense and a rock of stumbling" (2:34; 22:34) and Daniel 2:34ff where God's kingdom is described as a stone destroying all other rival kingdoms. Jesus' victory is certain despite his rejection which, however, will lead to the destruction of Jerusalem and of those who reject him (Rom 9;33).

(4) *Paying Tribute to Caesar—(20:20-26):*

The scene is like a modern angry press conference. The authorities had failed to intimidate Jesus and had instead provoked an unanswerable attack on themselves which must have embarrssed and discredited them in the eyes of the people. Now their tactic is to use spies to flatter and trap Jesus with a loaded question about a highly sensitive and explosive issue, the tax. Luke uses the correct Greek word "phoros" where Mark has a transliterated Latin word "kensos." This would either discredit him in the eyes of the people to whom the Roman "head" tax, symbolic of their loss of freedom, was hateful, or on the other hand incriminate him before the Roman authorities for speaking against the tax. This tax of one denarius a year per able adult, was levied when a Roman procurator took over Judea, Samaria and Idumaea in A.D. 6 when Archelaus was deposed. In particular, the fanatical Zealots, the most revolutionary sect among the Jews, who held that there was "no king but Yahweh," objected violently to paying taxes to Rome. Further, to the Jew, a coin bearing the king's head was a graven image especially as there was a tendency to deify the king. But there was also a subtle legal point which was convenient for legally-minded Jews, namely, that a coin stamped with the emperor's image belonged to him so that in taxes he was actually receiving back his own (v 25).

Luke's version is similar to Mark's but he emphasizes at the beginning and at the end that they were not able to catch him in their malicious trap so as to hand over lto the governor (v 20,26). In Mark the questioners were the unusual combination of Pharisees and Herodians, but in Luke they were men who pretended to be honest men, a decription more applicable to his own audience and their questions. They address Jesus as "teacher" of the Way of God in truth[9] and use a Hebrew expression lit, ' "do not lift up the face" for his lack of respect of persons.[10] Luke is particularly concerned to show both here and in the Passion that Jesus like the early Christians in Acts, is politically guiltless before the Romans of such accusations as Zealotry as they would later make (23:2; Ac 5:36). Jesus realizes their duplicity (v 23), asks for a coin which a true Jew would not have in his possession, and with a touch of irony commands them ' "to return" to Caesar his due—their expression was "to give." All three gospels stress that Jesus disconserted his critics and evidently escaped from the dilemma while emphasizing the paramount importance of loyalty to God, a theme that would be important in Acts (Ac 4:19-20; 5:29). His reply neither advocated insurrection nor complete submission to the Romans.

In Jewish history some other prophets had even suggested that a foreign ruler unknown to himself might be exercising the will of Yahweh, the lord of history in ruling the

Jews.[11] However, Jesus' reply is something of a riddle. Clearly all men owe a (limited) obedience to the political order which of necessity is imperfect. Is there an allusion to the Old Testament idea of man stamped with God's image and therefore belonging to God and to be returned to him? This reply of Jesus has been the basis of much subsequent discussion on the thorny problem of Church and State[12] but has often been pushed too far. Two distinct and separate spheres or kingdoms have often been advocated with religion, the future life and often also sexual morality left to the Church and its influence, while politics and economics are abandoned to Caesar. Clearly for Jesus all belong to God and should be under his rule but this does not mean that they should be directly under the Church. Yet is is amazing how like churches, many modern political parties are with their doctrines and saints, rites and duties, disciplines, rewards and even powers of intercession.

(5) *The Sadducees and the Resurrection of the Dead—(20:27-40):*

Jesus, having escaped attempts to discredit him with the people and to involve him in a treacherous answer against the Roman authorities, is now subjected by the Sadducees to a hypothetical, though not impossible question, about a woman who married seven brothers in turn. They attempt to ridicule the doctrine of the resurrection which Jesus held, in common with their great enemies, the Pharisees. These, like the Sadducees, seem to have originated in the second century, during the time of the Maccabees. The Sadducees, who are named only here in Luke's gospel believed neither in the resurrection nor in angels and spirits (Ac 23:8i; 4:1-2; 5:17) and are contradicted on both accounts by Jesus. Unfortunately, none of their writings have survived and we only know about their beliefs through non-friendly sources. They were wealthy priestly aristocracy who collaborated with the Romans to preserve Israel. It seems that they only held the Pentateuch as fully authoritative in religion and being of a fundamentalist tendency rejected many of the adaptations to contemporary times and newer ideas of the Pharisees, such as belief in the after-life which seems to have been stressed only late in Israel's history (Is 26:19; Dn 12:2).

Luke, in addition to some stylistic improvements on Mark, has a more tolerant Jesus as he omits the two blunt statements that the Sadducees are wrong. In v 34-6 Jesus' argument is developed differently from Mark and curiously, has some very semitic expressions, e.g. v 36, "sons of the resurrection."

The Levirate law ("levir" in Latin means brother-in-law) about which Jesus seems to have expressed no disapproval or reservations despite its polygamous implications,[13] is similar to the system of widow inheritance still found in many societies today. Its purpose was not just to provide a legal heir for a man's property but to prevent his name and his memory from being lost forever.

The Sadducees used their hypothetical case to show the impossibility of the resurrection which they did not find in the books of Moses. Luke's answer emphasizes more than Mark's the contrast between the two ages, showing how the Sadducees confuse them (1 Cor 15:35-50; Phil 3:21). The phrase "the sons of this age" is found only twice in the New Testament, here meaning all who are alive and in 16:8, as distinct from "the sons of light." The Pharisees also tended to picture the next world as a kind of indefinite continuation of the present good life and essentially the same. The answer here seems to correct Mark's ambiguity and only deals with "those judged worthy" who are "sons of the resurrection" and "sons of God" (see

14:14 Gn 6:1ff). They do not marry (14:26; 18:29) as they are no longer liable to death and become like the angels in whom the Sadducees do not believe (the word is "isaggelos"; "like an angel" is found only here but see Ac 6:15; 1 Cor 15:24ff).

Jesus quotes their highest authority, Moses, to show that the resurrection is contained in his writings, in fact, in his best known passage about his meeting with Yahweh at the burning bush (Ex 3:1-6, note the method of reference by content in a time when the Bible had neither chapters nor numbered verses. God does not say "I 'was' their God" but "I 'am' the God." A god of non-being is ridiculous. Death does not break man's relationship to God but only to his neighbor (Ps 16:8ff; 49:15f; 73:23ff). He is the God of the living, not of the dead, for "all are alive to him." This seems to be a quotation from 4 Macc 7:19; 16:25l, a pharisaical work roughly contemporaneous with Jesus (see 2 Cor 5:1ff; Gal 2:19; Phil 1:20ff). The argument from the literal words of the text is rabbinical in touch and pleases some of the scribes who congratulate Jesus. Note that this verse is found at the conclusion of Mark's next episode on the great commandment which Luke omits as he used it earlier to introduce the Good Samaritan (10:25ff). Jesus' answer completely reduces his opponents to silence.

(6) *Jesus, David's Son and Lord—(20:41-44):*

Now it is Jesus' turn to conclude the questions by asking a final question of the same audience to clarify the nature of his Messiahship (Mk 12:35). The question is an unanswered riddle based on Scripture which sums up the mystery of Jesus. It obviously posed difficulties for traditional Jewish messiology. The early Christians probably used it in their dialogues with their Jewish neighbors. Jesus quotes Psalm 110:1, from an enthronement oracle to a priest king and a verse frequently alluded to in the New Testament.[14] He accepts the common attribution in his time of the Psalms to David. Luke follows Mark closely here but omits the reference to the Scribes (Mk 12:35) and gives for his Gentile audience a more precise reference than Mark, replacing "in the Holy Spirit" with "in the book of Psalms." Compare Luke 11:20 and 212:25 with Matthew 12:28; Mark 13:11, where Luke also unexpectedly omits references to the Spirit, one of his favorite themes. Is Luke here emphasizing the fuller inspiration of Jesus as compared with mere statement of Scripture? In Acts 1:16 it should be noted that he accepts the inspiration of David.

Jesus challenges them to answer how the awaited Messiah could be called a mere Son of David when David himself had actually addressed him as "lord" and obviously superior to himself. The paradox is clearer in the Greek text quoted by Luke, where the same word "kyrios" is used twice. The question is left unanswered but probably the intention is to show that there is much more to Jesus than the nationalistic and political Son of David, of current Jewish expectation. Luke frequently emphasized Jesus' Davidic descent.[15] But for Luke, Jesus is Lord (Eph 1:20ff; Col 1:12ff) and much more than another warrior prince, another David,[16] even though Jesus had recently accepted the title (18:37ff). There is no answer from Jesus' audience. Later Christian theology would conclude that the Messiah was far more than the Son of David, in fact, the Son of God.

(7) *The Scribes are Denounced—(20:45-7):*

Here all three synoptics introduce a direct condemnation of the Scribes which is placed side by side with Jesus' praise of the poor widow, a good example of the reversing of popular values by the humbling and exaltation spoken of in the Magnificat. In an earlier denunciation (11:43; also 6:24f; 18:9-14), Luke is close to Matthew's longer version (Mt 23:1-14; Q), but here he follows Mark's account almost word for word(Mk 12:38-40). But in Luke it is addressed to the disciples, the "scribes" in the early church and "in the hearing of all the people." Three points are made: (i) the scribes' proud and self-advertised importance and love of externals, of ostentation and parading in long robes (11:43; 12:41ff; 22:24ff); (ii) their exploitation of vulnerable widows (8:3; Ac 16:15; hospitality?) for whom the law had commanded special concern;[17] (iii) their superficial prayers, emphasizing length rather than depth (18:9-14; Mt 6:5-15). Because of their special vocation of teachers for which it was forbidden to accept money they will receive a heavier sentence (Jam 3:1). The controversies end with a positive note as Jesus emphatically ("truly" 4:24) praises the poor widow.

(8) *The Widow's Mite—(21:1-4):*

The reference to widows and their savings in 20:47 leads Luke to one of his favorite themes, the reversal of the rich and the poor (1:52; 6:20; 4:18-19), as he tells the story of Jesus' approval of the poor widow's mite without significant variation from Mark. The poor widow who gives her everything to God (her "Bios" or life v 4) contrasts with the greedy self-important scribes and the self-sufficient rich with their gifts from their surplus funds (Rom 5:17; 2 Cor 8:2). The treasury is perhaps a section of the court of the women where there were thirteen trumpet shaped collection boxes (2 K 12:9ff), each marked for a different purpose. Sometimes the donor at the temple would declare both the amount and purpose of his gift to

Jerusalem

the presiding priest. The word translated "poor" (v 2) is found only here in the New Testament and signifies very poor in Greek literature. It's parallel in v3 (ptoche) was used of Lazarus (16:20) and in the great sermon (6:20). The word used for her gift (lepta) signifies a very small coin, the only Jewish coin mentioned in the New Testament and valued at about one-eighth of a cent. Mark translates it into the Roman "quadrans."

(9) *The Destruction of the Temple Foretold—(21:5-7):*

Luke's Eschatology:

This eschatological and apocalyptic discourse which is Jesus' last public discourse, exhorts Christians and describes the ultimate victory and deliverance of the Son of Man despite future suffering for his followers. This is Luke's third such discourse but here as in Mark and Matthew, it is closely associated with the destruction of the temple and Jerusalem (12:35-9; 17:20-18:8). A large part parallels. Mark 13, e.g. the first seven verses seem to be a revised version and to have characteristic Lucan emphasis which gives it a less Jewish character than Mark's account. In particular, Luke emphasizes the delay before the end (v 9,12) and separates more carefully than Matthew and Mark the destruction of Jerusalem from the predictions about the coming of the Son of Man in the distant future and the final event for which no precise date is given, but "until the times of the Gentiles are fulfilled" v 24. In Luke one must make a distinction between "the last days" of the early Church (Ac 2:17) and the final event of the coming of the Son of Man. Also, it is useful to remember that no gospel gives us a tape recording of Jesus' eschatological sermon but each gives, not a complete sermon, but, rather, a collection of sayings often somewhat awkwardly juxtaposed, e.g. v 16,17,25ff,32.

After an introduction (5-7) which includes both Jesus' foretelling of the destruction of the temple and the disciples' questions "when" and "what sign," there is an exhortation about false signs and cosmic disasters (8-11), leading to the center of the discourse describing the persecution of Christians (12-19) and the destruction of Jerusalem which will happen before the end of the world (20-24). This leads into another parallel section on cosmic disasters after which the Son of Man will come (25-8), a warning on the lesson of the fig tree (29-33), a further exhortation (34-6) and a conclusion summarizing the last days of Jesus.

The Destruction of the Temple Foretold—(21:5-7):

All synoptics begin the discourse with a prediction of the destruction of the temple, a prediction that would be fulfilled some forty years afterwards when the Romans entered Jerusalem on August 9, A.D. 70. In Luke this becomes a public discourse in the temple (20:45; 21:5,7), whereas in Mark it is a private teaching to Peter, James, John and Andrew (Mk 13:3) as they sit opposite on the Mount of Olives. Some, probably disciples (20:45), were admiring the noble stones and votive offerings (2 Macc 9:16; Mark mentions "buildings") of Herod's temple, the third Jewish temple which was being built during Jesus' lifetime. Begun in B.C. 20 it was completed only in A.D. 64 and only lasted until A.D. 70. The noble stones included the huge stones such as can still be seen at the "wailing wall" today and the forty foot columns which were carved out of single stones. Josephus tells us that those stones not covered with silver and gold, were so white that from a distance the temple gave the appearance of a snow capped

Jerusalem

mountain. Tacitus, the Roman historian described the temple as "a shrine of immense wealth." It is worth noting that in his description the temple was destroyed by fire and not pulled down stone by stone as the text has it here. The offerings would include Herod's golden vine which was set over the door and which according to Josephus, had "grape clusters as tall as man," a table given by Ptolemy of Egypt and a chair from Agrippa. Jesus' prediction, "the days will come" (17:22; Jer 26:6ff) must have been startling and led to the disciples "When?" and "What will be the sign?" for the destruction of the temple.

(10) *False Signs and Cosmic Disasters—(21:8-11):*

Jesus in his answer as so often before, gives more than the questioner required and diverts the questioner to more important matters. Luke's version seems to reduce the apocalyptic speculation and produce a public teaching to his community. His problem is not just false Messiahs who proclaim "I am" (Mt "the Christ," see Jn 4:25 f, etc.) but in particular some deluded and hyper-excited preachers who misread the signs of the times, proclaiming "the time" (the "kairos," the decisive Messianic time v28) "is upon us," a phrase found only in Luke and already corrected.[18]

Jesus seems to say that the end of the world will not come within the lifetime of his audience. Future history is under God's control. In addition to the destruction of the temple "first" as Luke adds (v 9), there will be wars and insurrection. They should not be terrified at these but the end does not follow immediately as there will be persecution first and then cosmic calamities (v 12). Note how Luke seems to omit Mark's "this is the beginning of the sufferings" (1:8) and substitutes the more exact "but before all these things." Many of his expressions here can be taken as referring to contemporary events such as the worldwide famines of the fifties and sixties, the Phrygian earthquake of A.D. 61, the eruption of Vesuvius A.D. 79, the wars in Britain and Parthia, the struggle between the four emperors in A.D. 69, the insurrection in Palestine. However, they are like standard and general descriptions of great sorrows in the Old Testament and are best not interpreted literally.[19]

(11) *Persecution of Christians—(21:12-19):*

However, before the destruction of the temple the followers of Jesus will be persecuted because of him (his name) at the hands of both Jews and Gentiles.[20] Luke interrupts his account of the cosmic disasters in verses 12-24 and returns to this theme in vv 25-33, to stress (v 12) that before they happen the persecutions and destruction of Jerusalem must first take place. Thus neither persecution nor the destruction of Jerusalem, not even the preaching of the gospel to the Gentiles, are the ultimate signs of the end of the world. Luke does not have Mark's 13:10 "But the good news must first be proclaimed to all the Gentiles," as perhaps it was already a reality and would imply that the end would come then (Ac 1:18; 28:30f).

Jesus bluntly spells out (9:23-7) the danger and the persecutions to come—prisons and synagogues which were, it should be remembered, not only places of worship but places where Jewish law was administered;[21] Kings and governors (Ac 24:10ff; 267:1ff). But such persecutions are not utter disasters but should be seen as occasions to bear witness to Jesus.[22] The book of Acts can be described as a study in witness, giving three kinds of witness, words, deeds and community life. There is no need to worry as

nothing will happen unless it is in God's plan and loving care (v 15,18 and 28 are Lucan additions). A technical term for preparing a court defense is used here, the only time in the New Testament. There is a note of confidence here and an assurance of ultimate victory. Jesus himself, who is parallel to the Holy Spirit (compare 21:12 and 12:12; also Ac 10:14 and 19), will give them a mouth of wisdom, a Semitic phrase for eloquence and understanding such as their enemies will neither be able to withstand or contradict.[24] Verses 16 and 17 are found almost identically in Mark 13:12 (see Lk 12:51-3). They will be hated by all and some will be put to death.[25] This verse 16 apparently contradicts v 18, where there is a promise that not a hair will perish.[26] Does Luke add v 18 to contrast the main group with a small group, i.e. "some" in v 16 introduces a parenthesis, or should some such addition as "without the special providence of God" be presupposed. Certainly Luke is stressing the control of God while he is not blind to the harsh realities of the early church, like Paul (e.g. Rom 8:39). Luke's emphasis on patient endurance to the end also recalls a favorite theme of Paul.[27] This word "hupomone" is especially connected in the New Testament with the future expectation of glory and greatness.[28]
'
(12) *The Siege and Destruction of Jerusalem Foretold—(21:20-24):*

Next we have advice to the followers of Jesus about what to do when they see Jerusalem being encircled by soldiers or army camps, a Roman technique "Know that devastation is near." This is the only prediction in Luke whose fulfilment is not recorded by the end of Acts. But considering the last scene in Acts about the rejection of the Jews, it seems inevitable or perhaps presumed, already known to the readers. Here, as one of the main highlights of the eschatological discourse, we are told in a verse proper to Luke, who gives a reason for the flight of the disciples, that the destruction represents the retribution of God and his wrath against the people[29] over the rejection of Jesus as was written in the scriptures.[30] Instead of Mark and Matthew's vague "abominable thing which destroys,"[31] we have the more direct and concrete prediction of the fall of Jerusalem. This seems based on prophetic descriptions in the Septuagint of the capture of Jerusalem in July B.C. 587, and thus not necessarily a prophecy after the events written in the light of the actual events of A.D. 70. None of the distinctive aspects of the siege as found in Josephus are described by Luke.

The historicity of some such prediction as given here is confirmed by Eusebius (3:5,3), who says that before the siege, the Christians fled towards the invaders some sixty miles to Pella, a trans-Jordan city of the Decapolis, in response to "an oracle given by revelation." During the destruction of Jerusalem, a city which normally had about 25-30,000 population, over a million were killed according to Eusebius and 97,000 taken to slavery. Mark 13:18 is omitted perhaps because it refers to the possibility of a winter siege when it was actually from April to September, also the merciful shortening of the final sorrows (Mk 13:20). The people are killed or enslaved and Jerusalem trampled by the Gentiles (Zech 12:3f; Apoc 11:2) "until the times of the Gentiles are fulfilled" (Dn 12:7). This somewhat enigmatic phrase seems to refer to an indefinite period (before 25ff), after the destruction of Jerusalem and also to Luke's hope of the ultimate restoration of the Jews.[32] Note that Luke uses "kairos" as in 21:8. He also omits Mark's reference to the shortening of the days (Mk 13:20) and instead calls for patience (v 34-6).

(13) *The Coming of the Son of Man—(21:25-8):*

Now he returns to v 10f, the real signs of the end, the convulsions of the natural world which will precede the triumphant coming of the Son of Man. The language used is from the common apocalyptic and poetic imagery used in Jewish writings.[33] Peter's quotation of the prophet Joel at Pentecost (Ac 2:16-21) shows perhaps that such literature was not taken literally even then. Luke has toned down the picture somewhat by omitting the moon giving no light and the stars falling from heaven (Mk 13:24f; Mt 24:29) and by adding in verse 25f to the cosmic disturbance some psychological observations on human distress (Dt 28:28; 2 Bar 70:2). "The roaring of the seas and the waves" must be understood against its Jewish background in which the sea was a great reservoir of evil bound by God at creation.[34] The powers in the heavens perhaps refer to the angelic beings permitted by God to preside over the destinies of the gentile nations.[35] The description of the Son of Man coming on a cloud suggests his coming from the mysterious, unseen realm of God (Dn 7:13; 1 Thess 4:16). Note the singular cloud (Dn 7:13 "clouds"), which recalls the cloud of the transfiguration (9:34) and also of the ascension which Jesus (Ac 1:9), not to mention the cloud symbolizing God's presence which guided the Hebrews through the wilderness (Ex 14:19; 34:5; Num 9:1ff).

When these things begin to happen, Luke emphasizes, then deliverance or redemption, an important Pauline word which he uses seven times but which is only found here in the gospels,[36] is near at hand.[37] Persecutions are then over and it is time "to hold your heads high" (Is 8:21). Luke believes in the historical return of Jesus and his final redemption of this world (3:21). Note that his use of the terminology of redemption is not applied to the death of Jesus.[38] The fact that there are signs does not contradict 17:20f and 21:34f, as it is insisted upon that nevertheless the end will come suddenly like a trap (v 34). In this section we have one of the two occasions in the gospel where the nearness of the kingdom of God and the coming of the Son of Man are associated side by side by the author.[39]

(14) *The Lesson of the Fig Tree—(21:29-33):*

Apart from Luke's introductory remark describing it as a parable, his Gentile application "or any other tree," and the substitution of "the kingdom is near" (Mk 13:29 "he is near even at the door"), there is a close similarity betwen the words of the parable in all synoptics. Mark's version could be applied to the destruction of Jerusalem but Luke has omitted "these things" from Mark's phrase "all these things," and introduced "the kingdom" to make his application to the story of redemption and the parousia clear. Most of the trees in Palestine are evergreen and the sudden burst of the fig tree which seems so dead signifies that summer is near. It was a good illustration of persecuted and perhaps seemingly dead Christianity looking forward to the sudden coming of the kingdom in its final parousia manifestation.[40] It has always been a problem to explain "this generation" not passing away until "all things have been accomplished" (v 36). Does it refer to the destruction of Jerusalem? Or does it refer also to the parousia with the phrase "this generation" meaning the eschatological generation, those living between the resurrection and the second coming? Does generation mean the Jewish nation or mankind (Ps 12:7; 14:5)? Certainly, we can rule out from Luke's point of view that Jesus made a prediction and was mistaken. Luke omits Mark 13:32 where Jesus seems to limit the son's knowledge about the time of the end. Luke concludes with an assurance that Jesus' words are eternal just like the old law was believed to be (Bar 4:1) and that they will last "even if the heavens pass away . . . " (a phrase also in 16:17; Mt 5:18).

(15) *Exhortation to Watch—(21:34-6):*

The discourse concludes with an exhortation to his follower to be watchful as Paul advised the Thessalonians (1 Th 5:1ff). Mark's parable of the man who went on a journey (Mk 13:33-7) is omitted as already it is given in a more developed form (19:11-18).[41] Luke in verses 34-6, collects here some of his important themes as he warns his audience not to let the remoteness of the Parousia make them like birds which fly unsuspectingly into a snare (Is 24:17). The Parousia will be sudden and universal (1 Thess 5:2; 2 P 3:1ff). Thus the debauchery and drunkenness recall the servants who abuse their absent master's trust(12:45). The worldly cares recall the parable of the sower (8:14) and the people of Noah's time (17:26ff) and the command to pray constantly recalls the parable in 18:1ff and the eschatological dimension of the Our Father whose center was the petition for the fullness of the kingdom which is being realized even now (see Rom 8;26ff; Eph 6:18; Phil 4:6f). The purpose of their vigilance and prayer which Luke alone stresses is to be able "to stand secure before the Son of Man,"[42] i.e. ultimate and full salvation.

(16) *The Last Days of Jesus—(21:37-8):*

The temple scene is concluded with a summary which recalls 19:47 in an "inclusion." Jesus teaches by day and spends the night on the hill called Olivet. The word can suggest camping out but Mark (Mk 11:1) tell us that Jesus spent the nights at Bethany which is on the far slopes of Mt. Olivet. The eagerness of the people who came early to hear and the openness of his teaching are emphasized as we enter the passion section. Thus Jerusalem and, in particular, the leaders, could never deny their opportunity to hear Jesus' message. The parallel situation and similarity between v38 and John 8:1f have led some scribes to insert here the account of the woman taken in adultery (Jn 7:53-8:11).

B. *The Passion of Jesus—(22:1-23:56):*

The story of the passion was important to the early Church. It is the longest individual section in each gospel. This is somewhat surprising in Luke and perhaps an example of his trustworthiness because in his version of the first sermons of the Apostles in Acts he seems to hurry over the humiliating suffering of Jesus.[43] It was, as Paul put it:

> "a stumbling block to the Jews and an absurdity to the Gentiles but to those who are called, Jews and Greeks alike Christ the power of God and the wisdom of God" (1 Cor 1:23f).

It was seen not really as a defeat but as a victorious battle in which God's plan was accomplished. All four gospels actually give more space to events like Jesus' trial than to the actual crucifixion itself so as to bring out the meaning of Jesus' mission and death in the face of subsequent misunderstanding and even distortion. The early Christians were especially witnesses to the Risen Lord.[44] But the light of the resurrection helped them not to run away from the reality of suffering but to face it and to learn from the example of Jesus. For Luke, as in the great journey narrative, the passion story is a personal invitation to his audience to carry one's cross and to follow Jesus on the way of the Cross, to suffer with Jesus (Ac 9:4f), to see oneself in such characters as Peter among the disputing and blind disciples at the last supper which is prepared "for us" (v 8), Simon the Cyrene, the good thief. His account is well organized but in no way the complete and cold objective account which historians sometimes attempt. Thus, he omits some of the cruel details which we find in the other gospels. It is a disciple's account of the Christian's path to glory (12:1-12; Ac 14:22).

Luke is unique among the evangelists in that he does not emphasize directly the connection between the cross and death of Jesus and salvation in the manner of a Paul or a John. Thus he does not have (Mk 10:45) "to give his life in ransom for the many," or explicitly say that Jesus died for our sins, but note Ac 20:28, which refers clearly to Jesus' artificial death. But there is the text 22:19f-20, on the redemptive aspect of the meal which though disputed, has in its support the overwhelming preponderance of external evidence. While Luke's other redemption terminology is not linked to the death of Jesus (see 21:28) yet his unique linking of redemption as tied to the second coming of Jesus (21:28) suggests that he sees redemption as tied to the whole process and only finally and fully achieved in the parousia. He does stress the place of suffering and the cross in the life of a disciple who truly follows Jesus (9:23ff; 12:49ff; 21:17; 23:26ff; Ac 9:16). In Acts he often joins the cross and resurrection with the offer of forgiveness, thus stressing their unity (Ac 2:36ff; 3:18f; 5:30f). He also identifies Jesus as the suffering servant of Isaiah (Ac 8:32f; 3:13; 26:4ff). Such texts were frequently used in the early church to explain the redemptive value of Jesus' death. Especially in his emphasis on Jerusalem and the divine necessity of Jesus going to die there, he does stress the passion of Jesus with his own theological insights. While John sees the suffering of Jesus as part of his glorification, Luke sees it in the light of his theology of reversal as an essential step to the glory of the resurrection and ascension (24:26).

For Luke, the passion is especially what the Messiah has to undergo so as to enter into his glory (24:26), into his kingdom (23:40-3), a kingship of service, unlike the earthly kings which are frequently found in Luke's pages (22:25-7; 4:5-6; 1:5 etc.). The kingship of Jesus, which will last forever (1:33), was stressed during the infancy reflections (1:32ff; 2:11; 3:22ff), as Jesus sets out on his great journey (9:21,35) and particularly during the entry to Jerusalem and during the Last Supper (18:38ff; 19:12ff; 22:29ff; 23:42f; 24:26ff).

Luke then has a passion theology of his own. Jesus' passion and death are a witness (martyr) to God and to his acceptance of God's will and plan.[45] But Jesus especially is the exemplar martyr for the early Christians. In Acts, Stephen is a martyr who exemplifies what the *imitatio Christi* should be: forgiving his enemies (23:34; Ac 7:60) and committing his spirit to his father.[46] Paul's journey to Jerusalem is modelled on that of Jesus.[47] Jesus is the model of those who suffer innocently (23:4,14ff,27,41,47), the victims of satanic evil (22:3,53). Similary, Paul will often be accused and declared innocent by the Roman authorities (e.g. Ac 24:2f; 25:18ff). Luke alone has Pilate's statement that he finds no crime in Jesus and also the centurion's verdict of innocence (23:47), thus preparing for one of his themes in Acts in which he denies that Christianity is subversive and that neither Jesus nor his followers were criminals or lawbreakers. But neither evil nor the suffering it brings will completely detroy Jesus or his followers (21:13f).

Other themes are also in evidence in Luke such as prayer (22:40ff; 23:34,46) and particularly the compassion of Jesus, as forgetful of himself, he reaches out to others, towards the High Priest's slave (22:50f), to Peter (22:31f,61), to the women (23:27ff), towards his enemies (23:34), the good thief (23:43). In Mark, Jesus seems much more isolated in his suffering. In his death he is identified with the disreputable outcasts of society (22:35ff; 23:32b).

The passion narrative is a particularly complex example of the synoptic fact and the synoptic problem. The three synoptics agree on the broad outline of episodes, beginning with the plot of the authorities to kill Jesus and the Lord's Supper where Jesus gives his life for the covenant to set up a new people of God. Next, all four gospels have the same arrangement—the arrest; a Jewish and a Roman trial; the execution on the Cross and the burial of the body in the tomb. Of the sixteen incidents in the crucifixion accounts, most are found in at least three gospels though not always in the same order. Of these 6 are found in all four gospels, 5 in all synoptics and one in Mark and Matthew alone. Reflecting on so deep a mystery many thoughts, insights and theologies are possible (Jn 21:25). Thus each evangelist, not least Luke, has his own personal reflections and unique elements. It is estimated, for example, that for about one quarter of his passion account, actually 27% of the vocabulary, and for the basic order, he used Mark as a source, which he does not hesitate to rearrange. For the rest, in addition to his creative writing and insights, it seems quite likely that Luke used an independent non-Markan source.

As compared with Mark, Luke does not have the

flight of the disciples at the arrest of Jesus (Mk 14:50ff; the false witnesses (Mk 14:55-9); the Roman soldiers' mockery (Mk 15:16-20); the offering of the wine drugged with myrrh (Mk 15:23); the praying of Psalm 22 from the Cross (Mk 15:34ff). Luke and Matthew do not have Mark's hour by hour structure of the passion or the names of Simon of Cyrene's sons (Mk 15:21). Further, they often agree on details against Mark.[48]

But in Luke where Jesus dies nobly concerned with others, he alone has additions to Jesus' address at the last supper (22:15,25-30,35-8); the angel at the agony (22:43); Jesus' look at Peter after the denial (22:61); Jesus before Herod (23:6-11); his conversation with the women at Jerusalem (23:27-31); words from the cross (23:34,43,46).

What is often noted is the relation between Luke's special tradition and John's narrative. Some 40 instances in fact can be pointed out where Luke and John have something in common with some of the instances too exact to be merely coincidences.[49] While there is no evidence that either knew the other's gospel it seems that there must have been contact at an earlier stage between the traditions available to both.

An Outline of Luke's Passion Account:

(1) The Plot of the Sanhedrin to Kill Jesus—22:1-6.
(2) The Preparation of the Passover—22:7-13.
(3) The Institution of the Lord's Supper—22:14-20.
(4) The Announcement of the Betrayal—22:21-23.
(5) The Dispute "Who is the Greatest"—22:24-30.
(6) Peter's Denials Foretold—22:31-4.
(7) The Hour of Testing—22:35-8.
(8) The Agony in the Garden—22:39-46.
(9) The Betrayal and Arrest of Jesus—22:47-53.

Jerusalem

(10) Peter's Denials of Jesus—22:54-62.
(11) The Mockery and Beating of Jesus—22:63-5.
(12) Jesus before the Sanhedrin—22:66-71.
(13) Jesus before Pilate—23:1-5.
(14) Jesus before Herod—23:6-12.
(15) Jesus Sentenced to Death by Pilate—23:13-25.
(16) The Way of the Cross—23:26-32.
(17) The Crucifixion of Jesus—23:33-8.
(18) The Penitent Thief—23:39-42.
(19) The Death of Jesus on the Cross—23:44-9.
(20) The Burial of Jesus—23:50-6.

(1) *The Plot of the Sanhedrin to Kill Jesus—(22:1-6):*

The story of the final events of Jesus' life is introduced with the plot of the authorities which culminates many attempts to silence the popular Jesus (e.g. 6:11) and, in particular, the treachery of Judas. Luke does not condemn but narrates and decribes Judas as one of the number of the twelve, perhaps signifying that he was not of their spirit.

Luke does not have Mark 14:2 "not during the feast . . ." because in fact all three synoptics, perhaps following the lunar calendar adopted by such as Qumran, describe the crucifixion as taking place on the feast of the passover, even though it seems extraordinary that the trial and crucifixion would take place during the solemn feast, not to mention the remark about Simon coming in from the country, as journeys were suspended during feasts. Some experts in ancient calendars suggest that the Passion meal could have taken place during the next three days. It is possible that Mark, influenced by liturgical considerations, telescoped the events somewhat. John, perhaps following the solar calendar of the temple authorities, seems to agree with a reference to Jesus in the Talmud according to which Jesus dies on the 14th Nisan, the day before the Passover. This was the day on which the paschal lamb was killed. Yet he agrees that Jesus died on a Friday (Jn 18:28; 19:14; 1:29; Mk 14:12). Mark, Matthew and Luke speak of Jesus' final meal as the Passover meal even though there is no direct reference to the eating of the Paschal Lamb. In the thinking of the early Christians, Jesus himself was the paschal lamb (1 Cor 5:7). It should be remembered that the Jewish day began with the previous sunset. Leviticus 23:5 commands the eating of the Passover meal for the evening which both concluded the 14th Nisan and began the 15th Nisan, the feast of Passover (Mt 26:17; Mk 14:12). The 15th Nisan (=March/April) was the day of the spring full moon. One might expect help from astronomy as to whether Nisan 15 was a Thursday or a Friday, but it seems the Jews had a custom of adding seven leap-months into the calendar to iron out differences between the solar and lunar years. The beginning of the month was the responsibility of two reliable witnesses who had the duty of spotting the new moon and foggy nights could easily lead to confusion here. In Mark 15:42, the day of the crucifixion is the day before the Sabbath. Mark and Matthew have "two days before," i.e. Wednesday, but Luke has the more vague "was drawing near." Luke does not describe the anointing at Bethany possibly because of its similarity with the event in 7:36-50 (Mk 14:3-9), but note 23:55f.

Actually there were two feasts at this time, the Passover, a one day feast which relived the great liberation from Egypt and the covenant by which they became the people of God (Ex 12:21-27) and the feast of unleavened bread (Mazzoth) or the feast of Omer. This latter began the very next day, the 15th Nisan and lasted until the 21st

Jerusalem

Nisan and which celebrated the harvesting of the first sheaf of barley and lasted seven days. In Exodus 12, both are combined.[50] The whole eight day feast could be described by either name. Thus, the Jewish historian, Josephus, writing for a non-Jewish audience like Luke's, sometimes simplifies and identifies the two feasts, like Luke (compare Antiq iii,10,5 with xiv,2,1). It should be remembered that the Passover Feast in which Jerusalem was thronged with pilgrims, many of whom had fulfilled their lifetime desire in coming, had an important future dimension as a feast of hope, of looking forward to the eagerly accepted messianic deliverance and the coming of God's kingdom. "On this night they were saved" said the Jewish proverb, "and on this night they will be saved."

The opponents are now the chief priests and the scribes. The officers (v 4) were temple guards chosen from the Levites and were permitted to keep order for the Sanhedrin (Ac 4:1; 5:24; Mt 27:65). The Pharisees, who were Jesus' great opponents during his ministry, now disappear. It seems that they were pacifists and non-violent in tendency. Luke seems to expand Mark's account of the betrayal by Judas (see v 3-6) and later he will tell of his replacement (Ac 1:15ff). Two suggestions are offered in the gospels as to why Judas betrayed Jesus. Luke gives no further explanation but that "Satan entered into him."[51] Satan has been almost absent from the intervening part of his story apart from 10:18 and 13:16. John further describes Judas as a greedy person (12:5f; Mt 26:124). But the sum of thirty pieces of silver which Matthew mentions is rather small (Mt 26:15; Zech 11:12). Other speculations have been made. Was Judas a militant zealot disillusioned with the non-violent Jesus? Was he trying to put Jesus on the spot so that he would have to make an extraordinary display of his miraculous power? Schweitzer suggests that he betrayed the Messianic secret to the high priests and that Jesus was secretly anointed in Bethany. Naturally, the Sanhedrin were delighted with Judas who became their spy, looking for a suitable opportunity away from the festival crowds, i.e. the garden of Gethsemane.

(2) *The Preparation of the Passover—(22:7-13:)*

This account is close to Mark's version except that here the two disciples sent out to make the preparations are identified as Peter and John, both of whom together are prominent especially in the early part of Acts.[52] There is a solemnity about the opening verse "The day of unleavened bread arrived on which the Passover had to be sacrificed." In the Greek text the victim, which could be a lamb or a kid (Ex 12:5f), is not specified and also another example of the "divine must" is found (17:25; 24:7,26,44). These are perhaps subtle allusions to Jesus as the Paschal Lamb. The question can be asked about the gospel accounts. "Why almost all the traditional elements of the Jewish Passover celebration are omitted?" e.g. the asking of questions about the significance of the observance, the recitation of the exodus narrative, the unleavened bread, the bitter herbs. The reason seems to be that later Christian worship did not use them but only the cup, the bread and the sayings of Jesus in its Eucharistic celebrations.

By leaving out Mark's question by the disciples (Mk 14:12 "Where do you wish . . . "), Luke shows Jesus himself in full command of events and not only taking the initiative, but freely facing his passion, a point which is clear from the Agony. Note how Jesus rises above his own sufferings to teach his disciples (22:35ff), remains a healer (22:51), can prophecy to the Jerusalem women (23:28-31), saves the penitent thief (23:43) and in death offers himself in trust to the Father (2:46).

The deliberate arrangements for the meal remind one of the previous arrangements for the triumphant entry into Jerusalem and show that this meal had particular symbolic importance for Jesus. This is the seventh in a series of meals in Luke which are continued after the resurrection.[53] It clearly must be understood against the background of the Passover meal which Luke alone emphasizes (v 11,15ff) and which celebrated the great liberation of Israel. Also one should remember the deeper meaning which table sharing had in the East, and in Luke in particular, where it is an acted parable symbolizing Jesus' mission, his acceptance of sinners into a new eschatological community of forgiveness, salvation and newness of life (19:1ff; 15:2).

The careful plans here, i.e. the unusual episode of the man carrying the water pot, who is identified in a sixth century tradition as Mark, show not only Jesus' extraordinary powers (19:30-34) but seem intended to conceal the place of the supper from plotters like Judas until Jesus is ready. A man carrying a water jar would be as unusual as a man wearing a hat in Church today. In the East women carried jars on their heads and men carried water in skins slung over their shoulders. The inhabitants of Jerusalem were obliged to provide rooms so that pilgrims could celebrate the passover. They received the lambskin as a donation in return. Peter and John are told that they will be shown a spacious upstairs room, (lit) "spread," i.e. with couches etc. Couches were used for reclining, which was, especially in the Roman custom, the position of free men (22:27). The Passover was especially a celebration of freedom. Their preparation would have included buying the paschal lamb, its slaughter at the temple, its roasting and also the purchase of unleavened bread, bitter herbs and wine (Ex 12:1ff).

(3) *The Institution of the Lord's Supper—(22:14-20):*

Lucien Deiss[55] reconstructs and compares the Lord's Supper and the Jewish Passover celebration in schematic form as follows:

The Jewish Passover Rite	:	*The Lord's Supper*
A. *Preliminary Ritual*		
Blessing of the feast day and of the first cup.		
Rite of Purification (ablution).	:	Washing of feet and catechesis (Jn 13:2ff; cf Lk 22:24-7).
Eating of bitter herbs.		
		Announcement of Judas' betrayal (?).
B. *Homily and Prayers*		
Passover story, haggadah, by the father (Ex 12:27; Dt 6:20).	:	Discourse of Jesus (Jn 14-17).
First part of the Hallel (Ps 113 or pss 113-114).		
Second cup (haggadah cup).		
C. *Passover Meal*		
Purification Rite (ablution). Blessing by the father over the bread.	:	Jesus' words over the bread: "This is my body ..."
Eating of the paschal lamb. Third cup (cup of blessing, 1 Cor 10:16; Lk 22:20).	:	Jesus' words over the wine "This is my blood ..."

D. *Conclusion*
Second part of Hallel (Ps 114-118 or 115-118) Fourth cup, celebrating God's kingdom (?). : Singing of Psalms (Mt 26:30; Mk 14:26).

All four accounts of the institution of the Eucharist have a remarkable agreement on the substance of both the words used and the meaning of the rite.[56] However, Luke, as may be expected, has his own characteristics. He postpones Mark's abrupt announcement of the betrayal until after the institution of the Eucharist thus agreeing with John that Judas shared in the actual meal. His meal begins quite formally and solemnly, "When the hour arrived" (Jn 2:4; 7:6ff; 8:20). Verses 15-18 are proper to Luke.

Jesus in a septuagintal phrase "with desire I have desired," shows his awareness of his imminent suffering and death[57] and his passionate desire to share the passover meal with his apostles, as they are called here (v 14f; 6:13; 9:10). Thus the meal opens by looking forward to the cross while the future celebrations of the Lord's Supper in the New Testament will look back to it (Heb 9:13-20). Mark and Matthew have the idea behind "I shall eat of it no more until . . . " (v 16,18) after the eucharistic words over the bread and wine (Mk 14:25; Mt 26:29). What was symbolized by both eating (v 16) and the drinking (v 17f) would be fulfilled (a divine passive) and become a reality through Jesus in the kingdom of God. Jesus, eating and drinking in the kingdom, seems to be a reference to the post-resurrection meals which only Luke and John describe,[58] which take place when Jesus has entered his kingdom. The old paschal meal is over and Jesus is instituting a new one for his disciples, the messianic banquet (13:28f; 14:15ff; Is 25:6), which will commemorate his sacrificial death and the salvation of the new Israel. This meal, like the Passover, looks forward to the final coming of the kingdom for all just as it has come for Jesus (22:16,18; 1 Cor 11:26; Rom 6:5). The thanksgiving (Greek Eucharistein, 17:16; 18:11) over the first cup[59] is given in eucharistic language, "took, gave thanks . . . said take, share" as in 9:16. Although originally it seems that this was one of four Passover cups and not actually the cup of the eucharist.

The synoptics, unfortunately, do not preserve Jesus' prayer of thanksgiving. It seems to have been unique as the disciples at Emmaus recognized him probably at the prayer "at the breaking of bread" (24:35). However, in Jewish tradition the prayer over the cup read:

> "Blessed be you, Yahweh our God, King of the universe, who gives your people Israel this feast of unleavened bread, for their joy and as a memorial. Blessed be you who sanctify Israel and its times."

Jeremias suggests that the request "divide it among you" may mean that Jesus did not share in the drinking at the last supper. Taken with 22:16,18 and Mark 14:25, it signifies an avowal of abstinence by Jesus. It seems also that the Palestinian Church similarly fasted at Passover.[60]

The textual problem of verses 18 and 19 has been much exaggerated by many scholars. The choice lies between two principal forms of the text: (i) the longer and until Hort in the last century, the traditional text which has the cup-bread-cup sequence (J.B. NAB. Common Bible); (ii) the shorter or Western text which stops after the words "This is my body" and omits the rest of v 19 and all of v 20, thus having a cup-bread sequence (R.S.V.; N.E.B.) but lacking the Eucharistic formula given in the other accounts (Mk 14:22ff; 1 Cor 11:23ff).

The Greek manuscript evidence is overwhelmingly in favor of the longer reading. Only one single Greek manuscript from some five thousand available in the New Testament, and that from the 5th-6th century, is in favor of the shorter reading together with a few texts among the Latin and Syrian versions. Actually, Justin, writing as early as A.D. 150 and before any of our existing Greek

Manuscripts, has the longer reading (Apology 66). It seems impossible that all the other texts are harmonizations with Mark and that this one Greek Manuscript and its few allies should alone have preserved the authentic text. Quite possibly, its scribe, confused by the sequence cup-bread-cup based on the Passover rite, eliminated the second cup to produce a sequence cup-bread as in 1 Cor 10:16,21 and the Didache (9:2-3). Another suggestion is that he wanted to avoid the suspicion that the early Christians were drinking blood.

In the climax of the meal, Jesus spoke something completely new as compared with the traditional Jewish liturgy when he proclaimed as he broke and distributed the bread, "This is my body to be given for you" and similarly with the cup "This cup is the new covenant in my blood which will be shed for you." This new kind of meal is clearly an interpretation of Jesus' coming death which will be both a kind of vicarious sacrifice and a redemptive death in fulfilment of the Passover expectations.

Also there is the command which is twice found in 1 Cor 11:24,25, to repeat his act in remembrance of himself. This looks forward to the breaking of the bread in Acts (Ac 2:42,46; 20:7) where the presence of Christ is celebrated and the final eschatological banquet is anticipated (22:16,18). A striking semitism is the absence of the verb "is" in the saying over the cup (lit "the cup of the new covenant." None of the evangelists or Paul gives us a full account of the Passover meal which Jesus celebrated as they perhaps presumed that much of the detail was familiar to their audience. What they give is the actual tradition as the eucharist was celebrated in their particular church. The different traditions fall into two main groups: (i) Mark and Matthew (Mk 14:22-4; Mt 26:26-8); (ii) Paul and Luke (Lk 22:19-20; 1 Cor 11:23-5). Scholars have attempted to get back to the original text but any such attempt as the following must be seen as a conjecture.[61]

> "And while they were eating, Jesus having taken bread and spoken the blessing, broke (it) and gave (it) to them and said 'Take and eat. This is my body (which is) given for you. Do this in my memory'. In the same way, having taken the cup after the meal, having given thanks, he gave (it) to them saying 'all of you drink this cup, the new covenant, my blood shed for many. Do this in my memory'."

Clearly there is symbolism here, a kind of acted parable looking forward to Jesus' atoning death for men. The bread which is broken and the wine which is poured clearly symbolize the crucifixion where Jesus' life (body and blood, Lv 17:11) is sacrificed, is broken and poured out (like the servant, Is 53:12) "for you," i.e. those present (v 19,20; 1 Cor 11:24; Ac 8:32-33). Matthew and Mark have "for many," an Aramaic expression meaning "all" (Is 53:10f).[62] But as to what Jesus actually meant by his words here has caused tremendous controversies among Christians, particularly since the Reformation.

However, in ecumenical discussions concerning the Eucharist, there seems to be a rather general consensus that:

> "Christ is really and truly present in the celebration of the Lord's Supper, which accordingly is not just a bare sign or commemoration in the psychological sense of remembering."
> "Christ is present whole and entire (and thus in his 'body and blood'), though not in a material way."[63]

Following Max Thurian's summary, Dulles finds three main schools of thought in Western Christianity on the relation between the real presence of Christ and the bread and the wine.

(1) *Transubstantiation:*

Although there is no physical or chemical change the profound reality (substance) of the elements (the bread and wine), is changed in a mysterious but radical way. They are converted into the body and blood of Christ and are no longer substantially what they were, bread and wine.

(2) *Consubstantiation:*

The profound being of the bread and wine subsists, but just as fire is present in heated metal so the profound reality or substance of the body and blood of Christ is closely united to the elements.

(3) *Concomitance;*

The bread and wine remain what they were but they become the vehicle of Christ's presence so that when we eat the bread and drink the wine we also spiritually receive Jesus Christ.[64]

Two phrases in Luke's text "new covenant" and "memory" or "remembrance" need to be carefully understood against their Jewish background. The words over the cup proclaim a new covenant[65] which constitutes a new people of God just as the covenant of the people of God at Sinai was constituted through sacrifice and blood.[66] The story of Israel is the story of "adoption, glory, covenants, law-giving, worship, promises, patriarchs" (Rom 9:4) and, of course, the story of failure which the Old Testament so vividly and honestly recorded. The covenant relationship was no natural relationship due to any evident reason, but the result of a free positive act on the part of Yahweh himself, and a free response of the part of man (Si 44:11). Moses and the Sinai covenant were the most familiar and important examples but the Old Testament also uses the term first of Noah (Gn 6:19; 9:12), then Abraham (Gn 15:17), Isaac and Jacob (Ex 2:24), Moses (Ex 24:1ff), Aaron (Num 18:19), Phinehas (Num 25:12-13), Levi (Mal 2:4-5). Joshua (Josh 24:25), David (2 Sam 23:5) and also the Servant of Yahweh (Is 42:6).[67]

Jesus then was the mediator of a new covenant at the climax of a long line of mediators and benefactors. He explains his sacrificial death in terms of a covenant, a word which occurs in all accounts of the last supper (1 Cor 11:25; Mk 14:24; Mt 26:28). Note v 29, lit, "I covenant for you." The "new" covenant recalls Jeremiah's attack, not on the old covenant but on the people's interpretation and rather legalistic fulfilment of it (Jer 31:31-4; 1 Cor 11:25; 2 Cor 3:6; Heb 8:8,13; 9:15). He hoped that God would make a new covenant, a real relationship of love, unlike the old one which was so often broken. In the new the people would obey because they really want to in their hearts, not because they have to. It would be a covenant based on forgiveness of the people's sin (1:77) and a proper understanding of what God really is like (Father).

The Passover meal was a "zikkaron" (Gk "anamnesis") of the great liberation from Egypt and the covenant at Sinai (Ex 12:14; 13:9; Ps 111:4; Dt 16:3). This word is weakly translated into English as a memorial or a remembrance because not only did it call to mind the great events but in some mysterious way it crosses the barriers of time and space to represent, to make present the saving event as both a present reality and a promise, a foretaste of the future (Dt 5:3). So also with the Eucharist (1 Cor 11:24ff; Rom 6:5; Heb 10:13).

This notion of an efficacious re-presenting, of making the past available in the present, was a fundamental notion in the cultic celebrations of Israel and is essential to an understanding of the Christian Eucharist. Davies comments that:

> "Do this in remembrance of me" means in part "Do this with a view to recalling me into your present life." ". . . it is not a figure of the past who is remembered only, but a Living Lord who is recalled so that his presence is experienced anew. Both Baptism and the Lord's Supper bring the Jesus of the past into the present."[68]

In the Bible there is a great emphasis on man's forgetfulness and his need to remember.[69] God alone is the one who does not forget, who remembers.[70] The life of Jesus is the example of God's unforgetting mercy (Lk 1:54).

(4) *The Announcement of the Betrayal—(22:21-23):*

Here we note how Luke, like John, has a farewell discourse at the last supper. Both stress the theme of service (Jn 13:1ff; Ac 20:17-38; Gn 49). This consists in four groups of sayings. (i) There is the announcement of the betrayal which is found in Matthew and Mark before the Eucharist. It seems a not so subtle warning to members of the early church that membership in the Eucharistic community is no guarantee against betraying Jesus. Judas' name is not mentioned and quite likely Luke intends his audience to read themselves into the situation and to question themselves. (ii) Then comes a lesson for the church leaders based on the service of Jesus. (iii) This is followed by a prediction of Peter's denial together with his conversion, "to strengthen his brothers." (v) The unusual section (v 35-8) which contrasts the success of their previous ministry with the tribulation to come. Some of the sayings are found in other contexts in Mark and Matthew[71] but many are found only in Luke, i.e. v 29,31-32, 35-8.

Luke's account is quite condensed. He does not have the unmasking of Judas or his uncomfortable presence thereafter nor the reference to dipping in the common dish, but the oblique reference in v 21 to the hand at the table has a similar meaning (Ps 41:10). His version stresses the free acceptance by the Son of Man of the course which God has appointed for him. "Determined" or "appointed" is the only use in the gospel of the frequent Lucan "divine passive" found in Acts (Ac 2:23; 10:42; 11:29; 17:26,31; Rom 1:4; Heb 4:7). Here it replaces Mark's "as is written about him."[72] The phrase "alas for that man" indicates the responsibility of the betrayer, yet Mark's harsh "better for that man . . . " is omitted (Mk 14:21). One argument now leads to another (v 23,24; Jn 13:22) and Jesus' references to the kingdom (v 16,17) lead them to an ambitious dispute about their respective positions in the coming kingdom and to forget their betrayal problems.

(5) *The Dispute "Who is the Greatest?"—(22:24-30):*

The association of the dispute with the previous announcement of the betrayal suggests that the power conflicts and concern about false greatness among the early Christians should be seen as a betrayal of Jesus. It is found at an earlier time in the Markan sequence after the request of the sons of Zebedee[73] and it is quite possible that Luke deliberately introduced it here with the catchword, table (v 27,30,21). It suggests too that at the eucharist Jesus is among Christians as "one who serves" (v 27; Is 25:6), to teach a vital lesson for church leaders. Here the service of Jesus is illustrated by his waiting at table (Jn 13) but in Mark it is illustrated by giving his life. Note that Luke does not have Mark 10:45 (Is 53) and that immediately after the

Eucharist Matthew and Mark have the journey to Gethsemane.

John does not have the dispute but he has the footwashing episode which teaches a similar lesson. As here Jesus silences them with a blunt criticism of wordly authorities, the so-called "Benefactors," a title like Savior, which was liked by kings of Syria and Egypt, who used their position to "lord it over" and tyrannize people. It must not be so among them. He reminds them of the kind of Master whose disciples they are. The only true greatness is humble service (9:48), like the youngest,[74] like a waiter at table, the way of Jesus himself (4:1-11). The word used is "diakonon," an allusion to Acts 6:1ff. The servant idea will be important in Acts (Ac ch 3,4,8) and here in 22:27, it replaces and clarifies Mark's "to give his life as a ransom for many," an idea which Luke may have found too difficult (but see Ac 20:28; Mk 10:45). The apostles must rule the kingdom which he now confers on them in the same spirit of service (v 29). They had continued with Jesus during his temptations to be a different kind of Messiah (4:1ff; 22:36; Ac 20:19). Therefore, appreciating their loyalty, Jesus now covenants (v 20,29) a kingdom to them, the dominion which the Father has assigned to himself, an allusion to Dn 7, also Lk 12:32; 13:25ff; 14:14ff; 16:9; 18:24. They will share with Jesus in the messianic feast (14:15ff) and will share in his rule over the new Israel, the church. This will be seen in Acts when the church is centered on Jerusalem. This promise, one of the few parallels to Matthew in these chapters, is found in another context in Matthew 19:28 and Luke's phrase " . . . who have continued with me . . ." replaces the phrase "my followers" in Matthew. Covenants were often sealed with a meal (Ex 24:9-11), and v 29 literally translates "I covenant with you a kingdom just as my Father covenanted to me." The verb is used also of disposing of one's property through a last testament or will. The conferring of his kingdom is associated in the context with the death of Jesus and the eucharistic meals of the community which will be a memorial of his service and at which he is present as host (13:29; 14:15ff; Apoc 19:7ff). This shows that Jesus in choosing twelve intended to set up a new Israel in which they will exercise authority (Apoc 7:4ff; 20:4; 21:12; 1 Cor 6:2f).

The term judging should be understood in the meaning of ruling as in The Book of Judges. It is not so much the modern idea of giving objective decisions but rather that of defending Yahweh's rights and in particular the poor. Actually, there were thirteen tribes if we count Levi but the popular designation was twelve. The text does not mean that each apostle judges one tribe but that together they share in Jesus' judgment as described in Dn 7:9f. That the twelve were not replaced after their deaths shows the uniqueness of their eschatological function which began in the Jerusalem church.

(6) *Peter's Denial Foretold—(22:31-4):*

Here Jesus describes Satan as in the book of Job as the accuser of the disciples ("you" in v 31 is plural, but singular in v 32) before God's throne and his own successful role as intercessor for Peter, setting free Satan's captives (13:16; 11:20; 22:3; Ac 26:18). All four gospels describe how Jesus predicted Peter's denial, but Luke alone describes Satan's role in it (23:3,31). In Matthew and Mark the prediction takes place on the way to Gethsemane but in Luke and John it takes place at the last supper. Luke, who unlike Mark, seems to omit such unfavorable comments on Peter such as the rebuke at Caesarea Philippi and at Gethsemane, puts the emphasis rather on Peter's recovery than on his fall. He is preparing the way for Peter's important role as leader and spokesman in Acts. A repentant Peter appears at three decisive moments in Luke (5:8; 22:32; Ac 10:1ff) and will be the first to be instituted an apostle by the risen Jesus (24:34; 1 Cor 15:5). Here, where Jesus confers on Peter a responsibility over the others, is Luke's equivalent of Matthew's famous "rock" saying (Mt 16:18). First Jesus begins with the affectionate repetition of Simon, a name symbolic of the old nature and then, the only time in the gospels, addresses him directly as Peter, symbolic of the new man created by Jesus (Jn 1:47).

(7) *The Hour of Testing—(22:35-8):*

In this rather difficult section which is peculiar to Luke, Jesus looks to the future even beyond the coming crisis, to prepare his disciples for what will be for them, a new experience of rejection, hostility and persecution. A distinction is made between the life of the twelve during the happier times in the earlier days of Jesus' ministry and the period of testing now beginning with Jesus' passion. The contrast in particular is with the mission of the seventy when they were sent out unarmed, without protection, purse, bag or sandals, with nothing and yet they did not lack anything but were well received (v 35). Their fears which had been due to lack of faith in God's protecting care will now be realized. Therefore, they should be prepared for hostility instead of welcome (9:22-7; 12:7; 21:18; Ac 27:34). Now things will be different and they will need everything they have, even a sword. The reason for the change will be that scripture "must" be fulfilled (Is 53:12; Ac 8:32f), that Jesus will be executed as a criminal.

His disciples can expect a similar fate. This, it should be noted, is the only direct quotation of an Isaian Servant Song on Jesus' lips in the gospels (Mk 15:28). Is Luke suggesting that the earlier instructions should not be applied literally to the missionaries of the Church? Some would actually see here words for a departure ceremony for missionaries in Luke's community. 380

All four gospels agree that at Jesus' arrest one of the apostles had used a sword. Here Luke, who stresses that there was nothing subversive about the Christians in his writings, seems to suggest that it was due to a misunderstanding of Jesus, a rather ironic and extreme metaphor, suggesting that they would need a sword (12:51; Mt 23:24; Mk 10:25; Neh 4:18). In Matthew a sword is used as a symbol for the opposite of peace (Mt 10:34ff).[77] Is it possible to interpret this section as Jesus making certain that his disciples were armed and ready to fight, to defend himself? The traditional interpretation of the purse, bag, sandals and especially the sword here as a symbolic warning of the conflict to come, in which everything will be at stake, fit in with Jesus' Passion prediction, his previous teaching on suffering service and on violence (6:27ff; 12:51) and the following emphasis on prayer and his subsequent rejection of the use of the sword at his actual arrest (v 49ff; Mt 26:52). Evidently, the disciples have, as is common in John's gospel, taken Jesus literally and misunderstood him "Look Lord here are two swords." Two swords which were perhaps fishing knives or possibly knives used to prepare the Paschal Lamb, would be of little use (14:31). Luke bluntly contrasts the disciples' misunderstanding (v 38 they said; v 39 but he said) with Jesus' closing words of dismissal "Enough" (v 39, it is used in Moses' farewell in Dt 3:26; 1 K 19:4; Mk 14:41).

Jerusalem

(8) *The Agony in the Garden—(22:39-46):*

Jesus now goes, not to hide, but as is his custom (1:9; 2:42) to the Mount of Olives (v 39; Jn 18:2) to "the place" (v 40) omitting Mark's Aramaic word "Gethsemane" as he omits "Abba" (Mk 14:36). In Luke's version which is much abbreviated as compared with Mark's, the disciples who "follow" Jesus (v 39) do not come out as badly as in the other versions where not once, but three times they are found asleep. Peter, James and John are not named and their failure is benignly interpreted as due to being exhausted with grief (v 45). The saying about the spirit and the flesh is omitted (Mk 14:38; Mt 26:41). Nor are they said at the end to abandon him completely (23:49). Jesus prayed once not three times as in Matthew and Mark. He does not seek their consolation by begging them to watch with him as his soul is sorrowful even unto death, but rather seeks to strengthen them. The scene begins and ends in Luke with its warning to pray that they may not enter into temptation or be put to the test (v 40,46), a prayer that is reminiscent of the Our Father (11:4). Prayer is in obvious contrast with the pathetic two swords just mentioned. Jesus' own prayer is an example of how to marshal one's strength to do the Father's will, to triumph over temptation (22:28).

Jesus withdraws from them (lit "was torn away from them" Ac 20:34; 21:1; Mt 26:51), a short distance "of a stone's throw," a biblical and classical Greek expression. He kneels down to pray, an unusual way for a Jew who normally prayed standing up (18:11,13; Jn 17:1), but an attitude which will be repeated four times in Acts by Stephen (Ac 7:60), Peter (Ac 9:20) and Paul (Ac 20:36; 21:5). Matthew and Mark have Jesus falling to the ground (Mk

14:35). All three synoptics have Jesus pray to the Father (10:22; 11:2) to remove the cup of suffering which was his lot[78] if it is his will but that the Father's will and not his own be done (Ac 21:14). The prayer clearly reflects the Our Father and it is interesting to note the verb "remove" is the same basic Greek verb used in the sixth petition and is translated "lead us not" into temptation. Verses 43-44, proper to Luke, which contain the only use of the Greek word agony in the New Testament, are absent in the most important manuscripts, all of which are later than A.D. 300 except the early third century Papyrus 75. They are at least very ancient as their quotation by many fathers such as Justin, Iranaeus, Hippolytus, Eusebius, attest. Their omission is more easily explained than their inclusion as they paint such a fully human and even shocking picture of extreme anguish, fear and mental suffering which could easily cause difficulty for anyone emphasizing the divine aspect of Jesus. He has already wept over Jerusalem (19:41-4) and his emotion here is quite different from either the "indifferent" courage of the Stoic or the rebellion of the Cynic. The angel, signifying strength from God, recalls the martyr stories in Daniel (e.g. Dn 3:25) and the consoling of the dejected Elijah (1 K 19:5ff). His sweat was not necessarily composed of blood as is often understood, but fell to the ground in quick succession (like great drops or clots of blood), a metaphor found in Greek literature as far back as Homer. These verses apart, Jesus appears quite calmly in control of himself and preoccupied with his disciples.

(9) *The Betrayal and Arrest of Jesus—(22:47-53):*

The arrest of Jesus is told simply but dramatically in all four gospels. It begins with "while he was still speaking" in the synoptics. Luke, who mentions that Judas was leading the crowd delicately avoids mentioning the swords and the club, the agreed signal and especially that Judas actually kissed Jesus, a customary greeting (1 Thess 5:26; 2 S 20:9; Gn 27:46) and called him Master. Instead he has a prophetic Jesus, knowing his intentions in advance, taking the initiative with his poignant question "Judas, would you betray the Son of Man with a kiss?" thus showing Jesus, as in John, in command of the situation (Jn 18:4-11).

The resistance of the disciples is more logically placed before telling of the arrest which he barely mentions in passing (22:54; Mk 14:46). He omits the flight of the disciples and the mysterious episode of the young man which Mark describes. Only John, writing much later, reveals not only the slave's name Malchus, but that it was the impetuous Peter who resorted to violence and agrees with Luke that it was the right ear. This possibly indicates either clumsiness or that the swordsman was left-handed (Jn 18:10).

Matthew expands Jesus' refusal to allow a defense with the saying about those who live by the sword and the legions of angels available to him (Mt 26:53-4). In Luke, however, the disciples, remembering v 36, ask permission to defend Jesus and receive the clearly negative reply. This is followed by the healing of the severed ear, the only miracle of its kind in the whole gospel tradition and the only miracle in the Jerusalem ministry. It emphasizes both the non-violence and compassion of Jesus (6:27-36). Jesus' words in v 51 can be translated simply as meaning "Enough," 'No more" or "let events take their course" or possibly "stop; while I do this," i.e. touch and heal the servant (5:13). Now Luke specifies the crowd of captors as the leaders of Judaism. They are not the "laos" of 21:38, but a mob ("ochlos"). While Mark avoids the term "disciple" throughout the whole passion narraive, Luke uses here a phrase which signifies solidarity "those who were about him" (v 49; Ac 13:13).

In Matthew and Mark the leaders send the crowds but in Luke they are dramatically present in fulfilment of the prediction of 9:22 and are directly rebuked by Jesus with blunt words for their cowardly arrest as if he was a robber (v 36; 19:47f; 20:19f; 22:2). Luke quotes Jesus' rebuke in exactly the same words as Mark but omits the final phrase "to capture me." Luke alone has the Temple police (Ac 4:1; 5:24). Behind them Jesus sees the powers of darkness and their temporary triumph (11:21ff). As in John, darkness symbolizes the evil which is hostile to Jesus and which explains his Passion.[79] But Luke omits Mark's reference to the fulfilment of scripture (Mk 14:49). Thus, he seems to distinguish between the freedom of such as Judas and the fulfilment of the divine plan as in Acts 2:23.

(10) *Peter's Denial of Jesus—(22:54-62):*

There are many variations in detail in the following episodes among the four evanglists. Matthew and Mark have three trials, one at night and one in the morning before the Sanhedrin and a third before Pilate. In John, Jesus is taken first to Annas then to Caiaphas, the actual high priest and finally to Pilate. Luke has a trial in the morning before the Sanhedrin, then a trial before Pilate who sends Jesus to Herod and finally the condemnation by Pilate. In Luke's clearer and more logical portrayal, Peter denies Jesus and the soldiers mock him during the night. Then he has only one Sanhedrin session "when day came" (22:26). Thus he only alludes (v 54,66) to the Mark, Mat-

Jerusalem

thew night trial before the Sanhedrin with its messianic charges and death verdict, or John's sessions before Annas and Caiaphas. It should be remembered when trying to put together the different items of information that none of the gospels give a full and detailed account of the whole proceedings which were clearly hasty and highly irregular by later Jewish laws and ideals. A legal trial could only be held by day, witnesses for the defense were called first and a sentence of condemnation had to be held over until the day after the trial. Like John he abbreviates the Jewish trial to emphasize the Roman trial whose charges he gives in greater detail.

He begins with the "trial of Peter," who at least had the courage and loyalty to follow Jesus at a distance right into the stronghold of Jesus' enemies, the house of the high priest (Jn 18:16; note "also" in Lk 22:56). All four gospels honestly record that Peter, the most prominent disciple, three times denied knowing Jesus, a serious sin according to 12:9 and that then the cock crew and he was reminded of Jesus' prediction. In Mark (Mk 14:53f,66) it is described after the first Sanhedrin session and in particular after the abuse and mockery of the servants with which it is associated. In John the examination before Annas comes between the first and second denials. The light of the fire in the middle of the courtyard gives Peter away as he sits there disguised. This is the only place in the New Testament where the word "periaptein," "to kindle" is used. Three times, i.e. completely and utterly, Peter denies—"I do not know him," "I am not one of them," "I do not know what you are talking about," to three different people, a slave girl, a little later to another man and then to a man who insisted also that he had a Galilean accent. In Mark 14:66,69,70 it is a slave girl who speaks twice and the bystanders. Luke's version which leads from a denial of

Jesus to a denial of membership among the disciples and to an absolute denial of even knowledge is much milder than Mark's as he does not have Peter cursing and swearing (Mk 14:71). The climax found in Luke alone is when "The Lord turned round and looked at Peter" (Jn 1:42). The verb "turned" is also found in 9:55; 10:23; 14:25; 23:28). Peter remembered "the word of the Lord." This phrase, apart from four passages in 1 and 2 Thess, is found only here and in Acts (e.g. 8:25; 12:24; 13:49; 15:35; 19:10,20) and is a synonym for "the gospel."

Typically in Luke's version Jesus in his Passion goes out in sympathy to others (e.g. 22:31f,51; 23:28ff,34,43). Verse 62 which describes how Peter went out and wept bitterly is found exactly the same in Matthew 26:75 and curiously has been omitted from a few lesser Lucan manuscripts giving rise to the possible conclusion that some copyists transferred it into the Lucan text from Matthew. Mark does not have "bitterly."

(11) *The Mockery and Beating of Jesus—(22:63-5):*

Luke records two mockings of Jesus, this one by the temple guards before the Sanhedrin trial, corresponding to Mark's after the trial at the hands of the Sanhedrin and the other by their servants (Mk 14:65; Mt 26:27). Luke (23:11) records another from Herod Antipas and his soldiers but conspicuously, does not have any mocking by the Roman soldiers and so only records mockeries by the Jews (see 23:25f,36,47).

Luke has (lit) "blaspheming many others" but does not mention the spitting and hitting (Mk 14:65). However, he explains the blindfolding as a sort of "blind man's bluff" mockery of Jesus the prophet when they taunt him "Which one struck you?" Compare the different synoptics here to see that Luke gives the only complete version.

(12) *Jesus Before the Sanhedrin (22:66-71):*

At daybreak the Sanhedrin assemble again. Subject to the Romans, it was the supreme authority in Judaism. However, as John points out (Jn 18:31; Joseph Antiq 20,9,1) and the lynching of Stephen notwithstanding, it seems that the Romans kept to themselves the power of capital punishment. Obviously if this power was in Jewish hands, the danger was that it could be used to eliminate Roman supporters. Here, however, due to the popularity of Jesus it would be quite convenient to have the Romans take the decision to execute Jesus.

Luke is clearly not giving us a reporter's account of the trial. It is scarcely a formal trial at all as there is no clear verdict: the decision was already reached (Ac 6:14). There are no false witnesses, no evidence presented, no accusation about Jesus destroying the temple (Ac 6:14) or no charge of blasphemy. He concentrates on the person and mission of Jesus and dividing Mark's single question into two, makes a clear distinction between the messianic titles, between popular messianism and his own divine sonship. The two parts of the dialogue recall the annunciation scene, 1:31 the son of his father David; 1:35 the son of God.

To their question (v 66,70,71) "Are you the Messiah?" Jesus gives a reply which has a very Johannine touch about it (see Jn 10:24ff), v 67f-68 is only in Luke. Jesus bluntly answers that it is useless to answer because they will not believe him and further if using a recognized method of self-defense, he questions them as he so often did, to try to bring out the real nature of his Messiahship in the face of popular misunderstanding, they will not answer him in turn (20;3ff; 41ff). Then to give a proper explanation of his Messiahship he typically switches to his favorite title, proclaiming the exaltation of the Son of Man to the right hand of God thus acknowledging his mysterious heavenly dignity because from now on the time of waiting "to be taken up to heaven" was over (9:51). Roles will be interchanged because Jesus is already (v 69; Jn 12:31) the ultimate judge not they.[80]

Note Luke's favorite phrase "From now on,"[81] also that he does not say "you will see,"[82] also that the Son of Man does not "come" with the clouds as in Mark's post-resurrection version (Mk 14:62), a phrase which could be interpreted that Jesus predicted a proximate parousia (7:34; Ac 1:11; compare Mt 26:64). This extraordinary statement leads all to the climactic chorus "So you are the Son of God," a phrase which has divine connotations as in 1:35; Ac 8:37. Does Jesus' somewhat ambiguous answer "You say that I am," contain the implication that they know but do not accept their own answer?" Certainly it is not a denial. It thus seems to be an open acknowledgment of divine sonship as Mark has simply "I am" (Mk 14:62). Evidently, the Sanhedrin are satisfied that they have their answer and are ready now to bring him to Pilate for the death sentence. A Roman authority usually did not institute proceedings but heard and pronounced upon the charges brought before him.

(13) *Jesus Before Pilate—(23:1-5):*

In the trial before Pilate it is significant that in Luke Jesus is charged and declared innocent of purely political crimes. The trial in Luke consists in three episodes. Jesus appears before Pilate and is sent by him to Herod Antipas, who sends him back to Pilate, who finally yields to the

Jews. There is a parallel between v 3 and Mark 15:2 but in general, Luke seems to be using his own unique tradition. Only Luke and John describe the charges laid against Jesus and both stress Pilate's proclamation of Jesus' innocence three times. Note the similarities between the accusations levelled against Jesus and those leveled against Paul in Acts (e.g. 17:7; 24:2ff; 25:7f). Similarly, in Acts Luke will show that the Romans always acquit Paul of the charges brought against him (e.g. Ac 16:35ff; 18:12ff; 19:31ff; 24:22f; 25:18ff; 26:31f). Clearly Luke wants to stress for Theophilus and his Gentile audience that Jesus, like the early Christians was no law breaker. He goes out of his way to show him innocent of any political ambitions and so to absolve the Romans as far as possible and lay the blame on the wickedness of the Jewish leaders.[83] Luke gives the impression that the Jews were the actual agents of the crucifixion (23:26).

Pilate pronounces Jesus innocent three times, v 4,14,22, and wants to release him (v 20). A similar verdict from the Roman centurion is found only in Luke (23:47). The three political charges are almost credible distortions for the benefit of the Roman judge; events already familiar to readers of Luke's gospel, i.e. creating a disturbance among the people (e.g. 19:42), forbidding the payment of tax to Caesar (20:25) and claiming to be the Christ, i.e. a King (22:67; 2:11), a revolutionary. This ironically many of them wanted Jesus to be, the kind Pilate would be obliged to get rid of immediately as a danger to the Romans (Ac 5:35ff; 17:6ff).

Jesus' answer to Pilate's question as recorded in all four gospels is the ambiguous "you say it" (see Jn 18:36f; Mk 15:3ff). Evidently, Pilate is satisfied with his interrogation that Jesus is not politically dangerous. They persist that Jesus has been stirring up the people throughout all

Judea beginning from Galilee as far as Jerusalem (6:17; 4:44; Ac 1:8; 10:37). The chance mention of Galilee, which was outside his jurisdiction, makes Pilate think of his enemy, Herod Antipas, who happened to be in Jerusalem (Ac 12:4,19) probably to keep up appearances at the feast and who might provide a convenient way out (13:1).

(14) *Jesus Before Herod—(23:6-12):*

Herod the tetrarch of Galilee is the second major witness (Dt 19:15) which Luke alone brings forward, to the innocence of Jesus (v 15). This scene which is found only in Luke has been criticized as a Lucan invention based on Psalm 2, the psalm quoted by Peter and John when saved from the Sanhedrin (Ac 4:27). However, in Acts the references to Herod and Pilate are almost the opposite of here as they are stated to be in league with both Gentiles and the peoples of Israel. The passage is very semitic in style and there is a reference to the relations between Pilate and Herod in the contemporary writer Philo. Acts 4:26 explains Luke's purpose here as Peter and John see Pilate and Herod fulfilling the prophecy of Ps 2 in their alliance against Jesus. Acts 25:13ff describes how later the Roman governor, Festus, consulted Herod Agrippa 11 in the case of Paul.

It is interesting to note how often Luke stresses the connection between the early Christians and the secular ruler, perhaps for the benefit of Theophilus. Possibly Luke had special sources of information about Herod (8:3; Ac 12:20; 13:1). He is mentioned in six passages in Luke (one in Matthew and two in Mark) and figures in each major section of Luke's gospel at 3:1,19; 8:3; 9:7-9 and lastly 13:31-5, where Jesus sent the fox a message that he was not intimidated. Herod was very pleased as he had long desired

Jerusalem

to see Jesus (9:9) and hoped to see "a sign" (Jn 10:41; Mk 8:11f; 13:22), a common word in John for a miracle (Lk 11:16,29). Herod typifies the insincere, superficial questioner who is not seeking to really see Jesus. He is the only one to whom Jesus does not speak (see Is 53:7 for the servant who does not speak; Mk 14:61; 1 P 2:21). Again the Jewish leaders are the villians with their vehement accusations. The scene ends with a verse telling how Jesus was mocked as a king, not by the Roman soldiers as in Mark, but by Herod and his guards as he is dressed in a white robe, the characteristic dress of the Jewish kings. The same word is used in Josephus' description of Solomon's robe (Mk 15:16ff; Mt 27:27ff). Herod cleverly renounces his jurisdiction and returns Jesus with a verdict of not guilty (v 15) to Pilate. Ironically, Jesus became the occasion of Pilate's being reconciled to Herod.

(15) *Jesus is Sentenced to Die by Pilate—(23:13-25):*

The second trial before Pilate begins in Luke with Pilate summoning the whole Jewish nation, the chief priests, the rulers and the people "laos." This is the only time in Luke that the "laos" and the Jewish leaders are united and that the people turn against Jesus (v 18). Elsewhere both before and after this episode they are in opposition (e.g. 19:49; 20:6,19,26,45; 21:38 and 23:17,35,48). Almost all this scene, particularly v 13-16, is in Luke alone apart from his reference to Barabbas. Curiously, Luke does not have Matthew's episode about Pilate's wife or the washing of Pilate's hands. John has expanded the dialogue here and unlike Luke, has a scourging before the sentence. Pilate repeats the charge (v 14) and not only twice (v 14,22) reaffirms his own verdict that their allegations are untrue, but also proclaims Herod's agreement, "for he sent him back to us," as the best manuscript tradition puts it (Dt 19:15). Pilate twice proclaims his intention to release Jesus after a light beating (v 16,22),[84] which the Roman magistrates sometimes gave as a warning to be more cautious in the future and possibly also as an appeasement to the accusers.[85] Verse 17 is omitted in a wide variety of Mss including the earliest and most important. Further it is sometimes inserted after v 19 and thus seems to be a gloss based on Mark 15:6 and Matthew 27:15, introduced to explain the rather abrupt request for the release of Barabbas, a custom which is surprisingly unexplained in Luke. The custom of releasing guilty prisoners at a celebration is described in several Roman writers such as Livy and the younger Pliny but no other example in Palestine is recorded. In Luke it is not a custom but the request of an emotional and aggressive mob. "Away with this man; release Barabbas for us."

Barabbas is a striking name for a revolutionary here (v 19) as it is the Armaic for "Son of the Father." Possibly there is an allusion here to the innocent Jesus setting free a man really guilty of what Jesus was charged, yet who is nevertheless, thanks to Jesus, a son of the Father (v 19; 4:18). In a few manuscripts of Matthew 27:16, he is called Jesus Barabbas and a marginal note interprets his name as "Son of the teacher" (son of a Rabbi). The contrasts in this whole section should be noted, Jesus and Barabbas, Jesus and guilty Jerusalem (v 28ff), the crowds (v 35), the two criminals. It is only when Pilate makes his third effort to release Jesus as a Passover gift, that in all gospels the mob demand crucifixion for Jesus.

Although Luke lays the blame squarely on the Jewish leaders, who initiated the capture of Jesus and were his persecutors at his trial,[86] this does not mean that he completely exonerates the Romans even though he barely refers to the soldiers' mockeries (v 36; Ac 3:13). Pilate, who takes the final decision, comes across as a character, morally weak under pressure, concerned with his future career and without the courage of his convictions (Jn 19:12). He has experienced a Jewish mob storming his palace in Caesarea for five days. Apart from the unique response of the centurion at the cross, the Romans are never portrayed as positively responding to Christ or Christianity in Luke. At best, they portray an uncomprehending impartiality and the prevarication which brings Paul to Rome. Quite likely it is at least impartiality and justice which Luke would like from such as Theophilus and other Roman officials.[87] In Acts Christians and especially Jesus and Paul, are portrayed as non-political persons who, though often accused, are never properly convicted of the charges against them.[88]

The obstinate and violent crowd prevails with its demands (the verb is found in the gospels only in 21:36 and Mt 16:18). Pilate acquiesces unwillingly and delivers Jesus up "to their wishes," not "to be crucified" as Mark puts it. The text is carefully written by Luke and almost suggests that the Jews actually crucified Jesus ("they led him away," v 36).

(16) *The Way of the Cross—(23:26-32):*

In presenting the tragic events to follow, Luke, who emphasizes personal reactions, makes a considerable unique contribution among the evangelists. Thus while Mark has one verse devoted to Simon of Cyrene (Mk 15:21), Luke alone has a section describing the way of the cross (v 26-31), which includes Jesus' prophetic warning to the daughters of Jerusalem. Later, we find such additions as the prayer for forgiveness (v 34), the episode of the penitent thief (v 39-45) and Jesus' committal of himself to God (v 46). Missing are the crowning with thorns and the Roman mocking (Mk 15:16-20; Mt 27:27-31).

It was normal for a condemned man to carry, not the whole cross, which would have been impossible for one man, but the cross piece (the "patibulum") to the place of execution. Jesus, "numbered among the transgressors" as he described himself (23:37; Is 53:12) is one of a group of three (v 32), who are led along together. The actual phrase, "two other criminals," has often caused difficulties here as it insinuates that Jesus was a criminal. He must have been considerably weak from his ordeal and mistreatment.[89] Mark mentions that Simon from the Greek colony of Cyrene on the North African coast and probably a returned exile (Ac 6:9; 11:20; 13:1) was compelled by the Romans to carry Jesus' cross (Mt 5:41). Mark, incidentally, seems to mention Simon's sons as if known to his readers (Mk 15:21; Rom 16:13). In John the Simon episode is omitted, probably to stress that Jesus is in full control of his destiny to suffer for the sin of the world (Jn 1:29; 10:18; 12:14; 18:6). But the scene is subtly changed in Luke and the description used suggests a mission rather than Mark's impressment. Simon becomes the first and the model disciple who fulfilled 9:23 by carrying his cross "behind Jesus," who is leading his disciples on the last part of the road to life, salvation and paradise.[90]

Luke typically mentions the crowd and the lamenting women. In Judaism the mourning for the dead was a pious act.[91] Here there seems to be clear allusion to Zech 12:10, a prophecy of mourning for the dead Messiah (Is 3:16;Ct 1:5; 2 S 15:30). Jesus' compassionate reply is a Semitism meaning "Weep not so much for me as for yourselves and for your children" (7:13). The situation is reversed as Jesus again predicts the destruction of Jerusalem.[92] Such disastrous "days are coming" (19:43) that barrenness, which was normally a great disgrace (1:25) will be a blessing (21:23) and people will cry out for death to escape. Note the many prophetic allusions in this section such as Hosea's description of God's judgment on Israel (Hos 10:8; 9:14; Apoc 6:16). Jesus' warning concludes with a proverb which in the Aramaic seems to have the traditional Jewish lament metre (kina). Its general meaning seems clear although typically there is variety in the detailed interpretations which are possible. "If they do these things" seems either a divine passive and/or a reference to the Romans crucifying the innocent Jesus (the green wood). The reference to the "dry" suggests the worse fate awaiting the Jews, the really guilty men or perhaps the real zealots to come. Other interpretations are also suggested, e.g. if the bringer of salvation is treated thus what will happen to those who destroy him? If the Jews behave like this now what will they be like when their evil gets worse?[93]

(17) *The Crucifixion of Jesus—(23:33-8):*

All four gospels describe the dreadful cruelty of a familiar scene in the ancient world with the fewest words. They neither mention here the divine purpose of Jesus' death or what it achieved. Matthew in particular never actually says that it happened. Yet they never forget that it was part of God's mysterious will (Ac 2:23; 4:28). It was considered by Jews, Romans and Greeks as not only the most cruel and agonizing form of execution at which one could barely move one's head, but also the most disgraceful (1 Cor 1:18,23; 2:2; Fal 5:11).[94]

Luke, however, softens the starkness and loneliness of Mark's portrayal omitting for example Mark's quotation from Psalm 22 which could be so easily misunderstood. Neither does he have Matthew's earthquake and appearances of the dead. Instead the dreadful event becomes a place of forgiveness and especially of entry into paradise. To the end Jesus continues his ministry of forgiveness, of saving the lost as he fulfills his own command "that he who seeks to save his life . . . ," his own recommendation that endurance brings real life (21:19), as he in one final act commits himself to the Father. Luke, in particular, notes the differing reactions of the people present, the elders, the crowd, the criminals, his acquaintances and particularly the centurion's pronouncement of innocence.

Luke begins with the scene: Jesus crucified between the two criminals at the "Skull Place" as he calls it, giving only the translation of the Aramaic name Golgotha as in John 19:17. the modern name comes from the Latin translation "Calvaria." From Luke 20:15 and Heb 13:12, the site seems to have been outside the walls of Jerusalem but there is no mention in the gospels of a hill or an explanation of its name. In recent times General Gordon proposed a rocky knoll some 250 yards northeast of the Damascus fate as the site. However, the traditional site, the Church of the Holy Sepulchre, which is inside the walls today, is the best attested site, as it was not only the site of Hadrian's Forum but also Constantine's basilica and would have been fixed in the memory of Christians from that day onwards.

The prayer for forgiveness, which is peculiar to Luke, is missing from many early and diverse manuscripts. Possibly its omission can be explained as due to some scribe who after the destruction of Jerusalem thought that Jesus' prayer was unanswered (20:16; 21:24; 23:31). Could its omission be due to some vindictive scribes who found it difficult to imagine Jesus forgiving at such a moment?

Probably on strict textual grounds it should be omitted from the text. However, this does not mean that it is not a very ancient saying, but like many other "floating" sayings, it quite likely goes back to Jesus himself. It is quoted in very many of the Fathers as far back as we can go, Hegesippus, Tatian and Irenaeus, which take us back to the beginning of the second century. Certainly it is in full agreement with Luke's language and thought and particularly his emphasis on intercession, forgiveness and mercy in his writings.[95] The tenses both here and in the request of the good thief (v 42) are the imperfect tense and thus can be translated "he kept saying." The prayer for forgiveness at first sight looks like a prayer for the Roman soldiers who perform the actual crucifixion but as Acts 3:17; 7:60; 13:26f; 17:27ff; 2:36ff, show, it probably includes both the Jews as well. They also acted through failure to understand Jesus although to a great extent his enemies understood him better than his disciples. Further, ignorance in the New Testament is often considered as culpable.[96]

The soldiers gambling for Jesus' clothes which are divided among them according to custom, are a good example of blind ignorance as compared with the centurion. Here Psalm 22 is used as also at v 35 (Ps 22:18,7). This Psalm about the innocent sufferer influenced all the gospel presentations, especially Mark.

Luke, at v 35, makes a clear distinction between the people standing there watching and the leaders (lit) "turning up the nose" at Jesus (Wis 2:13ff; Ps 22:7) with more knowledge than they realized or accepted. The title of Isaiah's servant "the chosen one" is only found here in Luke but the equivalent verb is found only once in the gospel, at the transfiguration (9:35; 6:13; Is 42:1; Ac 1:2,24). The form of their jeer here at v 35 is a reminder of the temptation at 4:1ff. Luke carefully removes Mark's suggestion that Jesus cannot save himself (Mk 15:31; Mt 27:42).

A third group is distinguished by Luke, the soldiers. They also join in the mockery and jeers both at Jesus and the Jews present using the ironic inscription over Jesus' head which called him the King of the Jews. He alone connects their mockery with the offer to Jesus of sour wine and their invitation to him to save himself (Ps 69:21). There is no indication whether Jesus accepted the wine or not. He rejected the drugged wine offered to relieve pain according to Mark 15:23; and Matthew 27:34. There is another offering of vinegar (Mk 15:36; Mt 27:48; Jn 19:28f) which Luke seems to omit as also Mark and Matthew's reference to Elijah which possibly would not suit Luke's Elijah portrayal of Jesus himself.

The account of the mockery reaches a climax with the inscription over Jesus' head "This is the King of the Jews." The title on the cross is not exactly the same in any of the gospels but all agree that Jesus is being put to death as a king and thus a possible threat to Caesar. In John, the inscription is trilingual as was common (Jn 19:20). In Luke it is the climax of the mockery scene. He writes it bluntly in non-Jewish style "The King of the Jews is this man." The Jews would have written "The King of Israel" (Mk 15:32). In this section we have together the title king three times (v 37,38,42 an "inclusion") and the cry "save yourself" which in comparison with Matthew and Mark is twice extra in Luke (v 36,39). The verb "save" is used four times in all in v 35-9. Ironically, but true, they know not what they do in Luke's eyes. Jesus is the king, savior as Luke has stressed so often in his gospel. Here especially his title is misunderstood and ironically they are right, unknown to themselves, but not in the political terms in which they think. Jesus has accepted the Father's will to be the suffering servant (22:27; Ac 8:32-5; 2:21). Jesus' way of kingship is not the way either the Jewish leaders, the Roman soldiers or the second crminal think the way of a king should be.

By losing his life he would save not only himself but others.

(18) *The Penitent Thief—(23:39-43):*

But the good thief alone accepts the kingship of Jesus and recognizes that Jesus' cross is his entry into his glory, where according to Luke Jesus is to remain an indefinite time. In Matthew and Mark we are only told that the thieves or possibly zealots who were crucified with Jesus also abused him. Here one proclaims the innocence of Jesus, confesses his own guilt and expresses faith in Jesus. The other echoes the Jewish insults and blasphemes while he evidently does not believe in Jesus' salvific power, even though he proclaims it; again an allusion to the temptation scene of 4:1ff. There is a typically Lucan contrast here, not to mention a resemblance to the repentant prodigal son and his elder brother. But in this extraordinary conversation which is peculiar to Luke, Jesus, the friend of publicans and sinners, is the savior of the despised to the end of his life (7:34). The penitent thief climaxes a long list of characters which includes a publican, a prostitute and such examples as the prodigal son and the unjust steward. It is a story which points out that there is always hope of forgiveness for those who repent.[97]

Different versions of the good thief's petition are found in the manuscripts. The best one, found in such MSS as P 75 and B is "remember me Jesus when you enter into your kingdom," as it agrees wth Luke's theology of the kingdom which is here but yet to come in its fullness (24:26; 22:18,29f; 19:38; 11:2). However, most witnesses read "when you come in your kingly power." It is the only place in the gospels where Jesus is addressed as simply

"Jesus." Evidently, Jesus' reply was more than the remembrance which the criminal expected. It is an immediate response, an emphatic "Truly I assure you, today you will be with me in paradise," words that every Christian would like to hear at the point of death, the gospel within the gospel as some describe it. There is a reflection of the image of the after-life found in the parable of Lazarus and the popular understanding in Palestine that immediately after death one was judged and rewarded or punished (Ac 3:15f; 4:10; 10:40f). It is a perfect example of salvation through faith without achievements (Eph 2:8).

Paradise, an old Persian word for a king's sumptuous garden, was used both for the original state of man in the Septuagint (Gn 2:8ff; Is 51:3) and also for heaven, for Abraham's bosom (16:23; 2 Cor 12:4; Apoc 2:7). It is found only here in the gospels. For Luke, the cross was the gateway to glory, to paradise (24:26; Jn 13:31ff). It was one of the popular contemporary expectations that the Messiah would reopen the gates of Paradise. Paradise is to be with Jesus (Jn 17:24; 2 Cor 5:8; Rom 8:38f; Phil 1:23).

(19) *The Death of Jesus on the Cross—(23:44-9):*

Jesus' death in Luke is a model of an innocent sufferer, as the centurion in particular stresses. Luke now ignores Jesus' enemies and mockers to emphasize its positive effects on those present, the centurion, the crowd, his friends and the women. He begins with a cautious statement about the hour, "about" the sixth hour or midday. See John 19:14 and note that he does not have the "darkness." There was darkness over the whole land until 3 p.m. These are the traditional three hours of the Passion which are passed over in silence. Darkness was the symbol of the apparent triumph of evil, just as bright light symbolizes the conquest of darkness (22:53; 24:4; Gn 1:2; Is 5:30). Perhaps the darkness here is a symbol of sorrow or an allusion to one of the Egyptian plagues (Ex 10:22).

His explanation of the darkness can mean either "the sun's light failed" or "the sun was eclipsed" or according to some manuscripts, "the sun was darkened." Whether we can say that this darkness was purely symbolic as described in Old Testament language[98] or something miraculous and mysterious, is difficult to answer. It seems that according to astronomers there is no possibility of an eclipse of the sun during Passover time when the moon is full and further, eclipses only last for a few minutes. An explanation is sometimes offered of a sirocco wind bringing dust with it from the desert.

Similarly with the second sign accompanying the death of Jesus, the tearing in two of the temple curtain. The choice is between a factual or purely symbolic event or both, as we have no more detailed evidence which would be necessary for a clear conclusion. Yet the symbolic explanation seems the more likely. Two interpretations of the symbolism involved are possible as no detailed identification of the veil is given. Veils symbolized both the remoteness of God and the division between the privileged Jew and the Gentile.

The Holy Place, where incense was offered by the priests, had a veil which hid the interior of the temple from the Gentiles. There was a further veil separating the Holy Place from the Holy of Holies, the special presence of Yahweh which was entered by the high priest once a year on the Day of the Atonement (Ex 26:31f; Lv 16). Rather it seems that the first veil is involved, thus removing the Jewish exclusiveness and their privileged access to Yahweh's presence (Eph 2:14; Gal 3:28; Heb 9:3ff; 10:9ff). This is the only reference to the temple veil in the New Testament. It tells us that the death and resurrection of Jesus opened up a new living way for all men into God's presence by the suppression of the Jewish cult. The tearing of the veil is the first stage in the destruction of the temple and henceforth entry into God's presence is through Jesus' death.

Mark and Matthew describe a loud cry or voice at Jesus' death (Mk 15:34,37; Mt 27:46,50). However, both Luke and John record words also. John 19:30 "It is accomplished" and Luke 23:46 "Father, into your hands I commend my Spirit." It should be remembered that the expression "a loud voice" is a frequent expression in Luke and has no special significance (e.g., 17:15; 19:37; Ac 14:10; 16:28; 26:24; Jn 11:43). Luke, who does not have Mark's psalm quotation (Mk 15:37), has another psalm quotation from psalm 31:6 (Ac 7:59f). This was the Jewish night prayer which they learned from childhood with the addition of the intimate "Father" which is found in all of Jesus' prayers in the gospels (except Mk 15:34). It seems to have been the actual time when the trumpet summoned the people to evening prayer. Jesus' last words affirm his sonship and recall his first words about his Father's business (2:49). Thus his whole life is dedicated to his Father. In total obedience he is not so much put to death by others in a deliberate and exemplar act of sacrifice (12:1ff; Ac 7:59)s; rather, he completely dedicated himself to and commends his spirit to the Father who will raise and exalt him making him Lord and Christ (4:43; Ac 2:33,36; 7:59f). Thus Luke, summarizing his own theology, gives three words to the dying Jesus which added to the three other found in John and the one given by Mark and Matthew, make up the traditional seven words on the cross. Who heard and preserved them or in what order, are questions which we cannot answer. The exact time and year are not fully certain but most scholars would agree to 3 p.m., April 7th, A.D. 30.

None of the evangelists actually say "Jesus died." Luke uses an unusual expression "exepneusen," which can be translated "expired" or "breathed his last." It is interesting to note that a modern medical report has concluded from an examination of evidence, that it is impossible to determine any physical cause which explains adequately the death of Jesus. Many possible factors have been given such as mental and spiritual agony, exposure, hunger and thirst, loss of blood, infection, shock as well as four main theories, rupture of the heart (a broken heart), embolism (the blockage of a blood vessel by a blood clot), asphyxia (lack of oxygen due to failure of respiration), acute dilatation of the stomach. None of these adequately explains the unexpectedly early death of Jesus (Mk 15:44; Jn 19:32ff) or the fact that Jesus was conscious to the end, that he spoke with a loud voice and seemingly died when he wanted to. Doctors tell of patients who decide to die and give up their lives with no evident physical reason. This conclusion has often been suggested in Christian writings down through the ages.[99]

The Roman centurion, for whom Luke uses a word (lit) "the commander of a hundred men," unlike Mark's translation of the Latin word, gives a final and "objective" verdict on the innocence of Jesus, that is, before God's verdict in the resurrection. Longinus, as he is traditionally called, praised God (2:20) saying "Truly this man was just."[100] The term "just" was a Christological title in the early church as can be seen in Ac 3:14; 7:52; 22:4 (see also Is 53:11; Sir 2:1ff). Only Luke describes the repentant beating of their breasts of the crowds as they returned home having seen what had happened (18:13; 20:1,38; Zech 12:10ff). The way is prepared here for the conversion scenes in Acts (Ac 2:41).

Finally, Jesus' friends and the women who we are told twice by Luke had come from Galilee (v 49,55) are mentioned, as in all the synoptics (the words here are based on Ps 38:11). Possibly some of these are the eyewitnesses whom Luke had emphasized in 1:2 (8:1ff; Ac 1:22). Here they are not called disciples as they were confused and with little hope left (24:17,21). Luke has not mentioned the fleeing of the disciples or their going to Galilee after the crucifixion (Mk 14:50; 16:7).

(20) *The Burial of Jesus—(23:50-6):*

His burial which stresses the finality of his death is one of the best attested historical facts about Jesus. All four gospels attest it and it is also recorded in our earliest summary of the Christian tradition which Paul himself received from the Jerusalem church some five years after it actually happened.[101] Luke emphasizes the integrity and importance of Joseph of Arimathea and also the witness of the women. Particular interest is shown in the details of the burial and especially the burial cloths now when the famous Holy Shroud of Turin is being given the first public display in recent years and is being examined with all the modern means of science.[102] The Holy Shroud of Turin is the one relic associated with the life of Jesus that is seriously claimed by scholars to be genuine. The well known John A.T. Robinson has an interesting comment on the relation between the Holy Shroud and the biblical evidence:

> "That the corpse of Jesus was enfolded in a single linen cloth passing lengthwise over the head and covering the whole body back and front is not, I submit, what any forger with medieval or modern presuppositions would have thought of; but it makes complete sense of the texts and fully comports with what other ancient evidence we have."[103]

Many scientists have concluded that it is the authentic burial cloth of Jesus. Thus the Swiss criminologist, Max Frei, has examined the pollen content which is almost indestructible, and concluded that it was about 2,000 years old and of a kind found almost exclusively in the Dead Sea area of Palestine.[104]

The journalist historian, Ian Wilson[105] has suggested that it was brought to Turkey before A.D. 50 as a gift to the Christian king of Edessa where it was dubbed in the sixth century the legendary Mandylion, the relic which Eastern Orthodox have long regarded as bearing Christ's image. In 944 it became part of the emperor's collection in Constantinople and may have been brought to Europe by a Knight Templar. It was first displayed in public in Europe in 1398. No rational explanation has been given of the enigmatic process by which the image was imprinted on the Shroud. One modern thermal chemist has suggested that it was imprinted by an intense burst of light.

Unlike the Roman custom, the Jewish law commanded that the body of an executed criminal be buried before nightfall as it was offensive to God and would pollute the land.[106]

All four gospels emphasize the role of Joseph from Arimathea, a Jewish town (Lk), unknown today. Luke omits the discussion with Pilate (v 52; Mk 15:44f) but, as if describing witnesses, he stresses the character and integrity of Joseph and the dedication of the women who had come from Galilee. Not unlike Gamaliel (Ac 5:34), Joseph was a member of the Sanhedrin but according to Luke it seems that he must have been absent when the unanimous vote against Jesus was taken (22:70; Mk 14:64). His character description in Luke puts him in the company of Zechariah (1:6), Simeon (2:25), Anna (2:38), Barnabas (Ac 11:24), Joseph of old (Gn 50:1ff) and those who hear the word properly (8:15). In Mark he is a respected member of the council (Mk 15:43), in Matthew he was rich and a disciple (Mt 27:57), in John he was a secret disciple (19:38). His influence with Pilate and his possession of a new rockhewn tomb (19:30; Jn 19:41), show a man of means (Is 53:9). He takes the body down, wraps (folds?) it in linen as is mentioned in all four gospels ("sindon" is found here but in 23:53 John's word "othonia" is used by Luke). Luke omits here the stone at the entrance to the tomb but mentions it at 24:2 (Jn 20:1). However, several witnesses at v 53 add a verse about a great stone rolled to the door of the tomb, based on Matthew 27:60 and Mark 15:46. The Codex Bezae adds that it was so big that twenty men could scarcely roll it. One can still see in Jerusalem rock-hewn tombs from the Roman period with round stones like large millstones which are rolled across the entrances in grooves.

It was the evening of the Preparation Day, a technical word for the Friday Passover, and the Sabbath was "dawning," a vivid expression which is possibly a reference to the evening star or to the lighting up time of the sabbath lights, as the sabbath began at sundown on Friday evening. Despite the urgency of the moment, Luke notes that the women have time to check the tomb, return home and prepare spices and ointments. All three synoptics mention the presence of the women at the burial. Evidently, they did not have time for an adequate care of the body; apart from the shroud there is no mention of washing the body (Ac 9:37). They went home to prepare the spices and the perfume which they intended to wrap with the body when they returned the morning after the sabbath, some 36 hours later (24:1). In Mark 16:1 they went by themselves early on Sunday morning, whereas in John, Nicodemus actually buried some spices with the body. Luke prepares his readers for the next episode by first noting that the women witnessed the tomb and how the body was buried so that they could find it on Easter morning. He also notes the precise time and how obedient the women were to the law (Gn 2:2). They would be the first to discover the empty tomb.

C. *After the Resurrection—In Jerusalem—(24:1ff):*

"We may be Protestants or Catholics, Lutherans or Reformed, to the right or to the left, but in some way we must have seen and heard the angels at the open and empty tomb if we are to be sure of our ground." (Karl Barth)[107]

Recent years have seen a veritable flood of books and articles devoted to the resurrection of Jesus after some seventeen hundred years of comparative neglect and emphasis rather on his Passion, particularly in Western Christianity. Today there is a return to the spirit of early Christianity where the emphasis was on the Resurrection, the basis of all true Christian life and worship. The preaching of the early Christians was essentially the preaching of the Resurrection.[108] It was not just proof of Jesus but the key to understanding the mystery of his life and death.

Early Christian Art for example, stressed the miracles and the healings of Jesus and particularly the Resurrection and Ascension. Today we are so accustomed to the crucifixion as the symbol of Christianity that we are surprised to learn how long it took to emerge in the history of Christian Art before its power was recognized. The problem with Christians is not to separate the Cross from the Resurrection, but to overemphasize one while ignoring the other. Thus, an over-emotional Christianity can produce Christianity such as existed at Corinth where the disorder and enthusiasm was based on a false understanding (1 Cor). They thought that with the Resurrection over the war of life was over and all they had to do was enjoy its results. For Luke, the Passion is a divine must before one enters into glory. It was the crucified Jesus who rose from the dead. Without the crucifixion the life of a Christian would be quite different.

Before we come to an actual examination of Luke's unique presentation of the post-resurrection events to see what he was trying to say, some general points should be recalled:

(1) Resurrection is a metaphor based on the everyday experience of awakening to a new day. In the hope of the Jewish people it was to be a communal experience which the faithful Jews in particular would experience at the end of time. Through some miraculous experience the dead would be brought back to life to share in the kingdom of God on earth (Is 26:19; Dn 12:2). They had no expectation as far as we know of an individual resurrection such as that of Jesus (see 9:7f). But the term as applied to Jesus should be carefully distinguished from the resuscitation of a corpse, like that of Lazarus, to continue this life. For Jesus it is the entering into glory as Luke puts it. In the New Testament apart from John 2:19 (10:17f; 1 Thess 4:14), it is always God's act. The New Testament expression used some 30 times is "God raised Jesus," or "Jesus was raised up by God." It is the conquering of death and the raising of Jesus to a sharing in the divine power so that he can make life available until he finally exercises his judgment at the end of time.

(2) The disciples and evangelists did not think in Greek philosophical terms such as our familiar dichotomy of body and spirit. Rather they saw man as a unity, as modern philosophers, psychologists and doctors tend to see him. They saw resurrection in terms of the body, i.e. of the total person and not merely of the soul. The theory of

immortality of the soul is of course, as has often been pointed out, a philosophical version of the shadowy survival after death found among many peoples. The gospel approach is then not a philosophical approach but nevertheless very profound, beginning with the fact of the empty tomb and especially in Luke using all the art of deceptively simple story telling and picture painting to deepen faith in the reader.

The well known Heidelberg Church historian, Von Campenhausen, has concluded on the most careful examination of the historical evidence alone that the tomb was really empty on Easter morning.[109] However, the evangelist writing a generation later to people who had no means of verifying the empty tomb, had other aims in view than just to give the facts of what happened, as Norman Perrin in his final book interprets:

> "Mark is attempting to convince his readers that they can experience the ultimacy of God in the concreteness, the historicality of their everyday existence: that wherever they are God is also there, and he is there in the form of the figure of Jesus known from the gospel stories. Matthew is attempting to convince his readers that the eternal ship of the church is the vehicle of salvation for all people everywhere, and that aboard that ship the risen Lord effectively sustains those who believe in him. Luke is attempting to convince his readers that Jesus effectively lived out the life of the first Christian in the world, and that the resurrection means that his spirit now empowers those who follow him truly to imitate his life."[110]

It is clear also that each evangelist is dealing with the objections and difficulties of his own community and possibly has anticipated many of ours also. Thus Luke stresses that the risen Jesus was no hallucination. The disciples were certain that Jesus was dead and were the last to expect a resurrection. Thus they were the most unlikely candidates as hallucinations come to those only who are conditioned to receive them.

Von Campenhausen makes the interesting point that many modern people who believe in a spiritual Resurrection are in the paradoxical situation of agreeing with the Jewish explanations of the empty tomb while on the other hand agreeing with the Christian description of the appearances of Jesus.

(3) While the Resurrection is the single most important fact in the Christian religion (Ac 10:40f; 1 Cor 15:12ff), nevertheless, only God knows what happened in the approximately thirty hours between Friday evening and Sunday morning. It was a unique event and thus outside the normal laws by which historians construct their hypotheses. This, of course, does not mean that it did not happen or that there is nothig which a historian can investigate, e.g. the empty tomb, the reliability of the witnesses. A historian perhaps could conclude that it never happened.

None of the canonical gospels attempts an actual description of the event itself (Mt 28:2-4). There is a fantastic description in the noncanonical Gospel of Peter where the risen Jesus towers higher than the heavens and the Cross follows Jesus from the tomb. Many reasons can be given such as the phenomenon of the Church, the changing of the Sabbath to the Sunday, the writing of the New Testament. However, no amount of historical analysis or philosophical speculation can convince a skeptic just as Pilate and Herod do not seem to have been convinced. A person's position depends so much on his presuppositions, his understanding of God and his activity in the world. The evangelists do not over concern themselves with such people or with the modern obsession with pure facts. Modern man likes to think that he is reasonable and to base his conclusions on observations which can be observed and on experiments which can be repeated. However, trust in the scientific approach to the problems of life has been shaken severely in recent years and a less rationalistic approach even to science itself is becoming common. Ultimately for a Christian it is a matter of faith based on the testimony of unimportant women and the apostles who handed on their witness to others down through the ages.

(4) It seems impossible to harmonize into a coherent whole the four gospel accounts and Paul's recording of the tradition which he received, i.e. 1 Cor 15. This account in Corinthians is our earliest account written probably some ten years before the first of the gospels. It records six appearances to Peter, the Twelve, the five hundred, James, all the apostles, Paul himself. Two of these, i.e. to James and the five hundred, are not recorded in our gospels. Paul's own clearly took place after the traditional forty days. One should also take into account the traditional ending of Mark which is found in a vast number of manuscripts, though not the two older, and which goes back at least to Irenaeus. It resembles Luke in that its appearances are in the Jerusalem area, to Mary Magdalene (Mk 16:9), to two disciples in the country (Mk 16:12-13) and to the eleven at table and it concludes with the ascension.

The difficulty of arranging all into a coherent sequence at least shows that there was no collaboration of witnesses, no committee document with the details laboriously worked upon and an agreed story produced. Quite unlike the Passion story, there is not only no common framework among the gospels, but quite a number of evident discrepancies as to place (e.g. Galilee or Jerusalem), people involved (e.g. how many angels?), as to what the women saw at the tomb,[111] sequence among the different gospels.

Nevertheless, all are united in believing and acknowledging the risen Jesus alive and active in the church and that thus the evil of man was reversed by God. They agree in not describing the actual Resurrection. There is basic agreement in the synoptics that the women discovered the empty tomb and that the Resurrection was announced to them by a young man (Mk), a messenger (Mt), two men (Lk), two angels (Jn).[112] It is evident that the New Testament writers did not suffer from our obsession with detailed accuracy. Certainly this variety in their details in no way discredits their central story no more than the fact that there are extraordinary discrepancies in the accounts of Waterloo as told by Wellington, Marshall Ney and Napoleon compels anyone to deny that a battle was fought there.

Luke gives an artistic yet artificial presentation (v 36,50) as he condenses all the post-resurrection events into one day of four scenes in and near Jerusalem on the eighth day. In Acts 1:3 he seems to suggest other appearances and many other days. It should be noticed how the story of the tomb is repeated during the Emmaus story (v 22-4), while the teaching of the Emmaus story is repeated in turn during the appearance to the eleven (4 44ff). Also the final verses are a summary of the first part of Acts. This one day is not just the end of Jesus' appearances but looks foward to the mission of the Church. The public witnesses who will dominate the early scenes of Acts are prepared. Peter is the first of them to see Jesus. According to his function he will confirm the others and all will receive a mission and wait to be empowered by the Spirit. Thus this chapter, while an artistic unity in itself, serves both as a conclusion to the first volume and also a bridge and an introduction to the second.

Luke goes beyond the empty tomb scene which seems to be the only one in the text of Mark available to him. Then he describes how the women bring the news to the incredulous eleven. Next he records three appearances, on the road to Emmaus (24:13-35), to Peter (24:34) and to the eleven "and the rest of the company" (v 33) in Jerusalem (24:36-49) and finally a brief note about Jesus' departure (24:50-53). The whole chapter is a unity in Luke, a unity of date and place and a repeated message about the necessity of the passion and the resurrection which is given by the two men at the tomb, on the road to Emmaus and to the eleven. This necessity is based on Jesus' own words (v 6-8,44 and 9:22) and on the Scriptures (v 26f,44ff). The basic appeal is not to the empty tomb nor even to the appearances of the Risen Jesus but to his word which he had spoken to them and which is put at least on a par with their Scriptures. Luke has emphasized the Scripture and its fulfilment right through his gospel especially in such scenes as the temptation scene and the Nazareth scene, where he prefaces and interprets Jesus' public ministry with a text from Isaiah.

Scripture is the clue to God's plan and the meaning of Jesus' life but it is in the Eucharist that Jesus is "made known" both to the two at Emmaus and, of course, to Luke's community (24:35). It is there especially that he is present to Luke's community. It is exactly the same Jesus that the disciples knew. For his final chapter Luke has used all his art, particularly for the Emmaus story and like the finale of a symphony, has interwoven all his basic themes e.g. reversal, insignificant people, women, the obtuseness of the disciples, Son of Man, Messiah, a journey, a meal, Jesus the host, God's plan and fidelity to his promises, mission, Gentiles, the Spirit. All events lead back to Jerusalem and to the eleven gathered there where the official apparition of the risen Jesus takes place and where they wait for the Spirit. Jerusalem, the place where God was especially to be found, is the climax of Luke's gospel and the place where Jesus enters his glory in paradise, there to remain until the consummation of the kingdom. It's emphasis is of course a simplification, as Luke, as a result of his "theological geography" must omit the many journeys to Jerusalem of which John speaks, and the appearances in Galilee such as are found in Matthew and in John's appendix (compare Mk 16:7 and Lk 24:6). It is from Jerusalem, where the Spirit, making a new beginning, will send forth the Christian movement in its inevitable way to Rome, the center of the Empire, the new symbolic center of Luke's world.

This last chapter of Luke has an unusual number of textual problems, e.g. v 3,6,12,36,40,51,52. These verses are missing in the Codex Bezae and the Itala type of the Old Latin version, inferior texts, which are usually characterized by additions or interpolations, hence their peculiar name "Western Noninterpolations." However, they are found in almost all the other manuscripts including those regarded as the best. At the end of the last century Westcott and Hort somewhat arbitrarily ruled in favor of the shorter readings and influenced many of the English translations. Nevertheless, although each must be evaluated separately on its own merits, in general it can be said that many scholars and translations have swung in favor of these longer verses.

(1) *The Women at the Empty Tomb—(24:1-12):*

Apart from a more artistic telling of the story there are quite a number of special features found in Luke's version by comparison with the parallel accounts in Mark and Matthew. As in Mark, the women come to the tomb on Sunday, quite early (v 1,22), but they do not need to buy spices as they have already prepared them on Friday (23:56). John agrees with the early hour and with Matthew and Mark mentions Mary Magdalene explicitly. Possibly there is a reference to the week of creation here (Gn 1) with the eighth day (lit) "the first of the Sabbath's" being the beginning of the new creation in Jesus. Luke summarizes Mark v 3-5 here but he alone emphasizes that when they found the stone rolled back and entered the tomb (Jn 20:1) they did not find the body "of the Lord Jesus"—"him they did not see." This is the best reading here. It uses an expression found also in Acts 1:21; 4:33; 8:16. It is noteworthy that only Luke and John describe Jesus' corpse as a body ("soma" 24:3,23; Jn 20:12).

The angelic announcement found in all four gospels is in many ways typical of many found in the Old and New Testaments and in particular not unlike those found in the early chapters of Luke.[113] Its purpose is to give God's interpretation of the sign of the empty tomb, that Jesus is the Living One, an Old Testament title used of God alone (Josh 3:10; Jg 8:19; 1 S 13:14). They are reminded of Jesus' prophecy about the Son of Man and the divine plan back in Galilee. Luke has three unique features here:

(i) The reaction of the women to the empty tomb is toned down from Mark's amazement and fright to perplexity and doubt (v 4,11) leading to remembering (24:8). In Matthew the reaction is worship (Mt 28:9, 17) and in John it is joy and faith (Jn 20:20,28). Neither do the women, who are terrified of the angels (1:12,30) and "look to the ground" (21:28), run away and keep silent, but they go back to bring the message to the eleven as in John (Mk 16:8).

(ii) He has two men in dazzling garments (Ac 1:10) instead of one in Mark. Matthew has one angel and John has two. However, it should be noticed that for Luke the words "man" and "angel" seem interchangeable as in Acts 1:10; 10:3,30. The dazzling color in Luke often suggests a supernatural visit.[114] The two men of v 4 remind one of Moses and Elijah, the Old Testament representatives who has foretold Jesus' exodus at the transfiguration (9:30; also Ac 1:10). In both cases as in Acts 1:10 the two men are introduced by precisely the same words (e.g. "and suddenly two men . . . stood by them"). Thus these three scenes are deliberately modelled on one another and linked by Luke. The angel's rhetorical question found here alone put the accent on "living," "alive," a favorite topic in Acts (Ac 1:3; 2:39).

(iii) This is the most radical diference from Mark's "he is going before you to Galilee." We find "Remember how he told you while he was still in Galilee" (9:22). Here not only is Luke emphasizing the importance of remembering Jesus' words but also his modification permits him to describe only events in and near Jerusalem. Luke has barely retained the word Galilee but there is also a subtle reminder that the witnesses in Galilee are also the witnesses of what is fulfilled in Jerusalem. The emphasis is not on the empty tomb but on remembering (11:28; 9:44; 22:61). The women are not given a message for the disciples as in Mark 16:7 and Matthew 28:7 (compare 24:8 with Mk 16:8 and Mt 28:7).

The first part of v 6 which is slightly different from Matthew and Mark should be included in the text as it is missing from only one fairly important Greek manuscript—"He is not here but has risen." The "sinful men" of v 7, to whom Jesus must be delivered, are probably an indirect reference to the Romans, typical of late Jewish literature.[115] The explanation given here of Jesus' suffering as his commitment to the divine plan, will become that of the apostles in Acts (Ac 3:18; 26:22ff).

The women more calm than in Mark, return to tell all to the eleven "and to others" (v 9,33). This seems to contradict Mark's rather abrupt ending (Mk 16:8; Mt 28:8). Luke's list here is close to that of Mark and Matthew but he has Joanna (see 8:2) for their Salome and mentions "other women." The Apostles (v 10) who will be the chief witnesses, do not accept the women's testimony and describe it in medical terminology as the babbling of a delirious person. They require first hand evidence for themselves. Here we have perhaps an apologia as to why the men had not gone to the tomb and why the women's testimony was not allowed.[116] Also there is a blunt emphasis as in all the gospels, on the incredulity of the disciples, pointing out that men are more skeptical and are not easily convinced.[117] It is not until they meet the risen Jesus who repeats his earlier words about the necessity of suffering that the break-through comes.

Verse 12, where Peter runs to confirm the story, is considered by some as a summary interpolation of John 20:3-10. Note the common use of the unusual word "othonia" for the wrappings. Yet Luke's version tells us, unlike John, that Peter went off "wondering at what happened' ' and at v 24 he says "some" went to the tomb. However, it is found in our best manuscripts and is omitted only in the Western tradition. It forms a necessary antecedent to v 24 and it seems likely that in these sections both Luke and John derive from a common tradition or source.

(2) *The Way to Emmaus—(24:13-35):*

This very beautiful recognition story told only by Luke has appealed to artists like Rembrandt, to writers like Malcolm Muggeridge, and has been one of the most loved Bible stories among Christians of all kinds down through the ages. Muggeridge's comment is worth quoting:

> "The story is so incredibly vivid that I swear to you that no one who has tried to write can doubt its authenticity. There is something in the very language and manner which breathes truth."[118]

Each evangelist selects the stories best suited to bring out his insight into the mystery of the risen Jesus.

Luke's artistry is at its best here as he weaves many of his most familiar themes into a consummate story which is both convincing and consistent—a journey, Jesus concerned with unimportant people, the Old Testament and God's plan, a meal, Jesus the host. Even though the reader is superior in knowledge to the participants, yet the story is so vivid and so well told, that he shares their desolation and sadness, their suspense and the wonderful climax of one of the greatest recognition scenes in literature as faith awakens in the hearts of the two disciples. One should notice the psychological observations about the human feelings made frequently and the wonderful "flashback" as they later relive their experience. Three parts can conveniently be distinguished, the opening walk with Jesus, the stranger (v 13-24), then Jesus' exposition of the Old Testament (v 25-7) and finally the climax, the recognition scene at table (v 28-32). The women did not see Jesus at the tomb and now in the next two appearances his followers will actually see Jesus and be persuaded that he has risen indeed.

It is a catechesis for Luke's community how to face the scandal of the Cross and find the risen Jesus by moving from the Scripture preparation to a real meeting in the "breaking of the bread," the two fundamental acts in the Christian celebration of the Eucharist. This incident seems to be summarized in Mark's longer ending (Mk 16:12-13; see Jn 20; Ac 8:26ff). It is the longest resurrection story in the gospels. Its importance for Luke is seen in the fact that he devotes to it 23 verses, almost half of his resurrection chapter.

Luke opens with a careful annotation of the day ' 'that same day,' ' "the third day' ' (v 21) and the length and destination of the journey. There are difficulties in identifying Emmaus today with some four possibilities to choose from but this difficulty in no way disproves the validity of the story (e.g. Mc 3:40; 4:3). It is possibly the modern Kulonich, some four miles from Jerusalem. It seems that the two were not members of the eleven (v 33) but were among the wider group (v 9). Possibly, they were husband and wife or brothers as they seemed to have a home in Emmaus. Cleophas is perhaps the Clopas of John 19:25. Hegesippus, quoted by Eusebius, identifies him as Jesus' uncle, Joseph's brother, the father of Symeon who succeeded James as leader of the Jerusalem church and who led the early Christians back to Jerusalem after A.D. 70.

The two travellers are so absorbed in their fallen hopes and their depression, as humans often tend to be, that they do not notice Jesus as he joins them. "What things," the stranger's question gives them the opportunity to show that they had little real understanding of Jesus' messiahship, but had stubbornly maintained the nationalistic Jewish expectations which he had tried to change with his teaching about the suffering Son of Man. Like many others, they did not recognize Jesus.[119]

It does not seem to be the case here that Jesus was disguised but the fault lay with their faith, their preoccupation with their despair (9:45; 18:34). Yet there always seems to be something mysterious about the appearances of the risen Lord in the gospels. Probably, the disciples were convinced despite Jesus' teaching that he could not rise. They saw Jesus of Nazareth as a prophet, another Moses in deed and in word (Ac 1:1) but no more (v 19,49).[120] But their expectations of political freedom were destroyed when Jesus was put to death, when "our chief priests and leaders delivered him up to be crucified." Possibly there is irony here in that the death which convinced them that Jesus was not the redeemer, was in fact the means of redemption which he actually used (1:68; Ac 28:20).

Here we have another of Luke's "Todays," signifying an important occasion and possibly the references to "the third day" is intended to refer back to 13:32 "on the third day I will be at my goal." The report of the women about the empty tomb and the angels message did not convince them. Nor did the others "of our members" who found (a frequent word) that the women were right, "but him they did not see" (v 24,12). The empty tomb is evidently not enough to convince people. The phrase "all the prophets" is Luke's frequent stereotyped phrase (e.g. v 27,44; 11:50; Ac 3:18).

Jesus' calling them "thoughtless," reveals to them once again the meaning of what had happened (8:10). If they had rightly understood the Old Testament they would have understood the sign of the empty tomb. Only when Jesus sets their hearts on fire by giving a christological explanation of the Scriptures to them are they ready to recognize him in the breaking of the bread. The angels had recalled Jesus' prophecy in Galilee, but here Jesus, in summary form, is speaking in the same way as Peter and Paul will speak in Acts (Ac 3:18; 2:23; 3:22ff; 4:28; 26:22f; 28:23). The Old Testament makes sense of the apparent scandal of Jesus. Its fulfilment for example made sense of the public ministry of Jesus (4:16ff). The phrase "all that the prophets have spoken" is found also in Ac 24:14, 26:22,27; 28:23.

Jesus here explains that the Messiah has completed his exodus, his great journey to Jerusalem by entering into his glory through his suffering which was part of God's plan (9:31; 1:52). This glory which was anticipated at the transfiguration, becomes permanent at the resurrection. This is the glory which Luke stresses whereas both Mark and Matthew tend to stress the glory of the future coming of Jesus, the parousia (9:36). Here we find the risen Jesus referring to himself as the Messiah (v 26,46; 2:11,26; 4:41) and also the ninth of the ten divine "musts" found in Luke. Jesus' exposition of the Old Testament probably means showing the constant pattern of God's plan which is fulfilled in his life and in his sufferings especially. Specific texts are not mentioned but such references to suffering as Ac 2:27; Ps 16; Is 40:1ff; 6:1ff; Jer 31:31ff; Hos 5:8ff; Zech 9:9-10; Dn 7:1ff; Dt 18:15; Exodus; Psalms 22,69,111 can be suggested. This is what Paul meant by his phrase "according to the Scriptures" (1 Cor 15:3ff).

The episode where they press Jesus to stay with them is typically oriental (Gn 19:3; Ac 16:15). However, suddenly Jesus' action shows that he is the real host (19:7ff; Jn 21:9ff). The Eucharist is the climax here just as Baptism is the climax of a similar scene, the meeting between Philip and the Ethiopian (Ac). Here the interpretation of the scripture is not sufficient so that the disciples recognize Jesus. For that the breaking of the bread is needed, a personal meeting with Jesus. They are given a clue to Jesus' identity perhaps by his action or prayer of blessing. The description of Jesus' action "took, blessed, broke, gave," clearly recalls Jesus' action at the last supper (22:14-27) and the great feeding of the five thousand (9:12-17). The "breaking of the bread," a common term for a meal, became a technical name for the Eucharist in the early church.[121] One recalls also Gen 18:1ff and Judg 6:11ff where God or his angels visit incognito and depart after a meal and a recognition. Once they have realized that Jesus is risen and present in the Eucharist they no longer need his visible presence. Again Luke is building a bridge both to Acts and to his own community. It is noteworthy that apart from Mark 7:35, the other seven New Testament uses of the verb, "their eyes were opened" are all in Luke with the meaning of a deeper view or insight into revelation (e.g. 2:23).

Their despair is over and the lateness of the hour is forgotten and they hurry back to Jerusalem to tell the eleven and the others. These will constitute the witnesses to the risen Jesus but as in the other gospels, will have their own apparition in which they will be commissioned (Mt 28:16-20; Mk 16:14-20; Jn 20:19-23). The scene when they meet the eleven is somewhat of an anticlima as they are greeted with the news that the Lord "has *really* appeared to Simon" (1 Cor 15:5; Jn 21:1ff). This "really" will be explained in the next episode. Evidently Luke is interested in stressing the priority of the appearance to Simon which must have been well known to his community. The appearance to Simon is a source of strength to the others (22:32). Only then could they tell their own story with an emphasis on "the breaking of the bread" (v 35). It is mysterious why Luke has not actually recorded the story of the appearance to Peter.

(3) *Jesus Appears to the Eleven in Jerusalem—(24:36-49):*

After the Emmaus story which stresses the recognition of Jesus through the Scripture and especially through "the breaking of the bread," Luke gives us an appearance scene of Jesus to the eleven and the others with them (v 33) which emphasizes the reality of the body of the risen Jesus and his continuity with the Jesus they knew in Galilee (v 37, 42f). Once convinced, the disciples are given an explanation of the Easter message (the kerygma) to which they will be witnesses when they receive the spirit.

A rather similar appearance story is told in the episode of doubting Thomas (Jn 20:19ff). It is an interesting example of how what was probably the same episode originally developed in independent traditions and was treated by each evangelist in accordance with his aims and theology. Both take place at the same time in Jerusalem on Easter Sunday evening. In both the disciples are startled by Jesus' sudden appearance as he "stood in the middle of them" (v 36; Jn 20:19) "one of the sabbaths" (v 1; Jn 20:19). Both have the same semitic greeting "and he says to them 'Peace to you' " (10:5f). This is missing in the Western text of Luke but found in a wide selection, including the earliest and best manuscripts and so should be read and considered another of the many points of contact between Luke and John in these chapters, probably due to a common source. In each there is an emphasis on the reality, yet mysteriousness of Jesus' body. Luke has a development about Jesus' ability to eat but substitutes "feet" for John's "side" (24:41f; see Ac 10:41) and also an instruction which is possibly influenced by his sermons in Acts.

In each there is a reference to the forgiveness of sins. John has a clear reference to the mission of the disciples and the conferring of the Holy Spirit. He describes Jesus as breathing on the disciples and a reference to sins being forgiven or retained. Luke has a statement that they are witnesses and "repentance and forgiveness of sins should be preached in his name to all nations," but that they should wait for "the promise of my Father . . . ". Both emphasize the joy of the disciples.

Luke links up the appearance story with the Emmaus episode by using one of his artificial transitions "as they were saying this" (see 8:49; 22:47,60). John's locked doors are not mentioned but are perhaps implied in v 36. The disciples are not easily convinced but are "startled and frightened," "disturbed," "have doubts," they think that Jesus is a ghost. The term for "doubts" or questionings (Gk dialogismoi) is found 6 times in Luke and only once in Matthew and Mark, e.g. in Simeon's prophecy in 2:35 also in 5:22; 6:8; 9:46f (Rom 1:21; 1 Cor 3:20; Phil 2:14). Their reaction is not unlike the natural reaction in the presence of the supernatural which we note in the annunciation scenes. It is one thing to hear about the empty tomb, it is quite another matter for a human person to experience the presence of the supernatural no matter how often it happens especially if one like Peter has denied Jesus. Luke gives a wonderful description of how their fear leads to faith and finally to joy and wonder and to future service. Jesus then gives what can be called a simple, three dimensional demonstration of the concrete reality of his body by first inviting them to touch his hands and feet ("hands and side" in John 20:27) and then asking for something to eat. A ghost is at most two dimensional. John 20:27 has "hands and side" which corresponds to his piercing of the side of Jesus episode (Jn 19:34) which Luke does not have.

He eats a piece of grilled fish in their presence in a scene reminiscent of the angel in Tobit 12:16-22, to stress that he has "flesh and bones" and to emphasize the identi-

Jerusalem 463

ty between his crucified and glorified body (22:16; 8:55; Ac 2:31; 10:41). Note how the Greek text contains the divine expression "I am" which only Jesus can legitimately use! despite the claims of many (21:8; 22:70). The verb used in the invitation to "handle" Jesus is found only three other times in the New Testament, one of which is the important opening verse of 1 John (also Ac 17:27; Heb 12:18). "That which was from the beginning, which we have looked upon and *touched with our hands* . . .". Many Greeks would have been familiar with the famous description of the dead in Homer's Odyssey (6, v 288) "they have no more flesh or bones" to which Luke perhaps alludes.

It is quite likely that for Luke this section was an apologia directed against the docetist tendencies of some of the Greeks in his community, who saw the resurrection as something purely spiritual which did not affect his body. The docetists tended to deny the full humanity of Jesus and to teach that he had only the appearance of a man, a divine spirit took possession of the man Jesus at the baptism and departed before the crucifixion. The Greek mind tended to distort the resurrection due to their traditions of religious heroes who escaped from the material world of flesh and blood into the somewhat unreal world of vague phantoms or embodied spirits.[122] Their pararoxical reaction is wonderfully described as disbelieving for sheer joy and wonder.

Unlike the Emmaus scene, the Scripture demonstration here comes after the revelation of Jesus and the meal. First they are recalled to Jesus' words while with them, that all which the Old Testament in its three divisions, the Law, the Prophets and the Psalms, had written about Jesus had to be fulfilled. This is the only place in the New Testament where the three-fold division is explicitly mentioned. The third division represented by the Psalms does not appear to have been clearly defined in Judaism until after the Christians had been expelled. The Psalms are probably mentioned because they provided the bigger number of Messianic texts. It all now becomes clear to them at last when Jesus removes their prejudiced reading of the Old Testament, opens their minds as on the road to Emmaus (v 32) and interprets it for them properly (Ac 8:31ff). Then a preview as it were, a bridge to Vol II, i.e. Acts, is given. Luke is evidently in a hurry here to get on to the story of Acts and the concluding part of the gospel after the apparition of Jesus is almost an anticlimax.

The brief discourse is both like the previous two (v 6ff, 24ff) and has basically the same argument which Peter will use at Pentecost. In the name, i.e. the person, of the dead and risen Messiah, the apostles' preaching and witness will take place, beginning at Jerusalem with the gift of the Spirit and going out thence "to all nations."[123] It gives the essentials of the Christian message or proclamation (kerygma) such as is found in Peter's five sermons in Acts (Ac 2:14ff; 3:13ff; 4:10ff; 5:30ff; 10:36ff) and Paul's speech at Antioch (Ac 13:17-41). Thus Jesus is shown to be the originator of the preaching and teaching of the Apostles whose mission will be to witness to the fulfilment of Scripture. It refers to the "divine must" of the suffering and Resurrection of Jesus which was also foretold in the Scripture,[124] to repentance and forgiveness of sins,[125] to the apostles, the witnesses (Is 43:10ff)[126] and to the spirit which Jesus himself will send down on them (11:13; Ac 1:4f; 2:33). It is still the same mission of Jesus but now it includes the Gentiles to which the Lucan Jesus in particular never went. This mission is founded in Scripture and is now guided by the Spirit. In fact, all three evangelists in whom the risen Jesus speaks, attribute to the risen Jesus or perhaps read back into these narratives as some would put

Jerusalem

it, instructions on the mission of the church as the immediate result of the resurrection. In each gospel the words of the risen Jesus reflect the style and theology of the particular evangelist. Acts, however, shows that convictions about this mission were only gradually attained by the early disciples.

The risen Jesus departs to be at God's right hand (Ac 7:56) but promises the Spirit before he goes as the beginning of the new movement to the Gentiles, which will be the real glory of Israel.[127] "The promise of my Father" is an unusual description of the Spirit (Joel 2:28ff). "Power from on high" (24:19; Ac 2:1ff) is a clear warning that the disciples' own resources are not sufficient for effective witness.[128] It reminds us too how Luke emphasized the descent of the spirit on Jesus himself almost to the exclusion of his baptism (3:21f). Note how Luke connects "power" and the "spirit" (1:35; 4:14; 24:49; Ac 1:8; 3:1-10; 2 K 2:9-13).

(4) *The Ascension—(24:50-53):*

The texts in the New Testament which deal with the ascension are classified by the biblical scholar, P. Benoit into three categories:

(a) Texts which affirm the exaltation of Jesus into heaven, to the right hand of the Father but do not mention the ascension.[129]

(b) Texts which mention the ascension as a purely theological or dogmatic fact but neither fix the time or place or describe witnesses.[130]

(c) There are two texts peculiar to Luke in which the ascension is represented as a sensibly observed fact (Lk 24:50f; Ac 1:9f).[131]

Benoit comments that "Luke is not giving us a journalist's account but a piece of theological teaching . . . ". "The earliest Christian theologians place the ascension of the Lord on Easter-Day itself. Theologically this is the only possible solution. Jesus does not wait in a cave in Jerusalem for the door of heaven to be opened. From the very instant that he issues from death, he enters into Life. What are we to make, then, of the ascension of the Mount of Olives? It is the final departure. Jesus who has ascended into heaven chooses to come down again—these are very clumsy expressions, God's world is not a world like ours, it has other dimensions—for a period of appearances. He lives in another world, but reveals himself still from time to time in this one in order to give proof that he is living and to instruct and encourage his faithful. Luke mentions a period of forty days, a figure which seems perfectly plausible."[132]

Possibly one could conclude from the forty days period in Acts that Luke intends the end of his gospel to be a somewhat artificial summary of and introduction to the events related in more detail in Acts. The Ascension here is pictured as taking place on Easter Sunday Evening (also 23:43). In the gospel the Ascension is clearly distinct from Jesus' vanishing at Emmaus. It has a finality about it signifying that Jesus has completed his missionary journey (9:51). One should note that our earliest account in 1 Cor 15:3ff presupposes a limited number of appearances.

In Acts, Luke makes a clear distinction between the Resurrection, Ascension and Pentecost as almost three separate events which have become three distinct feasts in the church's calendar. Some scholars would conclude that Luke is more concerned with theology than exact chronology (Note Ac 7:23,30,36; 13:21), that he has strung out as it were in chronological framework events that writers like John (Jn 20:17) have described on the evening of the first Easter.[132] Certainly in 1 Cor 15:3-8 and Matthew and the shorter Mark, there is no separation between the Ascension and the Resurrection. In Luke, unlike John, the Spirit is given after the departure of Jesus. Thus the Ascension is the

Jerusalem

key point in Luke's theological plan as it separates the era of Jesus from the era of his church guided by his spirit. However, at the conclusion of Matthew there is no Ascension or sending of the Holy Spirit as Jesus is already in heaven and promises his disciples that he will be with them until the end of time.

There is difficulty over whether to read v 51 "and he was taken up to heaven," but again our decision here is to include it with the vast majority of the readings from about A.D. 200 apart from the Western readings, even though they have a wider support here than in the cases treated above. Its inclusion fits in well with Luke's summary in Acts "all that Jesus began to do and teach until the day when he was taken up to heaven" (Ac 1:1f). It is the obvious climax to Luke's treatment of the gospel. Its omission can be explained as a "homoeoarcton," where the scribe accidentally jumped from one "kaia" to another "kaia" in the Greek text. Possibly they were also omitted by scribes who in view of Acts did not want to describe the Ascension on Easter Sunday (as in Mark 16:19 and also in the Epistle of Barnabas 15:9). Similarly, the phrase "they worshipped him," which was omitted when the scribe's eye jumped to a similar word, should be included in v 51 (see 4:7f, the only other place where Luke uses the phrase).

Finally, Jesus takes the initiative and "leads them out near Bethany" on the slopes of the Mount of Olives (Ac 1:12). This seems quite an artificial joining here as we have heard frequently even before the last apparition about the lateness of the time of day. No mention of the time is actually given. Jesus is pictured like a priest giving his blessing with uplifted hands at the end of a solemn celebration (Sir 50:19f; Num 6:23ff; Heb 8:1; see also Elijah's departure in 2 K 2). Quite possibly there is an allusion to the risen Jesus as replacing the traditional temple ritual and purpose as is explained in Hebrews. The expression "he was taken up" was often used in the Old Testament to describe sacrifices.[133] In contrast to Matthew's final scene Jesus departs from his disciples and no final words of his are recorded.

The parting of Jesus is not an occasion of sadness but they return to Jerusalem and its temple where it all began, according to Luke (1:5), with great joy, as they finally are able to understand the meaning of it all (Jn 14:28). Luke begins with praise (1:9) and leaves us with a vision of model Jewish disciples continually praising God in the temple (Ac 2:46; 3:1; 5:42). The tragic separation of Christianity from the synagogues will be told in Acts. There they wait the coming of the Spirit. Thus Luke ends both his gospel and his Acts on an incomplete note of waiting.

FOOTNOTES

INTRODUCTION
1. E.A. LaVerdiere S.S.S., & W.G. Thompson S.J., *New Testament Communities in Transition,* —A Study of Matthew and Luke in Theological Studies, p. 570ff.
3. A.J. Hultgren, *Interpreting the Gospel of Luke,* (Interpretation, 1976), p. 362ff.
4. Robert J. Karris, *Invitation to Luke,* (Doubleday, New York, 1977), p. 26.
5. *According to the Scriptures,* (London 1952), p. 110.
6. L.E. Keck, J.L. Martyn, (ed), *Studies in Luke and Acts,* (Abingdon Press, Nashville, 1966), p. 23.
7. *Ibid.,* p. 16.
8. C.H. Talbert, *Intepretation,* 1976, pp. 381-395.

CHAPTER ONE
1. The Expository Times, *Form Criticism,* February 1976, p. 137.
2. J. Jeremias, *The Parables of Jesus,* (1965), pp. 113ff.
3. H. Conzelmann, *The Theology of St. Luke,* (Faber & Faber, London, 1960).
4. W. Marxsen, *Mark the Evangelist,* (Abingdon Press, Nashville, 1969).
5. *Ibid.,* 5, p. 12.
6. E.g. Ac 2:23; Lk 1:68,78; 2:49; 4:43; 7:16 etc.
7. H. Flender, *Theologian of Redemptive History,* (S.P.C.K., London) p. 123ff.
8. *Ibid.,* p. 8ff.
9. O. Cullmann, *Christ and Time,* (S.C.M. London, 1962).
10. Compare Lk 9:27 and Mk 9:1; Lk 21:8 and Mk 13:6; read 12:49f; 19:11; 21:9-24; 22:69.
11. 10:9-11; 12:38-48; 12:54-13:9; 18:8; 21:32.
12. Roland Oliver, *The Missionary Factor in East Africa,* (Longmans, London, 1966) p. vii.
13. C.K. Barrett, *Luke the Historian in Recent Studies,* (Epworth Press, London, 1961).
14. Essays on New Testament Themes, (S.C.M. London, 1964), p. 29.
15. Barrett, *ibid.,* p. 53.

16. J. Jeremias, *Theology,* p. 41.
17. G.B. Caird, *St. Luke,* (Pelican Commentaries, London 1963), p. 20.
18. A.N. Sherwin-White, *Roman Society and Roman Law in the New Testament,* (Oxford University Press, 1963). He discusses for example, the best known contemporary of Jesus, the well-documented figure of Emperor Tiberius Caesar, p. 187. The story of Tiberius is known from four sources, the Annals of Tacitus and the biography of Suetonius, written some eighty or ninty years later, the brief contemporary record of Velleius Patercules, and the third century history of Cassius Dio. These disagree among themselves 'in the wildest possible fashion, both in major matters of political action or motive and in the specific details of minor events.' Tacitus is recognized as the best source, 'yet no serious modern historian would accept at face value the majority of the statements of Tacitus about the motives of Tiberius. But this does not prevent the belief that the material of Tacitus can be used to write a history of Tiberius.'
19. See John L. McKenzie in *The Jerome Biblical Commentary,* R.E. Brown etc., (ed) (Chapman, Dublin, 1968), p. 755f.
20. J.P. Kealy, *The Changing Bible,* (Dimension Books, New Jersey, 1977), p. 47ff.
21. Caird, p. 47f.
22. *Light on the Gospels,* (Thomas More Press, Chicago, 1976), p. 143.
23. E.J. Tinsley, *The Gospel According to Luke,* (Cambridge University Press, 1965), p. 7ff.
24. Eric Franklin, *Christ the Lord,* (S.P.C.K., London, 1975), p. 178.
25. J. Drury, *Tradition and Design in Luke's Gospel,* (Darton, Longman & Todd, London, 1976), p. XII.
26. M. Goulder, *Midrash and Lection in Matthew,* (S.P.C.K., London, 1974).
27. The existence of Q has been compared to the existence of the planet Pluto, which for many years was known only through its influence on Neptune.
28. See the chapter 'The Central Section of St. Luke's Gospel, in *Studies in the Gospels,* D.E. Nineham (ed), (Blackwell, 1955). Evans sees Luke as bringing out the truth that Jesus was the prophet like Moses described in Dt. 18:15.
29. P.R. Ackroyd etc., (ed), *Cambridge History of the Bible, Vol. I,* (1963-1970), p. 229.
29a. R. Le Deaut in "Apropos a Definition of Midrash", Interpretation 1971, pp. 268-9, well insists on the complexity of Midrash. "Midrash is in effect a whole world which can be discovered only

by accepting its complexity at the outset. It is pervasive throughout the whole Jewish approach to the Bible, which could in its entirety be called midrash. Technique and method cannot be separated, even if they lead to different literary genres. Midrash may be described but not defined, for it is also a way of thinking and reasoning which is often disconcerting to us."
30. John McHugh, *The Mother of Jesus in the New Testament,* (Darton, Longman & Todd, London, 1975), p. 22ff.
31. See Caird's balanced view in note 17 above.
32. H.H. Oliver, *The Lucan Birth Stories and the Purpose of Luke, Acts,* New Testament Studies, 10:202-226, (1964). See also the extensive treatment in John McHugh, note 30.
33. Quoted in McHugh, p. 133f.
34. *Ibid.,* p. 317.
35. *Ibid.,* p. 40ff, 57.
36. See Conzelmann, note 3, p. 14.
37. *Ibid.,* pp. 172, 118.
38. Charles, H. Talbert, *The Recent Study of the Gospel of Luke,* Interpretation, (1977), p. 385.
39. Keck & Martyn, *Studies in Luke-Acts,* (Abingdon Press, Nashville, 1966), pp. 113ff.
40. R.C. Fuller etc., *A New Catholic Commentary on Holy Scripture,* (Nelson, London), p. 859f.
41. *Ibid.,* pp. 988, 990.
42. Drury, p. 50.
43. R.E. Brown, *Virginal Conception of Jesus,* (Chapman, London/Dublin, 1973), p. 52, note 82.
44. R.E. Brown, *The Birth of the Messiah,* (Doubleday & Co., New York, 1976).
45. *Ibid.,* p. 8.
47. See Ac 2:23,32; 3:14-15; 4:10; 10:39-40; 1 Cor 15:3-4 and especially Gal 4:4-5.
48. The Greek New Testament edited by Black, Metzer, Wikgren and Aland, (Stuttgart, 1976). See also the companion volume to the third edition by Bruce M. Metzger, (United Bible Societies, London, 1971).
49. C.K. Barrett, *Luke the Historian,* p. 8.
50. M. Martini, S.J. II Problema della recensionalita del codice B alla luce del papiro Bodmer XIV, (Analecta Biblica, 26). See also Calvin L. Porter in J.B.L. (1962), pp. 363-376.
51. Porter, p. 37f.

CHAPTER TWO
1. Drury, p. 37f.

2. Caird, p. 15.
3. E.g. when he introduces 'Simon's house' in 4:38 he presupposes some knowledge of who Simon was.
4. Examples taken from W.J. Harrington, *The Gospel According to St. Luke*, (Chapman, London, 1968), p. 5,6.
5. See Lk 1:47-55; 2:14,32; 3:4.
6. Lk 8:13,15; Ac 4:4,20; 6:4; 11:19; Mt 23:1-6; Lk 11:37-54.
7. X. Leon-Dufour, *The Gospels and the Jesus of History*, (Collins, London, 1968), pp. 144-145.
8. See Lk 3:7-9; Mt 3:7-10; compare also Lk 11:15-15, Mt 12:24-30, Mt 23:1-6 and Lk 11:37-54.
9. "Whereas Q and to a lesser degree M concentrated on the sayings of Jesus, L is most noticeable for parables and stories of a memorable kind. M attacked the casuistry and frequent hypocrisy of Pharisees directly; L, indirectly by emphasizing the need for humility and the loss of self-righteousness through stories and parables (e.g. Lk 18:9). L is the comfort of the common man, remembering the friend of publicans and sinners. Jesus here emerges as a first-century prophet, surrounded by a band of simple disciples. He stays at the homes of rich friends; his message calls for faith in an uncomplicated manner; his tones are gentle; his raucous notes are few. No eschatological dogma or dream disturbs a Jesus who is sweet reasonableness itself and above all else, sympathetic." W.D. Davies, *Invitation to the New Testament*, (Darton, Longman & Todd, London, 1967), p. 95.
10. Ac 8:1ff; 21:8; 9:52-6; 17:11-19;
11. Lk 10:38-42; 11:27ff; 13:10-17; 23:27-31.
12. E.g. both put in only one multiplication of loaves before the confession of Peter—Lk 9:10-20; Jn 6:1-69.
13. Rom 2:16; 16:25; Gal 1:11; 2 Tim 2:8; 2 Cor 8:18; was translated 'the brother who is famous for the gospel that he wrote.'
14. W. Barclay, *The Gospels and Acts*, Vol. I, (S.C.M. London, 1976), p. 187f.
15. See Lk 7:9; 10:7ff,39; 11:13; 17:7-10; 18:1,14.
16. E.g. 3:15-16;4:14f; 9:43; 11:1,29; 13:1; 17:20; 18:1,9; 19:11; also his most cautious comments (1:56; 3:23; 23:44) contrast with Mark's hyperbolic 'everybody', 'all'.
17. E.g. 1:80 & 3:1-3; 3:20 & 9:9; 4:13 & 22:3; 5:33 & 11:1; 8:2b & 23:55b; 9:1-6 & 10:1; 9:9 & 23:8; 18:31 & 24:25b; 20:19 & 22:2; 20:25 & 23:2; 21:37 & 22:39; also compare the developing hostility in 6:11; 11:53f; 19:47f; 22:2,54.
18. Stephen Neill, *Jesus Through Many Eyes*, Vol. I (Fortress Press, Philadelphia, 1976), p. 130.
19. Found separately in Mark 1:1-8 and in 6:17-19, which describes his execution—omitted by Luke as he also omits the deaths of Peter and Paul.

Notes

20. 4:30; 9:31,51; 12:32; 24:26,51-3; Ac 1:1-11; 2:34-6.
21. See 9:51,53,56f; 10:1,38; 11:1; 13:22,31,33; 14:25; 17:11ff; 18:31; 19:1,11,28,41; 22:39; 24:50; Ac 1:8.
22. Lk 24:49; Ac 1:4; 2:46; 3:1-3; 5:20-42.
23. Ac 9:27; 15:2-22; see also 8:14-25; 11:1-22; 12:25; 13:13.
24. The oldest title which the early Christians used to describe themselves—Ac 9:2; 19:9-23; 22:4; 24:14-22;—this is an extension of a use wihch is found in the Old Testament in Dt 8:6; 26:17; 28:9; 30:16; Is 35:8; 40:3.
25. See the many *pro (pre)*compounds in Acts 2:23; 3:18ff; 4:28; 7:52; and his references to Jesus' 'appointed course' and God's plan Lk 22:22; Ac 2:23; 10:42; 17:26,31.
26. The verb 'to be filled with' is found almost exclusively in Luke's Gospel or Acts (22 times) with only two occasions in Matthew. Of sixteen instances of the adjective 'full' eleven are in Luke e.g. 4:1.
27. 2:49; 4:43; 9:22; 13:16,33; 17:25; 19:5; 21:9; 23:37; 24:7,26,44; Ac 10:8ff; 13:46; 26:14; and for Paul's 'must' 9:16; 14:22; 19:21; 23:11.
28. Caird, p. 34f points out that—
    "Jesus fulfilled not just a few isolated promises made by the prophets but the whole tenor, purport and pattern of Old Testament teaching and history. In particular he fulfilled the Exodus and the Passover. The Exodus in which God had brought his people through slavery to freedom, had made them a nation, had bound them to himself by a gracious covenant, and had provided the basic pattern for the interpretation of Israel's subsequent history. The Lord their God who had brought them out of Egypt would redeem them from every other humiliation, deserved or undeserved, and bring them in the end through the cleansing fires of affliction to their destined glory. The faith was kept alive by the annual memorial service of the Passover, which looked back to the historic emancipation and forward to God's future reign of righteousness and peace. Thus when Luke calls Christ's death his exodus which he was to fulfil in Jerusalem (9:31) and later links that death with the fulfilling of the Passover in the Kingdom of God (22:16), he means us to understand that in Christ God has brought to completion the great plan of redemption of which the whole story of the Old Testament was a prophetic forecast."
29. 7:19; 10:1,39,41; 11:39; 12:42; 13:15; 16:8; 17:5f; 18:8; 19:8; 22:61; 24:3,34.
29a. See also 1:47 where he uses the title of God, also 2:21 where he draws attention to Jesus' name, a noun for salvation is used at 2:30

and 3:6 and another in 1:69,71,77; in 19:9 Jesus is salvation for Zacchaeus' house.
30. Navone, pp. 88ff, A.R.C. Leaney, pp. 34ff, Marshall, pp. 89ff.
31. See also 9:21; 13:35; 19:42-5; 20:41-4; 22:67-70; 23:2-3; 35:8.
32. I de la Potterie, *Excerpta Exegetica ex Evangelio Sancti Lucae,* class notes, Rome 1963, pp. 17ff.
33. Gal 5:22; Eph 5:9; Lk 3:21; 5:16; 6:12; 11:1; 22:32,41; 23:34.
34. G.W.H. Lampe, *The Holy Spirit in the Writings of St. Luke,* in Essays in Memory of R.H. Lightfoot, D.E. Nineham (ed), (Oxford, 1963), p. 169.
35. 24:53—in the Temple speaking the praises of God—see Ac 10:23,30; 13:3f; Lk 2:14,29; 7:50; 8:48; 19:38,42; 24:36; Ac 7:26; 9:31; 15:23.
35a. Luke uses the more dynamic verb 'to proclaim the good news' 10 times in the gospel and 15 times in Acts. Mark only uses the noun 'good news' or 'gospel'. Matthew follows Mark apart from one use of the verb in a quotation (Mt 11:5). No adequate explanation of this phenomenon has been given. Luke's use of the verb seems due to the preference of the LXX for the verb.
36. Lk 2:14,29; 7:50; 8:48; 19:38,42; 24:36; Ac 7:26; 9:31; 15:23.
37. John Navone S.J. *Themes of St. Luke,* (Gregorian University Press, Rome, 1970), pp. 73ff.
38. Lk 1:46,48,68; 2:13,20,28,38; 5:25; 7:16; 13:13; 18:43; 23:37; 24:53.
39. Compare Mk 2:17; Mt 9:13 and Lk 5:32; also Mk 4:15; Mt 13:19 and Lk 8:12.
40. D. Macpherson, *Scripture Discussion Commentary, Luke,* (Sheed & Ward, London, 1971), p. 5.
41. Lk 7:11-17,35-50; 8:2f; 10:38-42; 11:27f; 13:10)17; 15:8-10; 18:1-8; 23:27f,49,55; 24:6-11.
42. See 4:16-30; 5:1-11 and Peter's reminder in Acts 10 and 11.
43. I de la Potterie, p. 6.
44. A common prophetic theme—Is 45:14-17; 49:12; Jer 12:15-16; Mal 1:11; Ps 106.
45. Lk 2:41ff; 4:4; 5:14; 6:1ff; 9:42; 12:24; 13:43; 14:1; 17:10ff; 21:20;
46. See Luke's texts on final salvation—9:26; 12:35-48; 17:22-37; 18:8; 19:11-27; 21:5,36.
47. Note how Matthew, probably writing much later, inverts the order of the words to emphasize repentance over an imminent judgement.
48. J. Kodell, *The Theology of Luke in Recent Study,* Biblical Theological Bulletin, Vol. I, n2, (June 1971), pp. 134ff.
49. Ac 1:8; 10;39; also Lk 24:48; and Luke's opening appeal to eyewitnesses 1:1-4.

Notes

50. John P. Kealy, & David W. Shenk, *The Early Church and Africa,* (Oxford University Press, Nairobi, 1975), pp. 54ff.
51. Xavier Leon-Dufour S.J., *The Gospels and the Jesus of History,* (Desclee, New York, 1968), p. 149.
52. 5:32; 7:36-50; 13:1-5; 15:1-32; 16:27-31; 19:1-10; 23:39-43.
53. 1:20,45; 7:50; 8:12f,48-50; 17:5-6, 12-19; 18:8-42; 22:32; 24:25.
54. 6:27-42; 10:25-37; 17:3-4.
55. 6:30; 11:41; 12:33; 16:9; 18:22; 21:1-4; Ac 9:36; 10:24,31; 11:29; 24:17.
56. 11:1-13; 18:1-8; 21:36; 22:40-6.
57. 5:11,28; 12:13-34; 14:25-35; 16:1-13; 18:24-30.
58. 1:14,28,41,44,47; 2:10; 6:23; 8:13.
59. 10;17; 13:17; 19:37.
60. 8:14; 10:14f; 12:11,22-5; 21:34.
61. A. George, *Pour lire L'Evangile selon Saint Luc,* (Editions du cerf, Paris, 1973), p. 9.
62. George, p. 64, Navone, p. 127. Drury, p. 70.
63. Flender, pp. 151f.

CHAPTER THREE

1. Ex 15; Num 23:25; Dt 33; Jdg 5; 2 S 22:23; Jonah; Daniel.
2. A.J. Hultgren, *Interpreting the Gospel of Luke,* Interpretation (1977), p. 357.
3. 1 Sam 1:2; 2 Sam 6:23; Pss 127:3-6; 128:3-4; Dt 7:11-13; 25:5-6; 1 Sam 24:21.
4. It should be noted also that in Acs, Cornelius is described in language similar to that of Zechariah (Ac 10:2,31,35).
5. Matthew also uses it in 1:20ff—see (Gn 16:7ff) Ishmael; (Gn 17:1ff) Isaac; (Jdg 13:3ff) Samson; also the divine commissions to Moses (Ex 3:2ff) and Gideon (Jdg 13:3ff).
6. Caird comments (p. 51)—
"It is inevitable that our religious experiences clothe themselves in garments provided by our habitual cast of thought. All those who have had any vivid sense of God's presence have wanted to speak of it in terms of seeing and hearing, though well aware that God himself can be neither heard nor seen. In early times the Israelites overcame this difficulty by speaking of God's presence as his 'angel' (Gn 22:11; Ex 23:20; cf Is 63:9), and this reverential manner of speech later developed into a belief that Gabriel was especially the angel or revelation."
7. Some would add up the various periods of time in these chapters—five months and sixth month (124,26), three months (1:56) eight days (2:21)—to a total of 490 days or seventy weeks of seven days till Jesus is presented in the Temple to fulfill the mysterious prophecy of Daniel.

8. Originally perhaps, abstention from wine (from grapes) and strong drink (other intoxicants), was a prophetic protest against the adaptation of Canaanite customs which led Israel away from God. In the desert, where there was no wine (Jer 2:2), Israel had been loyal to Yahweh. For John the only intoxicant will be the Holy Spirit. He is only taking part of the vow outlined in Num 6:1-8, yet, he is clearly calling to mind the Nazarites (Num 6:23; Jdg 13:4 and 1 Sam 1:11).
9. Dt 30:2; Hos 3:5; Chr 15:1ff; Lk 3:1-4; 7:24ff.
10. A phrase used in Zechariah 12:7,8,10,12; 13:1.
11. Some suggest that the translations should be "rejoice', a salutation based on Zeph 3:14-17, where the people of Israel are personified as the "daughter of Zion" who is invited to rejoice because the Lord is within her bringing victory. However, the connection of one word is somewhat tenuous—see Ac 15:23; 23:26, where the sense is a conventional greeting.
12. E.g. Moses (Ex 3:11ff), Gideon (Jdg 6:15f), Sion (Zeph 3:16f).
13. Luke does not explain the name which Mary is to give, just as he gave no explanation for John's name (in Matthew it is Joseph).
14. Is 9:6-7; Ps 132:11-12; Dn 7:14; Hos 3:5.
15. A Lucan title for God e.g. 1:35,76; 6:25; Ac 7:48.
16. 2 Sam 7:14; and such royal psalms as Ps 2:7, used by Luke in 3:22 and Ps 89:20ff.
17. Ac 9:20; 13:33; 20:28; Rom 1:3-4.
18. Some would see a reference to the struggle of the unborn babies in the womb of Rebekah (Gn 25:22) and that Luke is showing in anticipation of their careers, that John is already recognising that Jesus is "the mighty one" (3:15-16).
19. I.e. filled with the Holy Spirit—see also similar interpretations in the six texts—1:15,41,67; 2:25,26,27.
20. *Kyrios* clearly refers to Jesus here and is probably used in its post-resurrection meaning.
21. Consult a well referenced Bible such as the Jerusalem Bible for the veritable mosaics of allusions rather than direct quotations from the Old Testament and contemporary Jewish literature.
22. 4:18; 6:17ff; 12:16ff; 16:19ff; 18:19ff.
23. E.g. Ps 8,19,29,33,100,103,104.
24. 1 Sam 9:16; Dt 26:7; Ps 126:23.
25. Zeph 3:17; Ac 2:22; 10:38.
26. Lv 11:44-5; Ps 111:9; Lk 1:39; 11:2; Ac 3:14; 4:27,30.
27. Hesed, Covenant love, the Loving Kindness of Yahweh which initiates the covenant without any recognizable merit on the part of the people—Ex 34:6; 2 Sam 7:15.
28. Is 13:11; Ob 3; Job 15:29; Jer 17:11; Lk 20:10:11; Rom 1:30; 2 Tim 3:2; Jam 4:6; 1 P 5:5.
29. R.E. Brown, p. 363f.

Notes

30. A servant representative of what the servant Israel should be! v 48,54; Ac 3:13,26; 4:27,30.
31. Gn 17:9; Jer 9:25; Rom 2:25ff; Gal 2:7; Col 3:11.
32. Tobit was named after his father, Tob 1:19; See Josephus Ant, 14:1,3,10 and Jubilees 11:14f.
33. R.E. Brown pp. 386ff—a detailed analysis of sources.
34. Ex 4:31; Ru 1:6; Ps 65:10; 80:15; 106:4.
35. 1 Sam 2:10; Jdg 3:9; Ezek 29:21; Ps 18:3; Ps 132:16-17. The symbol of the horn was frequently applied to a king in near Eastern literature. It recalls the image of the sounding of the 'shofar' to announce the coming of the Messiah.
36. Ac 14:10-12; 5:31; 13:26,38.
37. See Mt 2:2 on the star at its rising, a reference to Num 24:17.
38. Is 9:2; 42:6-7; also Jn 1:5ff.
39. Lk 7:16; 11:34-5; 22:53; 23:44; Ac 26:18.
40. Michael Green (ed), *The Truth of God Incarnate,* (Hodder & Stoughton, London, 1977), p. 62—
    "We know that there is no example in the non-christian literature of anything that can be treated as a parallel to the birth-narratives in the gospels. The so-called parallels are for the most part what Dale Moody has elegantly called 'mythological fornication' or obvious compliments to a person regarded as specially eminent. There is nothing in the least like the sober and restrained dignity of the gospels. It is clear that there is no trace whatever of Hellenistic influence in these purely Jewish narratives; parallels to them are to be sought in the Old Testament and nowhere else; and they may well represent the convictions and experiences of those commonly called the 'quiet in the land'."
41. Augustus 2:1; Tiberius 3:1; Claudius, Acts 11:28; 18:2.
42. A term normally applied to Jerusalem—compare 2 Sam 5:7-9 and 1 Sam 16:1ff; 17:12; 20:6ff.
43. Jewish tradition had a very negative view of consensus (2 S 24; Ac 5:37). In Lk 23:4ff Pilate thrice affirms the innocence of Jesus of charges which included an anti Roman tax element.
44. A different word, pandocheion, is used of the Good Samaritan 10:34.
45. John Drury, opus cit, p. 61.
46. Ex 24:17; Ps 29:3; Ac 7:2,55; Rom 6:4.
47. 1:47; 13:17; it is God's own reaction 15:5,7,10,32.
48. Ac 2:36; 5:31; 12:32; Lk 3:22; Phil 2:11; 3:20; Eph 1:20f; Col 2:9ff; Is 9:5f.
49. The title savior is used in the LXX some 30 times of God but never of the Messiah. Neither Matthew nor Mark apply it to Jesus. Lord

is the LXX translation of Yahweh, although in LXX manuscripts before the first century A.D. we note, thanks to discoveries in the Judean desert, that the four letters YHWH regularly appear even in the Greek text. Matthew (21:3) and Mark (11:3) each use it once only of Jesus in contrast to Luke's 19 times in his gospel and more than 40 times in Acts (after Easter). Statistically Christ (12 times e.g. 2:26; 4:41 and 24:26,46, where Jesus speaks of himself as Messiah) and Lord are Luke's favorite titles for Jesus, but Savior is obviously very important to him and his audience.

50. The same word is in 2:13, of the shepherds 2:20, the crowds 19:37.
51. 1:77; 12:51-3; Eph 6:15; Is 9:5; 54:10.
52. 7:16; 13:13; 17:15; 18:45; 19:37; 23:47 (the centurion); 24:53 (the end of the gospel), Ac 2:47; 3:8-9; 4:21; 11:18; 21—20.
52a. The full form of the name, Yehoshua (Joshua) derives from the root 'to help' and originally meant 'Yahweh helps'.
53. 2:22,23,24,27,39 and also 41-2.
54. Luke does not record either a purification, presentation or redemption in the case of John.
55. The word can be translated as holy, righteous, pious, saintly and is also applied to Zechariah and Elizabeth in 1:6 and to Joseph in Mt 1:19.
56. In John, the Holy Spirit is paracletos (Jn 14:26; see 16:1; Jn 2:1).
57. And Joseph of Arimatheia is good and upright . . . waiting for the kingdom of God (Lk 23:50-51).
58. A term also found in Acts 4:24 and in the Septuagint it is applied to God.
59. See the final words of Paul at the very end of Ac 28:28 'salvation has been sent to the Gentiles.
60. 1:63; 2:18,33; 4:22; 8:25; 9:43; 24:12,41; Ac 2:7, 3:12; 4:13; 7:31.
61. Lk 11:29-32; Is 7:14; 11:10-12; 65:2.
62. 13 times in the New Testament, 6 times in Luke e.g. 1:51.
63. See John 5:23; 8:42-7; 9:39; 12:44-50.
64. Ex 22:22; Dt 24:17; Is 1:23; 10;2 2 Sam 14:4ff; Lk 18:3; 20:47.
65. Ac 6:1; 9:39ff; 1 Cor 7:8; 1 Tim 5:3-16.
66. Ac 2:17; 21:9; 1 Cor 11:5.
67. R.E. Brown p. 483.
68. The same expression as in Genesis 3:14; 4:10; 1 Sam 13:11.
69. E.g. 4:43; 9:22; 13:32; 17:25; 22:37; 24:7,26—Lk 18 times, Ac 22, Mt 8 and Mk 6.
70. Also used in 12:25 of one's lifespan and in 19:3 of Zacchaeus' stature.

CHAPTER FOUR
1. See Peter's speech in Ac 10:37 and Paul's 13:24 for Luke's summary of the early preaching.
2. R.E. Brown, p. 250 note.
3. 3:16; Ac 1:5; 11:16; 18:24-19:7.

Notes

4. 4:43; 10:9; 16:16.
5. Compare Luke 4:24-6; 7:11-17 with 1 K 17:18-24; also Lk 9:51 (going up) with 2 K 2:11; Lk 12:4 with 1 K 18:38.
6. Originally the ruler of a fourth of a region but commonly used for a ruler of a small kingdom.
7. Compare Luke 1:13 and Jer 1:5; Lk 3:9ff and Jer 1:10ff; Lk 1:14; 3:15f; 7:18ff and Jer 31:1ff.
8. Is 55:10-11; Ac 10:44; 11:15.
9. Ez 18:23; Amos 7:2ff; Hos 11:8ff.
10. John L. McKenzie, in the *Jerome Biblical Commentary,* pp. 759f.
11. T.W. Manson, *The Servant-Messiah,* (1953), pp. 44-5.
12. See also Is 42:16; 45:2; 49:11; Zech 4:7.
13. 3:4; 7:27; 18:31; 22:37.
14. In Is 40:4c—see Lk 24:26 for a possible explanation.
15. Which Mark attributes also to Isaiah, although it derives from Mal 3:1 and Ex 23:20.
16. McKenzie, *ibid.,* p. 753.
17. 16:29-31; 19:42; 13:16; 19:9.
18. 7:40-3; 14:28-30; 16:1-9; 16:19-31; 19:11-27.
19. See the story of Zacchaeus in 19:8 and the warning on covetousness in 12:15 and the unrighteous money in 16:11.
20. I.e. as the word Messiah means—priest, kings and even prophets (1 K 19:16) were anointed and were thus Messiahs.
   2Joel 3:1ff; Is 44:3; Ez 36:26ff.
38. 2:46; 21:37f; 24:53; Ac 2:46; 5:20-42.
39. E.g. the 'forty nights' (Dt 9:9,18; Ex 34:28), in fact his order of the temptations correspond with the order of the Exodus events (Ex 16:17; 23:24).
40. Jesus is stressed ate nothing but had the spirit.
41. 8:12; 10:18; 11:4,16,18,21; 13:16; 22:3,28,31,53; Ac 5:3; 26:18.
42. A reference to Jesus' baptism 3:22 or perhaps to be understood in the Old Testament sense of God's favorite chosen anointed and obedient one.
43. 19:12-15; 22:69; 23:42; 24:26; Ac 2:36.
44. 2:1; 21:26; Ac 11:26; 17:6,31; 19:27; 24:5.
45. 7:8; 9:1; 10:19; 12:11; 19:17; 20:20; 23:7; Ps 2:8; Dn 7:14; Mt 28:18.
46. 22:25,53; Ac 4:26-7; 26:18; Jn 12:31; 14:30; 16:11.
47. See Jesus' remarks to the sign seekers in 11:29ff; 12:54; 16:31; 2:34.
48. A. Schweitzer, *The Quest of the Historical Jesus,* (Macmillan, New York, 1966), pp. 270f.

CHAPTER FIVE

1. E.g. Lk 4:36,43; 5:17; 6:19; 7:16.39; 8:1,46; 9:2,6,11,43.
2. Compare Luke 4:16-22a with Matthew 4:13 with the unique spelling of the word "Nazara" in both. Augustine actually compared this visit with Matthew 13:54. See also Luke 4:22b-30 with Mark 6:1-6 and Mt 13:54-8.
3. Mk 1:21,39; 6:2; Mt 4:23; Lk 4:16,31,44; 6:6; 13:10.
4. I.e. attendance at the synagogue, a custom which the early church in Acts would follow—e.g. Ac 13:5,14,44; 14:1; 17:1ff; 18:4; 19:8.
5. Is 7:21; 18:35-43.
6. Is 5:17-26; Ac 3:1-10; 8:7; 14:8-10.
7. 5:12-16; 17:11-19.
8. No examples in Luke but in Mark 7:31-37; 9:25.
9. See the parallel scene with Paul's preaching at Antioch (Ac 13:15-51).
10. Mt 4:23; 9:35; 10:17; 12:9; 13:54.
11. This same word 'doxazein' was used of the Shepherds (2:20) and will be used of the paralysed man (5:25f), the people at Nain (7:16), the bent woman (13:13), the one thankful leper (17:15), the blind man (18:43).
12. E.g. the Shema, Dt 6:4-9; 11:13,21; Num 15:37-41.
13. The Torah, the first five books of the Bible which all accepted—Pharisees, Sadducees and Samaritans.
14. However, they had a paid official called a chazzan who looked after the buildings, the scrolls, for announcing the coming of the sabbath with the three blasts of the silver trumpet, for actually calling upon speakers and often also he was the teacher in the synagogue school.
15. Readings were in Hebrew with a running translation into the vernacular Aramaic. This is the only clear statement in the Bible that Jesus could read.
16. E.g. the Hebrew text from the Greek Septuagint was translated, the text which the Samaritans used, the text later canonized by the Hebrew tradition.
17. One notices the "a b b a" structure of Luke's text, as the first and last lines parallel as also the two central lines.
18. 4:18; 6:20ff; 14:12-24; 16:19-31; 1:46-55.
19. 24:47ff; see especially 5:30-32; 11:22; 19:1-10.
20. Dt 4:8,39; 9:3; 11:26,32; 27:9ff; 30:18f.
21. As they cannot see it like the Nazarenes.
22. It is interesting to note that the saying of Jesus discovered at Oxyrhynchus (Papyrus 1 Logion 6) gives a clearer text as it reads: "Jesus says 'A prophet is not acceptable in his own country, neither does a physician cure those who know him" (see also the Gospel of Thoman Logion 31; Mt 13:57; Mk 6:4; Jn 4:44).
23. 24:19; 7:16; 9:8,19; 13:31-3.

Notes

24. Ac 5:52; 3:22f; 7:37.
25. 12:37; 18:17,29; 21:32; 23:43—see also 9:27; 12:44; 21:3; where he translates the Aramaic term by the Greek 'alethos' 'truly'.
26. 1 K 18:12; 2 K 2:9-16; Ac 1:8.
27. 7:1-10; 13:29; 24:47.
28. Jn 7:30,45; 8:59; Dan 6:22.
29. Peter will say "at your word" in 5:5 and a leper will be cured in 5:13 as in the healings here, at the word of Jesus.
30. Jesus is the word of God in John 1:1-18.
31. Ac 6:7; 12:24; 19:20.
32. Ac 5:16; 8:7; 16:16-18; 19:11-17.
33. Lk 8:32; 10:18f; 11:14-23; Is 11:4; 1 Cor 15:25.
34. 4:14f,20,22,36f; 5:15f,26.
35. In blessing Gn 48:14; Mk 10:16.
36. 3:22; 4:3,9,41; 8:28; 9:35; 10:22; 22:70—it is found twice in Ac 9:20; 13:33.
37. 4:43; 8:1; 9:2,11; 16:16; 18:29.
38. 8:12; 20:25; 28:23,31.
39. Mt 11:5; Lk 9:2,11,60; 16:16.
40. 9:22; 13:33; 17:25; 19:5; 22:37; 24:7,26,44,46.
41. Ac 2:23; 3:18; 4:28; 5:29; 9:6,16; 13:27-33; 14:22 27:24.
42. E.g. 1:5; 6:17; 7:17; 23:5; Ac 10:37.
43. A frequent description of the Gospel in Luke which goes back to the prophets 4:32; 8:11,21; 11:28; Ac 4:4,29-31; 6:4; 12:24; 19:20.
44. Everything—5:11,28; 11:41; 18:15ff. Mark and Matthew say that they left their boat and their father.
45. A verb used in the Septuagint to describe not the catching of fish or animals but the saving of men from the danger of death—2 Tim 2:26; Num 31:15ff; Dt 20:16—Here Mark has "fisher of men" an expression whose negative implications Luke avoids.
46. Is 6:5; Gn 18:27; Job 42:6.
47. Here we find the first of seven uses found only in Luke in the New Testament (e.g. 8:24,45; 9:33,49; 17:13). It is the equivalent of 'Rabbi' which he does not use and is found only on the lips of disciples or near disciples (17:3).
48. R.E. Brown, *The Gospel According to John,* (Chapman, London, 1971), Vol. II, p. 1,900.
49. An Exodus reminiscence Ex 6:6; 14:16; 15:12.
50. From every village of Galilee, Judea and Jerusalem—clearly an exaggeration.
51. W. Harrington, *The New Catholic Commentary,* p. 1,002: 74f. V. Taylor, *The Gospel According to Saint Mark,* p. 91.
52. E.g. Mk 11:18 & Lk 19:47; Mk 12:12 & Lk 20:19.
53. See his Our Father, where the forgiveness of sins is included and

physical cures are not mentioned 11:4.
54. Dt 5:9; Ex 20:5; Job 3:3; but see also Jn 9:1 ff; Lk 13:1-5.
55. John P. Kealy, *Who is Jesus of Nazareth,* (Dimension Books, 1977).
56. 5:21; 7:49; 8:25; 9:9,18,20; 19:3.
57. As the shepherds 2:20; the people of Nain 7:16; the bent woman 13:13; the thankful leper 17:15; the blind man 18:43.
58. Which is only mentioned by Luke—he stresses repentance much more than the other synoptics e.g. 3:38; 5:31; 10:13; 11:32; 13:35; 15:7,10; 16:30; 17:34; 24:47.
59. 14:25-33; 18:18 but note that Zacchaeus does not give up everything 19:1-10.
60. 7:36-50; 19:12ff; 10:38-42; 11:37; 14:1ff; 19:7; 22:14-38; 24:30,41ff.
61. Is 25:6-12; 34:6; 55:1; 65:11; Dt 12:4; Zeph 1:7.
62. The Scribes and the Sadducees only appear in 20:27 and Acts.
63. 3:8; 13:1-5; 15:1ff; 16:30f 17:3f; 19:10; 24:27; Ac 19:19; 26:20.
64. G. Vermes, *Jesus the Jew,* (Collins, London, 1973), p. 79.
65. E.g. the betrothal between Yahweh and his people—Hosea 2:19-20; Is 54:5; 62:4-5.
66. Jn 3:28f; Mt 22:2-10; 25:1ff; Eph 5:23; Apoc 19:7; 21:2.
67. Here is the first hint of Jesus' violent death—see 23:18; Ac 8:33; Is 53:8,11; Septuagint.
68. John Drury, *Tradition and Design in Luke's Gospel,* p. 79.
69. 3:8; 5:32; 13:3,5; Ac 2:38; 3:19.
70. Ac 17:30; 20:21; 26:20.
71. In Mark it is Ahimelech's son, Abiather who was high priest.
72. Also the *right* ear in Lk 22:50f; Mk 14:47.
73. 7:19,49; 8:25; 9:9,18,20.
74. Ac 1:24; 6:5; 15:7,22,25.
75. Luke describes two missions 9:1-6 (Mk 6:7-13) and secondly the mission of the seventy 10:1-20; note 12:35 which is similar, is addressed to the twelve.
76. Gn 22:20-4; 25:12-15; 36:10-14.
77. Gn 49; Num 26; Deut 33: Jdg 5.
78. 28 times in Acts, 6 times in Luke 6:13; 9:10; 11:49; 17:5; 22:14; 24:10; but only once each in Mark 6:30 and Matthew 10:2.
79. Ac 1:21f; 14:4; 1 Cor 15:3-9; Gal 1:1; Rom 16:7; Apoc 21:14.
80. E.g. Jn 6:67; 20:24; but note that John has no list.
81. Mk 3:16-19; Mt 10:2-4 and two Lucan lists containing the same names but in different order, Lk 6:14-16; Ac 1:13 (without Iscariot).
82. Lebbaeus in some ancient MSS of Matthew.
83. Thus 6:38a,39,40,45 are found elsewhere in Matthew and some of

Notes

Matthew's extra material (e.g. Matthew 5:13-16 = Lk 14:34f; 11:33; Mt 5:25 = Lk 12:57-9; Mt 5:31 = Lk 16:18) is found later in Luke in his infancy narrative 9:51f.

84. E.E. Ellis, *The Gospel of Luke,* (New Century Bible, Oliphants, London, 1974), p. 109f.
85. Making no difference as to whether a person is a Gentile or a sinful prostitute (7:1-10, 36-50).
86. An expression which may also include Galilee, 4:44.
87. Mt and Lk usually have "all" for Mark's "many".
88. 16:23; 18:13; Jn 4:35; 6:5; 17:1.
89. E.g. Lk 11:28; 12:37; 1:45; Mt 11:6; Jn 20:29; See Ps 1:1; Is 56:2.
90. In Luke they are all in the second person while in Matthew they are in the third person and Luke's four correspond to 1,4,8 in Matthew with Luke 3 resembling Matthew 2. Most commentators favor Matthew's third person as the original version (see Dt 33:29; Is 32:20; Ps 128:2; Ec 10:17; Mal 3:12).
91. The same word is used for Lazarus 16:20 and in Jesus' program in 4:18 and 7:23. In Greek it means a destitute who is a beggar. In the Septuagint it translates " oni" (a dependent) 39 times; "dal" (lowly weak) 21 times; "ebyon" (poor man, beggar) 10 times. It generally has the connotation especially in Psalms (e.g. 86:1; 2:5) of a *non-violent* man, a pious humiliated person who calls on God for assistance.
92. Amos 5:12; Is 49:13; Ps 10:2; 86:1; 107:9ff; Matthew's synonymous "poor in spirit" is found in the Dead Sea Scrolls, meaning either "the faint hearted" or rather "the voluntary Poor" who consider worldly goods as nothing.
93. Ps 42:3; Is 49:10; 55:1; 65:13; Jn 6:35.
94. Ac 5:41; Jn 9:22; 12:42; 16:2; dt 22:13ff; Is 56:3.
95. 11:49-51; 13:34; Ac 7:9-10, 27-9.
96. According to A. Toynbee, *A Study of History,* (Oxford, 1939) pp. 245 ff, the impending reversal of roles is one of the main themes in the New Testament.
97. In Wisdom 3:9 it is used for the love of God and in Wisdom 6:18 for the love of wisdom but in fourteen uses e.g. Jer 2:2 it means sexual love.
98. Ac 10:38; Jn 18:22f; Lk 23:34; Ac 7:60.
99. Found first in Herodotus, also Tobit 4:15; Dt 15:13; Philo; Confucius; the Stoics. In its negative form it can be interpreted as mere cautious prudence.
100. Luke has "sinners" and omits Matthew's "Gentiles" but it is difficult to see him omitting Mt 5:45 "Who makes the sun to rise . . ." if he had to before him.
101. See Ac 5:1ff; 13:44ff; Rom 1:32; 12:19; 1 Cor 5:11ff; Jas 4:11ff.

102. In the Scribes' school the emphasis was not on originality but on handing on what was taught.—Mt 10:24f.
103. R.E. Brown, *The Gospel According to John,* Vol. I, pp. 192f.
104. 23:47; Ac 10:22; 22:26; 23:17,23; 24:23.
105. Compare 4:25 and 1 K 17:9; 8:55 & 1 K 17:21; 9:51; 24:49-51; Ac 1:10 & 1 K 19:7-8.
106. See 4:18,24; 6:22; 7:39; 9:8,30ff; 22:64; 24:19; Ac 3:22; 7:37.
107. Stretching on him three times—See Elisha's similar "kiss of life" 1 K 17:23; 2 K 3:4.
108. 23:47; 2:20; 5:25f; 13:13; 17:15; 18:43; Ac 11:18.
109. 7:19; 10:1.39.41 etc., Phil 2:9f; Eph 4:8; Heb 2:14f.
110. W. Barclay, *New Testament Words,* (S.C.M. London, 1971), p. 276ff.
111. Sean P. Kealy, *That You May Believe,* The Gospel According to John, (St. Paul Publications, Slough, London, 1978), p. 12f.
112. 3:16; 13:35; 19:38; Heb 10:37; Ps 118:26, originally probably from Mal 3:1,23.
113. Jer 20:14;18; 1 K 19:4; Num 20:12.
114. J.D.G. Dunn, *The Birth of Metaphor—Baptized in Spirit,* (Expository Times, February, 1978), p. 136f.
115. Is 35:3-5; 29:18-20; 61:1-2.
116. G. Vermes, *Jesus the Jew,* (Collins, London, 1973), p. 32-3.
117. Lk 10:21; 12:54-6; 1 Cor 1:21-5; Pr 1:8; Sir 1:24; Job 28.
118. Mk 14:3-9; Mt 26:6-13; Jn 12:1-8.
119. The other three evangelists place it late in the ministry, just before the Passion: Mark and Matthew at Bethany.
120. Luke has Simon the Pharisee; Mark has Simon; Matthew has Simon the leper; John names the woman Mary, the sister of Martha and Lazarus from Bethany.
121. In Luke and John she anoints the feet, whereas in Mark and Matthew she anoints the head.
122. See Gn 18:4; 29:13; 45:15; Jdg 19:21; Ps 23:5; 141:5.
123. Ac 10:43; 13:38; 26:18; 28:27-9.
124. See 5:21; 7:19,49; 8:25; 9:9,18ff; 19:3.
125. 8:1,22; 9:1,10,12,18,40,43,46,49.
126. 7:11,24; 8:4,18,40,45.
127. 1:3; Ac 3:24; 11:4; 18:23.
128. 8:9-10; 9:2; 10:9,11.
129. Ac 8:12; 20:25; 28:23,31.
130. 23:49,55; 24:10,33; Ac 1:14,21; 16:14; 18:2; Phil 4:2; 1 Cor 1:11; Rom 16:1; 1 Tim 3:11.
131. Fifty or seventy, according to how one counts them—other Jewish parables are quite inferior except 2 Sam 12; Is 5:17 and Ezech 16.
132. It is interesting to read some of the Fathers further allegorical in-

Notes

terpretations of the variety in the harvest. For Jerome the hundredfold meant virgins, the sixty fold widows and the thirty fold whose who married. For Augustin they were in turn, martyrs, widows and married. The interpretations given to Jesus in the Synoptics are much simplet and more obvious.

133. Mt 13:14f; Mk 4:12; Jn 12:20; Ac 28:26f; Rom 11:8.
134. Mk 4:13ff a parable; Mt. 13:36-43, 49-50.
135. E.g. 5:1; 8:21; 11:28; Ac 4:4; 6:4; 8:4; 10:36,44.
136. 8:13; 4:1-13; 22:28,40ff.
137. R.E. Brown, *The Birth of the Messiah,* p. 318.
138. See Mark 3:32; 6:3; Matthew 12:46; 13:55-6; Jn 2:12.
139. Compare Mark 6:3 and 15:40.
140. Gn 13:8; 37:16; Lev 10:4; 2 K 10:13; 1 Chron 23:22.
141. Ps 107:28ff; 8; 65:7f; 89:9f; 93; 104:5-9; Gn 1:26.
142. "Opposite Galilee", "swine", "among the tombstones".
143. 3:22; 4:3,9,41; 9:35; 10:22; 22:70; Ac 9:20.
144. John P. Kealy, *Who is Jesus of Nazareth?,* (Dimension Books, N.J. 1977), p. 43f.
145. Of the tassels which pious Jews wore Num 15:38ff; Dt 22:12.
146. Mk 5:31; but compare 22:46 with Mk 14:37.
147. 7:50; 8:12,26,48; 17:19; 18:42; Ac 16:31.
148. The order as in 9:28; Ac 1:13; also with James before John 5:10; 6:14; 9:54.
149. 4:15,43; 9:1,11ff; 10:9.
150. Ac 8:12; 10:38; 20:25; 28:23,31.
151. See also the question of Peter which is prepared here 9:18; 4:24.
152. Is 25:6-8; 49:8,10; Ps 23; 2 Bar 29:4; Ezr 6:52; Lk 14:15-24; 15:16-24; 23:30; Rev 7:16.
153. "Took . . . raised his eyes . . . blessed . . . broke . . ." i.e. the words and sequence 22:17ff.
154. 7:16 to the people; the leaders 6:11; 9:7-9.
155. "Anointed one" 2:26; 23:35; Is 61:11; Lk 4:18.
156. See Ac 3:18; 4:26; 17:3; 26:23.
157. 24:26; 2:49; 4:43; Is 53; Zech 13:7-9.
158. 24:25-7,44ff; 9:44ff; 17:25; 18:31ff.
159. See Rom 6:3ff; Col 1:24; Gal 2:20; 1 Cor 13:26; 15:31.
160. 14:26f; 23:26; Ac 9:2; 14:22; Is 40:3.
161. E.g. eight hundred Pharisees had been crucified by Alexander Jannaeus.
162. Lk 14:27; 17:33; Mk 8:34; Mt 10:38f; Jn 12:25.
163. A LXX phrase, Dn 10:6; Nahum 3:3; Exek 1:4-7;
164. Ex 34:29-35 *LXX;* Lk 21:27; 24:26; Ac 3:13; 7:55; 22:11.
165. 2 Mac 2:8; Ex 16:10; 24:15ff; 40:38; 1 K 8:12; Ps 97:2; Ac 1:9.
166. As on the Cross 23:35; Is 42:1,11; Mark has "the beloved".
167. The command of Dt 18:15; Ac 3:22f; 7:37.

168. "The Golden Calf" Ex 32:1-6; 34:29-35; Num 14:27.
169. 11:19; Ac 3:6; 16:18; 19:13f; 1 Cor 12:3—note the similar situation in Num 11:24ff.

CHAPTER SIX

1. An interesting suggestion by C.F. Evans has not gained widespread acceptance (The Central Section of St. Luke's Gospel in *Studies in the Gospels,* D.E. Nineham (ed), Oxford, 1967, pp. 37-53). He suggests that to emphasize the truth that Jesus Christ is the Deuteronomic prophet like Moses (Dt 18:5), Luke actually modelled this section on Deuteronomy as a Christian counterpart to Moses' instructions to the Israelites as they complete their journey to Jericho and the promised land. However, some scholars like John Bligh who has put the parallel passages side by side in his book *Christian Deuteronomy,* (St. Paul's, Langley, 1970) do not deny that some of the connections are too ingenious to be attributed to St. Luke. His parallels, which run from Lk 10:1-18:14, are as follows with Luke first and Deuteronomy and Kings in brackets:—9:51-6 (2 K 1:9-15); 9:57-10:1 (1 K 19:1-21); 10:1-3,17-20 (Dt 1:19-25); 10:14-16 (Dt 2:26-35; 3:1-3); 10:17-20 (3:3-7, 23-27); 10:21-24 (4:5-8,32-40); 10:25-37 (6:4-9; 7:1-6); 10:38-43 (8:1-3); 11:1-13 (8:5-20); 11:14-26 (9:1-7); 11:27-8 (10:12-15; 11:26-8); 11:29-36 (10:16-11:7); 11:37-12:7 (11:22-9: 27:14-26); 12:8-12 (12:1-11); 12:13-21 (12:10-14, 17-19); 12:22-34 (12:29-32); 12:35-48 (13:1-5); 12:49-53 (12:6-11); 12:54-13:9 (13:12-18); 13:18-30 (15:19-23); 13:31-5 (16:1,5-17); 14:1-6 (16:18-20; 17:8-13); 14:7-11 (17:14-20); 14:12-14 (18:1-8); 14:15-24 (18:9-14); 14:25-33 (18:15-22); 15:1-10 (19:1-13); 15:11-32 (19:15-21); 16:1-13 (20:1-8); 16:13-15 (20:19-20); 16:16-17 (21:1-9); 16:18 (21:10-17); 16:19-31 (21:18-22); 17:1-10 (22:1-12); 17:11-21 and 18:1-8 (22:13-21); 18:9-14 (23:2-6, 17-23); 18:15-17 (2 K 2:23-8).

   Certainly some of the parallels are striking but hardly sufficient to prove a detailed correlation.

   See also John Drury, *Tradition and Design in Luke's Gospel,* p. 138ff.
2. E.g. 9:60ff; 11:2ff; 12:8ff; 14:25ff; 16:10ff; 17:1ff; 18:15ff.
3. 10:3f; 11:29ff; 12:1f; 16:14f.
4. 9:51,53; 13:22,33f; 17:11; 18:31; 19:11.
5. 10:1,21; 12:1; 13:1,10,31f; 14:1.
6. Drury, pp. 144f.
7. 2 K 12:17; Ez 6:3; 13:17; 14:8, where the phrase denotes determination in the face of hostility.
8. 2 K 2:9-11; Sir 48:8; 1 Macc 2:58.
9. Jn 4:9,20; 2 K 17:24ff; Ezr 4:3ff; Neh 4:1ff.

Notes

10. E.g. "the Son of Man came not to destroy but to save" see 19:10; 23:34.
11. Gen 10 has 70/72 nations of the world; Num 11:16 has 70/72 (Eldad and Meded) elders assist Moses during the Exodus; the Septuagint was translated by 70/72 translators; the Sanhedrin had 70 members—in all there are about 20 instances in Jewish literature involving 70/72.
12. 1 Cor 9:7,14; 1 Tim 5:18; Mt 10:10 has food for wages.
13. Mt 9:37; Jn 4:35; Joel 3:13; Apoc 14:18.
14. E.g. the symbols of demonic forces, snakes and scorpions, Ac 28:3-5; Mk 16:18.
15. Ex 32:32-33; Is 4:3; Dn 10:21; 12:1; Ps 69:28; 87:4-6; 139:16; Phil 4:3; Heb 12:23; Apoc 3:5; 13:8; 17:8; 20:15—ancient cities put up a list of their citizens.
16. J.D.G. Dunn, *Spirit and Kingdom,* Expository Times, Vol 80, pp. 26-40.
17. Quoted in A.M. Hunter, *Teaching and Preaching the New Testament,* (Westminster Press, Philadelphia, 1963), p. 41.
18. John Reumann, *Jesus in the Church's Gospels,* (Fortress Press, Philadelphia, 1973), p. 292f.
19. The basic verb as in the temptation scene—4:2; also 22:28.
20. See also the question to John "What shall we do?" in Luke 3:10ff; Ac 2:37; 16:30.
21. For St. Augustine, the centrality and supremacy of the love commandments meant that one did not really understand any section of the Bible properly unless it taught love of God and love of one's neighbor, *De Doctrina Christiana,* 1.36. His allegorical interpretation, for which he found justification in 2 Cor 3:6, is famous. The man on the Jericho way is mankind (Adam) attacked by the devil and his angels, uncared for by the Old Testament priesthood and ministry but rescued by Jesus, the Good Samaritan and brought to the Church (the inn) whose function is the refreshment of travellers on their way to heaven.
22. Thus the phrase "Love the Lord and your neighbor" is found twice in *The Testaments of the XII Partriarchs,* but the dating of this work is disputed and Christian influence is quite possible.
23. A key word repeated three times in 10:25,28,30; 6:31ff,46ff.
24. E.g. Lev 18:5; Dt 30:15ff; Rom 10:5; Gal 3:12.
25. 12:13ff,42ff; 13:23ff; 14:15ff.
26. See 2 Chron 28:14ff1 for a similar story about compassionate Samaritans.
27. See also 7:13; 1:78-9; Dt 22:4; Is 58:7.
28. 10:33-5—Luke's medicine was the disinfectant of his time, not ours—Is 1:6; Mk 6:13; Jas 5:14—the two denarii, or two days wages would pay for about twenty four days rations, Mt 20:2.

29. 4:4; 6:46ff; 16:19ff; Dt 8:3ff.
30. 4:39; 7:36-50; 11:37; 14:7-14; 19:5; 22:14-28; Ac 16:14f.
31. 8:14; 12:11,22ff; 21:34; Mt 6:25ff.
32. See Ac 6:1ff; Gn 43:34; Eccles 11:10.
33. Bligh,—41f.
34. 6:35; Rom 8:15; Gal 4:6; Jn 14:13f; 15:7; 16:23f.
35. Compare Matthew's 7:21 and Luke 6:46; Mt 12:50 and Lk 8:21; Mt 18:14 and Lk 15:7; Mt 21:31 and Lk 15:11ff.
36. For Matthew's today Luke has daily as in 9:23, to bring out his emphasis on discipleship each day.
37. Jn 6:54; Lk 14:15; Mt 15:26; 1 Cor 11:26.
38. 18:33; 6:35; 23:34; Eph 4:32; Col 3:13.
39. Gn 22:1; Ex 17:7; Ac 5:9; 1 Cor 10:9; Heb 3:9.
40. James 1:13; 1 Cor 6:18; 10:14; 1 Tim 6:11; 2 Tim 2:22.
41. Lev 16:10; Is 13:21; Tob 8:3; Bar 4:35; 2 Cor 5:1; Apoc 18:2.
42. See Mt 7:22; 1 Jn 4:1; 2 Thess 2:9; Apoc 13:13ff.
43. For Bultmann, this saying can—
    "Claim the highest degree of authenticity we can make for any saying of Jesus; it is full of that feeling of eschatological power which must have characterized the activity of Jesus."
    The History of the Synoptic Tradition, (Blackwell and Harper, 1963), p. 162.
    According to W. Wilkinson, (p. 73 note)
    "Luke never uses the phrase 'Spirit of God', or 'God's Spirit'. For Luke, the Holy Spirit is always connected with Jesus; preparing men for his coming into the world; fully incarnate in him during his earthly life; and filling his followers after Pentecost."
44. 4:9-12; 2:34; Jn 4:48; Ac 2:22; 1 Cor 1:22ff.
45. 1:78-9; 8:15; 11:34-5; 16:15.
46. Jn 1:7ff; 3:19; 8:12; 9:40f; 1 Jn 1:5; Jam 1:17.
47. See Mt 23:13-21—the end in particular, 23:4,6,7,13,25,27,29-31, 34-6, also Mk 76:1-9 and not Luke's changes at Lk 11:37,41,49.
48. 7:4ff; 12:21,33; 16:9,19ff; Ac 2:41-7; 4:31-5; 8:27; 10:2ff.
49. Lev 27:30; Dt 14:22 which concerned the main crops.
50. Mt 23:23—"have neglected the weightier matters of the law, justice, mercy and faith', Mic 6:8; Amos 5:21ff; Hos 6:4-7; Is 1:10ff.
51. See Kealy, *Who is Jesus of Nazareth?,* p. 93ff.
52. 2 Chron 24:32; note that Mt 23:35 calls him the son of Barachiah, making his identification uncertain (Zech 1:1). He could in fact be the Zechariah killed in the temple by guerillas in A.D. 68.
53. 13:28; 18:31; 24:25ff; Ac 3:18,24; 10:43; 24:14.

Notes

54. Wilkinson, *Good News in Luke,* p. 77f.
55. 2:35; 8:17; Heb 4:13; 1 Cor 4:5; Rom 2:16.
56. Gn 39:9; Ezra 8:22; Neh 6:11; Heb 12:28; 1 Jn 4:18; Jam 4:7; 1 P 5:9.
57. Lev 18:21; John 15:8; 18:16; 1 K 11:7; 2 K 23;10; 2 Chron 28:3; Jer 7:31ff; 10:6; 32:35; 1 Enoch 27:2.
58. Mt 10:32; Rom 10:9; Phil 2:11; 1 Tim 6:13; Apoc 3:5.
59. Ac 4:8; 6:8ff; 19:21-41; 23:1-11; the final verse of Acts.
60. E.g. 7:40-43; 14:28-30;16:1ff,19ff; 19:11ff.
61. E.g. Lk 12:15ff; Mt 18:21ff; Mk 3:23ff; Jn 3:8 and Lk 12:27ff.
62. J. Jeremias, *New Testament Theology,* (S.C.M. London, 1972), p. 9ff.
63. 12:22-32; Ac 5:1ff; 8:9ff; Mt 6:19-21; 1 Tim 6:17ff; Jam 2:5.
64. Dt 4:29; Amos 5:4; Mt 6:33 adds "and his righteousness".
65. See Acts 20:28; Lk 10:21; 2:14; Mt 10:42; 1 P 5:2-4—in the Old Testament it signifies the people of Israel, Zech 10:3;11:11; 13:79; Dn 7:27.
66. See v 31; 10;38; Jn 13:29; 19:27; Ac 2:41ff; 4:31-5; Rom 15:25-8; 1 Cor 16:1-4; 2 Cor 8:1-4; 1 Tim 6:9ff.
67. 17:20-18:8; 21:5-36; Mt 24:25-31; Mk 13:33-7.
68. The five parables in the gospels which deal especially with this problem are: The Wise and Foolish Virgins (Mt 25:1-13; Lk 12:35); The Thief (Lk 12:39-40; Mt 24:43-44); The Doorkeeper (Mk 13:33-7; and par); The Faithful and Wise Servant (Lk 12:41-6; Mt 24:45-51): The Talents (Lk 19:12-27; Mt 25:14-30).
69. Mt. 24:51 "with the hypocrites"; Is 56:3; 59:2; 2 P 3:4.
70. The Expository Times, (February 1978), pp. 137ff.
71. Is 1:25; Jer 6:29; Zech 13:9; Mal 3:2-4.
72. Is 66:15-16; Ez 38:22; Mal 3:19.
73. Mk 10:38; Rom 6:3; Heb 9:12ff; Ps 125:4-5.
74. See 1:17,79; 2:14; 19:38; Jn 14:27; 16:33; Eph 2:14-18; Is 9:5-6; 11:6-9; Mi 5:4.
75. Mi 3:5-8; 7:6; Jer 6:14; 8:11ff; Ez 13:8-16.
76. Jn 1:5ff; 5:24; 7:12-13; Phil 4:2-3.
77. A.M. Hunter, *The Parables Then and Now,* (S.C.M., London 1971), pp. 90f.
78. Ps 37:25; Job 4:7; Jn 9:2; Ezek 18:1-32; Jer 31:29.
79. 13:24; 3:8; 5:32; Ac 5:31; 2:38; 3:19½.
80. 24:47; 15:7ff; 16:30; 17:3ff.
81. Jer 8:13; Hos 9:10; Joel 1:7; Rom 11:17ff.
82. 13:25,34f; 19:41-44; 21:20-24.
83. Note 11:14; 14:1-6; 17:11-19; 18:35-42.
84. 10:31ff; 4:40; 5:13; 8:54; 7:14; 24:50; Gen 48:14-20; Lev 9:22; Mk 1:41; 5:23; 6:5; 7:32; 10:13ff.
85. 13:13; 2:20; 5:25; 7:16; 17:15; 18:43.

86. 13:29; Ezek 17:22f; 13:3-9; Dn 4:10-21; Apoc 7:9.
87. Mt 7:13f; 25:10f; 7:22f; 8:11f.
88. E.g. 10:25ff; 7:50; 8:12; 19:10; 4 Ezra 7:45 ff; Sanhedrin 10:1,97b.
89. 16:16; Jn 18:36; 1 Cor 9:25; 1 Tim 4:10; 6:12.
90. Luke typically adds all the prophets 11:50; 24:27; Ac 3:18,24; 10:43.
91. Is 2:2-3; 11:9-10; 25:6-7; 45:6; 49:12; Mi 4:1f; Apoc 7:9f.
92. E.g. Nicodemus, Gamaliel; 7:36; 12:37; 14:1; Ac 5:34; 15:5; 23:6ff; 26:5.
93. Ac 1:4ff; 9:6ff; 17:3; Lk 9:22; 17:25; 22:37; 24:7,26,44.
94. 6:23; 11:47-51; 22:67-71; Ac 3:22; 7:37-52.
95. Dt 32:11; Ruth 2:12; Ps 57:1; 61:4; 91:4.
96. 11:50; Jer 26:20f; 2 K 21:16; 2 Chron 24:20f.
97. Jer 22:5; 12:7; Ac 7:48; 1 Cor 3:10f.
98. 5:29; 7:36; 9:16; 10:39; 11:37; also 22:14; 24:30.
99. E.g. Is 25:6; 34:6; 55:1; 65:11; Dt 12:4; Zeph 1:4; Ps 22:27; 23:5; 78:24ff.
100. 10:12; 11:31f; Ac 24:15; Jn 5:28f; Rom 2:5ff; 2 Cor 10:2; 2 Tim 4:1.
101. See Sean P. Kealy & David W. Shenk, *The Early Church and Africa,* (O.U.P., 1975), p. 319.
102. 7:9; 9:55; 10:23; 22:61; 23:28.
103. Mk 8:34; Mt 10:38; 16:24; also Jn 19:16 where the same word is used.
104. E.g. 11:31f; 13:18f; also 12:24ff; 14:28ff.
105. 15:7,10; 13:3,5; 16:30; 17:3f.
106. Quoted in A.M. Hunter, *The Parables Then and Now,* (S.C.M., London, 197i), p. 57.
107. Gen 25:27; 33:4; 41:42; 46:29; Ex 10:16; 1 K 8:47ff; Tobit 7:6; Esth 8:2; Gen 25:29; Prov 29:3.
108. See Drury, p. 75ff.
109. Hunter, opus cit., p. 60.
110. Sir 33:19-24; Tobit 4:3-21; Dt 21:15-22; 1 K 1-2; Heb 9:16-17.
111. Ac 20:37; Tob 11:9; Gen 3:21; 41:42; 45:14f; Zech 3:3-5; Ezek 16:10.
112. Michael Green, *You Must be Joking,* (Hodder & Stoughton, London, 1977), p. 43.
113. The modern scholar, Rudolf Bultmann in his writings curiously tends to place the shift from the old to the new between Jesus and Paul.
114. Sean P. Kealy, *That You May Believe,* The Gospel According to John, (St. Paul's Publications, London, 1978), pp. 104ff.
115. E.g. Lev 9:18; Is 58:7f; 68:7f; Amos 6:4ff; Dt 24:6ff; Ex 22:25.

Notes

116. A.M. Hunter, *The Parables Then and Now,* (S.C.M., London, 1971), p. 155.
117. 1:38; 12:35ff; Ac 2:18; 4:29; 16:17.
118. 5:24; 6:5; 7:34; 9:58; 11:30; 12:10; 19:10.
119. 9:22,44; 17:25; 18:31; 22:22,48; 24:7.
120. 9:26; 12:8,40; 17:22-30; 18:8; 21:27,36.
121. E.g. 1 Thess 5:1ff; 2 Thess 2:1ff; 2 Pet 3:3ff; Apoc 1:7.
122. 11:16; 12:56; 19:11; 21:7; Ac 1:6—the same verb is used in 6:7; 14:1; 20:20; Ac 9:24.
123. E.g. Amos 4:2; 8:11; Jer 7:32; 1 S 2:31; Lk 19:43; 21:6; 23:29.
124. 9:22,44; 17:25; 18:32ff; 22:37; 24:7,26,46; Ac 17:3; Is 53:3ff.
125. The same word both in Greek and Hebrew described vultures and eagles.
126. On constant prayer see Rom 1:10; 12:12; 1 Thess 5:17; 2 Thess 1:11; Eph 6:18.
127. Gal 6:9; 2 Thess 3:13; 2 Cor 4:1ff; Eph 3:13.
128. Ex 22:2; 23:6; Dt 10:18; 16:19; Is 1:17; 10:2; Jer 22:3; Ps 68:5.
129. John R.H. Moorman, *The Paths to Glory,* (S.P.C.K., London, 1963), p. 209, points out how this parable is—
    "perfectly portrayed by Beethoven in the slow movement of his piano concerto in G major (No. 4), where the orchestra represents the judge, loud, noisy and emphatic, saying 'No! No! No! while the widow is represented by the solo instrument which gently and softly pleads her cause until the opposition of the judge is finally worn down and the voice of hope and thanksgiving soars over a silenced and defeated adversary."
130. 9:35; 23:35; Rom 8:33; Mk 13:20ff; Mt 24:22.
131. 10:25; 18:18; Gal 3:18; Col 3:24; Eph 1:14.
132. 5:11; 12:33f; 16:14; Ac 2:44; 4:32ff.
133. 13:25-30; 14:14ff; 16:9; 19:11-27; 22:28-30.
134. 5:11,28; 9:57-62; 14:25-33.
135. 5:35; 9:22,43ff; 12:50; 13:32f; 17:25; See Mk 8:31; 9:31; 10:33f; 9:12.
136. 9:22; 22:22,37; 24:25ff; 3:4; 7:27; Ac 2:22ff.
137. 11:50; 13:28; 18:31; 24:25ff; Ac 3:18,24; 10:43; 24:14.
138. See 20:17; 23:35f; Ac 4:11; 5:30; 10:39; 13:29.
139. The Son of Man is a triumphant figure in Jewish writing which say almost nothing about his sufferings. See Kealy, *Who Is Jesus of Nazareth?,* p. 184ff.
140. *Ibid.,* p. 164ff, 173ff.
141. 4 Ezra 13:32; Mk also has one use of the title but in Matthew it is more frequent—see Lk 1:27,32,69.

142. 4:18f; 7:21; Is 29:18; 35:5.
143. 4:35,41; 9:21,36; 22:67ff.
144. Ezra 2:9; Neh 7:14; 2 Mc 10:19.
145. 3:12; 5:27; 7:29; 15:1; 18:10.
146. 19:5,11; 2:11; 22:61; 23:43.
147. Ex. 21:37; 2 Sam 72:6; Prov 6:31.
148. Ac 10:2; 11:14; 16:15ff; 18:8.
149. 13:16; Rom 4:11ff; Gal 3:9ff.
150. 15:4-7; 2:14; 10:21; 12:32.
151. 1:33; 19:38; 22:29-30; 23:42; Ac 17:7.
153. 19:11; 9:45; 18:34; Ac 1:6.
154. 1:35; Ac 2:18; 4:29; 16:17.
155. Gn 49:11; 1 K 1:38; Lk 18:31.
156. Zech 9:9-10; 11:4-14; 12:10; 13:7.
157. Num 19:2; Dt 21:3; 1 Sam 6:7; Lk 23:53.
158. 7:39f; 22:13,21,34; Jn 14:29; 1 Sam 10:2-9.
159. 7:13,32,38; Ac 21:13; Mk 5:38f; 1 Sam 1:7; Lm 1:16.

CHAPTER SEVEN
1. A.J. Hultgren, Interpreting the Gospel of Luke, Interpretation, 1978, p. 360.
2. "My house" v 46; 19:48; 20:1,9,45; 21:38.
3. 24:53; Ac 2:46; 3:1-3; 5:20,25,42,46.
4. 19:47f; 20:6; 19:26.
5. Note Mark's references at 11:1,11,19,20; 14:1,12,72; 15:1,47; 16:1.
6. See the parable in 13:6-9; Mk 11:12-14,21ff.
7. Is 5:1-7; Jer 2:21; 12:10; Ezek 15:1-6; 19:10-14; Hos 10:1; Joel 1:7; Dt 32:32f; Ps 80:8ff.
8. Amos 3:7; Apoc 10:7; 11:18; Ac 7:52; Heb 11:36f; Mt 23:34; Jer 9:25; Neh 9:26.
9. 1:79; 3:4; Ac 9:2; 18:25f; 19:9; Dt 8:6; 10:12f; Job 23:11; Ps 27:11; 119:15.
10. See Ac 10:34; Rom 2:11; 11:11; Gal 2:6; Eph 6:9; Col 3:25; Jas 2:1ff; Dt 1:17; 10:17; 16:19; Sir 4:27; Lv 19:15; 2 K 3:14; Job 42:8.
11. Jer 27:6; Is 10:5-7; 44:28; 45:1; 2 Chron 36:22ff.
12. Jn 19:11; Rom 13:1-7; 1 Pet 2:13-17; Tit 3:1.
13. Gn 38:8-10; Dt 25:5-10; Lv 18:16; 20:21; 25:25ff; Ruth.
14. Ac 2:34f; Rom 8:34; Heb 1,3,13; 8:1; 10:12f; 12:2.
15. 1:27,32,69; 2:24; 3:23ff; 18L38f; Rom 1:3.
16. 9:20ff; 22:69; 2 S 7:8-16; Is 9:5-7; Mic 5:2 etc..
17. Ex 22:22-4; Ac 6:1; 9:39ff; 1 Tim 5:3-16; Jam 1:27.
18. 19:11; 17:23; Ac 5:35-7; 21:38; Dn 7:22; Apoc 1:3; 22:10.
19. Ac 2:16-21; 2 S 24:13; Is 8:21f; 13:13; 19:2; Jer 21:9; 34:17; Ez 5:12; 2 Chron 15:6.

Notes

20. This is the story of Acts—e.g. Ac 4:1ff; 3:17ff; 7:1ff; 14:19; 16:19-24; 17:6ff; 18:12ff.
21. Ac 4:3; 5:18; 16:22f; 22:19; 2 Cor 6:5; 11:24.
22. 12:2-12; 24:28; Mk 13:9; Ac 4:5ff.
23. J.P. Kealy & D.W. Shenk, *The Early Church and Africa*, p. 55.
24. The same word in the New Testament only here and in Acts 4:14; see also Ac 3:12ff; Jn 16:13-15.
25. 9:23-7; Ac 28:22; Jn 15:18ff; 1 Cor 15:16ff.
26. 12:4,7; Ac 27:34; Mt 28:10ff; 1 Cor 15:16ff; 1 S 14:45; 2 S 14:11; 1 K 1:52.
27. 8:15; 9:24; 17:33; Rom 2:7; 5:3; 8:25; 15:4f; 2 Thess 1:4; 2 Cor 6:4.
28. Rom 2:7; Heb 10:36; 12:1; 2 Tim 2:10ff; Ham 1:12; 5:11.
29. V 23; 2 K 3:27; Lk 19:41ff; 4:18.
30. 11:49-51; 13:34f; 19:41-4; Dt 32:35; Hos 9:7; Is 34:8; 63:18; Jer 5:29; Ez 9:1; Ps 94:1 Zech 12:3; 14:2.
31. Dn 9:27; 11:31; 12:11; 1 Mc 1:54; 6:7.
32. 13:29f,35; 20:16; Rom 9:1ff; 11:25.
33. Is 13:10; 27:13; 34:4; Ps 65:8; Jer 4:23-6; Ezek 32:7f; Dn 7:13; Am 8:1; Joel 2:10; Mic 1:3f; Hab 1:8; 4 Ezra 13:30ff.
34. Ps 65:7; Job 38:8-11; Apoc 4:6; 13:1.
35. Dt 32:8; Is 13:26; 24:21; 34:1ff; Joel 2:10; Gn 37:9.
36. e.g. Rom 3:24; 8:28; 1 Cor 1:30; Eph 1:7,14; 4:30; Col 1:14.
37. Note the 'inclusion' with v 31 where 'the kingdom is near'.
38. 1:68; 2:25,38; 21:28; 24:21; Ac 7:35.
39. 21:27,31; 17:21,22; Mk 8:38/9:1; 10;7,23; 13:37,43; 25:31,34.
40. 28; 9:27; 17:20f; Joel 2:22.
41. 12:4ff,35ff; 17:26ff; Rom 13:11-13.
42. 2 28,35; 6:20ff; 8:14; 9:23-7.
43. Ac 2:23ff; 3:13ff; 10:39; 13:28.
44. Ac 1:22; 2:32; 3:15; 1 Cor 15:14; Rom 10:9.
45. Ac 2:23; Lk 22:22; 18:31; 20:17; 22:37; 24:26f,44f; 9:22,31,51; 12:50; 13:33; 17:25; 24:7.
46. 23:46; Ac 7:59; 23:4,14ff,27,41,47.
47. Ac 19:21; 20:16,22f; 21:4,10ff,13, 14ff.
48. e.g. Lk 22:47f & Mt 26:47,50; Lk 22:62 & Mt 26:75b; Lk 22:64 & Mt 26:68.
49. The Jerome Commentary, p. 156 lists some of the points of contact as follows: *negatively;* no explicit naming of the garden as 'Gethsemane' (Lk 23:39; Jn 18:19-24); omission of the cry "My God, why have you forsaken me?"; no rendevous in Galilee after the resurrection; *positively:* the attitude of the apostles at the announcement of Judas' betrayal (Lk 22:23; Jn 13:22); a farewell discourse (Lk 22:24-38; Jn 14-17); Jesus' custom of praying in the garden (Lk 22:39; Jn 18:2); the specification of Malchus' 'right'

ear (Lk 22:50; Jn 18:10); the triple declaration by Pilate of Jesus' innocence (Lk 23:4,14,22; Jn 18:38; 19:4,6).
50. Ex 12:6,15; Lv 23:5-9; Num 28:16ff; Dt 16:3.
51. See Jn 13:2,27f; 6:70; 1 Cor 2:8,28,53; Ac 26:18.
52. Ac 3:1,3,11; 4:19; 8:14; Lk 8:45.
53. Note the parallels with the banquet scene and table talk in 14:1ff, the concern about status, and Jesus' reflections on service, the eschatological reward and the kingdom.
54. e.g. Gn 26:30ff; Jer 52:31ff 2 K 25:27ff.
55. Lucien Deiss, *It's the Lord's Supper,* (Paulist Press, N.Y. 1976) pp 37ff.
56. Lk 22:14-20; Mk 14:22-5; Mt 26:24,29; 1 Cor 11:23-5.
57. As also Mk 14:21,25; Mt 26:24,29; Jn 13:33.
58. 24:30,41ff; Ac 10:41; Jn 21:9ff.
59. Luke and Paul, where Matthew and Mark have a blessing.
60. J. Jeremias, *New Testament Theology,* Vol 1, (S.C.M. London, 1971), p. 189f.
61. Lucien Deiss, *God's Word and God's People,* (The Liturgical Press, Collegeville, 1976), p. 240.
62. Actually John's word 'flesh' is quite likely the word Jesus actually used as neither Hebrew nor Greek seem to have a suitable word for body here (Jn 6:51ff).
63. Avery Dulles S.J. *The Resilient Church,* (Doubleday, N.Y. 1977). p. 167.
64. 1) is the catholic church; 2) Luther was inclined to this view; 3) Calvanists and other Reformed Christians.
65. Jer 31:31; Heb 9:18ff; 2 Cor 3:6-18; Tit 2:14; 1 P 2:9-10.
66. Ex 24:3ff; 19:3-6; Dt 7:6-8; 14:2; Is 53:11ff.
67. Deiss, ibid, p. 232.
68. W.D. Davies, *Invitation to the New Testament,* (Darton, Longman & Todd, London, 1967).
69. Dt 8:2,18; 19:7; 1 Cor 4:17; 2 Tim 2:8; 2 P 1:12ff; Jn 14:26.
70. Gn 8:1; 19:29; 1 S 1:19; Ps 8:5; Jer 2:2.
71. Mk 10:42-52; 14:25,29f; My 19:28; 20:25-8; 26:29,33-4.
72. Mk 14:21; Lk 18:31; 7:30; Ac 12:36; 20;22.
73. Mk 10:41-5; Mt 20:25,28; also Lk 9:48ff; 12:37; 14:7ff; Ac 20:30.
74. Ac 5:6,10; 1 Tim 5:1ff; 1 P 5:5; Heb 13:7ff.
75. Heb 7:28; Jn 17:1ff; Lk 13:8; Ex 18:19; 32:30ff; Num 27:5; Dt 9:18ff; 1 K 13:6; 2 K 19:4; Jer 7:16; 11:14; 14:11.
76. 24:34; 1 Cor 15:5; Mic 5:3-4; Jn 21:15ff.
77. Rom 13:12; 2 Cor 6:7; Eph 6:11-17.
78. Is 51;17; Ezek 23:33; Jer 25:15; 49:12; Ps 11:6; Mk 10;38; Jn 18:11.
79. 1:78f; 11:33ff; 22:3,32; Jn 12:31; 14:30; 16:11; Col 1:13; 2 Cor 4:4; Eph 6:12; 1 P 2:9.

Notes

80. 20:42; Ac 2:34ff; 5:31; 7:53ff.
81. 1:48; 5:10; 12:52; 22:18; Ac 18:6.
82. Mk 14:62; Ps 110L1; Lk 20;42; 22:30; Dn 7:13; Ac 2:33f; 7:55.
83. 23:5,18,23; 20:19-26; Ac 2:23; 3:14ff.
84. This is what the text means according to A.N. Sherwin White, who also comments—"Luke is remarkable in that his additional materials—the full formulation of the charges before Pilate, the reference to Herod, and the proposed acquittal with admonition—are all technically correct." *Roman Law in the New Testament,* (Oxford University Press, 1963), p. 27.
85. Jn 19:1; Ac 16:22ff; 22:24; Is 53:5.
86. 24:20; Ac 2:23; 3:13-17; 4:10; 5:30; 10:39; 13:28.
87. Ac 24:26f; 4:25ff; 17:6f; 18:12ff.
88. Ac 16:39; 18:14ff; 19:37; 23:29; 25:8,25; 26:32.
89. 21:37; 22:39,63ff; 23:11; Jn 19:1.
90. 12:49ff; 14:27; 23:26ff; 21:17; Ac 3:15; 5:31; 9:16.
91. 7:11ff; 8:52; Mk 15:23; Prov 31:6, but see Dt 21:22f.
92. 13:1ff; 11:49ff; 19:43-44; 21:20-24; Ac 6:14.
93. Ezek 21:3; 20:47; Is 10:16ff; Prov 11:31; 1 P 4:17f.
94. See the Supplement to the Interpreter's Dictionary of the Bible, p 199, for a brief account of the new archaeological information due to the discovery of the skeletal remains of a crucifixion from a first century A.D. tomb near Jerusalem. It is to be noted that the subject had actually been buried in a family tomb.
95. 23:34; 24:47; 6:26-36; 7:48; 17:3; Is 53:12.
96. 12:8ff; Rom 2:4; 10;3; i Cor 2:8; Eph 4:18; 1 P 1:14; Num 15:24ff.
97. e.g. 6:36; 7:36-50; 15:1ff; 18:9-14; 19:1-10.
98. e.g. Amos' description of the coming day of the Lord, Am 8:9; Jer 15:8f; Joel 2:10,31; 3:15.
99. John Wilkonson, *The Physical Cause of the Death of Jesus,* The Expository Times, p 104, January 1972.
100. 2:25; 15:7; Ac 3:14; Mk has the less probable 'Son of God'.
101. 1 Cor 15:3f; Gal 1:18; Ac 13:39; 5:50; 10:39; Gal 3:13; 1 P 2:24; Apoc 1:18.
102. This linen cloth, about fourteen feet long and less than four feet wide, is stained and bears the barely discernible image of an apparently crucified man. It is like a photographic negative and when photographed, yields a positive image. Further, it gives three dimensional information and incredibly precise anatomical details. "The face and body are marked by wounds and lesions in uncanny correspondence with the Gospel accounts of Jesus' scourging and crucifixion. The back is covered with sores of dumbbell-shaped marks suggesting flogging by a Roman flagrum. Both shoulders are bruised by the weight of a heavy

object, such as a cross. The wrists and feet are pierced and, between the fifth and sixth ribs on the right side of the body, there is a slanting wound that could have been made by a lance. One final group of details distinguishes the man in the shroud from the usual crucified Roman criminal. These are apparent bloodstains on the hairline and forehead as if caused by a crown of thorns." (Newsweek, September 18, 1978,) p. 58.

103. The Tablet, 26th August, 1978, p. 818, also to be published in *Face to Face with the Turin Shroud,* Peter Jennings (ed), (Morbrays and Mahew McCrimmon).
104. Newsweek, ibid, p. 58.
105. Ian Wilson, *The Shroud of Turin,* (Doubleday, N.Y. 1978).
106. Dt 21:22ff; 2 S 21:1ff; Ac 5:30; 10:39; Gal 3:13; 1 P 2:24; Jn 19:31.
107. Quoted on p V, G. O'Collins S.J., *The Easter Jesus,* (Darton, Longman & Todd, London, 1973).
108. e.g. Ac 2:24,32; 3:15,26; 4:10,33; 5:30; 10:40; 13:30ff; 17:31.
109. H. Von Camphausen, *Tradition and Life in the Church,* (Collins 1968), p 77.
110. Norman Perrin, *The Resurrection,* (Fortress Press, Philadelphia, 1977), p 83f.
111. 24:22f; Mt 28:9; Jn 20:14ff.
112. The individual narratives of the appearances have certain common features which suggest to some scholars that one basic appearance is behind all the main appearances to the Eleven, described in the gospels e.g. Mt 28:16-20; Jn 20:19ff. In the regular pattern at least four features are normally found—1) A brief description of the disciples in sorrow, bereft of Jesus (Lk 24:13ff, 36); 2) The appearance of Jesus (24:15,30,36); 3) A greeting from Jesus and a recognition of him (Lk24L381 Mt 28:9; Jn 20:21); 4) A command or a mission (Lk 24:48f; Mt 28:10,19f; Mk 16:7; Jn 20:22ff; 21:15).
113. 1:8ff; Ac 1:10f; 10:30ff; Dn 10:5ff; 2 Mc 3:26ff; Apoc 3:5 etc.
114. e.g. 9:29; 10:18; 11:36; 17:24; Ac 9:3; 22:6.
115. 18:32; 24:20; 1 Mc 1:34; 2:48ff; Ps 9:18; LXX.
116. Dt 17:6; 19:15; Ac 1:10; Mk 16:14; Mt 28:17; 18:16; 2 Cor 13:1; 1 Tim 5:19; Heb 10:28.
117. 11:25,41; 9:43ff; 18:31ff; Mt 28:17; Mk 16:10ff; Jn 20:18ff.
118. *Another King,* (St. Andrew Press, 1968), p. 14.
119. Jn 20:14; 21:4; Mt 28:17; 2 K 6:17.
120. 4:36; 7:16; 9:19,35; 19:32; 1 Cor 10:16.
121. Ac 2:42,46; 20:7,1; 27:35; 1 Cor 10:16.
122. Jn 1:14; 6:53; 20:24ff; 1 Jn 2:22; 4:2f; 1 Cor 15:42ff; Ac 2:25-31; Ac 17:18.

Bibliography

123. Ac 1:8; 2:32,38; 3:6,15; 4:10,30.
124. 24:44,6; 19:5; 22:37; Ac 2:22-32; 3:15f; 4:10f; 5:30f; 10;39f 13:2,8-30; 26:22.
125. 24:47; Ac 2:38; 3:9; 5:31; 10:43; 13:38-41; 26:18.
126. 24:48; 1:2; Ac 1:22; 2:32; 3:15; 5:32; 10:41; 13:31; 22:15: 26:16.
127. 2:32; Gn 12:3; 2 Sam 22:50; Is 49:6.
128. ac 19:2; 1 Thess 1:5; Heb 2:4; Eph 1:21; Rom 14:9.
129. Ac 7:55; Rom 8:34; Eph 1:20; 2:6; Phil 2P9f; Col 3:1 1 P 1:21; 1 Jn 2:1.
130. Eph 4:10; 1 Tim 3:16; 1 P 3:22; Heb 1:3,13; 2:7-9; 4:14; 6:19f; 7:26; 8:1; 9:24; Jn 3:13; 6:61; Ps 110:1; Ac 2:32-4.
131. John L. McKenzie, *Dictionary of the Bible,* (Chapman, London, 1965), p. 59.
132. P. Benoit, *The Passion and Resurrection of Jesus Christ,* (Herder & Herder, N.Y. 1969), p. 341f.
133. J. Reumann, *Jesus,* (Fortress Press, Philadelphia, 1968), p. 132f.
134. Lv 2:16; 3:5ff; Is 53:11; Heb 7:27; 1 P 2:24; Jam 2:21.

SELECT ENGLISH BIBLIOGRAPHY

General Works

W. Barclay, *The Gospels and Acts,* 2 Vols, (S.C.M. London, 1976).

P. Benoit, *The Passion and Resurrection of Jesus Christ,* (Herder & Herder, N.Y. 1969).

R.E. Brown, *The Birth of the Messiah,* (Doubleday, N.Y. 1977).

R.E. Brown, *The Gospel According to St. John,* 2 Vols., (Geoffrey Chapman, London, 1971).

M. Burrows, *Jesus in the First Three Gospels,* (Abingdon, Nashville, 1977).

D.G. Buttrick, (ed), *Jesus and Man's Hope,* (Perspective, Pittsburgh, 1970).

A.M. Greeley, *The Jesus Myth,* (Search Press, London, 1972).

A.E. Harvey, *Companion to the New Testament,* (Cambridge, 1970).

A.M. Hunter, *The Parables Then and Now,* (S.C.M. London, 1971).

The Interpreter's One-Volume Commentary on the Bible, C.M. Laymon, (ed), (Collins, London, 1971).

The Interpreter's Dictionary of the Bible, Supplementary Volume, (Abingdon, Nashville, 1976).

J. Jeremias, *New Testament Theology,* Vol 1, (S.C.M. London, 1972).

The Jerome Biblical Commentary, R.E. Brown etc., (ed), (Chapman, London, 1968).

S.P. Kealy, *The Changing Bible,* (Dimension Books, N.J. 1975).

S.P. Kealy and D. Shenk, *The Early Church and Africa,* (Oxford University Press, Nairobi, 1975).

S.P. Kealy, *Who is Jesus of Nazareth?* (Dimension Books, N.J. 1977).
S.P. Kealy, *Jesus the Teacher,* (Dimension Books, N.J. 1978).
S.P. Kealy, *That You May Believe,* The Gospel According to John, (St. Paul Publications, Slough, 1978).
H.C. Kee, *Jesus in History,* (Harcourt Brace Jovanovich, N.Y. 1977).
G. Kittel, (ed), Theological Dictionary of the New Testament, 10 Vols., (Eerdmans, Michigan, 1977).
E.A. La Verdiere, W.G. Thompson S.J., *New Testament Communities in Transition,* in Why the Church?, (Paulist Press, N.Y. 1977).
X. Leon-Dufour, *Resurrection and the Message of Easter,* (Chapman, London, 1974.
R.P. Martin, *New Testament Foundations,* Vol. 1, (Paternoster Press, Exeter, 1975).
J.L. McKenzie, Dictionary of the Bible, (Chapman, London, 1965).
B.M. Metzger, *A Textual Commentary on the Greek New Testament,* (United Bible Societies, London, 1971).
A New Catholic Commentary on Holy Scripture, R.C. Fuller etc. (ed), (Nelson, London, 1975).
G. O'Collins, *The Easter Jesus,* (Darton Longman & Todd, London, 1973).
N. Perrin, *The Resurrection,* (Fortress Press, Philadelphia, 1977).
J. Reumann, *Jesus,* (Fortress Press, 1973).
B.H. Throckmorton, *Gospel Parallels,* (Nelson, Camden, N.J. 1967).
A. Vanhoye, *Structure and Theology of the Accounts of the Passion,* (The Liturgical Press, Collegeville, 1967).
B. Vawter, *The Four Gospels,* (Gill & Sons, Dublin, 1966).

Books and Articles on St. Luke

C.K. Barrett, *Luke the Historian in Recent Studies,* (Fortress Press, (Philadelphia, 1970).
J. Bligh, Christian Deuteronomy, (St. Paul's Publications, Slough, 1970).
F. Bovan, *Recent Trends in Lucan Studies,* (Theology Digest, 1978).
W.R.F. Browning, *The Gospel According to St. Luke,* (S.C.M. London, 1960).
H.J. Cadbury, *The Making of Luke-Acts,* (S.P.C.K. London, 1968).
G.B. Caird, *Saint Luke,* (Penguin Books, Middlesex, 1968).
F.W. Danker, *Luke,* (Fortress Press, Philadelphia, 1976).
J. Drury, *Tradition and Design in Luke's Gospel,* (Darton Longman & Todd, London, 1976).
E.E. Ellis, *The Gospel of Luke,* (New Century Bible, Oliphants, London, 1974).
H. Flender, St. Luke, *Theologian of Redemptive History,* (SPCK London, 1967)

Bibliography

E. Franklin, *Christ the Lord,* (S.P.C.K. London, 1975).

R.H. Fuller, *Luke's Witness to Jesus Christ,* (Lutterworth Press, London, 1963).

W.J. Harrington, *The Gospel According to St. Luke,* (Chapman, London 1968).

A.J. Hultgren, *Interpreting the Gospel of Luke,* (Interpretation, 1976, pp. 353-365).

R.J. Karris, *Invitation to Luke,* Doubleday, N.Y. 1977).

A.R.C. Leaney, *The Gospel According to St. Luke,* (Black, London, 1971).

D. Macpherson, *Luke, Scripture Discussion Commentary,* (Sheed & Ward, London, 1971).

I.H. Marshall, *Luke, Historian and Theologian,* (Zondervan Grand Rapids, London, 1971).

I. H. Marshall, *The Gospel of Luke,* (The Paternoster Press, Exeter, 1978).

D.G. Miller, *Saint Luke,* (S.C.M. London, 1966).

J.R.H. Morris, *The Gospel According to St. Luke,* (Eerdmans Grand Ripands, 1974).

J. Navone, *Themes of St. Luke,* (Gregorian University Press, Rome, 1970).

C.H. Talbert, *Shifting Sands,* The Recent Study of the Gospel of Luke, (Interpretation, 1976, pp. 381-395).

E.J. Tinsley, *The Gospel According to Luke,* (Cambridge University Press, 1976).

W. Wilkinson, *Good News in Luke,* (Collins Fontana, 1975).